Paul, G.

I bought

Ma...
United

POCKET ANNUAL
1996-97

*Lots of love
now and always
Laura xxx*

Phil Bradley
Andy Bradley

Manchester United Pocket Annual 1996-97

Copyright © Phil Bradley – 1996

ISBN: 1-898351-45-7

Typeset by Bruce Smith Books Ltd
Editorial Director: Mark Webb
Cover Photo: Eric Cantona, SpedeGrafix

First published in 1996 by
Words on Sport

Words on Sport Ltd
PO Box 382
St. Albans
Herts, AL2 3JD

Registration Number: 2917013

Registered Office:
Worplesdon Chase, Worplesdon,
Guildford, Surrey, GU33LA

Printed and bound in the UK by The Lavenham Press, Suffolk.

CONTENTS

Acknowledgements

Many thanks to all those who, in one way or another, have contributed something to this third edition of the Manchester United Pocket Annual and I am most grateful to those readers who have taken the time and trouble to write in with suggestions etc. I would like to thank, in particular, Andy and Erica Bradley for their help in compiling the Records Section along with Bill and Audrey Johnson for their help with the Diary of the Season. Thanks is also due to my ever suffering wife, Carole, who rarely complains when I disappear for hours on end to work on the publication. Last, but not least, thanks most of all to Bruce Smith and Mark Webb and everyone at Words on Sport for making it all happen at the sharp end.

Introduction

The 1995/96 season was the stuff that dreams are made of. This third edition of the *Manchester United Pocket Annual* chronicles the highs and lows of an incredible season, match by match, blow by blow, kick by kick. If this isn't your first Manchester United Pocket Annual then rest assured there are many new features, including the Manchester derbies, all League results since the war and much more. And the Annual includes much else besides: all the records, facts and statistics associated with this great football institution including how the world's most famous club was saved from extinction by a dog! Read on.

Manchester United are probably the best known football team in the world and, since the Munich Air Disaster, have held a special place in the hearts of most neutrals. No club has appeared in more FA Cup Finals, nor won the coveted trophy on more occasions than the Old Trafford side. They have conquered not only the domestic scene but also, on two occasions, Europe.

The common denominator in all their successes has been flair. Many players such as Duncan Edwards, Bobby Charlton, Denis Law and George Best became household names and are now replaced in the modern side by Ryan Giggs and Eric Cantona. Unfortunately, of course, the Frenchman has his dark side but, say what you will about that, there is no doubt that he falls into the category of the United greats when it comes to football flair.

The bulk of United's achievements have come in the last fifty years after Sir Matt Busby founded his dynasty in 1945 when he inherited a club with no ground and very little cash. It was a fitting tribute to the great man that the year of his death, 1994, should see his beloved Reds lift the double.

Unfortunately 1994/95 saw the now infamous Eric Cantona kung-fu attack at Crystal Palace and, bearing in mind that the Reds needed just one more goal at West Ham in the last game of that campaign to retain the title, and that they were beaten 1-0 in the FA Cup Final by Everton, that one incident almost certainly cost them another double. But, as we now know, their place in football's history books was only delayed for twelve months. What *can* the next twelve have in store for this Manchester United side?

Disclaimer

In a book of this type it is inevitable that some errors will creep in. While every effort has been made to ensure that the details given in this annual are correct at the time of going to press, neither the editor nor the publishers can accept any responsibilities for errors within.

If you do notice any mistakes then please write in and we will try to rectify them for future issues. In addition, if there are other areas of information about Manchester United Football Club that you feel should be included in future editions then please let us know of your choices.

The Season Reviewed

The 1995/96 campaign turned out to be Alex Ferguson's greatest triumph yet but, strangely, the season had begun with United in a state of turmoil and Ferguson's position under pressure, at least as far as the fans were concerned. After the United boss had allowed Paul Ince, Mark Hughes and Andrei Kanchelskis to all depart Old Trafford without signing any replacements, a poll conducted by the *Manchester Evening News* revealed time was running out for the Scot who had brought so much success to the club with supporters unable to believe that the Reds could possibly regain their Premiership supremacy and reclaim the title.

At 3.45pm on the opening day of the season United, who in addition to the three transferred stars, were also destined to be without Eric Cantona until October as he served out his suspension for his Kung Fu attack at Crystal Palace, were three down at Villa Park with plenty of people prepared to write off the campaign there and then. Among them was BBC TV's pundit Alan Hansen whose quote of "You don't win anything with kids" that evening was to haunt him for the rest of the winter.

Five straight league wins, including one over reigning Champions Blackburn, plus a goalless draw in Russia in the 1st Leg of the UEFA Cup against Rotor Volgograd put hope in the hearts of United followers everywhere only for them to be shot down immediately as the Reds climbed aboard their 1995/96 roller coaster. And they were shot down in some style with little York City humbling the mighty Old Trafford outfit 3-0 in their own backyard, if you can describe the Stadium of Dreams in those terms, as the visitors produced the Coca Cola Cup shock of 1995/96, or any other season for that matter.

A lifeless, and goalless, draw at Sheffield Wednesday in the league failed to lift spirits and worse almost followed when United's unbeaten home record in Europe was really on the line with a couple of minutes to go against Volgograd. It was saved by a goal from, of all people, Peter Schmeichel! But whilst it saved United's proud home record, it wasn't enough to prevent the Russians going through on the away goals rule.

By now Eric was back and it took just seconds for the Frenchman to make his mark on his return against Liverpool by creating a goal for Butt and then crowning his comeback with success from the penalty spot in a 2-2 draw. With Cantona in harness, United began to reel in the points, picking up 12 in the next five games during which time they found the net four times against Chelsea, Southampton and Coventry City, losing only once, to the only goal of the game, at Arsenal.

Hopes were again high as United were now only three points behind a Newcastle side that looked quite outstanding and five points in front of Arsenal in third. But then Forest, Chelsea and Wednesday all conspired to hold Ferguson's team to draws whilst the next two games brought defeats against Liverpool and Leeds that were much worse than the two goal margins suggested.

The Reds were still in second but ten points adrift of the North East side when Kevin Keegan's outfit visited Old Trafford. It was a game that the Reds had to win and they put on a tremendous performance to reduce the gap and promptly followed up with a home win over QPR in the final game of 1995. The New Year, however, got off to a disastrous start with Peter Schmeichel injured during the pre-match warm-up at Spurs resulting in the Londoners blasting four past United. A fortunate home draw against Sunderland in the FA Cup, followed by the dropping of two more home points in a dour draw against Aston Villa, began to suggest that the season was over for Ferguson's fledglings.

It appeared even more that way when Sunderland went ahead in the FA Cup replay at Roker Park only for super sub Paul Scholes to save the day. But he more than saved the day with that much needed equaliser because the win that ensued set United on the path to glories unimaginable at the time.

Eight straight wins, culminating in a 6-0 rout of Bolton Wanderers at Burnden Park, saw United into the last eight of the FA Cup and within striking distance of league leaders Newcastle when the Reds visited St James Park in early March. Ferguson's side took a battering in the first half when Peter Schmeichel stood firm against everything Kevin Keegan's outfit could throw at him and a strike early in the second period from Cantona was the decisive goal. United were now just one point behind the Geordies with what appeared, on paper, to be a much easier run in as Newcastle still had tricky looking trips to Liverpool, Blackburn and Arsenal.

A win over Southampton in the FA Cup gave United a semi-final berth but they failed to make it eleven successive victories when they needed a last gasp Cantona effort to even save a point at QPR, who were later to be relegated. It was Cantona again with the only strikes in 1-0 wins against Arsenal and Spurs and, as United headed to the FA Cup semi-final showdown with Chelsea and Mark Hughes, the Frenchman had scored all but one of United's goals in the month of March. Cole and Beckham took the weight off him at Villa Park as United came from behind to clinch their third successive FA Cup Final appearance. The Frenchman continued his incredible scoring record against Manchester City and then netted the only goal of the Easter Monday clash with Coventry City.

United now had the title within their grasp for the Coventry victory put them six points ahead of Newcastle who had sensationally slipped up in the last minute against both Liverpool and Blackburn to lose games they had been winning. But the Reds never do anything the easy way and in their next game took a first half hammering at the Dell against relegation candidates Southampton. After trailing in at half time some three goals adrift of the Saints, United changed their grey kit but a late Giggs goal was only a consolation affair.

United recovered to edge nervously past a Leeds United team reduced to ten men in the first twenty minutes after goalkeeper Mark Beaney was dismissed but until Roy Keane's second half winner it had looked as though the Yorkshire side would stifle the Reds. A brilliant performance against Forest followed and the 5-0 victory was made even better when the Midlands side then held Newcastle to a draw just four days later.

United now made their first ever visit to the Riverside Stadium in the knowledge that the title was in their own hands and goals from May, Cole and Giggs gave the

Reds the first part of the double. For the man of the season, Eric Cantona, it was an incredible fourth title in five campaigns, having won the Championship with Leeds before his trans-Pennine move. For David May it was his dream come true at the third time of asking. In 1993/94 he had been pipped at the post for the title by United when a Blackburn player and then lost out on the last day in 1994/95 after switching camps.

Alex Ferguson and his side were now just one game away from taking United into the history books as the first club to ever do the double twice and, whilst the FA Cup Final itself was not a classic, the goal that won it certainly was. In an ending of almost fairytale proportions, it was a fabulous volley from Eric Cantona that completed the dream.

The 1995/96 season surely put Alex Ferguson on the same pedestal as Sir Matt for not only had his side done the double for the second time in three years, they had done it Sir Matt's way with kids – much to the chagrin of Alan Hansen!

'Red Devils' Diary 1995-96

June

1st   Inter Milan bid £3.5m for Paul Ince. United turn the offer down but hint they might do business at double the amount.

3rd   Gary Neville is a surprise choice to gain his first full international cap after only 19 FAPL appearances. He is on the winning side as England scrape a 2-1 victory over Japan in the Umbro Cup thanks to a penalty two minutes from time. Andy Cole misses the game as he undergoes an operation to cure his shin splint problem. Denis Irwin plays for the Republic of Ireland who are shocked by Liechtenstein. The goalless draw gives the tiny Principality their first ever Championship point in any competition. They had conceded thirteen goals in their previous two games.

5th   Inter Milan make an offer in the region of £7m for Paul Ince but United boss Alex Ferguson says "There has been a lot of speculation about Paul but we are not interested in selling him. We want all our players to stay at Old Trafford". However, it was strongly rumoured that some of the hierarchy at the club were in favour of letting the deal go through.

6th   Leeds United make a bid of £4m for Andrei Kanchelskis but United refuse to comment. David Beckham and Phil Neville are given debuts at Under 21 level by England but are on the wrong end of a 2-0 defeat by Brazil.

7th   Former United player Steve Coppell returns to a managerial role at Crystal Palace, the club that sacked him as manager two years previously. His new title is Director of Football. Young reserve player Pat McGibbon plays for Northern Ireland who are humbled at home by Latvia. Mark Hughes is another to suffer as Wales are beaten at home by Georgia.

8th   Gary Pallister is substituted as England give three soft goals away against Sweden. It is the first time an England team has conceded three goals in an international for seven years but there is a sensational finish as former United apprentice David Platt and Darren Anderton both score during injury time to salvage a 3-3 draw.

9th   The funeral of Bobby Stokes takes place at Portchester Crematorium, Hampshire. The 44 year old Stokes, who scored the only goal of the 1976 FA Cup Final as Southampton, then a Second Division team, beat United, had passed away suddenly from pneumonia a week earlier.

10th   Inter Milan make further overtures for Ince and are encouraged by United who say they can talk to the player. Ferguson now says he has a ready made replacement in Nicky Butt if Ince decides to go to Italy. Ince says he is amazed that United are prepared to release him. David Beckham misses a penalty against Angola as England Under 21s struggle to beat the African nation 1-0 to qualify for the semi-final of the Toulon Under 21s Tournament. He said afterwards "That's the first spot kick I've missed in nearly three years". Also in a spot of bother is Wesley Brown, an Associate Schoolboy at Old Trafford, when he gives away a second minute penalty at Wembley as England Schoolboys go down 4-2 to Germany.

11th   Gary Neville is recalled to the England team that are beaten 3-1 at Wembley by Brazil after being left out of the side that drew with Sweden. Also beaten 3-1 at home are the Republic of Ireland who have Denis Irwin in their team as they go down to Austria.

12th   United refuse rivals Manchester City permission to approach Brian Kidd with a view to becoming their new manager.

13th   Derby County make an official approach to United to request permission to offer Steve Bruce the position of player manager at the Baseball Ground. United turn the request down and Bruce himself says "I am happy to stay and fight for my place. It is nice to know that at 35 years of age I am still wanted".

15th A Press Conference in Milan to announce the signing of Paul Ince by Inter Milan is cancelled at the last minute when the player says he wants more time to think over the move.

16th United assure Paul Ince that he is more than welcome to stay at Old Trafford if he does not fancy the proposed move to Italy. Chairman Martin Edwards says "He has not become a bad player overnight. If he does not want to go then it is not an embarrassment to us. It just means we will not be able to spend heavily in the short term."

17th Brian Kidd states he is not prepared to resign his position at Old Trafford in order that City can approach him to become their manager. "I have absolutely no intention of leaving Old Trafford" says the United number two. United Chairman, Martin Edwards says he is hopeful that Andrei Kanchelskis will stay at Old Trafford.

21st Inter Milan lay on luxury hotel accommodation overlooking Lake Como for Paul Ince and his family for three months as part of a deal designed to entice him to sign. It is thought that this will cost the Italian giants a further £450 a day on top of the transfer fee. The hotel has three pools, eight tennis courts and a gymnasium.

23rd Paul Ince signs at last for Inter but an even bigger shock is the departure of Mark Hughes to Chelsea. Glenn Hoddle lets it slip that he went after Hughes because he was out of contract. United had paraded Hughes on the pitch at Old Trafford in February saying that the player had agreed to sign a new contract. Whilst they never actually claimed he had signed the document everyone was led to believe, in the absence of news to the contrary, that he was under contract to the Reds. The club admitted he had never signed the contract "for various reasons". Many fans say they feel duped.

24th United's teenage striker David Johnson who failed to break into the first team squad signs on a free transfer for Bury. The powerfully built 18 year old had not been able to agree a new contract at Old Trafford and opted for the 'Shakers' ahead of a host of other clubs. He had, of course, tasted life at Gigg Lane with United's Reserve team who played most of their games in 1994/95 at Bury.

25th Wimbledon lose 4-0 to Turkish outfit Bursaspor at Brighton's Goldstone Ground in the Inter Toto Cup. They include in their side three United youngsters John O'Kane, Michael Appleton and Graeme Tomlinson all of whom were loaned to the Dons. Wimbledon coach Ernie Tippett, in charge of the side in the absence on holiday of Joe Kinnear, said he was delighted with the contribution of the young

Reds. Reports surface that Italian star Roberto Baggio wants to move to Old Trafford "for the challenge of playing in the FA Premiership".

26th   United youngster Mark Rawlinson signs for Bournemouth on a free transfer.

27th   United state that they are not interested in signing Baggio.

28th   Andy Cole's agent Paul Stretford runs into trouble with FIFA as he had not registered with the FA by the respective deadline issued by FIFA under their new regulations governing agents requiring them to lodge a bond of 200,000 Swiss Francs.

July

1st   United's Youth team coach 'Pop' Robson resigns after four years at Old Trafford to become Sunderland's Reserve team coach in place of Jim Montgomery. "We are sorry to see him go but we fully understand his desire to return to his native North East" said a United spokesman.

4th   England Under 16 captain John Curtis, who played in the Reds FA Youth Cup winning side in May, heads a five strong Old Trafford contingent to receive their 'caps' on graduation day at Lilleshall. The others are Stuart Brightwell, Mark Wilson, Matthew Wicks and Elliott Dickman. Wicks is the son of Steve Wicks the former Chelsea and QPR defender.

7th   Alex Ferguson says he wants a meeting with Andrei Kanchelskis when the winger arrives back from Russia to try to resolve the problems the Russian seems to have in staying at Old Trafford.

8th   Roy Keane is cleared of defamation by an Irish court which rules that he doesn't have to pay anything to a woman he called a 'whore' when hurling abuse and fighting with the woman's brother in a busy street in Cork, Keane's native city.

12th   Kanchelskis says he is not interested in meeting Ferguson and claims the manager has not spoken to him for five months. He says he cannot stay at Old Trafford because of the manager. The Russian's agent Grigoriy Esaulenko also issues what appears to be a provocative statement saying "If the manager goes, Kanchelskis will stay". Kanchelskis again reiterates he cannot forgive Ferguson for leaving him out of the team at Everton in February. Ferguson refuses to get into what he calls a slanging match simply saying "It doesn't serve any useful purpose going over all this old ground".

14th	A poll conducted for the Manchester Evening News shows the fans to be still divided over the sale of Ince and Hughes. With Kanchelskis obviously next to leave, 53% said they thought Alex Ferguson should be shown the door.
20th	Eric Cantona plays in the first of the weekly practices arranged to get him match fit. The game at The Cliff reveals a new look Frenchman as he has his head shaved almost bare. His side win 3-0.
21st	Andrei Kanchelskis becomes the latest star to leave Old Trafford when he signs for Everton in a £5m deal.
22nd	Reserve striker Richard Irving who never made a first team appearance signs for Nottingham Forest in exchange for a fee of £75,000.
24th	United reveal that Andy Cole is behind with his rehabilitation programme as a virus has halted his efforts to regain fitness following his close season shin operation. He is unlikely to make the club tour of Malaysia.
25th	England Under 21 player David Beckham signs a new four year deal with the Reds to end speculation that he may be returning to his native London to join either Spurs or Arsenal. Cantona is in action for a United side against Rochdale in a game behind closed doors at The Cliff which the Reds win 3-2. Meanwhile Mark Hughes scores on his debut for Chelsea in a friendly at Gillingham which attracts a full house of 10,400. The game ends 3-1 for Chelsea. Leeds United state that they will file an official complaint to United regarding remarks made by Alex Ferguson in his new book *A Year in the Life* in which he says "I almost want Leeds to be relegated because of their fans. You can feel the hatred and animosity".
26th	Ashley Westwood follows in the footsteps of David Platt when leaving Old Trafford for Crewe Alexandra. Platt went on a free transfer but the Reds receive £40,000 for the young defender.
27th	Exactly half of the United squad that flies out to Malaysia have come through the Youth ranks as Kevin Pilkington, Gary and Phil Neville, Nicky Butt, David Beckham, Paul Scholes, Ben Thornley and Terry Cooke all make the trip. United leave Gary Walsh at home so that he can play some Reserve games and put himself in the shop window. The 27 year old has refused new terms and is on a weekly contract with United boss Alex Ferguson saying "The lad deserves first team football. I am mystified as to why we have not received any enquiries for him".

28th   Alex Ferguson sends a letter of apology to Leeds Chairman Leslie Silver regarding his remarks about their fans saying that he does not consider there is any ill feeling between the clubs and that the offending paragraph was written at an emotional time.

29th   A United XI beat North West Counties League side Blackpool Mechanics 5-3 after going two goals down. Simon Davies opens United's account with the other strikes coming via Des Baker, Michael Appleton and two from Jonathon Macken who was only denied a hat-trick when his shot hit the bar to provide Appleton with his goal.

30th   It is revealed that Andrei Kanchelskis is due a massive £1.2m signing on fee as part of his move to Everton. The Goodison Park outfit agree to pay this on top of their £5m outlay to United.

31st   The FA step in to reprimand United for playing Cantona in the closed doors friendly at the Cliff. The FA say the inclusion of the Frenchman in games against other clubs even behind closed doors is in breach of the suspension. Meanwhile, at Stamford Bridge, Mark Hughes scores a goal on his home debut that is described as a "Hughes classic". His header gives Chelsea the lead against Porto who fight back to gain a draw. United call off a closed door friendly with Preston following pressure from the FA and FIFA. In Malaysia, Steve Bruce scores twice as the Reds beat a Selangor State Select 4-1. Also on target are Nicky Butt and Lee Sharpe. United announce they have captured one of the country's most successful developers of young football talent in Neil Bailey who has made a huge impression in his time at Blackpool.

August

1st   Andrei Kanchelskis fails to make the line up for Neville Southall's Testimonial game against Celtic. He is introduced on the pitch with the explanation that his work permit has not cleared. He is given a muted response from the Celtic fans after saying all summer he wanted to play for Rangers. The Reds, meanwhile, unveil their seventh new kit in four years. In Wales, United's shadow squad beat Flint 1-0 with Michael Appleton heading the only goal of the game in the 63rd minute. But the star was again second year apprentice Jonathon Macken who supplied the cross for Appleton's goal as well as hitting the woodwork himself.

2nd   United beat the Selangor State Select again, this time by 2-0 thanks to goals from Steve Bruce and Paul Scholes.

3rd   Former United goalkeeper Alex Stepney signs up as goalkeeping coach for Manchester City. He played more than 400 games for the Reds before retiring in 1977 and is still remembered for his fantastic save from Eusebio in the 1968 European Cup Final.

5th   United call off the Kanchelskis move to Everton saying that the Goodison side will not pay the £1.1m sell on clause that his former Russian club had put in the original contract with the Reds. Apparently, although terms had been agreed, no contracts had been signed with the result that the Old Trafford side withdrew from the deal when the add on clause came to light. They instruct Kanchelskis to report to the Cliff for training.

7th   Kanchelskis fails to report to United for training and trains with Everton. United boss Alex Ferguson is told he could face a disrepute charge after criticising the FA in article in which he says "I can see no reason for them at all. It should be a professional body, not self electing. The structure is too tightly knit with too many friendships". Adding to United's woe are the first team who lose at Birmingham to the only goal of the game from Chris White just before half-time. United's Youth team beat Trafford of the North West Counties League with the only goal coming from Jonathon Macken who is rapidly making a name for himself.

8th   United are rocked further when Eric Cantona issues a "let me play or I'm quitting" ultimatum regarding the closed doors friendlies. It came just hours after the FA announced that they would not be taking any further action over the player having appeared against Rochdale but that any further appearances would be viewed in a different light.

9th   Cantona disappears to France and Inter Milan are reported to be tabling a big offer for him. United beat Bradford City 1-0 thanks to a Roy Keane goal whilst Macken is again on target as the Youth side beat Bristol City Youths 2-0 with the other goal being scored by Tommy Smith.

10th   Manager Alex Ferguson flies to France to meet Cantona and announces that the player will be staying at Old Trafford. A crowd of almost 1,500 watch a United XI draw one all at Altrincham. David Beckham scores United's goal and Chris Casper has an effort disallowed for pushing.

11th   The Kanchelskis transfer saga takes a new twist when it emerges that Rune Hauge, the agent involved in the George Graham affair and now banned by FIFA from working as an agent in football, was involved in the original deal that brought the Russian to Old Trafford. Meanwhile, United announce that they will not be attending an arbitration hearing planned by the FA Premiership for 14th August to sort out the transfer argument and say they have not even named their nominee for the panel. Everton appeal to the FA to invoke Rule 41 which allows the FA to arbitrate and reach a binding decision without the club's consent. Both clubs name Kanchelskis in their lists of players submitted to UEFA as the deadline for European competitions is reached. In Ireland, United need a 65th minute equaliser from David Beckham to grab a two all draw with Shelbourne. Nicky Butt scores United's other goal as the Reds take the field minus Peter Schmeichel, Ryan Giggs, Andy Cole and Gary Pallister. Middlesbrough boss Bryan Robson signs United Reserve team 'keeper Gary Walsh for £250,000 with a further £250,000 after 50 games.

13th   United beat East Fife 4-0 with two goals from David Beckham and one each from Brian McClair and Lee Sharpe. A United X1 beat GM Vauxhall Conference Champions Macclesfield Town, who are managed by former Red Sammy McIlroy, 4-3.

14th   United announce that they have signed up to show twelve home games live on cinema screens at Manchester's G-Mex centre and Salford Quays. Tickets will be priced at £8 to £10 for adults and £4 to £6 for children. Eric Cantona trains at The Cliff to dispel any immediate fears over a departure.

15th   United bring the curtain down on their pre-season friendlies with a 2-0 win at Oldham Athletic in a fixture to mark the 'Latics Centenary. The goals come from Sharpe and an own goal by Richard Jobling.

16th   United Reserves get their Pontin's League campaign underway by beating last season's Champions Bolton Wanderers 1-0 with Graeme Tomlinson getting the all important goal in the 83rd minute against a side that included five first team regulars.

19th   United are comprehensively beaten 3-1 by Villa as they set out on their attempt to regain the title.

23rd   The Reds win their first home game when they beat West Ham 2-1. Marco Boogers is dismissed for the visitors after fouling Gary Neville.

25th   The Andrei Kanchelskis deal finally goes through when Everton agree to indemnify United up to the amount of £550,000 of any add on fee the Old Trafford club have to pass on to the Russian's former outfit.

26th	United spoil Wimbledon's 100% start to the season when they beat the London side 3-1 at Old Trafford. Incredibly, for a game against the Dons, not a single player from either team is booked.
27th	Paul Ince gets off to a winning start in the Serie A when a goal by Roberto Carlos gives Inter a 1-0 victory over newly promoted Vicenza. Ince is reported as having had "a solid game in midfield".
28th	United beat Blackburn Rovers 2-1 but their joy is dampened by the dismissal of Roy Keane for a second bookable offence.
29th	The funeral of former United captain Johnny Carey takes place at Handforth, Cheshire. The 76 year old Carey had died a week previously. A full obituary appears elsewhere in this Annual.
31st	Ryan Giggs continues his build up to full fitness with a Reserve team outing against Notts County that sees him get booked for retaliation after a foul by County's Chris Marsden before he scores a 66th minute goal in a 2-2 draw.

September

1st	Paul Scholes is forced to miss England's Under 21 trip to Portugal with a leg strain.
2nd	United are without a game due to midweek internationals but the Reserves lose 3-2 to a Liverpool second string that includes Stig Bjornebye, Mark Walters, Nigel Clough, Jan Molby and Michael Thomas. Ryan Giggs nets one of the United goals as his come back gathers momentum. In Portugal, England Under 21s include Nicky Butt, David Beckham and Phil Neville in the side that goes down 0-2 in a European Group qualifier.
4th	Rachel Viollet, the former Lancashire Under 14s Lawn Tennis Champion, leaps into the game's World Rankings at No 513 from nowhere after winning a ranking tournament in San Salvador. Now aged 23, she is the daughter of former United forward Dennis Viollet and lives with her parents in Jacksonville, USA.
6th	Gary Neville is United's sole representative in the England team that is held to a goalless draw by Colombia at Wembley.
7th	Gordon Hill, nicknamed 'Merlin' when he played in the United side under Tommy Docherty in the Seventies is back at Old Trafford as a match day host to the Old Trafford Executive Box holders. He had just returned to England from a five year coaching stint in Canada.

8th	The Neville brothers have their FA Youth Cup medals stolen by a sneak thief at their home in Bury.
9th	United play Everton for the first time since the Kanchelskis transfer saga but it is not a happy day for the Russian who leaves the field after just thirteen minutes with a dislocated shoulder. United go on to win 3-2.
12th	United play out their third consecutive goalless draw against Russian opposition in European competition when they visit Volgograd.
15th	Eric Cantona confirms that he will attend a meeting in Paris called by Diego Maradona to attempt the formation of a World-wide Players Union. The Frenchman says "Of course I shall be there. Even if he only has one ally on the day, it will be me".
16th	United beat Bolton 3-0 to stay right in contention at the top of the FAPL.
18th	Cantona attends the launch of Maradona's International Association of Professional Footballers in Paris. Also in attendance are Italy's Gianluca Vialli, Brazil's Rai, Sweden's Tomas Brolin, Germany's Michael Rummenigge, and Abedi Pele of Ghana amongst others.
20th	Disaster hits United as debutant Pat McGibbon is sent off and the Reds crash 0-3 in the Coca Cola Cup to York City. The result equals United's worst ever home defeat in the competition against Everton and Spurs.
22nd	United sign York City's third choice goalkeeper Nick Culkin. They pay around £250,000 for the 17 year old.
23rd	United draw 0-0 against Sheffield Wednesday in the only goalless game of the afternoon in the FAPL but the point is good enough to take the Reds to the top.
26th	A last gasp goal from Peter Schmeichel saves United's unbeaten home record in European competition but it is not enough to put the Reds through as Volgograd win on the away goals rule. For the record, it is not Schmeichel's first goal from open play as he apparently once also scored in a Danish Third Division match. He is also not the first United 'keeper to score a goal, either, as Alex Stepney notched up some penalties in the Seventies. Meanwhile in Italy, Paul Ince serves out his suspension incurred after being sent off in the Champions League with United in 1994/95 as his Inter Milan team mates lose 1-0 at home to Swiss side Lugano and go out 2-1 on aggregate in a tie they were expected to win in a canter.

| 27th | Peter Schmeichel lands a hat-trick of Best European goalkeeper awards. Following his 1992 and 1993 awards, the big Dane missed out in 1994 but was again top dog in 1995 just ahead of Gothenburg's Thomas Ravelli and Michel Preudhomme of Sporting Lisbon. He finishes second in the World rankings calculated by the International Federation of Football Historians and Statisticians who name Argentinian Jose Luis Chilavert of Velez Sarsfield as the World No 1. |

| 29th | United's conquerors, Volgograd, are drawn to meet Bordeaux in the next Round of the UEFA Cup. |

| 30th | Former United Reserve 'keeper Gary Walsh plays superbly to keep a clean sheet as Middlesbrough beat Champions Blackburn Rovers whilst Mark Hughes scores the only goal of the game as Chelsea put an end to Arsenal's unbeaten start to the season. United's Juniors play South Africa's Under 23's in Johannesburg drawing 1-1 with a Michael Twiss goal. The game is watched by 12,000 despite being shown live on TV. |

October

| 1st | Eric Cantona makes a sensational comeback after his eight month suspension taking just sixty seconds to lay on an opening goal for Nicky Butt against arch rivals Liverpool. But the Anfield side come back to lead 2-1 before the Frenchman puts Giggs through to win a penalty which Cantona then converts for the equaliser. |

| 2nd | United's Juniors play the second of their two games against South Africa's Under 23's and this time go down 2-1 in front of a 20,000 crowd. |

| 3rd | United announce a massive £20m profit as income jumps 38% from £43.8m to £60.6m. Merchandising sales play their part by racing ahead by over 65% to a total of £23.5m. Television income rose from £4m to £6.8m and gate and programme receipts rose 10% to £19.6m. A player transfer surplus of £3.7m boosted the fund available to Alex Ferguson for incoming players to £8m. Andy Walsh of the United Independent Supporters Association says "We congratulate the club on the profit they have made but now it is time to reward the loyalty of the fans who have made it possible by announcing that season ticket prices will be frozen". |

| 4th | United beat York City 3-1 at Bootham Crescent but go out of the Coca Cola Cup 4-3 on aggregate. They are not the only FAPL club, |

however, to crash out to lower opposition with Mark Hughes making a mistake to gift Stoke City the only goal of the tie against Chelsea, Wimbledon lose 8-7 on aggregate to Charlton, Everton go down 4-2 after being two up at home to Millwall and Nottingham Forest lose 5-4 on aggregate to Bradford City.

5th   Man City supporters are busy gloating they are still in the Coca Cola Cup whilst United are not when the Blues score their first win of the season by beating Wycombe Wanderers.

6th   City's glee soon turns to tears when they are drawn to play Liverpool at Anfield in the next Round. Please don't laugh.

7th   An amazing crowd of 21,502 turns out at Old Trafford for a Reserve match against Leeds United. The attraction is Eric Cantona as he continues his come back but he limps off injured after just 18 minutes after a tackle by Leeds youngster Jason Blunt. As well as Cantona, United's second string includes Phil Neville, Lee Sharpe, Brian McClair, Paul Scholes and Terry Cooke of the current first team squad whilst Leeds have David White, Phil Masinga, Noel Whelan and Rod Wallace in their line up. The Reds win with two late goals from Cooke and Graeme Tomlinson.

10th   Arthur Albiston, who appeared in no fewer than four FA Cup Finals for United between 1977 and 1985, signs for Witton Albion in the UniBond League from Scottish club Ayr United. Ryan Giggs has an outstanding game for Wales against Germany earning the following tribute from German boss Bertie Vogts "The only problem for Ryan Giggs is that he doesn't have a German passport".

13th   United introduce their latest merchandising line, two new isotonic sports and vitamin drinks.

14th   United beat City 1-0 in the 'Derby' match which leaves the Blues with just one point from nine matches and is their eighth successive league defeat. Former Red Keith Gillespie scores twice as league leaders Newcastle come back to win 3-2 at QPR whilst Mark Hughes sets up Denis Wise for the only goal of the game at Aston Villa.

17th   United's UEFA Cup conquerors, Rotor Volgograd, lose 2-1 in the First Leg of their tie against Bordeaux.

18th   Deniol Graham, who made one league appearance for the Reds in 1987 against Wimbledon plus one as substitute against Derby County in 1989 along with one substitute appearance in both the FA Cup and League Cup against QPR and Hull City respectively, signs for GM

Vauxhall Conference club Dagenham and Redbridge from Halifax Town. Graham also won one Welsh Under 21 cap in 1990 whilst still with United.

21st   Mark Hughes scores against United at Stamford Bridge but the Reds run out 4-1 winners as the Londoners have Frank Sinclair sent off. They don't, however, make up any ground on leaders Newcastle who blast six past Wimbledon who have Vinny Jones as stand-in goalkeeper following the dismissal of Paul Heald for a second bookable offence. United lose an FAPL record as Forest beat Bolton to make it 23 games unbeaten since February overhauling the Reds 22 game run from September 1993 to February 1994.

23rd   United bring over two South African teenagers for trials. They are 17 year old Junaid Hartley, a goal scoring winger from Wits University and 16 year old defender Japie Motale from Mameladi Sundowns FC. Hartley was his country's leading goalscorer when South Africa won the recent African Nations Youth Tournament by beating Mozambique in the Final. It was South Africa's first ever football tournament success at any level. Motale, despite his age, has represented Northern Transvaal Under 20's and is the brother of Edward Motale a current full South Africa international.

24th   City fans, having gloated at United supporters as their team stay in the Coca Cola Cup for one match more than the Reds, are quickly silenced when beaten 4-0 by Liverpool. Unlucky Paul Parker, having missed most of the 94/95 campaign, now enters hospital for a cartilage operation.

25th   United's summer target, Ajax winger Marc Overmars, says he is willing to drop his wage demands by £10,000 a week and Ajax drop his fee by £4m, just over half the original asking price.

28th   United welcome back Bryan Robson and Gary Walsh as Middlesbrough bring the meanest defence in the country to Old Trafford. But the hospitality doesn't extend to the points as Gary Pallister scores against his old team whilst Andy Cole adds a second against a side that had only conceded four goals in ten games. Bad news, however, as Roy Keane is dismissed for the third time in six months after striking Fjortoft. City deprive United of another record as they are thrashed at Anfield for the second time in five days. This time it is 6-0 which is City's heaviest ever FAPL defeat thus removing the 5-0 debacle at the hands of United from the Maine Road record books.

29th	Paul Ince, having a desperate time in Italy, finally elicits some praise from the Italian press after helping his side to a 1-1 draw against arch rivals AC Milan. The former Red, who has consistently picked up the lowest marks in the media's post match assessments, is awarded his side's highest marking.
30th	Ince is linked with Arsenal but United say they have to be approached first before any deal can take place.

November

4th	With Newcastle not playing, United lose out on the chance to go top when they go down 1-0 at Arsenal thanks to an uncharacteristic mistake from Denis Irwin.
5th	Newcastle beat Spurs to go five points clear at the top.
6th	Roy Keane is the latest player to enter hospital. He is to undergo a hernia operation and will be out for six weeks. His loss, however, is reduced by the fact that he would have missed four games due to suspension. Alex Ferguson enters his tenth year at Old Trafford. His first nine years saw him take charge for 482 senior games which produced 254 victories and just 94 defeats of which 42 came prior to the start of the 1990's when his policies really began to bear fruit.
7th	United send 20 year old Ben Thornley on loan to Stockport County to gain first team experience as they did with Keith Gillespie and David Beckham who went on loan from Old Trafford to Wigan Athletic and Preston North End respectively.
8th	Denis Irwin signs a new contract that will take the former Oldham Athletic defender up to the summer of 1998. Newcastle beat Blackburn Rovers 1-0 to go eight points clear of United whilst at Middlesbrough, Bryan Robson plays his first game in six months and lays on the opening goal in a 2-0 Coca Cola Cup victory over Crystal Palace. The daughter of former Red Denis Viollet, Rachel, moves into the World's top 300 ladies tennis players at 299.
9th	United say they are not interested in taking up their option on Paul Ince and free him to enter in to discussions with Arsenal, Spurs, Blackburn and Newcastle.
10th	United win against Newcastle but the success comes off the pitch as the FA agree that the Red's Christmas clash with their rivals should

be put back 24 hours. Newcastle didn't want a change but United were adamant that they were at a disadvantage playing Newcastle just 48 hours after meeting Leeds whilst Newcastle had no game.

11th No game for United but two members of United's 1977 FA Cup winning side are involved in the First Round of the FA Cup with differing fortunes. Arthur Albiston is on the losing side as Witton Albion are beaten 2-1 but David McCreery, now coaching at Blyth Spartans, sees his side humble Bury 2-0. Two of his players, Mark Telford and Tommy Ditchburn, work a night shift until 8.00am, are met at the factory gate and are then driven to Bury on a mattress in the back of a van to enable them to get some sleep before playing. A million miles away from McCreery's Wembley victory! United's surprise signing from York City, teenage 'keeper Nick Culkin, is sent off as the 'B' team defeat Manchester City 2-1 with Culkin outstanding until dismissed in the 86th minute for handling the ball outside his area. The 'A' team win 6-1 at Marine Reserves to cap a bleak day for the Merseyside non-leaguers whose first team are swamped 11-2 in the FA Cup by Shrewsbury Town.

13th Inter Milan announce that Paul Ince is definitely staying in Italy despite all the conjecture. Nearer home, United say they are amazed at rumours circulating that Lee Sharpe is unsettled and has appointed Mark Hughes's agent Dennis Roach to find him another club. Ferguson slaps a "not for sale" notice on the midfielder and says "The squad is already lightweight and needs strengthening rather than weakening".

14th Nicky Butt and David Beckham gain further international caps at Under 21 level in a 2-1 victory over Austria at Middlesbrough but Portugal beat the Republic of Ireland 3-1 to win the group which leaves England in second place and out of the European Under 21 Championships. Former United star Maurice Setters, now managing the Republic's Under 21s is incensed at Portugal's decisive second goal which is scored with one of his players, Tottenham's, Owen Coll, lying injured with the referee refusing to allow him to be substituted or to receive attention even though the ball had gone out of play just prior to the goal!

15th Gary Pallister, Gary Neville, Peter Schmeichel, Ryan Giggs and Denis Irwin are all away on international duty with mixed results as England and Denmark win, Wales draw and the Republic of Ireland lose in Portugal which means they have to play off with Holland for the last place in the 1996 European Championships. Former Red, Paul

McGrath sets a new record of 79 caps for the Republic overtaking Pat Bonner's total.

18th A great day for second place United as they score three goals in the first eight minutes against Southampton and they are the only one of the top seven teams before play begins to win. Former United junior, David Johnson scores the only goal (the first League goal of his career) as Bury beat Cardiff City whilst Andrei Kanchelskis scores both Everton goals as they beat Liverpool at Anfield for the first time in eight years. One of the Russian's goals is a header and nobody can recall Kanchelskis scoring with his head in all his time at Old Trafford!

20th It is revealed that Nicky Butt is to face police charges after a man is injured during an argument in a city centre restaurant. Better news comes when United's second string sweep to the top of the Pontin's League with a 2-0 win over Wolves at Gigg Lane. Terry Cooke and Lee Sharpe are the goalscorers.

22nd United close the gap on Newcastle to just three points when they beat Coventry City 4-0 at Highfield Road. Facing Cantona is Richard Shaw who was at the centre of the incident that sparked off the trouble at Crystal Palace that led to Cantona's ban.

23rd Ferguson now scotches rumours that Paul Parker is having talks with a view to a possible move to Sunderland. "I am not aware of anything happening and I'm sure that Sunderland would not make an approach without informing us".

24th United's 'A' team win 2-0 away to Morecambe Reserves where the attendance of over 800 is more than the first team's normal home gate.

25th Newcastle come from behind with two goals in the 71st minute to beat Leeds United and increase their lead over United to five points with a game more played.

27th United dominate the game against Forest but can only draw 1-1. It could have been much worse but for ex United youth player Richard Irving missing a sitter in the last minute on his debut.

28th Peter Schmeichel flies home to Denmark for an operation on a troublesome elbow. He is likely to be out of action for two weeks.

29th Paul Ince suffers another blow to his Italian career when he picks up a one match ban for his fourth yellow card of the season. Alex Ferguson's son, Darren, scores what proves to be the winner as First Division Wolves beat Premiership Coventry City in the 4th Round of the Coca Cola Cup.

30th   United are told that their game against Sheffield Wednesday on 9th December will go ahead despite Jack Charlton invoking the "five day rule" that means United must do without both Denis Irwin and Roy Keane who will be required to play for the Republic of Ireland against Holland on 13th December. Had it been an England match, United could have got a postponement.

December

1st   United announce massive profits of £20m at their AGM. But fans hoping to hear that ticket prices would be frozen were in for a disappointment. They are told that no decision would be made until April at the earliest.

2nd   United fail to close the gap significantly on league leaders Newcastle United when they are held to a 1-1 draw at Old Trafford by Chelsea. The Londoners have an astonishing record at Old Trafford losing just twice in the past thirty years. Newcastle have a good day all round without even playing as not one of their nearest eight challengers win!

3rd   Wimbledon, who start the game third from bottom, do United a big favour when they hold Newcastle to a 3-3 draw to prevent the Geordies taking a seven point lead on level games.

5th   United lose 2-1 to an International Select X1 in Belfast. The Reds had sent a team for the game staged by Cooperation North, a non-political organisation for the promotion of understanding between the two communities of Northern Ireland. United's goal came from Paul Scholes in the 54th minute sandwiched between strikes from Phil Masinga (Leeds United) and Northern Ireland international Jimmy Quinn. The match raises £160,000 for the charity.

9th   United can only draw at home to Sheffield Wednesday but close the gap on Newcastle to four points as the Geordies lose at Chelsea. Ryan Giggs is injured and put down. The horse named after the United player is hurt at Haydock Park and the vets cannot save him.

12th   United are beaten 3-1 by Celtic in Paul McStay's testimonial match. Paul Scholes scores the Red's goal against two from Dutchman Pierre Van Hooijdonk and Chris Hay. But the Old Trafford outfit are without most of their big names including Gary Neville and Denis Irwin on international duty and Roy Keane, Eric Cantona and Ryan Giggs injured. Neville wins his sixth cap as England draw 1-1 with Portugal.

13th Denis Irwin is in the Republic of Ireland side that loses 2-0 to Holland at Anfield in the play off for the last place in Euro '96.

14th Roy Keane breaks down with an ankle injury in his come back match for United Reserves against Oldham Athletic at Gigg Lane. Des Baker, who comes on in place of Keane, scores a last gasp equaliser just after Jovan Kirovski had scored what looked likely to be merely a consolation effort after the young Reds side had gone two behind to a team that included six of Oldham's first team party to Genoa a couple of days previously.

16th Newcastle increase their lead to seven points over second placed United when they beat Everton 1-0 despite having to play with ten men after Beresford is dismissed in the first half.

17th United put on a poor performance to lose 2-0 at Anfield where Denis Irwin is on the losing side at the ground for the second time in five days. The result leaves Newcastle seven points clear. Better news for Old Trafford is that they will play hosts to Germany in the Group matches at Euro '96. The Germans opponents will be Italy, Czech Republic and Russia.

18th Christmas comes a week early across the city at Maine Road. Seven days before Christmas the Sky Blues score their TENTH league goal of the campaign when drawing 1-1 with Forest! And to think in that time Alan Ball had won a Manager of the Month Award!!

19th UniBond League club Frickley Athletic announce that former United player Mark Dempsey will take over as player-manager until the end of the season. Dempsey played two first team games during his time at Old Trafford and scored in both legs of the 1981/82 FA Youth Cup Final which the Reds lost 7-6 to Watford.

20th 28 year old French international central defender William Prunier begins a fortnight's trial at Old Trafford with a debut for the Reserves in a 3-1 win over Derby County. If United like what they see, Prunier is available from Bordeaux on a free transfer. The game also sees the return from suspension of Nicky Butt as United go three up in 27 minutes helped by an own goal from Wayne Sutton after just 99 secs.

21st Matthew Wicks, one of the youngsters at the centre of the allegations against United that they are poaching other club's promising teenagers, is said to be homesick and wanting to return to London. Alex Ferguson says reports that he will be allowed to return to Arsenal are not correct until "we are satisfied that everything is alright and we have certain guarantees". Spurs and Chelsea (for whom his father, Steve, played for many seasons) are also said to be monitoring the situation.

23rd   Newcastle go ten points clear of United at the top of the Premiership when they beat Forest 3-1. Paul Ince is sent off in Italy.

24th   United put in another pretty poor performance and lose 3-1 at Leeds to leave themselves ten points adrift of Kevin Keegan's men.

26th   United, without Pallister, Bruce and Parker all injured, desperately try to contact Bordeaux to get permission to play Prunier against Newcastle but, because of the Christmas holidays, cannot make contact.

27th   United with Gary Neville and David May filling the gap left by Bruce and Pallister put on a superb display to beat leaders Newcastle 2-0 and reduce the gap at the top to 7 points.

30th   The Reds claw back another three points with a 2-1 win over QPR that sees Prunier almost mark his debut with a goal that is eventually put away by Andy Cole for his third goal in successive games. The win reduces Newcastle's lead to four points.

31st   The year ends with United having won more points (83) in 1995 than any other club in the FAPL, scored more goals (74) than other FAPL club, and conceded fewer goals (32) than any other FAPL outfit. The next best on points are Newcastle with 78 whilst the Geordies and Notts Forest had the second highest number of goals with 67. The next best defence to United's was Liverpool who conceded 36. Man City came bottom of the points pile with a miserable 36 whilst only Coventry City and Sheffield Wednesday conceded more than their 56 goals against and only three clubs scored fewer goals than City's 48.

January

1st   Having ended 1995 on a high note, the Reds promptly begin the New Year by conceding four goals in an FAPL game for the first time when they crash 4-1 at Spurs but it could have been even worse as the London side also hit the woodwork twice! Peter Schmeichel is injured in the warm up and has to be replaced at half time by Kevin Pilkington whilst the Reds have a makeshift back four of Parker, Prunier, and the Neville brothers. Had United won, they would have closed the gap on Newcastle to a solitary point. Amazingly, the last time United conceded four goals in a league game was also on New Year's Day and also against a London club managed by Gerry Francis when he brought QPR to Old Trafford in 1992!

2nd	Newcastle open up the gap at the top to seven points again when they outplay Arsenal. After the disastrous game at White Hart Lane, United refuse to offer Prunier a long term contract and say they want to see him play further games before making such a commitment. Prunier takes exception and returns home to France. The Reds are now understood to be targeting 24 year old Danish international Diego Tur of FC Copenhagen.
6th	Pallister, Bruce and Irwin all return for the Reds but they need a late equaliser from Eric Cantona to stay in the 3rd Round of the FA Cup against Sunderland. Former United player Denis Law loses his FA Cup goalscoring record as Ian Rush hits one of Liverpool's seven against Rochdale to take his tally of FA Cup goals to 42, one more than Law.
7th	United are drawn away to Reading in the 4th Round if they can survive the replay at Roker Park.
9th	Central defender Chris Casper scores the only goal of the game at Goodison Park as the Reserves win to go back to the top of the Pontins League. It is Casper's first goal of the season and is the start of an eventful five days for the youngster.
10th	Former United striker Andy Ritchie is given a free transfer by Scarborough.
11th	Casper is sent on a month's loan to Bournemouth to get first team experience. Ben Thornley's loan to Stockport County is extended to the maximum three months.
12th	United are found guilty by an FA Commission of "poaching" Matthew Wicks, the sixteen year old son of former Chelsea star Steve Wicks, from Arsenal. With the teenager having recently returned to the London club because of home sickness, United escape any financial penalties but the FA say that they didn't impose any sanctions solely due to the fact that Wicks had returned. That doesn't bode well for the other cases that United have to answer.
13th	United close the gap on Newcastle by a solitary point as they are held to a goalless draw at home by Aston Villa. Former Red Mark Hughes, now with Chelsea, is sent off at Goodison Park in his side's 1-1 draw. Strangely, his namesake who plays for Altrincham in the GM Vauxhall Conference, is also sent off in his club's game at home to Slough as Altrincham finish up with eight men. Chris Casper makes his debut for Bournemouth who have a sensational 5-4 win at Peterborough with Casper marking his debut with a goal.

27

16th	United come back from a goal down to win a cup-tie at Roker Park for the first time ever when they beat Sunderland 2-1 to earn a 4th Round FA Cup visit to Reading. Former United player Paul Ince is called back up for England training by Terry Venables after a year in the international wilderness.
19th	Manchester City 'keeper Tony Coton, unable to stake a first team spot due to the form of Eike Immel, signs for United in a £400,000 deal to act as understudy to Peter Schmeichel. He is the first City player to move to Old Trafford since Wyn Davies in 1972.
20th	United lose second spot on goal difference to Liverpool when the Anfield outfit hammer Leeds 5-0. Newcastle beat bottom team Bolton 2-1 at St James Park to go 12 points clear of Liverpool and the Reds.
21st	United could have lost third place to Spurs if the London club had beaten Aston Villa but the Birmingham outfit come out on top by two goals to one with former Red Paul McGrath on the scoresheet for both sides.
22nd	United win at Upton Park in the league for the first time since 1989 with Eric Cantona scoring the only goal of the game. Nicky Butt is sent off in controversial circumstances as the Reds receive six bookings from Referee Stephen Lodge whilst the worst tackle of the night, a two footed lunge at Andy Cole by the Hammers' Julian Dicks goes completely unpunished and leads directly to the Butt sending off. The win puts the Old Trafford side back in second place but still nine points adrift of Newcastle.
24th	Former United player Mark Hughes fails in his appeal to have his sending off for stamping on Everton's David Unsworth overturned. He will have to serve a five match suspension, three games for the sending off offence and two for being booked nine times to date in 1995/96! Peter Schmeichel signs a boots and kit deal with Reebok worth £300,000 over the next five years. The Dane immediately promises to donate £5,000 per year to the costs of setting up a goalkeeping foundation school in his homeland.
25th	United's opponents in the FA Cup have a goalkeeping crisis on their hands. Reading's number one choice Bulgarian Bobi Mihaylov is extremely doubtful with a thigh strain whilst number two 'keeper Nicky Hammond has chicken pox.
26th	Matthew Simmons, the man who provoked the Eric Cantona kung fu attack at Crystal Palace loses his appeal against not standing trial for his part in the incident. He had based his appeal on the fact that he

alleged he would not get a fair hearing because of all the media attention the case had received.

27th   Hammond plays in goal for Reading but United go through 3-0 with Paul Parker scoring his first ever FA Cup goal for United and only his second for the club in all his years at Old Trafford.

28th   Incredibly, United are drawn against Manchester City in the 5th Round of the FA Cup providing City overcome Coventry City when they meet in their re-arranged tie after the first meeting was postponed due to snow. The last time United played and beat Reading in the FA Cup was in 1954/55 and they promptly got knocked out in the next Round by Man City!

29th   United are found guilty by an FA Inquiry of poaching schoolboy David Brown from Oldham Athletic. They are fined £20,000, ordered to pay the costs of the Inquiry and told to agree compensation with Oldham. United refuse to comment saying they are "seriously thinking about making an appeal". Former United captain Bryan Robson also appears before the FA and is fined £750 along with two of his players, Neil Cox and Nigel Pearson, for using foul and abusive language to Referee Paul Danson after Middlesbrough's 1-0 defeat at Blackburn in December. It is Robson's first disrepute charge in his long and distinguished career. In a busy day for the diary, United turn down a request from Burnley to take 'keeper Kevin Pilkington on loan despite the arrival of Tony Coton from Man City. On the subject of Man City, their players are thrown out of the Meon Valley Golf and Country Club where they were preparing to play Southampton after other guests complain about some of the City player's conduct in the early hours of the morning.

30th   United announce that Nicky Butt has lodged an appeal against his sending off at West Ham.

31st   With rumours raging about the formation of a European Super League, United announce that they will be one of three English clubs invited to Switzerland in February for talks with UEFA regarding the proposal. The other two English clubs at the forum will be Liverpool and Arsenal.

February

1st   The FA state they will not even ask referee Stephen Lodge to review the Nicky Butt dismissal against West Ham. They say the dismissal was for a second yellow card and there is no right of appeal in the laws against a yellow card offence! United are very upset especially as the referee had said he was more than willing to study the incident on video and, if necessary, to review his decision. Butt will miss the game against Blackburn as a result. The Reds come to the rescue of Oldham Rugby League club when they allow the rugby boys to train at the Cliff to prepare for their cup-tie against Warrington. Oldham's own ground has been covered in snow for days. In Germany, former Manchester City import Maurizio Gaudino, who played against United in last season's 'derby' match at Maine Road, is given a suspended three year jail sentence for his part in a car insurance fraud.

2nd   United announce they have applied to the relevant authorities for a licence to enable the ground to be used as a venue for 'matches' of another kind. If granted the licence, Old Trafford will be able to hold Civil Wedding ceremonies. Meanwhile, Blackburn reveal what it cost them to deny United a hat-trick of Championships when they announce a loss of £3,954,000 for their year ending June 1995. This is in addition to a loss the previous year of £8.2m.

3rd   Eric Cantona returns to Selhurst Park for the first time since his infamous 'kung fu' attack on a spectator a year earlier. With his bodyguard Ned Kelly constantly eyeing the crowd for any attempt to provoke the Frenchman, Cantona scores twice as the Reds beat Wimbledon 4-2. But they do not cut the gap on Newcastle who make it thirteen home wins in as many games when they defeat Sheffield Wednesday.

4th   United deny any interest in Roberto Trotta, an Argentinian international whose club Velez Sarsfield were World Club Champions in 1995. Trotta, who had scored the opening goal when the South American Champions beat AC Milan for the title, is a central defender available for £2.5m.

5th   After the previous day's denials, the Old Trafford outfit admit they are trying to to get South African international Mark Fish to come to Manchester. The central defender had a great African Nations competition keeping Ghana's Tony Yeboah under lock and key in the semi final and then playing a commanding role in his side's victory over Tunisia in the Final. Several other clubs, however, are also interested in the player who is rated as worth £1m by his club Orlando Pirates.

6th   Nicky Butt is arrested and charged with causing damage to a car as he left a night club in Hale Barns in the early hours of the previous Sunday morning after celebrating his side's win at Wimbledon. It is alleged that he kicked the car causing damage to the value of £250. Better news, though, for Ryan Giggs. He signs a contract with Reebok that assures him of a minimum £1.8m whilst his earnings from it could be swelled to a staggering £6m by the year 2002 if he and United are successful in their bid for honours.

7th   United look to be assured of a place in the 1996/97 European Champions League even if they don't catch Newcastle after UEFA unveil plans to expand the competition in order to head off the ambitions of the major European clubs to start a League of their own. As well as the Champions, UEFA will select a second club based on the past five season's domestic and European form leaving the Reds an automatic selection for the second English spot. Former United striker Dion Dublin scores a 93rd minute equaliser to force a replay for Coventry against Man City in the FA Cup as United wait to see which of the two sides they will face in the Fifth Round.

8th   South African Mark Fish agrees to visit Old Trafford for talks ahead of a possee of Italian clubs. Meanwhile, United's rivals for the title, Newcastle United, spend another £7.5m to strengthen their squad still further when they land Columbian Faustino Asprilla from Italian club Parma.

9th   United strike it rich by signing a record sponsorship deal with kit manufacturers Umbro that is rumoured to be worth £60m over six years. Umbro make the move even though their present deal with the Reds still has two years to run in order to head off offers from other sports wear makers such as Nike, Adidas and Reebok.

10th   United beat Blackburn with a Lee Sharpe goal that is his first for five months. But the Reds don't close the gap on Newcastle as former United 'keeper Gary Walsh, now playing for Middlesbrough, gifts a winning goal to Les Ferdinand after new record signing Asprilla had set up an equaliser for Kevin Keegan's side.

11th   Ex Red Frank Stapleton is appointed head coach of New England Revolutions in the US Major League.

12th   Former United junior Alan Wardle becomes a millionaire when he sells his company Caldwell's the Stationers to an American concern for £1.47m. The 54 year old former defender started work at the company on a part time basis whilst still training at Old Trafford. After failing to make the grade at football he took over Caldwells with the help of a business friend and built it up from a staff of five to a position where it employed 56 people. Wardle, who went on to play for Altrincham, Northwich Victoria and Winsford United, is the present Chairman of the Manchester United Former Players Association.

14th   Manchester City beat Coventry City 2-1 in their replay to earn an all Manchester 'Derby' Fifth Round FA Cup tie with United. Everton, who denied the Reds a second successive FA Cup success at Wembley the previous May, crash out to humble Port Vale.

15th   UEFA change their thinking on qualification for the 96/97 League of Champions and United are now far from certain to qualify as the fresh edict indicates it will be this season's runners-up who qualify as well as the Champions rather than the club with the best record over the past five seasons. There is also bad news for Eric Cantona who isn't included in the French squad to play Greece in a friendly. There had been considerable speculation that Cantona would be recalled.

16th   Former Red Lee Martin links up with Ron Atkinson at Coventry City after being given a free transfer by Glasgow Celtic to whom United sold him for £350,000 in January 1994. Martin's claim to fame at Old Trafford was his goal that won the 1990 FA Cup for United in the 1-0 replay victory over Crystal Palace. It was the only goal he scored in the competition during his United career.

17th   The all Manchester FA Cup 5th Round tie is announced as a sell out. All 42,000 tickets are sold with gate receipts of almost £675,000. TV Fees and perimeter advertising take the total income generated to £1m which is believed to be a record for any tie other than a Final or semi-final.

18th   United beat City 2-1 but it takes a controversial penalty decision to get United level after the Blues had taken an early lead. Sharpe scores the winner in the second period. It extends Ferguson's brilliant record against City to just one defeat in sixteen derby games. The Reds then promptly receive more good news when they are drawn at home in the last eight to either Southampton or Swindon Town.

20th   United are stunned when South African defender Mark Fish cuts short his visit to Old Trafford in order to fly to Europe for talks with a top Continental side, believed to be Lazio.

21st   United beat Everton 2-0 in a re-arranged league game and then learn they have cut Newcastle's lead to six points as Kevin Keegan's team slump 0-2 at West Ham. It is a seventh straight win for the Reds.

22nd   Ben Thornley goes out on loan again, this time to Huddersfield Town after his two month spell at Stockport County.

23rd	United skipper Steve Bruce signs an astonishing footwear deal with Diadora that sees him pocket a six figure sum for a contract that is longer than the one he actually has to play for United!. The 35 year old was given an 18 month contract in August 1995 when Derby County, Wolves and Sheffield United all tried to lure him into management but the contract signed with Diadora is for two years.
24th	City do United a big favour when they draw 3-3 with leaders Newcastle but it could have been so much better as Kevin Keegan's side come from behind on three occasions. Newcastle actually therefore increase their lead to seven points despite dropping two points.
25th	United smash six past bottom club Bolton Wanderers at Burnden Park to record their biggest FAPL away victory and also their biggest ever win at the ground where they have only twelve wins in 47 visits. The three points obtained slashes Newcastle's lead at the top to four points.
26th	Simon Davies asks to be placed on the transfer list and promptly alerts interested parties to his potential by scoring two cracking goals as the Reserves register their sixth Pontins League victory on the bounce when beating Sheffield United 3-0 at Chesterfield. Gary Neville, unable to regain his first team berth after suspension, scores the other.
27th	Mark Fish's agent, Josie Pinnock, reveals that the highly rated South African has signed for Lazio. Pinnock then says "Fish would have been happy to sign for United but Alex Ferguson suddenly demanded a trial period. When we came over it was specifically stated there would be no trials because the lad has played in 17 of his country's last 19 internationals during which time they have proved to be the best team in Africa. When Ferguson went back on this precondition it was a real disappointment but we simply took the lad to Lazio who couldn't believe their luck". Lazio paid out £1m for his transfer from South African club Orlando Pirates.
28th	Southampton overcome Swindon Town to earn a trip to Old Trafford in the Sixth Round of the FA Cup.
29th	Alex Ferguson is named Carling Manager of the Month for February. It is the first time he has won the award during 1995/96 season.

March

4th	United close the gap on Newcastle to just one point when they beat their rivals for the title with Eric Cantona scoring the only goal of a pulsating game at St James Park.

33

5th	The Stock Market reacts to United's win the previous evening by marking up their share price by 13p which adds £7.9m to the value of the club as the shares reach their highest point of the campaign at 280p each. United's share issue is 60.8m which at 280p a share values the club at £170m. After they were knocked out of the UEFA Cup by Rotor Volgograd in September the share price plummeted to 197p. United's Youth team relinquish their grasp on the FA Youth Cup when they are beaten in the last minute at Anfield. Liverpool owe their victory to 16 year old FA School of Excellence pupil Michael Owen who notches a hat trick. Grant Brebner and Michael Twiss had put the young Reds in front after Owen had drawn first blood early in the second period but Owen equalised from the penalty spot and then hit the winner in the final seconds of the tie.
10th	United are drawn to play Wimbledon or Chelsea in the semi-finals of the FA Cup providing they can overcome Southampton at Old Trafford. The Sunday papers run a drugs story concerning Lee Sharpe and Man City's Nicky Summerbee.
11th	United beat Southampton 2-0 with Eric Cantona scoring yet again.
13th	Liverpool, chasing Newcastle and the Reds hard for the title, are held at home by Wimbledon who maintain their impressive record against the Anfield side in a 2-2 draw. The Dons have lost only twice in the last fifteen meetings with the Merseysiders.
14th	Former United full back Arthur Albiston is appointed manager at UniBond League outfit Droylsden.
16th	Alex Ferguson makes unforced changes to a team that has just won ten games on the bounce for the visit to QPR. He leaves out Nicky Butt, Phil Neville and Lee Sharpe and the Reds lose two vital points as they only draw with the next to bottom London side. It could have been much worse, however, as Cantona only scores the equaliser in the fourth minute of stoppage time. Some small consolation is that the point is sufficient to take the Reds to top spot on goal difference although Newcastle have two games in hand.
18th	Former United 'keeper Les Sealey gives a brilliant display on his debut for West Ham against United's major rivals Newcastle at St James Park. He keeps the Magpies at bay almost singlehanded for more than thirty minutes but the incessant pressure tells and the Hammers eventually go down 3-0 despite Sealey's heroics. Newcastle have an incredible 41 attempts on goal during the game and they return to top spot on goal difference.

19th	United's Reserves lose for the first time in two months despite going a goal up through Terry Cooke against Derby County who fight back to win 2-1. Nicky Butt, who himself is facing two Court appearances, one for damaging a car outside a nightclub and another for assault in a City centre Chinese restaurant, has his car broken into. The thieves cause £90s worth of damage and steal golf clubs, a radio and match tickets.
20th	The Neville brothers are both included in the England squad named by Terry Venables to take on Bulgaria. They celebrate by helping United beat Arsenal with an Eric Cantona wonder goal taking United back to the top.
21st	Three of United's reserve team players are named in Northern Ireland's B team squad to take on Norway. Belfast born midfielder Philip Mulryne is joined by defenders Pat McGibbon, who hails from Lurgan, and Colin Murdock of Ballymena.
23rd	A terrific day for United as Newcastle lose at Arsenal and Liverpool crash at Forest. United return to top position on goal difference without even playing!
24th	United's weekend is complete when they beat Spurs 1-0 to go three points clear of Newcastle although they have played two games more. But Keane picks up a caution which means a one match ban. In the PFA Awards, Gary Neville, surprisingly, is the only Red to feature when he is named in the Player's FAPL select side. Neville also comes second to Liverpool's Robbie Fowler in the Young Player of the Year Award with Nicky Butt in third spot. In Italy, former United star Paul Ince is sent off at Udinese and it is reported that the Italian FA are likely to take a dim view of the fact that Ince takes a long time to leave the field.
25th	The Stock Market reacts to the weekend results by marking the club's shares up by a massive 28p to a year's high of 286p. United announce that because of the increased capacity at Old Trafford they are holding prices at current levels for the 1996/97 season. In Italy, Ince is reported to say that if the Italian FA take strong action against him he will invoke a clause in his contract that allows him to leave Italy after one season of his three season contract. Cissie Charlton, mother of former Red Bobby Charlton and his brother Jack, dies on Tyneside aged 84. United express fears after learning that some tickets for the semi final against Chelsea have been allocated by the FA placing 3,000 United fans in front of Chelsea supporters at the Holt End of Villa Park. The Football Supporters Association also describe the move as "a recipe for disaster".

26th	Young reserve player Phil Mulryne comes on as sub for Northern Ireland's B team and scores an 87th minute goal against Norway's Olympic team in a 3-0 victory. United announce half time operating profits of over £8m.
27th	In a topsy turvy few days for Paul Ince, the former United player regains his England place for the first time since February 1995 when he plays against Bulgaria with Gary Neville. Roy Keane is sent off, however, when captaining the Republic of Ireland against Russia.
28th	Paul Ince escapes with a one match ban for his dismissal at Udinese.
30th	United starlet Ben Thornley, on loan to Huddersfield Town, is sent off at Sunderland. But he isn't on his own as former Man City player Gary Flitcroft is also dismissed just three minutes into his new career at Blackburn!
31st	The Reds continue their remarkable record at Villa Park where they beat Chelsea 2-1 to reach the FA Cup Final for the third successive season. United have never lost a semi-final at Villa Park. The semi final appearance enables the Reds to close the gap on Everton who have played in 23 semis against United's 21. Liverpool, who beat Villa 3-0 at Old Trafford in the other semi, are third in the all time list of semi-final appearances with 20.

April

1st	It is revealed that Martin Edwards and his family made £4.4m from a sale of their shares. However, he retains overall control of the club with the shares retained by the family still worth some £41m.
2nd	Steve Bruce, who missed the semi final win over Chelsea due to a thigh strain picked up in training, is ruled out of the vital Easter programme. The FA announce that they have closed the book on the drug allegations concerning Lee Sharpe and City's Nicky Summerbee.
3rd	Liverpool have a sensational 4-3 win over Newcastle with Stan Collymore scoring the winner during stoppage time. The result, probably the first time United supporters have ever wanted the Anfield side to win, leaves United three points clear of the North East side and a slightly better goal difference although Newcastle still have one game in hand. There are more celebrations at Old Trafford as the Reds score a double in the Carling Monthly awards. Alex Ferguson picks up the Manager's prize for March whilst Eric Cantona scoops

the player's award. Ex Red Mark Hughes is fined £1,000 by the FA and suspended for two games after topping 45 disciplinary points in the campaign for Chelsea.

5th   United are presented with a hefty bill by the FA for allegedly poaching Michael Brown from Oldham Athletic. They have to pay £75,000 plus a further £25,000 if the youngster, who is currently the B team's leading scorer, makes five first team appearances followed by another £100,000 after 25 games and similar amounts after 50 and 75 appearances. If he is capped at Under 21 level it will cost United £25,000 whilst a full cap will take another £100,000 out of the United coffers.

6th   United win a thrilling Derby match when they overcome City 3-2 at Maine Road. It is very nearly so much better still but Newcastle, after trailing QPR at home for nearly all the game, come back to win with two goals from former United player Peter Beardsley in the last thirteen minutes. Liverpool, however, drop out of contention when they are surprisingly beaten 1-0 by relegation threatened Coventry City. In Italy, Paul Ince scores his first goal for Inter with a fierce first time effort from just outside the area as his side beat Cremonese 4-2.

8th   A brilliant day for the Reds as they beat Coventry City with yet another only goal of the game from Eric Cantona and then sit back in the evening to watch Blackburn Rovers score twice in the final four minutes through substitute Graham Fenton to beat Newcastle 2-1 after trailing. A Geordie himself, Fenton had only ever scored one goal previously for Rovers!

11th The Republic of Ireland are informed by FIFA that it is up to the Irish FA to impose any punishment on Roy Keane for his dismissal against Russia in March. They say they will not suspend the United midfielder but hand out a hefty fine instead.

13th United crash 3-1 at relegation threatened Southampton. They go three down before half time whereupon they change their kit from Grey to Blue. They have never won in the grey kit with four defeats and one draw. Former Red Mark Hughes scores a hat-trick for Chelsea against Leeds.

14th Newcastle beat Aston Villa with a solitary goal from Les Ferdinand to close to within three points of the Reds and with a game in hand.

15th United announce they are to discard the grey kit in which they have never won and will introduce a white kit for the following season with a £10 discount as a gesture to fans who have bought the grey.

16th	United win the toss to wear Red in the FA Cup Final against arch rivals Liverpool.
17th	It's as you were at the top as United and Newcastle both win 1-0. The Red's opponents, Leeds United, are reduced to ten men after just nineteen minutes when 'keeper Mark Beeney is dismissed but make hard work of it whilst only the woodwork stops Southampton nicking a point at St James Park against United's rivals for the title.
20th	Eric Cantona is voted Footballer of the Year by the Football Writer's Association just 15 months after his kung-fu attack on a Crystal Palace had seemed likely to drive him out of the English game. He won the PFA version of the Award in 1994 and becomes the fourth United player to win the Football Writer's vote following in the footsteps of Johnny Carey (1949), Bobby Charlton (1966) and George Best (1968). He wins 36% of the vote ahead of Ruud Gullit and Robbie Fowler with United's Steve Bruce and Peter Schmeichel fourth and fifth ahead of Peter Beardsley.
22nd	United's young Reserve Terry Cooke is called up for England's Under 21's for the match against Croatia at Sunderland.
23rd	Cooke's debut is not a happy one as England go down 1-0. But even unhappier is another United youngster Graeme Tomlinson who suffers a badly broken leg whilst playing his first full game on loan for Luton Town. He fractures his leg in two places just below his right knee in Luton's 1-0 defeat against Port Vale.
24th	Gary Neville is the only United representative in the England team held to a goalless draw at Wembley by Croatia. Peter Schmeichel keeps a clean sheet in Denmark's 2-0 win over Scotland but there is bad news for the Reds as Denis Irwin suffers a calf injury in the Republic of Ireland's 2-0 defeat in Czech Republic. He is immediately flown back in a private jet to England to receive treatment. Back in England, United's Reserves and A team make it a double celebration as they win their respective titles on the same street! United's Reserves beat Newcastle 2-0 at their second home of Gigg Lane whilst the A team hammer Bury 6-1 at Lower Gigg Lane.
27th	United unveil their tribute to Sir Matt Busby when the wraps are pulled off the nine foot statue that will stand forever outside the East Stand overlooking Sir Matt Busby Way. The statue, which is hollow, has been filled with memorabilia and souvenirs left outside Old Trafford by fans in tribute to Sir Matt when he passed away in 1994.

28th   United put five past Nottingham Forest to put real pressure on Newcastle United who are left six points behind the Reds with an inferior goal difference of seven although the North East side have three games left as opposed to United's one. Prior to the game Reserve team captain Chris Casper is presented with the Pontin's First Division Championship Trophy whilst Ronnie Wallwork receives the Lancashire League Division One Cup on behalf of the A team. It is the ninth time in thirteen seasons that the A side have captured their title.

29th   Newcastle reduce the points deficit to three when they beat Leeds with the only goal of the game coming from ex-Red Keith Gillespie. Leeds had hit the woodwork twice in the opening ten minutes. The 'Magpies' manager Kevin Keegan flips his lid in a TV interview after the game clearly indicating that Alex Ferguson has at least won the psychological battle. United's Youth team come from two down inside 16 minutes against Blackburn Rovers at Ewood Park to win the Lancashire Youth Cup Final.

30th   United announce that 2,300 seats in the lower tier of the new stand are set to triple in price to £1,169 per season. The same spots in the old cantilever stand had cost £340. Fans relocated when the old stand was demolished had been told they would be able to claim their old seats back but have now learned it is going to cost them dearly to do so. In addition, ordinary supporters are to be excluded from 1,300 seats in the first twelve rows of the second tier of the new North Stand as these are to be reserved for development of executive seating.

May

1st   Despite living in Jacksonville, USA, Rachel Viollet, the daughter of former United striker Denis Viollet, becomes Lancashire's number one ranked tennis player and under a new International Tennis Federation ruling can now expect to be called up by Great Britain. Until now, players residing overseas have not been eligible.

2nd   The man at the centre of the Eric Cantona kung fu attack at Crystal Palace pleads not guilty to charges arising from the incident in January 1995 saying he was merely on the way to the toilet when Cantona was sent off and that all he said was "Off, off, off, Cantona. Go and have an early bath". He is found guilty and fined £500 with £200 costs as well as being banned from all football grounds for twelve months. He then immediately assaults the prosecuting officer and is sentenced to seven days imprisonment for contempt of court.

On the field of play, an Ian Woan thunderbolt later timed at 91 mph equalises an earlier Peter Beardsley strike as Nottingham Forest deny Newcastle two points. Kevin Keegan refuses to appear in TV after the game. United now only need to draw their last game at Middlesbrough to regain their title. Incredibly, the 2nd May has proved to be a very lucky day for the Reds in the past few years for in 1993 it was this day that saw Oldham Athletic beat Aston Villa 1-0 to give United the title whilst on the same date in 1994 United took the Championship when Coventry City defeated Blackburn Rovers 2-1. Nottingham Forest just failed to repeat the performance but the draw certainly helped United's cause no end!

4th 25 year old Angela McDonough and 35 year old Gerry McKenna become the first couple to tie the knot at Old Trafford since the ground was granted a licence to perform wedding ceremonies. Later in the day, United Associate Schoolboys Paul Wheatcroft and Lee Fitzpatrick also tread the hallowed turf when they represent England in the Under 15s international against Holland in front of a crowd in excess of 12,000.

5th United beat Middlesbrough 3-0 to take their third FA Premiership in four years. They finish four points in front of Newcastle who are held at home by Spurs. At the other end of the table Manchester City become the fifth club that Alan Ball has led to relegation following in the footsteps of Blackpool, Portsmouth, Stoke City and Exeter City. That is a real run of bad luck! United's title win earns them £983,300 in prize money.

11th Brian Kidd is involved in a dramatic rescue on the River Thames just hours before United take on Liverpool in the FA Cup Final. Strolling along the banks of the river near the Windsor Hotel where the players were staying prior to the big game, Kidd spotted a young canoeist in the water and in some trouble after capsizing. The Assistant Manager went in and pulled the canoeist to safety. Ryan Giggs, who was with Kidd at the time, said the canoeist asked "Are you lads down here for the Cup Final?". Later in the day United beat Liverpool 1-0 with an Eric Cantona special to put themselves in the record books as the first club ever to do the 'double' twice.

16th Just days after steering United to a historic second double, Alex Ferguson is, amazingly, embroiled in talks regarding his future at Old Trafford. He wants a six year contract to take him up to retirement but Martin Edwards and the Board only offer a three year deal despite insisting they want the Scot to stay until he retires.

17th	Brian Kidd, having helped Ferguson plot United's path to the double, now has his eyes set on the World Cup. He has been enlisted by Ghana to prepare them for their World Cup qualifier against Tanzania during the summer.
18th	The squabble over Alex Ferguson's contract is ended with a compromise that sees him win a four year deal reputed to be worth as much as the six year deal he was originally seeking.
20th	The Paris headquarters of the French FA was under siege by angry fans after confirmation that Eric Cantona was not included in the French squad for Euro 96. But French manager Aime Jacquet was unmoved, saying that he did not doubt Cantona's qualities but his team had built an unbeaten run of twenty games without Cantona and he was not prepared to alter his system to accommodate the United player.
21st	United release Paul Parker on a free transfer with Derby County and his former club QPR both rumoured to be keen on acquiring the services of the 32 year old. The Reds also release youngsters Des Baker, Danny Hall, Phil Whittaker and Heath Maxon.
22nd	Nicky Butt pulls out of the England Under 21 squad for the annual Toulon tournament but United still have three players, David Beckham, Ben Thornley and Terry Cooke in the 18 strong party. One of United's all time greats, George Best, celebrates his 50th birthday. He played 466 games for United, scoring 178 goals before moving on to play briefly for Fulham, Hibernian, Motherwell, Cork Celtic and Bournemouth. A little known fact about the 37 times capped Best is that his mother was an Irish international at hockey.
23rd	Steve Bruce shocks United by accepting an offer to join Birmingham City on a free transfer and earns himself £2. The Neville brothers play in the same England team against China to equal a 120 year old record. Not since 1876 have a pair of brothers played in a Cup Final winning side and then appeared together for England. Frank and Hubert Heron of The Wanderers were the last pair to achieve this feat.
24th	Roy Keane is the latest Old Trafford double hero to become embroiled in contract talks. He tables a demand for a new million pound a year deal some twelve months before his current contract expires. United are in danger of losing the midfielder for nothing under the new freedom of movement should his contract expire, and it is known that a number of wealthy Italian and Spanish clubs are interested.

The Season
Match by Match

United flew half way round the world to kick off their 1995/96 campaign with two games in Malaysia against the host country's Champions, Selangor. The opening game saw Paul Parker play his first match after missing virtually all of the 1994/95 season through injury. The former England player lasted just over an hour and was "quite outstanding" according to Brian Kidd who was in charge of the touring party in the absence of Alex Ferguson who missed the trip due to an ear infection.

This game also saw the introduction of United's new grey strip that was only officially launched back in Britain the following day. With both Giggs and Cantona missing due to injury and suspension this was a good performance with Keane looking superb whilst old hand Bruce opened the scoring after 48 minutes with a header. Butt added the second four minutes later when he raced onto a through ball to slide it past the 'keeper in a one on one situation before Bruce's central defence partner, Gary Pallister copied his captain's header to make it three in the 64th minute. Sharpe was the crowd's favourite and a spectacular fourth goal from him was just what the screaming fans wanted before Ollerenshaw reduced the deficit 12 minutes from time.

The second leg for the Glamoir Invitation Cup came two days later but, after United's comprehensive first leg win two days earlier, many of the locals stayed away for the return. Bruce quickly increased United's aggregate lead with a diving header and Scholes made certain with a deadly finish on the half hour.

Back in England, United lost their first friendly to Birmingham City when the Reds looked somewhat jaded after their Far East trip. Nevertheless, it took an outstanding performance from City 'keeper Ian Bennett to keep United out. He made a fine stop from Scholes in 17th minute but shouldn't have stood a chance with the rebound had Butt found the target instead of firing wildly over. But Bennett's best effort was saved for a 54th minute point blank save from Roy Keane that had the Irish international holding his head in disbelief. By then United were a goal down courtesy of Birmingham substitute Chris Whyte who had only been on the pitch six minutes when he latched on to a quickly taken free kick by Hunt just prior to the interval with United's defence taken by surprise at the quickness of the kick and that was how the scoreline stayed.

Next stop on a hectic schedule was Bradford City and the Reds were very fortunate not to go behind again after only six minutes when Ian Ormondroyd missed an open goal. United got over their slow start and took the lead after 38 minutes with a gem of a goal. Butt lofted the ball into Steve Bruce who had stayed forward after a corner and the central defender squared the ball into the path of the onrushing Keane. The Irish international hit a superbly struck shot for the only strike of the game. But within a minute Keane's Jekyll and Hyde character was again revealed when he reacted badly to a clumsy challenge from behind by City's giant Eddie Youds that resulted in both players going in the book where they were later joined by Butt.

Alex Ferguson took in his first game of the campaign when United stopped off in Ireland to take on Shelbourne. After missing the trip to Malaysia with his ear infection, the United manager was then pre-occupied with chasing Cantona to France when United played Birmingham and Bradford. United included Terry Cooke, a member of the 1995 FA Youth Cup winning side in their starting line up and it was a cross from the youngster that gave Butt the opportunity to head home an equaliser in the 27th minute after Vinnie Arkins had given the locals a 12th minute lead. United then gifted the Irish part-timers the lead back again when Geoghegan robbed Gary Neville seven minutes into the second period and easily beat Pilkington. United's blushes were spared when Beckham controlled a through ball and took it round the 'keeper before cooly stroking his shot home.

United's geography lesson continued with a trip to Scotland to meet East Fife in a game which was a Testimonial for Alex Ferguson's one time coaching mentor, Jimmy Bonthrone. The Scottish side, however, had opened their domestic league campaign only twenty-four hours earlier and looked tired. Beckham opened the scoring after twenty minutes with a shot from just outside the area after being *teed up* by Sharpe and he was to round off the scoring in the 72nd minute with an identical effort. In between, McClair and Sharpe found the net to give the Reds an easy victory.

The final pre-season game was nearer home at Oldham Athletic for a fixture to mark the East Lancashire club's Centenary. The celebrations, however, were muted in a tame game in which the sole highlight was a fabulous strike from Lee Sharpe after 26 minutes. Ten minutes after half-time the tone for the match was confirmed when Ben Thornley's cross was pushed out by Oldham 'keeper Jon Hallsworth against the legs of his own defender Richard Jobson who looked on in horror as the rebound finished up in the Ol Oldham net. The real thing was now about to begin.

Results Summary

Date	Type	Opposition	Ven	Score	Scorers	Att
31/07/95	Friendly	Selangor StateSelect	(a)	4-1	Bruce, Butt, Pallister, Sharpe	n/k
2/08/95	Friendly	Selangor State Select	(a)	2-0	Bruce, Scholes	n/k
7/08/95	Friendly	Birmingham City	(a)	0-1		n/k
9/08/95	Friendly	Bradford City	(a)	1-0	Keane	n/k
11/08/95	Friendly	Shelbourne	(a)	2-2	Beckham, Butt	n/k
13/08/95	Friendly	East Fife	(a)	4-0	Beckham 2, McClair, Sharpe	n/k
15/08/95	Friendly	Oldham Athletic	(a)	2-0	Sharpe, Jobson (og)	n/k
19/08/95	FAPL	Aston Villa	(a)	1-3	Beckham	34,655
23/08/95	FAPL	West Ham Utd	(h)	2-1	Scholes, Keane	31,966
26/08/95	FAPL	Wimbledon	(h)	3-1	Keane 2, Cole	32,226
28/08/95	FAPL	Blackburn Rovers	(a)	2-1	Sharpe, Beckham	29,843
9/09/95	FAPL	Everton	(a)	3-2	Sharpe 2, Giggs	39,496
12/09/95	UEFA 1 (1)	Rotor Volgograd	(a)	0-0		40,000
16/09/95	FAPL	Bolton Wanderers	(h)	3-0	Scholes 2, Giggs	32,812
20/09/95	CCC 2 (1)	York City	(h)	0-3		29,049
23/09/95	FAPL	Sheffield Wednesday	(a)	0-0		34,101
26/09/95	UEFA 1 (2)	Rotor Volgograd	(h)	2-2	Scholes, Schmeichel	29,724
30/09/95	FAPL	Liverpool	(h)	2-2	Butt, Cantona (Pen)	34,934
3/10/95	CCC 2 (2)	York City	(a)	3-1	Scholes 2, Cooke	9,386
14/10/95	FAPL	Manchester City	(h)	1-0	Scholes	35,707
21/10/95	FAPL	Chelsea	(a)	4-1	Scholes 2, Giggs, McClair	31,019
28/10/95	FAPL	Middlesbrough	(h)	2-0	Pallister, Cole	36,580
4/11/95	FAPL	Arsenal	(a)	0-1		38,317
18/11/95	FAPL	Southampton	(h)	4-1	Giggs 2, Scholes, Cole	39,301
25/11/95	FAPL	Coventry City	(a)	4-1	McClair 2, Irwin, Beckham	23,400
27/11/95	FAPL	Nottingham Forest	(a)	1-1	Cantona (Pen)	29,263
2/12/95	FAPL	Chelsea	(h)	1-1	Beckham	42,019
9/12/95	FAPL	Sheffield Wednesday	(h)	2-2	Cantona 2	41,849
17/12/95	FAPL	Liverpool	(a)	0-2		40,546
24/12/95	FAPL	Leeds United	(a)	1-3	Cole	39,801
27/12/95	FAPL	Newcastle United	(h)	2-0	Cole, Keane	42,024
30/12/95	FAPL	QPR	(h)	2-1	Cole, Giggs	41,890
1/01/96	FAPL	Spurs	(a)	1-4	Cole	32,852
6/01/96	FAC 3	Sunderland	(h)	2-2	Butt, Cantona	41,563
13/01/96	FAPL	Aston Villa	(h)	0-0		42,667
16/01/96	FAC 3 R	Sunderland	(a)	2-1	Scholes, Cole	21,378

44

Date	Competition	Opponent		Score	Scorers	Attendance
22/01/96	FAPL	West Ham United	(a)	1-0	Cantona	24,197
27/01/96	FAC 4	Reading	(a)	3-0	Giggs, Parker, Cantona	14,780
3/02/96	FAPL	Wimbledon	(a)	4-2	Cole, Perry og, Cantona 2	25,380
10/02/96	FAPL	Blackburn Rovers	(h)	1-0	Sharpe	42,681
18/02/96	FAC 5	Manchester City	(h)	2-1	Cantona (Pen), Sharpe	42,692
21/02/96	FAPL	Everton	(h)	2-0	Keane, Giggs	42,459
25/02/96	FAPL	Bolton Wanderers	(a)	6-0	Beckham, Bruce, Cole, Scholes 2, Butt	21,381
4/03/96	FAPL	Newcastle United	(a)	1-0	Cantona	36,610
11/03/96	FAC 6	Southampton	(h)	2-0	Cantona, Sharpe	45,446
16/03/96	FAPL	QPR	(a)	1-1	Cantona	18,817
20/03/96	FAPL	Arsenal	(h)	1-0	Cantona	50,028
24/03/96	FAPL	Spurs	(h)	1-0	Cantona	50,157
31/03/96	FAC SF	Chelsea	(n)	2-1	Cole, Beckham	38,421
6/04/96	FAPL	Manchester City	(a)	3-2	Cantona (Pen), Cole, Giggs	29,688
8/04/96	FAPL	Coventry City	(h)	1-0	Cantona	50,332
13/04/96	FAPL	Southampton	(a)	1-3	Giggs	15,262
17/04/96	FAPL	Leeds United	(h)	1-0	Keane	48,382
28/04/96	FAPL	Nottingham Forest	(h)	5-0	Scholes, Beckham 2, Giggs, Cantona	53,926
5/05/96	FAPL	Middlesbrough	(a)	3-0	May, Cole, Giggs	29,921
11/05/96	FAC Final	Liverpool	(n)	1-0	Cantona	79,007

Aston Villa
Manchester United

(3) 3
(0) 1

Saturday, 19th August 1995, Villa Park   Att: 34,655

ASTON VILLA

1	Mark	BOSNICH
2	Gary	CHARLES (Y)
14	Alan	WRIGHT
4	Gareth	SOUTHGATE
5	Paul	McGRATH
16	Ugo	EHIOGU
7	Ian	TAYLOR
8	Mark	DRAPER
9	Savo	MILOSEVIC *52
18	Dwight	YORKE +87
11	Andy	TOWNSEND

Subs

10	Tommy	JOHNSON *
1	Nigel	SPINK (G)
20	Riccardo	SCIMECA +

MANCHESTER UNITED

1	Peter	SCHMEICHEL
2	Paul	PARKER
20	Gary	NEVILLE
6	Gary	PALLISTER +59
3	Denis	IRWIN
16	Roy	KEANE
19	Nicky	BUTT
23	Phil	NEVILLE *45
5	Lee	SHARPE
9	Brian	McCLAIR
22	Paul	SCHOLES (Y)

24	David	BECKHAM *
18	Simon	DAVIES
30	John	O'KANE +

Match Facts

• Having lost to Everton in the 1995 FA Cup Final, the defeat against Villa was the first time in over 150 games that United had lost two consecutive competitive matches. Strangely, the last time it happened in 1993, Aston Villa were again the villains defeating United in the league just days after Wimbledon had beaten the Reds.

• FAPL debut for John O'Kane.

• First time in a FAPL fixture that United had not named a goalkeeper amongst the substitutes.

• Yorke's goal was the 100th conceded by United in the FAPL.

Score Sheet

I. TAYLOR 14mins —1-0
M. DRAPER 27 mins — 2-0
D. YORKE 37 mins (pen) — 3-0
D. BECKHAM 84 mins — 3-1

Referee

Mr R.Hart (Darlington)

Young Reds Slaughtered

The learner driver who unwisely chose to take the Trinity Road next to Villa's ground for a Saturday afternoon driving lesson set the tone for the afternoon as United's young side were also given a lesson, albeit of a footballing nature. Villa, unlike the driver or United, were very quickly out of second gear and cruising along in top to take a three goal interval lead whilst the Reds were bogged down in traffic.

Villa paraded their £9.2m trio of new boys, Gareth Southgate, Savo Milosevic and Mark Draper to a sell out crowd and the carnival atmosphere was increased further with the arrival of the match ball delivered onto the centre circle by helicopter. The match kicked off with Keane being abused every time he went near the ball, a backlash to United's match at Villa Park with Crystal Palace in the FA Cup semi-final in April when the United star had been sent off after clashing with Southgate, now of course a Villa player.

But United, shorn of most of their double winning side, were to suffer worse than abuse when they went behind in the fourteenth minute. Yorke, who had been causing problems for the visiting defence from the start, slung over a high cross from the left which eluded everybody except Charles who retrieved the ball from the right. He drove the ball in hard and low for Taylor to stick out a foot and turn the ball home from just inside the six yard box. Butt, set free by Scholes, missed a glorious opportunity to equalise when he blasted wildly over the bar and the Reds paid dearly for the mistake when they went two down after 27 minutes. United were themselves attacking near the corner flag down Villa's left flank when Phil Neville lost the ball to Wright. The full back's long clearance found Draper who cut in from the left past both Irwin and Pallister before curling the ball into Schmeichel's net. United's problems were compounded just over ten minutes later when their Danish number one felled Villa's new foreign star, Milosevic, leaving Yorke to make it three from the spot.

At half time, Ferguson withdrew Phil Neville and replaced him with David Beckham but within five minutes of the resumption Villa made an enforced change when Milosevic was hurt in a challenge from Parker. Bosnich made a point blank save from a Keane header but United's woes continued when Pallister was carried off following a tackle from Taylor to give substitute John O'Kane his FAPL debut. United salvaged something from the wreckage with a spectacular first time effort from over 25 yards out by David Beckham six minutes from time but it was too little, too late.

League Record

		Home					Away				
	P	W	D	L	F	A	W	D	L	F	A
95/96 FAPL	1	0	0	0	0	0	0	0	1	1	3
All time FAPL	127	44	15	4	119	31	33	18	13	105	69
FAPL +FL	3683	1080	425	336	3670	1815	565	480	797	2511	3123

FAPL Attendances	Home	Away	Total
	—	34,655	34,655

Manchester United (0) 2
West Ham United (0) 1

Wednesday, 23rd August 1995, Old Trafford   Att: 31,966

MANCHESTER UNITED			WEST HAM UNITED		
1	Peter	SCHMEICHEL	1	Ludek	MIKLOSKO
20	Gary	NEVILLE	2	Tim	BREACKER
4	Steve	BRUCE	4	Steve	POTTS
6	Gary	PALLISTER	8	Marc	REIPER
3	Denis	IRWIN	3	Julian	DICKS
24	David	BECKHAM	6	Martin	ALLEN
16	Roy	KEANE	7	Ian	BISHOP
19	Nicky	BUTT	10	John	MONCUR
5	Lee	SHARPE	20	Danny	WILLIAMSON *74
9	Brian	McCLAIR	9	Tony	COTTEE
22	Paul	SCHOLES *68	16	Don	HUTCHISON (Y)

Subs

13	Kevin	PILKINGTON (G)	11	Marco	BOOGERS * (R)
17	Andy	COLE *	13	Les	SEALEY (G)
28	Ben	THORNLEY	5	Alvin	MARTIN

Match Facts

- United have not failed to beat West Ham at Old Trafford since 1986.
- First Old Trafford goal for the 'Hammers' in the FAPL.
- Boogers manages to get sent off after only 15 minutes of just his second appearance as a substitute since his £1m summer transfer from Sparta Rotterdam.

Score Sheet

P. SCHOLES 50 mins — 1-0
S. BRUCE og 56 mins — 1-1
R. KEANE 67 mins — 2-1

Referee:
Mr. D. Gallagher (Banbury)

Keane Saves Bruce's Blushes

After their comprehensive set back at Villa Park on the opening day of the campaign, United needed to come back in style in their first home fixture at an Old Trafford stadium that resembled more of a builder's yard than a football ground. The partly built new stand saw the attendance reduced drastically to just under 32,000 but United failed to turn in the performance expected of them and were probably fortunate that the opposition was not of the highest calibre.

The Londoners were first to attack and Moncur had Schmeichel on his knees at his left hand post with a 20 yarder. A clearance from the big 'keeper saw Sharpe lose out to Breaker with the ball falling free to Allen way out on the West Ham right touchline. Quickly sensing that the Dane was still off his line having made the original clearance, Allen tried to chip home but, although Schmeichel finished up in the net after back pedalling furiously, the ball just cleared the bar. United's only clear cut chance of a ragged first period fell to Keane who was thwarted at the expense of a corner by Breaker after rounding Miklosko.

Soon after the interval, however, United went in front when Beckham put in a long cross from deep on the United right. The headed clearance was won back by Sharpe who found Irwin on the left. A fast one two with Scholes saw the full back cutting into the six yard box and, as defenders rushed across to cut out the threat, Irwin slotted the ball across the face of goal to the far post where the West Ham defence was non-existent, leaving Scholes an easy tap in from seven yards.

The Hammers, however, were back on level terms within five minutes when United's defence allowed the ball to bob around the edge of the area. It fell eventually to Moncur who beat Irwin and drove the ball in hard and low. The cross beat Schmeichel and, as Bruce attempted to stop Cottee getting on the end of it, he only succeeded in placing the ball in his own net. United hit back to regain the lead when Sharpe switched play from United's left with a long ball to Scholes on the right. Beckham and Butt were involved in a quick exchange of passes before the latter tried to find Scholes in the area. The youngster was bundled off the ball but it ran to Keane on the United left just inside the area leaving the Irishman to cut in and score with a right foot drive from ten yards. West Ham introduced new signing Boogers into the action with sixteen minutes left but just before the final whistle he committed an outrageously high tackle on Neville to get a red card. Although they took the points it had been a far from convincing performance by United.

League Record

	Home					Away				
	P	W	D	L	F	A	W	D	L	F	A
95/96 FAPL	2	1	0	0	2	1	0	0	1	1	3
All time FAPL	128	45	15	4	121	32	33	18	13	105	69
FL/FAPL	3684	1081	425	336	3672	1816	565	480	797	2511	3123

	Home	Away	Total
FAPL Attendances	31,966	34,655	66,621

Manchester United (1) 3
Wimbledon (0) 1

Monday, 26th August 1995, Old Trafford   Att: 32,226

MANCHESTER UNITED

1	Peter	SCHMEICHEL
20	Gary	NEVILLE
4	Steve	BRUCE
6	Gary	PALLISTER
3	Denis	IRWIN
24	David	BECKHAM
16	Roy	KEANE
19	Nicky	BUTT
5	Lee	SHARPE
17	Andy	COLE +77
22	Paul	SCHOLES *77

WIMBLEDON

13	Paul	HEALD
3	Alan	KIMBLE
4	Vinny	JONES
7	Oyvind	LEONHARDSEN *77
8	Robbie	EARLE
9	Efan	EKOKU +77
10	Dean	HOLDSWORTH
12	Gary	ELKINS
15	Alan	REEVES
16	Andy	THORN
21	Chris	PERRY

Subs

2	Paul	PARKER
11	Ryan	GIGGS *
18	Simon	DAVIES +

32	Steve	TALBOYS *
14	Jon	GOODMAN
25	Gary	BLISSETT +

Match Facts

- First double strike in the FAPL for Roy Keane since his home debut against Sheffield United in August 1993.
- The defeat shattered Wimbledon's 100% start to the campaign.
- Strangely, for a United v Wimbledon game, there were no bookings.

Score Sheet

R. KEANE 27 mins — 1-0

A. COLE 60 mins — 2-0

R. EARLE 65 mins — 2-1

R. KEANE 80 mins — 3-1

Referee:

Mr P.Durkin (Portland)

FA Carling Premiership

	P	W	D	L	F	A	Pts
1 Newcastle United	3	3	0	0	8	1	9
2 Leeds United	3	3	0	0	5	1	9
3 Wimbledon	3	2	0	1	7	5	6
4 Liverpool	3	2	0	1	4	2	6
5 Manchester United	3	2	0	1	6	5	6

Cole Back with a Goal

Andy Cole was back in United's starting line up for the first time in the season whilst Ryan Giggs occupied one of the substitute spots. And the good news for the home fans was that Cole looked as sharp as ever but it was Wimbledon who were first to attack with Pallister forced to concede an early corner by Hallsworth. Kimble's kick was met by Thorn whose header had Schmeichel arching his back spectacularly to tip over. United hit back to have a penalty claim denied when Thorn seemed to bring down Neville and Jones joined in to give the young United player plenty of verbals and a push which brought the Wimbledon player nothing more than a long talking to by the referee. A Roy Keane header was United's first attempt on goal after six minutes and brought a corner and ten minutes later Scholes set Irwin free who squared to Beckham but the youngster's shot was blocked.

Scholes was behind most of United's attacking moves at this stage and another deft touch almost got Cole in. The youngster's perseverance paid off after 27 minutes when he slid the ball through to Keane at the edge of the penalty area and, although it looked as if his way forward was blocked by a line of defenders, the Irishman somehow threaded his shot through the mass of bodies and past Heald in the Londoners' net.

United held their lead until the interval but Wimbledon immediately took the initiative at the start of the second period with Earle forcing a block from Schmeichel and Irwin clearing Leonhardsen's follow up effort. Cole began to get really into his stride and sent a shot just wide and then danced his way past several defenders before Wimbledon managed to clear the danger. There was no stopping Cole in this mood and there appeared little danger when Butt won the ball 30 yards out. He played the ball into Cole at the right hand side of the area and the record signing seemed to be well marked until he turned Thorn inside out before cutting in and unleashing a shot that defied an acute angle to nestle in the far corner.

But Wimbledon refused to lie down and Earle reduced the arrears five minutes later when he easily beat Schmeichel from about twelve yards after a cross from Kimble had set him up. It would now be a stern test for the young United side and Ferguson withdrew Cole to save him presumably for the following game against Blackburn Rovers. The striker left to a standing ovation and there was a big cheer for his replacement, Ryan Giggs. With just over ten minutes left, United made the game safe when Heald couldn't hold onto a fierce 25 yard drive from Sharpe and Keane had the easy task of tapping home from five yards into an empty net.

League Record

	Home					Away				
	P	W	D	L	F	A	W	D	L	F	A
95/96 FAPL	3	2	0	0	5	2	0	0	1	1	3
All time FAPL	129	46	15	4	124	33	33	18	13	105	69
FL/FAPL	3685	1082	425	336	3675	1817	565	480	797	2511	3123

	Home	Away	Total
FAPL Attendances	64,192	34,655	98,847

Blackburn Rovers (0) 1
Manchester United (0) 2

Match Four

Monday, 28th August 1995, Ewood Park   Att: 29,843

BLACKBURN ROVERS

1	Tim	FLOWERS
20	Henning	BERG
5	Colin	HENDRY
6	Graham	LE SAUX (Y)
7	Stuart	RIPLEY +76
4	Tim	SHERWOOD (Y)
23	David	BATTY (Y)
15	Matt	HOLMES *57
25	Ian	PEARCE
9	Alan	SHEARER)
16	Chris	SUTTON

MANCHESTER UNITED

1	Peter	SCHMEICHEL
20	Gary	NEVILLE (Y)
4	Steve	BRUCE
6	Gary	PALLISTER
3	Denis	IRWIN
24	David	BECKHAM +76
16	Roy	KEANE (Y/R)
19	Nicky	BUTT (Y)
5	Lee	SHARPE
17	Andy	COLE (Y)
22	Paul	SCHOLES *76

Subs

13	Bobby	MIMMS (G)
22	Mark	ATKINS *
10	Mike	NEWELL +

11	Ryan	GIGGS *
18	Simon	DAVIES +
2	Paul	PARKER

Match Facts

- Roy Keane's 20th booking, and his second sending off in his last seven appearances.
- Gary Neville's ninth booking in 12months.
- Second consecutive meeting at Ewood Park to see a player dismissed.
- Seven of United's first eight FAPL goals have now come in the second half.

Score Sheet

L. SHARPE 46 mins — 0-1

A. SHEARER 58 mins — 1-1

D. BECKHAM 67 mins — 1-2

Referee:

Mr D.Elleray (Harrow)

FA Carling Premiership

		P	W	D	L	F	A	Pts
1	Newcastle United	3	3	0	0	8	1	9
2	Leeds United	3	3	0	0	5	1	9
3	**Manchester United**	4	3	0	1	8	6	9
4	Wimbledon	3	2	0	1	7	5	6
5	Liverpool	3	2	0	1	4	2	6
13	**Blackburn Rovers**	4	1	0	3	4	6	3

Keane Off

The meeting of the only two teams to have won the FA Premiership at the time of the match produced an ill-tempered game as is par for the course between two sides with a genuine antagonism towards one another. But away from the bitter feuding there was plenty of exciting football action as United registered their third successive FAPL victory since the opening day setback at Villa Park and, at the same time, consigned Rovers to their third successive defeat.

United's stars were Cole and Keane with the former Newcastle player's speed causing all sorts of problems for the reigning Champions whilst Keane dominated midfield before being unluckily dismissed in the 75th minute for a second bookable offence. Both Sutton and Shearer gave United early scares but once the Reds settled down they looked the more likely to score. Scholes twice released Cole with Hendry at the first time of asking just nicking the ball away in time and then hacking the second effort off the line after Cole had successfully evaded a crude attempt by Flowers to impede him. Beckham, Scholes and Butt's interpassing movements were leaving Blackburn exposed but Rovers, having started the first half well, finished it on a high with Neville lucky not to be sent off when he pulled Shearer back by the shirt.

United went into the lead shortly after the break with a goal that would have done justice to a pinball machine. Butt and Scholes combined once more to give Cole an opportunity which Flowers first parried and then palmed away. The follow up shot from Scholes was partially cleared by Berg off the line only for Keane to hammer it goalwards again. This time Flowers was in the way but once more couldn't do anything other than parry to give Sharpe a fourth chance to put it away as the home defence finally capitulated. Rovers now fought back and within fifteen minutes were level when a poor attempt at a clearance by Neville from a Ripley corner gave Shearer the chance to shoot left footed between Schmeichel and the 'keeper's left-hand post.

The game ebbed and flowed between both ends but it was the Reds who regained the lead after another pinball episode. Several efforts were blocked before Hendry's final tackle on Sharpe saw the ball rebound to Beckham on United's left. The youngster defied the crowded area by simply curling a majestic strike around everybody including Flowers. Then came the Keane dismissal after he was alleged to have taken a dive as Hendry tackled him. Having booked Le Saux earlier in the game for a similar offence, Mr Elleray had little option other than to book the United player but the Irishman paid a far heavier penalty than Le Saux for it was his second caution and dismissal was inevitable.

League Record

| | Home | | | | | | Away | | | | |
	P	W	D	L	F	A	W	D	L	F	A
95/96 FAPL	4	2	0	0	5	2	1	0	1	3	4
All time FAPL	130	46	15	4	124	33	34	18	13	107	70
FL/FAPL	3686	1082	425	336	3675	1817	566	480	797	2513	3124

	Home	Away	Total
FAPL Attendances	64,192	64,498	128,690

Everton   (1) 2
Manchester United   (1) 3

Saturday, 9th September 1995, Goodison Park   Att: 39,496

EVERTON

1	Neville	SOUTHALL
34	Paul	HOLMES
6	Gary	ABLETT (Y)
4	David	UNSWORTH (Y/R)
5	Dave	WATSON (Y)
17	Andrei	KANCHELSKIS *13
10	Barry	HORNE
18	Joe	PARKINSON
11	Anders	LIMPAR
12	Daniel	AMOKACHI
8	Paul	RIDEOUT

Subs

3	Andy	HINCHCLIFFE *
19	Andy	BARLOW
13	Jason	KEARTON (G)

MANCHESTER UNITED

1	Peter	SCHMEICHEL
20	Gary	NEVILLE
3	Denis	IRWIN (Y)
4	Steve	BRUCE
6	Gary	PALLISTER (Y)
24	David	BECKHAM
19	Nicky	BUTT (Y)
16	Roy	KEANE (Y)
5	Lee	SHARPE (Y)
22	Paul	SCHOLES *66
17	Andy	COLE +74

2	Paul	PARKER
11	Ryan	GIGGS *
18	Simon	DAVIES +

Match Facts

- First time in 1995 that United have as many as five players cautioned in a game. The previous occasion had been on 31st December 1994 against Southampton at The Dell.
- Giggs scores his first FAPL goal for over 12 months. The last time he found the net in the FAPL was against Wimbledon on 31 August 1994. The last time he scored in the FAPL away from Old Trafford was on 30 April 1994.

Score Sheet

L. SHARPE 3 mins — 0-1
A. LIMPAR 27 mins — 1-1
L. SHARPE 49 mins — 1-2
P. RIDEOUT 55 mins — 2-2
R. GIGGS 74 mins — 2-3

Referee:
Mr G. Poll (Tring)

FA Carling Premiership

		P	W	D	L	F	A	Pts
1	Newcastle Utd	5	4	0	1	9	2	12
2	**Manchester United**	5	4	0	1	11	8	12
3	Wimbledon	5	3	1	1	10	7	10
4	Leeds Utd	5	3	1	1	7	4	10
9	**Everton**	5	2	1	2	6	5	7

KO Blow for Kanchelskis

Although both parties tried to play it low key during the build up, this game was billed as the grudge match of the season with, so the reasoning went, the former United winger Andrei Kanchelskis out to prove a point to Alex Ferguson whilst the Reds themselves were not only keen to prove to the departed Russian that they could manage without him but also to gain revenge for the FA Cup Final defeat at the hands of the 'Toffees' four months previously.

As it happened, Kanchelskis played little part as he was taken off with a suspected dislocated shoulder after only thirteen minutes following a touchline tackle by Lee Sharpe. By then, United were already in the lead thanks to a third minute goal from Lee Sharpe and it was the Russian's replacement at Old Trafford, David Beckham, who helped the Reds on their way. Andy Cole split the home defence with a through ball to Beckham and the young winger's hard, low cross whistled across the area to the far post where Sharpe was waiting to ram the ball home from close quarters.

Keane earned the first booking of the game for a tackle on Limpar but Ablett equalised that out with a caution on twenty minutes for felling Beckham in full flight. Everton, however, came back into the game when Limpar robbed Bruce at the edge of the United area and placed the ball past Schmeichel from just inside the eighteen yard box. The Reds almost regained the lead when Beckham struck the bar with a twenty yard free kick but it was still all square at the interval.

Beckham was having an excellent match and he set up Cole straight after the break but the striker couldn't quite control the ball as Southall was quickly out. Then it was Everton's turn to attack with Pallister heading back to Schmeichel under pressure. The big Dane's kick upfield caused all sorts of problems for Unsworth whose poor header only found Beckham. The ball was played quickly back into Scholes who fed Cole and the former Newcastle man sidestepped Unsworth to find Sharpe bursting through at speed to pinch the ball away from them both and hammer it home left footed past a bemused Southall from eight yards. Everton responded six minutes later with their second equaliser from a disputed free kick against Pallister for hand ball which seemed a dubious decision that saw Bruce booked for arguing the point. Limpar's free kick hit the bar but there was to be no reprieve as the ball was again punted goalwards to fall nicely for Everton's FA Cup goalscoring hero Rideout to score from ten yards. United introduced Giggs and the move paid immediate dividends when Beckham brilliantly robbed the Everton defence of possession before slipping the ball to the Welshman who stroked the ball home left footed from eighteen yards for his first league goal for twelve months.

League Record

| | Home | | | | | | Away | | | | |
	P	W	D	L	F	A	W	D	L	F	A
95/96 FAPL	5	2	0	0	5	2	2	0	1	6	6
All time FAPL	131	46	15	4	124	33	35	18	13	110	72
FAPL/FL	3687	1082	425	336	3675	1817	567	480	797	2516	3126

	Home	Away	Total
FAPL Attendances	64,192	98,994	163,186

Rotor Volgograd   (0) 0
Manchester United   (0) 0

Tuesday, 12th September 1995, Volgograd   Att: 39,396

ROTOR VOLGOGRAD			MANCHESTER UNITED		
1		SAMORUKOV	1	Peter	SCHMEICHEL
2		GERASTCHENKO	2	Gary	NEVILLE
3		SHMARKO	3	Denis	IRWIN
4		ESTCHENKO	4	Steve	BRUCE
5		JUNENKO	5	Lee	SHARPE
6		ESIPOV	6	Gary	PALLISTER
7		BURLATCHENKO	7	David	BECKHAM
8		ZERNOV *79	8	Nicky	BUTT
9		VERETENNIKOV	9	Roy	KEANE *23
10		KORNIETS	10	Paul	SCHOLES +71
11		NIDERGAUS	11	Ryan	GIGGS

Subs

12		KRIVOV *	12	Paul	PARKER +
13		TCHINENOV (G)	3	Kevin	PILKINGTON (G)
14		BERKETOV	14	Simon	DAVIES *
15		MENSTCHIKOV	15	Phil	NEVILLE
16		TSARENKO	16	Terry	COOKE

Match Facts

- United's third game in Europe against Russian opposition and their third goalless draw.
- First time in six European outings that United had not had a player booked.
- First start in five months for Ryan Giggs.

Score Sheet

Referee:
Mr P.Mikkelsen (Denmark)

United Stop Rotor Motor

United went into their third European conflict with Russian opposition in the knowledge that they had yet to score against a Russian side. But neither had they conceded a goal and the Red's defence was to again come out on top as United stopped the Rotor motor up front. Ferguson assembled one of United's youngest ever European squads for the tie with nine players aged 21 or under either in the starting line up or on the bench but the fledglings were to stand firm in a test of their character.

Torrential rain throughout the day turned the pitch into a quagmire and Giggs used the greasy surface to good advantage as early as the seventh minute to skip past his marker and deliver a low cross to Irwin who was wide with his shot from ten yards. Two minutes later, United saw another chance go begging when Keane set up Neville for a shot from twenty yards that tested Samorukove but didn't find him wanting. Rotor hit back and Schmeichel did well to smother a near post shot from Nidergaus after a free kick had taken a deflection to wrong foot the United rearguard. United then had a major set back with the loss of Roy Keane who pulled up sharply and was clearly in distress with his hamstring which led to the introduction of Simon Davies.

United reached the halfway mark with their goal still intact and within a minute of the restart should have taken the lead through Giggs. Beckham's cross from the right was inch perfect but, after rising unmarked to head home, the Welshman once again confirmed that heading is not one of his strong points as he placed the ball tamely over the bar to squander a glorious opportunity. He acknowledged his miss by promptly putting his head in his hands in disbelief.

United almost paid for the miss when a Korniets corner fell to the unmarked Veretennikov at the edge of the area. His low shot was only just wide but was so powerful that it would certainly have beaten Schmeichel had it been just a foot to the right. Ferguson decided with twenty minutes left to keep what he already held and sent another defender in the shape of Paul Parker for an attacker (Paul Scholes) but both sides had good chances in the last ten minutes. Samorukov, who had looked distinctly shaky, distinguished himself with a fine one handed save from a Giggs header before Veretennikov forced Schmeichel to make a magnificent diving stop whilst in the last minute the big Dane had to be alert to keep out a sliced clearance from Pallister. Alex Ferguson's verdict was "It was a good result with the kids coming through their test well".

European Record

	P	W	D	L	F	A	W	D	L	F	A
		Home					*Away*				
All comps	112	40	14	0	142	36	18	18	22	78	85
Inter City/UEFA Cup	30	8	6	0	25	7	4	6	6	15	17

European Attendances	*Home*	*Away*	*Total*
	—	40,000	40,000

Manchester United (2) 3
Bolton Wanderers (0) 0

Saturday, 16th September 1995, Old Trafford   Att: 32,812

MANCHESTER UNITED

1	Peter	SCHMEICHEL
2	Paul	PARKER
4	Steve	BRUCE
6	Gary	PALLISTER
23	Phil	NEVILLE
24	David	BECKHAM (Y)
19	Nicky	BUTT
5	Lee	SHARPE
22	Paul	SCHOLES
27	Terry	COOKE *74
11	Ryan	GIGGS

Subs

18	Simon	DAVIES *
25	Kevin	PILKINGTON (G)
21	Pat	McGIBBON

BOLTON WANDERERS

1	Keith	BRANAGAN
2	Scott	GREEN
3	Jimmy	PHILLIPS
5	Gudni	BERGSSON
8	Richard	SNEEKES
10	John	McGINLAY +71
11	Alan	THOMPSON (Y)
14	Fabian	De FREITAS
7	David	LEE
21	Chris	FAIRCLOUGH
22	Gerry	TAGGART *53

15	Mark	PATTERSON *
13	Aidan	DAVISON (G)
6	Alan	STUBBS +

Match Facts

- First team debut for Terry Cooke.
- First FAPL start for Ryan Giggs since 2nd April.
- First time since April 1994 that Giggs had scored in two successive FAPL matches.
- United leading FAPL goalscorers after six games.

Score Sheet

P. SCHOLES 19 mins — 1-0

R. GIGGS 34 mins — 2-0

P. SCHOLES 85 mins —3-0

Referee:

Mr S.Dunn (Bristol)

FA Carling Premiership

		P	W	D	L	F	A	Pts
1	Newcastle United	6	5	0	1	12	3	15
2	**Manchester United**	**6**	**5**	**0**	**1**	**14**	**8**	**15**
3	Aston Villa	6	4	1	1	8	4	13
4	Arsenal	6	3	3	0	6	2	12
18	**Bolton Wanderers**	**6**	**1**	**1**	**4**	**6**	**12**	**4**

What an Anniversary!

The proud parents of Terry Cooke received the best 25th Wedding Anniversary present any mother and father could wish for when, on their big day, they sat in the stands at Old Trafford and watched their son make his debut for the most famous club in the world, Manchester United. Indeed, Cooke was to play a starring role in a team that saw seven players 21 or under take part in the game while another two remained on the bench. It had only been four months since both Phil Neville and Cooke were in the United Youth side that won the FA Youth Cup.

Without Roy Keane due to suspension, Denis Irwin (flu) and the injured Gary Neville, United turned to Phil Neville, Cooke and Paul Parker with David Beckham slotting into Keane's midfield spot from where he emerged as the man of the match as he sprayed passes across the field in a splendid imitation of Cantona at his best. At other times he would join in the crisp, short, fast passing game that United's youngsters had played together for some three years. In fact, the highlight of the game came when Pallister picked the ball up in his own half of the field before playing it forward to Scholes on the halfway line. A nonchalant flick found Cooke facing the wrong way but, in almost Brazilian style, a back heel from the debutant played the ball to Beckham. He rolled the ball back with his first touch to Scholes who promptly dispatched the now flying Cooke down the right wing. The inevitable low cross evaded everybody but Giggs who scored from five yards at the far post to put United two up. Earlier, Giggs himself had turned Phillips inside out down the left flank before hitting a vicious cross that Fairclough could only slice against his own 'keeper. The parry fell to Scholes who had a straight forward task of tapping home from a couple of yards to give United an early lead.

The second period saw Bolton regroup with Patterson introduced for captain Gerry Taggert with obvious instructions to batten down the midfield. The move probably prevented Wanderers getting a good hiding but saw the end of the game as a spectacle as the visitors were then unable to offer any threat to the United goal whilst the Reds themselves became somewhat bogged down. Cooke was withdrawn to a tremendous round of applause in the 74th minute and ten minutes later Scholes added United's third with yet another quick, decisive move. There seemed little problem for Bolton when Beckham received the ball on United's right for they had plenty of men back but his inch perfect chip to the left was stabbed first time by Giggs into the path of the onrushing Scholes who scored from eight yards. The Theatre of Dreams, which had resembled a builder's yard before the kick off due to the rebuilding work going on, had been turned into a playground by the kids.

League Record

	Home						Away				
	P	W	D	L	F	A	W	D	L	F	A
95/96 FAPL	6	3	0	0	8	2	2	0	1	6	6
All time FAPL	132	47	15	4	127	33	35	18	13	110	72
FAPL/FL	3688	1083	425	336	3678	1817	567	480	797	2516	3126

	Home	Away	Total
FAPL Attendances	97,004	98,994	195,998

Manchester United (0) 0
York City (1) 3

Wednesday, 20th September 1995, Old Trafford   Att: 29,049

MANCHESTER UNITED

25	Kevin	PILKINGTON
2	Paul	PARKER
21	Pat	McGIBBON (R)
6	Gary	PALLISTER
3	Denis	IRWIN
24	David	BECKHAM (Y)
23	Phil	NEVILLE *46
18	Simon	DAVIES +57
5	Lee	SHARPE
9	Brian	McCLAIR
11	Ryan	GIGGS

YORK CITY

1	Dean	KIELY
2	Andy	McMILLAN
3	Wayne	HALL
4	Darren	WILLIAMS
5	Steve	TUTILL
6	Tony	BARRAS
7	Nigel	PEPPER (Y)
8	Scott	JORDAN
9	Graeme	MURTY
10	Nick	PEVERILL * 67
11	Paul	BARNES +89

Subs

4	Steve	BRUCE +
27	Terry	COOKE *
15	Graeme	TOMLINSON

12	Paul	BAKER * (R)
13	Andrew	WARRINGTON (G)
14	Paul	ATKIN +

Match Facts

- Pat McGibbon dismissed on his debut.
- A first start for Kevin Pilkington.
- First ever meeting of the clubs in either the League Cup or FA Cup.
- United's 100% record in competitive games against York is smashed (they had met twice on league business in 1974/75 with United winning both games).
- Only the third occasion that United had conceded three goals at home in the League Cup. The other occasions were Everton in 1977 and Spurs in 1989. Both those games also finished 0-3 to the visitors.

Score Sheet

P. BARNES 24 mins — 0-1

P. BARNES 51 mins (pen) — 0-2

T. BARRAS 53 mins — 0-3

Referee:

Mr J.Rushton (Stoke on Trent)

Yorked

Just days after the cricket season officially finished United were comprehensively 'yorked', to use a cricket expression, when the boys from Bootham Crescent all but booted the Reds out of the Coca Cola Cup. It was a disastrous night for the new boys in particular with Northern Ireland international Pat McGibbon receiving his marching orders on his debut and goalkeeper Kevin Pilkington making a hash of two of the goals in his first start.

The extent of the humiliation could be gauged from the fact that York arrived at Old Trafford occupying next to bottom place in the Second Division and had cost just £100,000 to assemble. The game was a personal triumph for manager Alan Little, brother of Aston Villa boss Brian, whose game plan of hitting United on the break after sucking them forward worked perfectly.

There was little to indicate the calamity that was to befall United as they took the game to York and McClair almost gave the Reds the lead only to see his looping header pushed over the bar by Manchester born Kiely. But that was to be as near as the Reds got to scoring until ten minutes from time when the same player rounded the 'keeper only to push the ball into the side netting with an open goal beckoning.

The visitors took the lead in the 24th minute when Barnes hit a shot, in hope more than anything else, from outside the area. Pilkington, making his first start for the senior team, should surely have dealt with the weak effort despite being wrongfooted when the ball took a deflection off a United defender. However, he failed to do so and the ball squirmed under his body to give York a shock lead.

It hardly panicked United but two goals in as many minutes just after the interval certainly did, especially as the first also resulted in United being sensationally reduced to ten men with the dismissal of Pat McGibbon on his debut. Barnes had burst through the middle on a counter attack and there could be little argument that he was wrestled to the ground by the young debutant. What was in dispute, however, was the penalty award as the incident clearly took place well outside the area. Barnes was not going to dwell on that for too long and smartly dispatched the spot kick beyond Pilkington. United were to quickly feel aggrieved again two minutes later when the referee again appeared to treat them harshly with the award of a free kick just outside the area for a tackle on Peverill. Whatever the rights and wrongs of the decision, when the ball was floated over from the right Pilkington should have easily claimed it but was late in coming and finished up in no man's land as Barras, completely unmarked, headed home. York substitute Paul Baker, after coming on in the 67th minute, managed to earn himself two cautions to get dismissed but even then United failed to make any inroads as York cantered to the shock of the season.

League Cup Record

	Home					Away				
P	W	D	L	F	A	W	D	L	F	A
125	45	11	9	136	56	23	14	23	81	77

	Home	Away	Total
CCC Attendances	29,049	—	29,049

Sheffield Wednesday (0) 0
Manchester United (0) 0

Match Nine

Saturday, 23rd September 1995, Hillsborough   Att: 34,101

SHEFFIELD WEDNESDAY			MANCHESTER UNITED		
13	Kevin	PRESSMAN	1	Peter	SCHMEICHEL
2	Peter	ATHERTON	2	Paul	PARKER
4	Mark	PEMBRIDGE *82	4	Steve	BRUCE
5	Dan	PETRESCU	6	Gary	PALLISTER
17	Des	WALKER	3	Denis	IRWIN
3	Ian	NOLAN	24	David	BECKHAM
6	Chris	WADDLE	19	Nicky	BUTT
12	Andy	PEARCE	9	Brian	McCLAIR
14	Marc	DEGRYSE	18	Simon	DAVIES *66
16	Graham	HYDE	22	Paul	SCHOLES
9	David	HIRST +86	11	Ryan	GIGGS

Subs

10	Mark	BRIGHT +	23	Phil	NEVILLE
11	John	SHERIDAN	26	Chris	CASPER
29	Lee	BRISCOE *	27	Terry	COOKE *

Match Facts

- Only scoreless game in the FAPL.
- Only one win in last six league trips to Hillsborough for United.
- First game of United's 95/96 FAPL campaign in which there has not been at least three goals.
- United failed to score in three of their last four starts.

Score Sheet

Referee:
Mr K.Burge (Tonypandy)

FA Carling Premiership

		P	W	D	L	F	A	Pts
1	**Manchester United**	7	5	1	1	14	8	16
2	Newcastle Utd	6	5	0	1	12	3	15
3	Liverpool	7	5	0	2	13	5	15
4	Arsenal	7	4	3	0	10	4	15
12	**Sheffield Wednesday**	7	2	2	3	8	9	8

United Stumble to the Top

Following their shock defeat at the hands of York City in midweek, United travelled to Yorkshire to try to regain their composure but unfortunately still seemed to be suffering a hangover as they put on a limp performance against a Sheffield Wednesday side that seemed equally inept. Wednesday had also experienced midweek Coca Cola problems only drawing with Crewe Alexandra and it was easy to see how they had lost their last two home FAPL games to Spurs and Newcastle.

The home crowd was roaring for a penalty when a shot from Degryse struck Pallister but generally chances were few and far between as play got bogged down in midfield. Wednesday came closest when Pembridge's free kick took a deflection and clipped the crossbar whilst seven minutes from the break Hirst was put through on goal only for Schmeichel to smother the ball at his left-hand post. United's reply was for Parker to slide a cross in to the area for Giggs who cleverly beat a couple of defenders before rolling a pass into the path of the onrushing Butt, only for the midfielder to be hopelessly high with his final effort.

The second half produced some better football but it was Wednesday who threatened most to break the deadlock. Parker appeared to hold Degryse but no penalty was given and then Petrusco was allowed to run almost half the length of the field before firing against Schmeichel's body as the big Dane spread himself.

Wednesday then won a series of corners without creating any chances from them but Hirst did look likely to score when Pallister slipped to let the Wednesday striker get a clear sight of goal. Once again, however, Schmeichel spread his giant body to block. Then it was Hirst again who broke down the left and United were let off the hook when the big striker chose to go for glory himself as he closed in on goal. His shot was tame and easily pushed away by Schmeichel as Petrusco, to the right, was left fuming as Hirst's better option was clearly to roll the ball across to him for an easy tap in.

United had by now thrown on teenage prodigy Terry Cooke to try to liven things up but to no avail and United were glad to hang on to the point that saw them stumble to the top of the Premiership for the first time in 1995/96.

League Record

| | Home | | | | | | Away | | | | |
	P	W	D	L	F	A	W	D	L	F	A
95/96 FAPL	7	3	0	0	8	2	2	1	1	6	6
All time FAPL	133	47	15	4	127	33	35	19	13	110	72
FAPL/FL	3689	1083	425	336	3678	1817	567	481	797	2516	3126

	Home	Away	Total
FAPL Attendances	97,044	133,095	230,139

Manchester United   (0) 2
Rotor Volgograd   (2) 2

Tuesday, 26th September 1995, Old Trafford   Att: 29,724

MANCHESTER UNITED			ROTOR VOLGOGRAD
1	Peter	SCHMEICHEL	1	SAMORUKOV
2	John	O'KANE *26	2	SHMARKO
4	Steve	BRUCE	3	JUENENKO (Y)
6	Gary	PALLISTER	4	BERKETOV (Y)
3	Phil	NEVILLE	5	ESTCHENKO *69
7	David	BECKHAM +83	6	BURLATCHENKO
8	Roy	KEANE	7	KORNIETS
10	Nicky	BUTT	8	ESIPOV
5	Lee	SHARPE	9	VERETENNIKOV
9	Andy	COLE	10	ZERNOV +73
11	Ryan	GIGGS	11	NIDERGAUS #78 (Y)

Subs

12	Paul	SCHOLES *	12	TSARENKO *
13	Kevin	PILKINGTON (G)	13	TCHICHOV (G)
14	Brian	McCLAIR	14	ILUSHIN +
15	Terry	COOKE +	15	KRIVOV #
16	Chris	CASPER	16	MENSTCHIKOV

Match Facts

- United stretch unbeaten home record in European competition to 55.
- European debuts for Terry Cooke, Phil Neville and John O'Kane.
- Peter Schmeichel first United 'keeper to score in a European game in open play and first United 'keeper to score in a match since Alex Stepney took a penalty against Birmingham City in 1973.
- First European goal for Paul Scholes.

Score Sheet

NIDERGAUS 16 mins — 0-1
VERETENNIKOV 24 mins — 0-2
P. SCHOLES 59 mins — 1-2
P. SCHMEICHEL 89 mins — 2-2

Referee:

Mr B.Heynemann (Germany)

Molotov Cocktails Wreck the Reds

United were hit by two Molotov cocktails in the first half of a game they had been expected to win without too much trouble following the goalless first leg in Russia. They were thankful in the end to escape with their unbeaten European home record still intact thanks to a goal from a Peter Schmeichel header a minute from time.

Eighteen corners to one and something like thirty shots against five told the story of United's territorial advantage but once the Russians had gone two up with decisive counter attacks, the Reds were always going to struggle to get the three goals needed to go through. The first Volgograd goal came as early as the sixteenth minute when United tried to work the offside trap but failed to come out as a unit allowing Nidergaus to score after a one-two with Zernov had left United's back line flat footed. But worse was to come eight minutes later when a poor ball from Beckham put Steve Bruce in trouble on the half-way line. Veretennikov seized on the chance to dispossess the United captain before running almost half the length of the field to despatch a fifteen yard thunderbolt past Schmeichel and in off the post.

With goals now desperately required, Ferguson quickly whipped off European debutant John O'Kane after just 26 minutes to put on an extra forward in the shape of Paul Scholes but the Reds looked for the remainder of the half as if they had accepted their fate.

They returned after the interval with a hungrier appetite and went close on several occasions before Scholes reduced the deficit on 59 minutes. The goal came when Cole tested Samorukov with a powerful shot that the 'keeper could only parry leaving Scholes to tap in from close range. Soon after the Reds had bad luck when from Keane's throw-in on the right, Shmarko handled in the area only for a free-kick to be given on the edge of the area. It had clearly been inside the area and it didn't need television replays to confirm the fact. United's luck, however, got worse when from the free-kick Bruce rattled the bar with a header. Next, television replays seemed to confirm a Pallister header from a Giggs corner had crossed the line before being hooked away but again the match officials didn't agree.

United threw everything forward including goalkeeper Peter Schmeichel leaving the Red's net virtually without a custodian for the final five minutes. The giant Dane got his reward a minute from time when nodding home a Giggs corner but it wasn't enough to stop United from failing to progress past the Second Round for the fifth consecutive season since winning the European Cup-winners Cup in 1990/91.

European Record

	Home						Away				
	P	W	D	L	F	A	W	D	L	F	A
All European Comps	113	40	15	0	144	38	18	18	22	78	85
UEFA Cup	31	8	7	0	27	9	4	6	6	15	17

	Home	Away	Total
European Attendances	29,724	40,000	69,724

Manchester United (1) 2
Liverpool (1) 2

Sunday, 1st October 1995, Old Trafford   Att: 34,934

MANCHESTER UNITED			LIVERPOOL		
1	Peter	SCHMEICHEL	1	David	JAMES
20	Gary	NEVILLE	5	John	SCALES
4	Steve	BRUCE	25	Neil	RUDDOCK
6	Gary	PALLISTER	6	Phil	BABB
23	Phil	NEVILLE +72	4	Jason	McATEER (Y)
16	Roy	KEANE (Y)	15	Jamie	REDKNAPP
19	Nicky	BUTT *45	17	Steve	McMANAMAN
5	Lee	SHARPE	16	Michael	THOMAS (Y)
11	Ryan	GIGGS	22	Steve	HARKNESS
7	Eric	CANTONA	23	Robbie	FOWLER
17	Andy	COLE	9	Ian	RUSH

Subs

2	Paul	PARKER	8	Stan	COLLYMORE
22	Paul	SCHOLES +	26	Anthony	WARNER (G)
24	David	BECKHAM *	19	Mark	KENNEDY

<hr>

Match Facts

- First time United had scored in the first minute during Alex Ferguson's tenure.
- United only lost once to Liverpool at Old Trafford since 1982
- £8m signing Stan Collymore, who scored for Forest against United in both games the previous season remained on the bench!

Score Sheet

N. BUTT 1 min — 1-0
R. FOWLER 33 min — 1-1
R. FOWLER 52 min — 1-2
E. CANTONA 71 min (pen) — 2-2

Referee
Mr D.Elleray (Harrow on the Hill)

FA Carling Premiership

		P	W	D	L	F	A	Pts
1	Newcastle United	8	7	0	1	17	3	21
2	Aston Villa	8	5	2	1	12	5	17
3	**Manchester United**	**8**	**5**	**2**	**1**	**16**	**9**	**17**
4	**Liverpool**	**8**	**5**	**1**	**2**	**15**	**7**	**16**
5	Leeds United	8	5	1	2	14	9	16

Cantona Back at the Double

After 248 days, 18 hours 57 minutes, a Court case, and 120 hours Community Service, it seemed almost suitable that the Frenchman should emerge from the darkness of the tunnel into the light of day given his trials and tribulations of the previous eight months. His 32 match long sojourn now over, Cantona took just sixty seconds to stamp (in the best sense possible) his mark on the game. Straight from the kick off, Cole flashed the ball out to United's left from where United's most enigmatic character since the days of George Best swept the ball across the edge of the Liverpool area. If Butt's first touch then left something to be desired as he appeared to push the ball too far in front of himself, his second definitely did not. The Liverpool 'keeper James had spotted Butt's apparent error of control and took his one chance of preventing a goal by throwing himself forward at Butt who, to his credit, recovered quickly to smartly lift the ball over the custodian to give the Reds a sensational start.

But Liverpool came back to gradually take control. Slowly, but ever so surely, the Anfield side gained the ascendancy and the writing was on the wall when Rush missed from only a couple of yards after Fowler's cross beat Schmeichel. The Reds could then have conceded a penalty as Bruce appeared to pull back Fowler but Referee Mr Elleray later said he had considered it to be "six of one and half a dozen of the other". But there was no escape from Fowler's 33rd minute strike as he cut in from the left. Schmeichel seemed to think the Liverpool striker would cross to Rush and began to move to his left whereupon Fowler launched an Exocet missile of a shot past the big Dane's right that left the 'keeper sprawled on his back.

Soon after the interval, Liverpool were in the lead but there was definitely a question as to whether it was legal as the push interpreted by the referee as a "shoulder charge" could quite clearly be seen to be a swipe around the neck of Gary Neville. Once bundled out of the way, Neville could not get near Fowler who easily beat the exposed Schmeichel. Despite the dubiousness of the goal it was, in fairness, no more than Liverpool deserved at that point. But the Reds dug deep, none more so than Cantona who was lasting his first full game without any signs of tiredness. Gary Neville took his revenge by winning a tackle on the half way line before supplying Cantona. The Frenchman ran at the Liverpool defence before slipping the ball through to Giggs who was left clear on goal only to be hauled to the ground from behind by Redknapp. The penalty decision was obvious but it was somewhat of a mystery, given the situation in which the foul had been committed, as to how the culprit stayed on. Cantona tends to score from penalties awarded by Mr Elleray and put the ball to the left of James as the 'keeper went right to send the crowd into raptures and ensure a fair result over the ninety minutes. The long wait was over.

League Record

| | Home | | | | | | Away | | | | |
	P	W	D	L	F	A	W	D	L	F	A
95/96 FAPL	8	3	1	0	10	4	2	1	1	9	6
All time FAPL	134	47	16	4	129	35	35	19	13	110	72
FL/FAPL	3690	1083	426	336	3680	1819	567	481	797	2516	3126

	Home	Away	Total
FAPL Attendances	131,978	133,095	265,073

York City (0) 1
Manchester United (2) 3

Tuesday, 3rd October 1995, Bootham Crescent   Att: 9,386

YORK CITY

1	Andrew	WARRINGTON
2	Andy	McMILLAN
3	Wayne	HALL
4	Darren	WILLIAMS
5	Steve	TUTILL
6	Tony	BARRAS (Y)
7	Nigel	PEPPER (Y)
8	Scott	JORDAN (Y)
9	Paul	ATKIN
10	Nick	PEVERILL (Y) +90
11	Paul	BARNES *89

Subs

12	Paul	BAKER *
14	Scott	OXLEY
15	Glenn	NAYLOR +

MANCHESTER UNITED

1	Peter	SCHMEICHEL
20	Gary	NEVILLE
4	Steve	BRUCE
6	Gary	PALLISTER
5	Lee	SHARPE +67
27	Terry	COOKE *54
24	David	BECKHAM
11	Ryan	GIGGS
7	Eric	CANTONA
17	Andy	COLE
22	Paul	SCHOLES

23	Phil	NEVILLE +
16	Roy	KEANE *
9	Brian	McCLAIR

Match Facts

- First senior goal for Terry Cooke.
- Debut game for 19 year old York 'keeper Andrew Warrington.
- First goal of the season for York's Scott Gardner.
- 58 places between York and United in the English League set up.
- Second time in only five Coca Cola Cup appearances that Paul Scholes had hit two goals in a game.
- First time since 1981 that United had been knocked out of the League Cup as early as the Second Round.

Score Sheet

P. SCHOLES 7 mins — 0-1

T. COOKE 14 mins — 0-2

S. JORDAN 39 mins — 1-2

P. SCHOLES 80 mins — 1-3

Referee

Mr J.Winter (Middlesbrough)

York Hold On

United won the battle but not the war as they went out of the Coca Cola Cup 4-3 on aggregate to a side some 58 places below them in English football's pecking order. After the damage inflicted by York City at Old Trafford in the First Leg two week's earlier, United needed the impetus of an early goal but did even better by grabbing two that set the night up for a terrific climax.

York were giving a debut to teenage goalkeeper Andy Warrington and the youngster twice did well to thwart Andy Cole and Terry Cooke in the opening minutes. But United's thrilling start would not be denied and they took the lead after only seven minutes when Cantona unhinged the home side's defence. From out on United's left flank near the corner flag, the Frenchman curled the ball right footed towards the penalty where Scholes was lurking. The youngster has all the instincts of a predator and his speed left a defender flatfooted to give himself room to pick his spot.

Just another seven minutes had passed when United made it two with a first senior goal for Terry Cooke. This time it was Andy Cole who took up position down United's left wing and he played the ball into the path of Ryan Giggs who took it to the byeline before crossing to the far post for Cooke to cleverly lob over the diving Warrington from close range.

The outcome now seemed a formality but, as they pushed forward, United were caught out and Barnes brought a tremendous save out of Schmeichel. The Reds did not heed the warning and were again facing an uphill climb when Jordan made the score 4-2 on aggregate just before the break with his first goal since March. United defended poorly when Peverill broke clear with neither Bruce nor Pallister looking to clear his cross. Barnes beat them both to it, leaving Pallister facing in the wrong direction whilst Bruce slipped to allow the York player sight of goal. But Barnes' glory was snatched away from him when Jordan arrived on the scene to just beat his team mate to stab the ball past Schmeichel.

United pressed hard in the second period but the York defence held firm until ten minutes from time when Scholes reduced the deficit to the minimum. Again Cole was the provider with a ball in from the left that found Scholes at the edge of the area confronted by a wall of defenders. But the youngster still took aim and, with the aid of a deflection, found the net to set up a grandstand finish. But there were no excuses from Alex Ferguson who said afterwards "We are out and that's that. We had enough chances but we failed to take them. York deserve their bit of glory".

League Cup Record

| | Home | | | | | | Away | | | | |
	P	W	D	L	F	A	W	D	L	F	A
	126	45	11	9	136	56	24	14	23	84	78

	Home	Away	Total
CCC Attendances	29,049	9,386	38,435

Manchester United (1) 1
Manchester City (0) 0

Saturday, 14th October 1995, Old Trafford   Att: 35,707

MANCHESTER UNITED

1	Peter	SCHMEICHEL
20	Gary	NEVILLE (Y)
4	Steve	BRUCE
6	Gary	PALLISTER
23	Phil	NEVILLE
24	David	BECKHAM
16	Roy	KEANE +76
19	Nicky	BUTT
11	Ryan	GIGGS
22	Paul	SCHOLES *63
17	Andy	COLE

MANCHESTER CITY

21	Eike	IMMEL
2	Richard	EDGHILL
3	Terry	PHELAN (Y)
4	Steve	LOMAS (Y)
5	Keith	CURLE (Y)
7	Georgi	KINKLADZE
9	Niall	QUINN +80
0	Garry	FLITCROFT
11	Peter	BEAGRIE *59
14	Kit	SYMONS
28	Uwe	ROSLER

Subs

2	Paul	PARKER
5	Lee	SHARPE *
9	Brian	McCLAIR +

8	Gerry	CREANEY +
55	Alan	KERNAGHAN
6	Nicky	SUMMERBEE *

Match Facts

• City have not won at Old Trafford since Denis Law's back heel helped send United down 21 years previously.

• City not yet beaten United in the FAPL.

• First 'derbies' for Butt, Gary Neville and David Beckham.

Score Sheet

Paul SCHOLES 4 mins — 1-0

Referee:

Mr R.Dilkes (Mossley)

FA Carling Premiership

		P	W	D	L	F	A	Pts
1	Newcastle Utd	9	8	0	1	20	6	24
2	**Manchester United**	9	6	2	1	17	10	20
3	Arsenal	9	5	3	1	13	5	18
4	Liverpool	9	5	2	2	15	7	17
5	Nottm Forest	9	4	5	0	15	9	17
20	**Manchester City**	9	0	1	9	3	15	1

The Little Giant

City had not won at Old Trafford since Denis Law's back heel helped send United down some twenty-one years previously and, given that they arrived in 1995 with just one point from 27 and on the back of eight straight defeats, nobody gave the Blues much chance of reversing that run against a United side that lay third in the table. But if a goal after only four minutes, along with the sight of Clive Lloyd and Mike Atherton in the Directors Box, gave visions of a cricket score, the thoughts evaporated as the afternoon wore on and the Reds were very grateful by the end as the early strike from the smallest man on the pitch, Paul Scholes, played a giant role in the hard won victory.

With no City fans present, there was a strangely one-sided atmosphere for a 'derby' match and the delivery of the only goal of the game after just four minutes also had a strange look about it. Butt played the ball across field to Beckham on the right and his attack down the flank won a corner which Giggs went across to take. The corner kick was high and only just outside the six yard box but, despite the presence of numerous six footers in the City penalty area, the diminutive Scholes was left completely unmarked to stoop and head home with the aid of a deflection off Curle's shoulder as City's tallest defender stood rooted to the goal line. As City manager Alan Ball said afterwards "These things are the bane of a manager's life".

City however, to their credit, did not fold. Indeed, they should have equalised when Pallister slipped to let in Quinn but, as Schmeichel came out to narrow the angle, the City striker was hopelessly off target when it looked as if he must score. Just minutes earlier there had been another scare for the Reds when Gary Neville clearly fouled Rosler when the German was through but the card was only yellow when it could have easily been red. Then it was a case of the hero turning villain as Scholes completely missed his kick three yards out with the goal at his mercy from a Phil Neville cross that was knocked down by Cole.

Early in the second period Quinn again fluffed a good opportunity when his effort to place the ball past Schmeichel from fifteen yards resembled more of a pass back than a serious effort to score and the Reds accepted the let off to get on top. Phelan, Curle, Lomas and Flitcroft all found themselves in the referee's notebook in the space of fifteen minutes as City began to lose their cool. Cole was guilty of a glaring miss from a header and was then denied by a fine save from Immel who also thwarted Giggs as the Reds finished strongly without being able to add to their goal tally.

League Record

	Home						Away				
	P	W	D	L	F	A	W	D	L	F	A
95/96 FAPL	9	4	1	0	11	4	2	1	1	6	6
All time FAPL	135	48	16	4	130	35	35	19	13	110	72
FL/FAPL	3691	1084	426	336	3681	1819	567	481	797	2516	3126

	Home	Away	Total
FAPL Attendances	167,685	133,095	300,780

Chelsea   (0) 1
Manchester United   (2) 4

21st October 1995, Stamford Bridge   Att: 31,019

		CHELSEA			**MANCHESTER UNITED**
1	Dmitri	KHARINE	1	Peter	SCHMEICHEL
2	Steve	CLARKE (Y)	20	Gary	NEVILLE
4	Ruud	GULLITT	4	Steve	BRUCE
5	Orland	JOHNSEN	6	Gary	PALLISTER
6	Frank	SINCLAIR (R)	3	Denis	IRWIN
8	Mark	HUGHES	16	Roy	KEANE
10	Gavin	PEACOCK +63	9	Nicky	BUTT (Y)
11	Dennis	WISE *45	11	Ryan	GIGGS
14	Paul	FURLONG (Y)	22	Paul	SCHOLES *79
15	Andy	MYERS	17	Andy	COLE
18	Eddie	NEWTON	7	Eric	CANTONA

Subs

7	John	SPENCER +	5	Lee	SHARPE
12	Craig	BURLEY *	9	Brian	McCLAIR *
13	Kevin	HITCHCOCK (G)	24	David	BECKHAM

Match Facts

- Biggest league win over Chelsea since a Law inspired 4-1 win in 1965.
- United's biggest win at Stamford Bridge since their 6-3 victory in 1959.
- First home defeat of 1995/96 for Chelsea.
- For Eric Cantona's first away FAPL game since his sending off at Crystal Palace, the referee was Mr Wilkie who was in charge on that fateful night! Mr Walsh was the linesman nearest to the Cantona sending off.

Score Sheet

P. SCHOLES 3 mins — 0-1

P. SCHOLES 9 mins — 0-2

M. HUGHES 75 mins — 1-2

R. GIGGS 78 mins — 1-3

B. McCLAIR 85 mins — 1-4

Referee:
Mr A. Wilkie (Co. Durham)

FA Carling Premiership

		P	W	D	L	F	A	Pts
1	Newcastle United	10	9	0	1	26	7	27
2	**Manchester United**	**10**	**7**	**2**	**1**	**21**	**11**	**23**
3	Arsenal	10	6	3	1	15	5	21
4	Middlesbrough	10	6	3	1	11	4	21
9	**Chelsea**	**10**	**4**	**3**	**3**	**11**	**11**	**15**

Scholes at the Double

Many thought that Paul Scholes would be the one to make way for United's returning stars such as Eric Cantona and Denis Irwin but not only did he figure in the starting line up, he also scored a brace of goals at the double to put the Reds two up inside the first ten minutes at Stamford Bridge.

The first strike came after just three minutes when a long ball from the half way line by Gary Neville was stepped over by Cantona to leave Scholes in the clear. He didn't seem to hit the ball that sweetly but Kharine was unable to get it round his left-hand post despite getting a hand to it. Worse was to follow for the London side when United scored a truly memorable goal six minutes later. The Reds strung together twenty-one consecutive passes with the last one from Cantona again putting Scholes clear. He cut in from the right and, just when it seemed his best option was to turn the ball square for either of the unmarked Cole or Cantona to convert, the youngster blasted the ball home past Kharine at his near post.

Chelsea had started with a 3-5-2 system that seemed to be confusing their own players more than United and quickly reverted after the interval to a 4-4-2 set up. But that didn't stop Scholes from almost completing his hat-trick when yet again he was released by Cantona but this time his thunderous shot smashed against the bar with Kharine well beaten and rebounded to safety. Chelsea got back into the game with fifteen minutes left when Hughes got the goal he wanted so much against his old team mates. A cross from Spencer on the right was knocked down by Furlong to Hughes on the penalty spot leaving the Welshman with a clear sight of goal and he was able to beat Schmeichel with ease. It quickly proved to be a false dawn, however, for Chelsea who three minutes later again went two down thanks to a superb individual strike from Giggs. He picked the ball up on the left just inside the Chelsea half before setting off on a run that saw the Londoners' defence retreat in front of him. He wrong footed Clarke and, as Kharine came out, made an early stab at the ball that fooled the 'keeper for an outstanding goal.

United scored a fourth when another exquisite passing move again left Kharine completely exposed. The ball had found its way out to Keane on the left touchline and the Reds worked it across the edge of the penalty area via Cole and Cantona before the Frenchman's final ball left McClair clear to score easily. There was still time for one final nail in the Chelsea coffin when Sinclair was dismissed for a high tackle surely committed out of frustration that just about summed up Chelsea's day.

League Record

	Home					Away				
	P	W	D	L	F	A	W	D	L	F	A
95/96 FAPL	10	4	1	0	11	4	3	1	1	10	7
All time FAPL	136	48	16	4	130	35	36	19	13	114	73
FAPL/FL	3692	1084	426	336	3681	1819	568	481	797	2620	3127

	Home	Away	Total
FAPL Attendances	67,685	164,114	331,799

Manchester United (1) 2
Middlesbrough (0) 0

Saturday, 28th October 1995, Old Trafford   Att: 36,580

MANCHESTER UNITED			MIDDLESBROUGH		
1	Peter	SCHMEICHEL	13	Gary	WALSH
20	Gary	NEVILLE	2	Neil	COX (Y)
4	Steve	BRUCE (Y)	3	Chris	MORRIS +70
6	Gary	PALLISTER	4	Steve	VICKERS
3	Denis	IRWIN	5	Nigel	PEARSON
16	Roy	KEANE (R)	7	Nicky	BARMBY
19	Nicky	BUTT (Y)	8	Jamie	POLLOCK (Y)
7	Eric	CANTONA	9	Jan	FJORTOFT (Y) *70
17	Andy	COLE	11	Robbie	MUSTOE
22	Paul	SCHOLES *45	15	Phil	WHELAN (Y)
11	Ryan	GIGGS	21	Craig	HIGNETT

Subs

5	Lee	SHARPE	14	Alan	MOORE
9	Brian	McCLAIR *	19	Jaime	MORENO *
24	David	BECKHAM	22	Craig	LIDDLE +

Match Facts

- Return to Old Trafford for Bryan Robson and Gary Walsh.
- Gary Pallister opens his account for the season with a goal against his old club.
- Middlesbrough not won at Old Trafford in 65 years.
- Third dismissal for Keane in six months.
- Only second goal of season for £7m striker Andy Cole.

Score Sheet

G. PALLISTER 44 mins — 1-0

A. COLE 87 mins — 2-0

Referee:
Mr S. Lodge (Barnsley)

FA Carling Premiership

		P	W	D	L	F	A	Pts
1	Newcastle Utd	10	9	0	1	26	7	27
2	**Manchester United**	**11**	**8**	**2**	**1**	**23**	**11**	**26**
3	Liverpool	11	7	2	2	24	8	23
4	Arsenal	10	6	3	1	15	5	21
6	**Middlesbrough**	**11**	**6**	**3**	**2**	**11**	**6**	**21**

Pointless Return for Robson

Bryan Robson was given a standing ovation all the way from the players' tunnel to the dug out when he returned to Old Trafford in charge of the resurgent Middlesbrough who arrived boasting the best defensive record in British senior league football with just four goals conceded in ten FAPL games. But he would have been disappointed when he left with his side defeated by ten men after the early dismissal of Roy Keane for retaliation following a shirt pulling tackle from behind by Jan Fjortoft who was booked for his part in the incident which saw the United player clearly strike his opponent in the face.

With the dismissal, Middlesbrough, on the back of five straight wins and their excellent defensive record, must have fancied their chances but a goal at the end of each half gave the Reds a well deserved victory. Indeed, such was their superiority that it appeared it was the North East outfit who were reduced to being a man short. From the start former Red, Gary Walsh, denied Andy Cole with a smart stop but it was nothing to the brilliant save he produced after 13 minutes to prevent Cantona giving United the lead. A long ball into the area was controlled in a flash by the Frenchman who exploded a ferocious shot with goal written all over it until Walsh somehow tipped it over. Bruce was the first player into the book but was quickly followed by Middlesbrough's Phil Whelan on his FAPL debut for a foul on Cantona. Cox suffered the same fate when he caught Irwin and the game was in danger of boiling over. On the half hour it did that with the dismissal of Keane.

The sending off, however, only served to make United more determined and the Reds almost took the lead just before half time when Cantona cleverly chipped Walsh only to see Pearson clear off the line at the expense of a corner. But there was to be no reprieve for Robson's men. The flag kick from Giggs was poorly punched by Walsh under strong pressure from Cole and fell to Pallister about fifteen yards out. The big defender had to stoop low to head the ball back over Walsh and, for a moment, it didn't look as if it would elude a defender on the goal line but the former Middlesbrough player had directed his effort perfectly to give United an interval lead.

The Reds had a big let off in the second period when Pallister clearly felled the Bolivian, Jaime Moreno, only for Mr Lodge to wave away the claims for a blatant penalty. On such decisions are games won and lost and United capitalised to make the game safe three minutes from time with Cantona again the playmaker. A superb through ball from midfield split the Middlesbrough defence but Cole still had a lot to do. He beat Whelan and then rattled in a shot that Walsh partially blocked only to see it loop up in the air and bounce slowly over the line for what was only Cole's second goal of the season.

League Record

	Home						Away				
	P	W	D	L	F	A	W	D	L	F	A
95/96 FAPL	11	5	1	0	13	4	3	1	1	10	7
All time FAPL	137	49	16	4	132	35	36	19	13	114	73
FAPL/FL	3693	1085	426	336	3683	1819	568	481	797	2620	3127

	Home	Away	Total
FAPL Attendances	204,265	164,114	368,379

Arsenal
Manchester United

Saturday, 4th November 1995, Highbury   Att: 38,317

ARSENAL

1	David	SEAMAN
2	Lee	DIXON
5	Steve	BOULD
6	Tony	ADAMS
3	Nigel	WINTERBURN
9	Paul	MERSON (Y)
14	Martin	KEOWN
7	David	PLATT
11	Glenn	HELDER
8	Ian	WRIGHT *80
10	Dennis	BERGKAMP

Subs

16	John	HARTSON *
19	John	JENSEN
13	Vince	BARTRAM (G)

MANCHESTER UNITED

1	Peter	SCHMEICHEL
20	Gary	NEVILLE (Y)
4	Steve	BRUCE (Y)
6	Gary	PALLISTER
3	Denis	IRWIN **79
16	Roy	KEANE
19	Nicky	BUTT *64
22	Paul	SCHOLES +64
11	Ryan	GIGGS
7	Eric	CANTONA
17	Andy	COLE

5	Lee	SHARPE *
9	Brian	McCLAIR +
24	David	BECKHAM ** (Y)

Match Facts

- No presents for Alex Ferguson on his ninth anniversary of being appointed boss.
- First win for Arsenal over United in FAPL.
- Bergkamp only second Arsenal player to score against United in the FAPL.
- First time in three seasons that no United player had been sent off in the league fixture at Highbury!

Score Sheet

D. BERGKAMP 14 mins — 1-0

Referee:
Mr P.Durkin (Portland)

FA Carling Premiership

		P	W	D	L	F	A	Pts
1	Newcastle United	12	10	1	1	29	9	31
2	**Manchester United**	**12**	**8**	**2**	**2**	**23**	**12**	**26**
3	**Arsenal**	**12**	**7**	**3**	**2**	**16**	**6**	**24**
4	Liverpool	12	7	2	3	25	10	23
5	Aston Villa	12	7	2	3	17	9	23
6	Middlesbrough	12	6	4	2	12	7	22

Reds Outgunned by Bergkamp

United arrived in London attempting to extend their unbeaten run in the FAPL to eleven games and Alex Ferguson named an unchanged line up for the third successive match. But Arsenal were unbeaten at home and had taken over from United's previous opponents, Middlesbrough, as the Division's meanest defence. They also had former United trainee David Platt, who was allowed to leave Old Trafford for nothing before going on to become the world's most expensive player after a series of big money moves, for the first time since August following a knee injury.

But it was Arsenal's other big name summer signing, Dennis Bergkamp, who was to prove the match winner when he latched on to a dreadful mistake by Denis Irwin to score the only goal of the game after just fourteen minutes. United had started well and there appeared little danger when a long ball from midfield was played down United's left flank. Irwin had half a yard on Bergkamp and seemed in total control of the situation as he attempted to play the ball back to Schmeichel. But his foot barely made contact with the ball and, as Irwin slowed instinctively thinking he had got the ball back to the Dane, Bergkamp pounced on the error to nip past the Eire international and find the net from about ten yards. It was a rare mistake from Irwin but sufficient to give the Gunners their first win over the Reds in the FAPL.

Following the strike, Arsenal got on top and it was only some stirling work from Pallister and Schmeichel that prevented the London outfit from extending their lead. But United came back and on the half hour Irwin almost made amends when he cut in from the left to send a shot crashing just wide. Cole thought he had equalised after being set free by Cantona but, as the ball hit the net, United's costliest player turned to see a linesman's flag raised for offside. Cantona again freed Cole with a gem of a pass and the former Newcastle player should have scored but fired a weak effort straight at Seaman.

Immediately after the interval Seaman again denied Cole and, as United began to turn the screw, Merson was booked for pulling Irwin back by the shirt. It was a good spell for United and Keane had a smart effort saved before play switched to the other end where Schmeichel brought off the save of the day from a Wright header that even had the Arsenal man applauding in admiration. In a desperate last gamble, Ferguson used all three of his subs for the first time since the rules were changed but, despite some devastating attacks from the Reds, it was Arsenal who came closest to scoring in the final few minutes when Merson hit a post and from the rebound Schmeichel grabbed Bergkamp's follow up.

League Record

	Home						Away					
	P	W	D	L	F	A	W	D	L	F	A
95/96 FAPL	12	5	1	0	13	4	3	1	2	10	8
All time FAPL	138	49	16	4	132	35	36	19	14	114	74
FL/FAPL	3694	1085	426	336	3683	1819	568	481	798	2620	3128

	Home	Away	Total
FAPL Attendances	204,265	202,431	406,696

Manchester United (3) 4
Southampton (0) 1

Saturday, 18th November 1995, Old Trafford   Att: 39,301

MANCHESTER UNITED

1	Peter	SCHMEICHEL
20	Gary	NEVILLE
4	Steve	BRUCE
6	Gary	PALLISTER
3	Denis	IRWIN *46
24	David	BECKHAM
19	Nicky	BUTT (Y)
22	Paul	SCHOLES +50
11	Ryan	GIGGS **66
17	Andy	COLE
7	Eric	CANTONA

Subs

5	Lee	SHARPE **66
9	Brian	McCLAIR +
23	Phil	NEVILLE *

SOUTHAMPTON

13	Dave	BEASANT
2	Jason	DODD
3	Francis	BENALI
64	Jim	MAGILTON
5	Richard	HALL
6	Ken	MONKOU
8	Gordon	WATSON +55
9	Neil	SHIPPERLEY
11	Neil	HEANEY *55
12	Tommy	WIDDRINGTON
16	David	HUGHES

1	Bruce	GROBBELAAR
10	Neil	MADDISON +
21	Frankie	BENNETT *

Match Facts

- First time visiting supporters had been allowed in at Old Trafford for an FAPL game in 95/96.
- Seventh consecutive Old Trafford league victory over Southampton.
- United's 50th home win in the FAPL.

Score Sheet

R. GIGGS 1 min — 1-0

R. GIGGS 4 mins — 2-0

P.l SCHOLES 8 mins — 3-0

A. COLE 69 mins — 4-0

N. SHIPPERLEY 85 mins — 4-1

Referee:

Mr P.Danson (Leicester)

FA Carling Premiership

		P	W	D	L	F	A	Pts
1	Newcastle United	14	11	2	1	31	10	35
2	**Manchester United**	13	9	2	2	27	13	29
3	Arsenal	13	7	3	3	17	8	24
4	Aston Villa	13	7	3	3	18	10	24
5	Leeds United	13	7	3	3	19	14	24
15	**Southampton**	13	3	3	7	14	24	12

Saints Blitzed

On the day that United allowed visiting fans in Old Trafford for the first time in 95/96 for a FAPL game, the Southampton supporters who made the long haul from the South coast must have quickly wished they hadn't bothered. Already without their star player Matt Le Tissier, through suspension, the Saints were also hit by the loss of new signing Barry Venison who reported indisposed with flu although he could not have been as sick as the rest of his team mates who found themselves three down inside eight minutes.

The blitz began within sixteen seconds of the kick off and making that time even more incredible was the fact that it was Southampton who actually kicked off! But they had barely got the ball more than a yard inside the United half before it was intercepted by Paul Scholes on the right. The youngster slung a long crossfield ball to Cantona on the left-hand side of the area where the Frenchman chested it down before slipping it to Giggs to finish from just inside the penalty box. Barely had the cheers died down when Giggs added a second with just four minutes gone. This time it was kamikaze play from Widdrington and Dodd who confused one another with a square ball just inside their own half. Giggs seized on their indecision to intercept and set off towards goal before beating Beasant with a rising shot from just inside the box. Incredibly, United went three up after eight minutes with Gary Neville given a couple of bites of the cherry by a bemused defence that was giving the ball away with abandon. His cross from the right was cleverly stepped over by Cantona who took two men out with the move to leave Scholes unmarked to slot home from ten yards out. There were now thoughts of the nine goals that United slammed past Ipswich but the Reds went off the boil and the Saints survived to the interval without further mishap.

With the game wrapped up, manager Alex Ferguson quickly used all three of his substitutes early in the second period but the changes didn't alter the flow of the ball towards the Southampton area and the fourth goal came after 69 minutes when Southampton were again guilty of slapdash marking as a David Beckham corner was headed home by the unmarked Cole.

United, having received so many presents, were hospitable hosts and, with the game drifting towards its foregone conclusion, gave away a present of their own to allow Southampton a sloppy consolation strike with five minutes left. Phil Neville failed to intercept on the left of United's penalty area when he slipped to allow Shipperley in. Gary Neville made a mash of two attempts to dispossess the Southampton player whilst Schmeichel also failed with a couple of tackles that left Shipperley barely able to believe his luck as he managed to bundle the ball past Bruce on the line for the scrappiest goal seen at Old Trafford all season.

League Record

	Home						Away				
	P	W	D	L	F	A	W	D	L	F	A
95/96 FAPL	13	6	1	0	17	5	3	1	2	10	8
All time FAPL	139	50	16	4	136	36	36	19	14	114	74
FL/FAPL	3695	1086	426	336	3687	1820	568	481	798	2620	3128

	Home	Away	Total
FAPL Attendances	243,566	202,431	445,997

Coventry City   (0) 0
Manchester United   (1) 4

Wednesday, 23rd November 1995, Highfield Road   Att: 23,400

COVENTRY CITY

1	Steve	OGRIZOVIC
24	Richard	SHAW
5	David	RENNIE
4	John	WILLIAMS
18	Marcus	HALL
26	Gordon	STRACHAN
6	Kevin	RICHARDSON
8	Marques	ISAIAS * 69
11	John	SALAKO
9	Peter	NDLOVU
10	Dion	DUBLIN

Subs

15	Paul	COOK *
30	John	FILAN (G)
17	Ally	PICKERING

MANCHESTER UNITED

1	Peter	SCHMEICHEL
20	Gary	NEVILLE *57
4	Steve	BRUCE **79
6	Gary	PALLISTER
3	Denis	IRWIN
24	David	BECKHAM
19	Nicky	BUTT +63
9	Brian	McCLAIR
11	Ryan	GIGGS
7	Eric	CANTONA
17	Andy	COLE

23	Phil	NEVILLE *
5	Lee	SHARPE +
12	David	MAY **

Match Facts

- Equalled United's biggest winning margin away from Old Trafford (FAPL) previously achieved against Leicester City.
- United maintain their 100% record at Highfield Road (FAPL).
- Coventry still to beat United in FAPL.
- United conceded just one goal to Coventry in FAPL.

Score Sheet

D. IRWIN 27 mins — 1-0

B. McCLAIR 47 mins — 2-0

D. BECKHAM 57 mins — 3-0

B. McCLAIR 76 mins — 4-0

Referee:
Mr K.Burge (Tonypandy)

FA Carling Premiership

		P	W	D	L	F	A	Pts
1	Newcastle United	14	11	2	1	31	10	35
2	**Manchester United**	14	10	2	2	31	13	32
3	Arsenal	14	8	3	3	21	10	27
4	Aston Villa	14	8	3	3	19	10	27
5	Spurs	14	7	4	3	22	17	25
20	**Coventry City**	14	1	5	8	11	29	8

United Close the Gap

United, who just five days previously had trailed leaders Newcastle United by eight points, cut the gap at the top to just three with a scintillating display that dropped their hosts, Coventry City, to the bottom rung of the Premiership and left the home side without a league victory since August. The Midlands club had an Old Trafford Old Boys look about them with Ron Atkinson, Gordon Strachan and Dion Dublin all involved at Highfield Road in one capacity or another but they certainly did not make life for United as easy as the scoreline suggests, especially in the early stages.

After Cole's first touch had let him down to allow a golden opportunity of opening the scoring get away, Coventry almost made United pay for their record signing's indiscretion on more than one occasion. Dublin sent in a scorcher from fully thirty yards that produced a wonderful tip over from Schmeichel which had the Dane still wringing his fingers a good minute later. The United 'keeper, however, had little time to recover before Salako was bearing down on him from the right and the Danish international was again at his brilliant best to deny the City player at the expense of a corner. From the flag kick, Schmeichel made a poor punch and Dublin quickly seized on the half chance to beat the 'keeper from some ten yards only for Bruce on the line to hack the ball to safety. Having survived by the skin of their teeth United, with Giggs outstanding, began to take control and Cantona was only just over with a header from a Cole cross. A Giggs effort was then touched away for a corner and when the Welsh international's kick was only partly cleared, some quick thinking by Pallister saw the ball laid back to Irwin who thumped home a right foot daisy cutter from about 25 yards to give the Reds an interval lead.

Within three minutes of the restart, United had increased their lead when an awful clearance by young Marcus Hall fell to Giggs who seemed to try to find Cole only for the ball to fall conveniently into the path of McClair who drove home left footed from fifteen yards.

An offside decision against Dublin led directly to United's third when Bruce's quickly taken free kick found Cantona. A super pass from the Frenchman played in Butt who was tackled just inside the area as he was about to shoot. The ball broke to Beckham out on the right who unleashed a powerful shot from an awkward angle that gave Ogrizovic no chance. The Reds signed off in style when a mazy run by Giggs ended with a pass to Cantona on the left wing and his subtle cross was met by McClair arriving late to head home from around the penalty spot. In the end it was a comfortable win but, if Coventry had accepted one of their early chances, it might have been entirely different.

League Record

| | Home | | | | | Away | | | | |
	P	W	D	L	F	A	W	D	L	F	A
95/96 FAPL	14	6	1	0	17	5	4	1	2	14	8
All time FAPL	140	50	16	4	136	36	37	19	14	118	74
FAPL/FL	3696	1086	426	336	3687	1820	569	481	798	2624	3128

	Home	Away	Total
FAPL Attendances	243,566	225,831	469,397

Nottingham Forest (1) 1
Manchester United (0) 1

Monday, 27th November 1995, City Ground   Att: 29,263

NOTTINGHAM FOREST

1	Mark	CROSSLEY
2	Des	LYTTLE
3	Stuart	PEARCE
4	Colin	COOPER
5	Steve	CHETTLE
14	Ian	WOAN
8	Scott	GEMMILL
21	Chris	BART-WILLIAMS
11	Steve	STONE
20	Paul	McGREGOR *73
19	Stephen	HOWE +88

Subs

18	Alf-Inge	HAARLAND *
24	Richard	IRVING +
7	David	PHILLIPS

MANCHESTER UNITED

1	Peter	SCHMEICHEL
20	Gary	NEVILLE
4	Steve	BRUCE
6	Gary	PALLISTER (Y)
3	Denis	IRWIN
24	David	BECKHAM +81
19	Nicky	BUTT
9	Brian	McCLAIR *45
11	Ryan	GIGGS
17	Andy	COLE
7	Eric	CANTONA

5	Lee	SHARPE +
22	Paul	SCHOLES *
23	Phil	NEVILLE

Match Facts

- United remain unbeaten at the City Ground in the FAPL.
- Cantona's 50th goal for United and his 50th goal in English league football.
- Full FAPL debut for former United junior Richard Irving who left Old Trafford for Forest in July 1995 without ever tasting first team football.

Score Sheet

P. McGREGOR 19 min — 1-0

E. CANTONA 66 min (pen) — 1-1

Referee:

Mr K.Cooper (Mid-Glamorgan)

FA Carling Premiership

		P	W	D	L	F	A	Pts
1	Newcastle United	15	12	2	1	33	11	38
2	**Manchester United**	15	10	3	2	32	14	33
3	Arsenal	15	8	4	3	21	10	28
4	Aston Villa	15	8	3	4	19	11	27
7	**Nottingham Forest**	14	6	7	1	24	21	25

Robbed in the Forest

Despite totally dominating the game, United failed to close Newcastle's lead at the top by more than a solitary point when they were robbed by a Forest team that was only interested in defending. That said, Forest then committed blue murder at the end when substitute Richard Irving, who left Old Trafford six months previously without figuring in the first team, should have marked his first ever two minutes of FAPL action with a winner that would have been a total injustice to a team whose point away from home was already a raw deal.

Although facing the massed ranks of a Forest defence provocatively waving a "No Entry" sign, United sent wave after wave of men forward in an attempt to break down a side who had just taken away from the Reds the FAPL record for the longest unbeaten run in the fledgling competition. But after nineteen minutes the Old Trafford side were hit by a sucker punch when Forest broke free down the inside right channel. Lyttle's free kick was helped on by Cooper to Howe on whom Pallister made a lunging tackle. He cleared the immediate danger but only across the face of his own goal and straight to Paul McGregor who, like Howe, was making his first FAPL start although from the classic finish he applied nobody would have guessed.

United's attacking resolve grew even more intense after the goal but on 32 minutes Alex Ferguson's men almost fell two behind when, on a rare Forest sorty, McGregor got in front of Bruce to send a header flashing just over. Butt replied with an excellent run and then Neville (one of only two United players on the pitch not to have scored in the FAPL so far in 95/96, Bruce surprisingly being the other) sent in a 30 yarder straight at Crossley. Minutes later, Cantona was only just wide from outside the area and on 40 minutes a marvellous move involving Cole, Cantona and McClair got Giggs through but, although he beat Crossley, the ball rebounded to safety off the post. Cole then just cleared the bar with a header but on the odd occasion Forest attacked they seemed likely to score, and right on the halftime whistle, Woan's flag kick curled out of reach of Schmeichel and bounced fortuitously in United's favour off the post.

Scholes was thrown on for McClair at the start of the second period and almost immediately got the ball in the net after a class move down the left by Cantona and Giggs which he followed up when Crossley dropped Cole's header from Cantona's cross. Relentless United pressure finally paid off when Chettle tripped Cantona and the Frenchman himself stepped up to send the ball to Crossley's right as the 'keeper went left. It was no more than the Reds deserved but they almost lost everything in the last seconds when former United junior Irving missed a wonderful opportunity of scoring the winner against his old club on his debut as he sent a header wide when it looked easier to score.

League Record

	Home						Away				
	P	W	D	L	F	A	W	D	L	F	A
95/96 FAPL	15	6	1	0	17	5	4	2	2	15	9
All time FAPL	141	50	16	4	136	36	37	20	14	119	75
FL/FAPL	3697	1086	426	336	3687	1820	569	482	798	2625	3129

	Home	Away	Total
FAPL Attendances	243,566	255,094	498,660

Manchester United (0) 1
Chelsea (0) 1

Saturday, 2nd December 1995, Old Trafford   Att: 42,019

MANCHESTER UNITED			CHELSEA		
25	Kevin	PILKINGTON	1	Dimitri	KHARINE
20	Gary	NEVILLE (Y)	24	Dan	PETRESCU
4	Steve	BRUCE	20	David	LEE
12	David	MAY	26	Michael	DUBERRY
3	Denis	IRWIN	5	Andy	MYERS
24	David	BECKHAM	7	John	SPENCER *82
22	Paul	SCHOLES	12	Craig	BURLEY
9	Brian	McCLAIR	18	Eddie	NEWTON (Y)
5	Lee	SHARPE	11	Dennis	WISE
17	Andy	COLE *75	23	Gareth	HALL (Y)
7	Eric	CANTONA (Y)	8	Mark	HUGHES

Subs

21	Pat	McGIBBON	6	Frank	SINCLAIR
18	Simon	DAVIES	13	Kevin	HITCHCOCK (G)
27	Terry	COOKE *	14	Paul	FURLONG *

Match Facts

- First FAPL start for Kevin Pilkington
- First booking of the season for Cantona
- Chelsea's amazing form at Old Trafford continues – just two defeats in twenty games spanning thirty years
- Only second league game that Gary Pallister has missed since formation of FAPL in 1992.

Score Sheet

D. WISE 53 mins — 0-1
D. BECKHAM 61 mins — 1-1

Referee:
Mr M.Bodenham (East Looe)

FA Carling Premiership

		P	W	D	L	F	A	Pts
1	Newcastle United	15	12	2	1	33	11	38
2	**Manchester United**	16	10	4	2	33	15	34
3	Arsenal	16	8	5	3	22	11	29
4	Aston Villa	16	8	4	4	20	12	28
11	**Chelsea**	16	5	6	5	15	18	21

Sharpe's Pass Not Wise

United went into this game very much up against it for not only had the Londoners travelled North in the knowledge that they had the best record of any club at Old Trafford in recent times with just two defeats at the Theatre of Dreams in the last thirty years, but United were shorn of Schmeichel, Giggs, Pallister, and Butt whilst the Reds were also still missing the suspended Keane. Thus Ferguson was able to name only five of the side that had beaten Chelsea 4-1 at Stamford Bridge barely a month earlier with Pallister missing only his second FAPL game since the new League was introduced in 1992 whilst, at the other end of the scale, Schmeichel's elbow operation gave a first ever FAPL start to Kevin Pilkington. The game also saw the return to Old Trafford of Mark Hughes whom the visitors made captain for the day but the Reds were not without hope of breaking the hoodoo as Chelsea had scored only six times in their previous eleven games.

Chelsea quickly revealed their intentions from the kick-off when they piled everybody behind the ball whilst it took Eddie Newton just 54 seconds to get his name in the referee's book after upending Beckham. Chelsea's defensive tactics were frustrating United and the crowd with the only magic coming from a couple of Cantona gems, one a deft back heel that sent Neville free to send in a cross that came to nothing. But the first period was poor and neither 'keeper was severely tested.

United attacked straight from the restart and almost went ahead when Bruce, who hadn't scored all season, sent a header screaming just past the post. Chelsea, however, quickly hit back to take a shock lead. There appeared absolutely no danger when Sharpe had the ball just inside his own half on the United left but an inexplicable pass-back fell well short of its intended target to let in Spencer. It appeared as though Pilkington had spared Sharpe's blushes when he spread himself to block Spencer's shot but the rebound fell kindly to Wise and the England international slotted the ball into the unguarded net from just inside the area.

Cantona's response was to lose his cool for the first time since his come back and he was rightly booked for a two footed tackle on Newton within a minute of the Reds going behind. But the Frenchman made amends a few minutes later when he freed Neville on the right. The youngster's cross caused problems in the Chelsea rearguard who could only clear it as far as Beckham dead centre of goal at the edge of the area. United's long range specialist was confronted by a mass of blue shirts but somehow whacked the ball into the top corner past a bemused Kharine for a superb equaliser.

League Record

	Home						Away				
	P	W	D	L	F	A	W	D	L	F	A
95/96 FAPL	16	6	2	0	18	6	4	2	2	15	9
All time FAPL	142	50	17	4	137	37	37	20	14	119	75
FL/FAPL	3698	1086	427	336	3688	1821	569	482	798	2625	3129

	Home	Away	Total
FAPL Attendances	285,585	255,094	540,679

Manchester United (1) 2
Sheffield Wednesday (0) 2

Saturday, 9th December 1995, Old Trafford   Att: 41,849

MANCHESTER UNITED			SHEFFIELD WEDNESDAY		
25	Kevin	PILKINGTON	13	Kevin	PRESSMAN
20	Gary	NEVILLE	2	Paul	ATHERTON
4	Steve	BRUCE (Y)	17	Des	WALKER
12	David	MAY	29	Lee	BRISCOE
23	Phil	NEVILLE	3	Ian	NOLAN
24	David	BECKHAM (Y)	8	Chris	WADDLE *74
9	Brian	McCLAIR	5	Steve	NICHOL
22	Paul	SCHOLES *51	14	Marc	DEGRYSE
5	Lee	SHARPE +82	9	David	HIRST
17	Andy	COLE	10	Mark	BRIGHT
7	Eric	CANTONA	19	Guy	WHITTINGHAM

Subs

2	Paul	PARKER	11	John	SHERIDAN *
18	Simon	DAVIES *	15	Andy	SINTON
27	Terry	COOKE +	16	Graham	HYDE

Match Facts

- Only six wins in over 50 league visits to Old Trafford for Wednesday.
- First goal for Cantona in open play since his return from suspension in October and his first double strike since converting his two penalties against Chelsea in the 1994 FA Cup Final.
- Whittingham's goal is first header conceded by United in 95/96.

Score Sheet

E. CANTONA 19 mins — 1-0

M. BRIGHT 59 mins — 1-1

G. WHITTINGHAM 78 mins — 1-2

E. CANTONA 83 mins — 2-2

Referee:

Mr P.Jones (Loughborough)

FA Carling Premier

		P	W	D	L	F	A	Pts
1	Newcastle Utd	17	12	3	2	36	15	39
2	**Manchester United**	**17**	**10**	**5**	**2**	**35**	**17**	**35**
3	Arsenal	17	8	6	3	22	11	30
4	Middlesbrough	17	8	6	3	19	11	30
14	**Sheffield Wednesday**	**17**	**4**	**6**	**7**	**20**	**25**	**18**

Cantona Rescues Sad Reds

United were without no fewer than six first team regulars for this fixture and it proved to be too much as they failed to beat a Wednesday team that would have been cannon fodder for a first choice line up. Pallister, Irwin, Schmeichel, Keane, Butt and Giggs were all missing and, as hard as their replacements tried, it was too great a number of players to cover at this level of the game. Fortunately, Eric Cantona was at his brilliant best to rescue the Reds with two goals that at least salvaged a point when it looked likely that United would lose all three. It was, however, United's third draw in a row and even more annoying was the fact that, with Newcastle losing at Chelsea, Alex Ferguson's side could have reduced the gap on the leaders to just two points.

Scholes and Cantona linked up well as United made the early running but when the Frenchman laid the ball into what he thought would be the chosen path of Cole, United's record signing failed to read it and the chance went begging. But Cole made amends after 17 minutes when he made the last pass of an intricate movement started by Sharpe to find Cantona bursting into the area. As Pressman ran out, Cantona waited for him to commit himself and then calmly lifted the ball over the 'keeper's body as Wednesday's custodian spread himself at the Frenchman's feet.

United had a remarkable let off five minutes later when Bright headed a Nolan cross well wide when he should have certainly scored and then just before the interval Cantona was unable to get enough power in a header after stretching to reach a Sharpe cross. The Frenchman then set up a sitter for McClair but the Scot put his header over from the edge of the six yard box.

The equaliser that Wednesday had threatened came on the hour in bizarre style. As Bright shaped to shoot after Hirst had headed on to him, Bruce got in a tackle that appeared to have saved the day only to see the ball loop up in the air from the tackle and float gently over the stranded Pilkington before coming to rest in the net. Matters were to get worse for the Reds when Degryse, who had been threatening down the left flank all afternoon, opened the United defence up again and from his cross Whittingham's header was unerring in its accuracy.

With time running out, Cantona saved United's blushes by scoring a gem of a goal fashioned from nothing. Gary Neville's long throw from the right was only partially cleared as far as the Frenchman at the edge of the area and despite numerous bodies of both sides between him and goal, Cantona hit a crisp volley past a bewildered Pressman.

League Record

| | Home | | | | | | Away | | | | |
	P	W	D	L	F	A	W	D	L	F	A
95/96 FAPL	17	6	3	0	20	8	4	2	2	15	9
All time FAPL	143	50	18	4	139	39	37	20	14	119	75
FL/FAPL	3699	1086	428	336	3690	1823	569	482	798	2625	3129

	Home	Away	Total
FAPL Attendances	327,434	255,094	582,528

Liverpool
Manchester United

(1) 2
(0) 0

17th December 1995, Anfield   Att: 40,546

LIVERPOOL

1	David	JAMES
2	Rob	JONES
5	Mark	WRIGHT
12	John	SCALES
4	Jason	McATEER
22	Steve	HARKNESS
16	Michael	THOMAS
10	John	BARNES
17	Steve	McMANAMAN (Y)
8	Stan	COLLYMORE
23	Robbie	FOWLER (Y)

Subs

19	Mark	KENNEDY
21	Dominic	MATTEO
26	Anthony	WARNER (G)

MANCHESTER UNITED

1	Peter	SCHMEICHEL
20	Gary	NEVILLE
4	Steve	BRUCE
12	David	MAY
3	Denis	IRWIN
24	David	BECKHAM
9	Brian	McCLAIR (Y)
5	Lee	SHARPE (Y)
11	Ryan	GIGGS
17	Andy	COLE *52
7	Eric	CANTONA

25	Kevin	PILKINGTON (G)
22	Paul	SCHOLES *
23	Phil	NEVILLE

Match Facts

• Robbie Fowler becomes first player to score four goals against United in a single FAPL season. His second goal was his 50th in the FAPL.

• Only Sharpe's second booking of season but both on Merseyside and both by Mr Poll!

Score Sheet

R. FOWLER 44 mins — 1-0

R. FOWLER 88 mins — 2-0

Referee:
Mr G.Poll (Tring)

FA Carling Premiership

		P	W	D	L	F	A	Pts
1	Newcastle United	18	13	3	2	37	15	42
2	**Manchester United**	18	10	5	3	35	19	35
3	Spurs	18	9	6	3	24	17	33
4	Aston Villa	18	9	5	4	25	14	32
5	**Liverpool**	18	9	4	5	31	15	31
6	Arsenal	18	8	7	3	23	12	31

Limp Reds Suffer Fowler Blues

United had Schmeichel and Giggs back for their visit to arch rivals Liverpool but were still without Pallister, Keane and Butt from their first choice line up. Despite the game resembling a personal battle between Liverpool's record signing Stan Collymore and Peter Schmeichel, it was actually won by a young man who seems likely to become a thorn in the side of United for years to come, the fast developing Robbie Fowler whose two goals took his tally against the Old Trafford side in 95/96 to four.

It was a limp display by United who were totally outclassed in the first half with the alarm bells ringing as early as the 10th minute when Fowler was left alone to head wide from an excellent position. Five minutes later Collymore forced Schmeichel to the first of many fine saves that were to deny the former Forest man all afternoon and almost immediately the Dane repeated his effort, also against Collymore. It took United twenty minutes to win a corner but it was only a brief respite and back at the other end Beckham was relieved when his attempted chip back to Schmeichel beat the 'keeper but also just cleared the bar. Schmeichel thwarted Collymore yet again but, just when it seemed that United would reach the interval on level terms, they conceded a free kick some 25 yards out. Schmeichel was at his right-hand post lining the wall up and then moved to his left to take up a more central position. As he made the move, Fowler also made his to cleverly curl the ball to Schmeichel's right clearly wrong footing the United 'keeper.

United responded well after the break and came more into the game especially after Scholes was brought on for Cole, whose memories of Anfield in a United shirt are not the best as the previous season he was on the bench to start off with! But the Mancunians didn't look like scoring and the duel between Schmeichel and Collymore resumed with the Dane blocking an effort on the hour and then having to rely on the woodwork when the Liverpool player did eventually beat him! Tempers were beginning to get frayed and, in the space of five minutes, four separate incidents saw the names of McManaman, McClair, Fowler and Sharpe all go into the referee's book. McManaman, who hadn't scored a home goal for over 14 months, showed why when he hit the side netting. After 72 minutes came United's first real chance only for James to bring off a fine save from Cantona's drive. Almost immediately Scholes fashioned another opportunity, this time for Giggs, but the Welshman's shot was narrowly wide. Schmeichel twice more denied Stan the Man and then Mark Wright came within an inch of putting through his own goal. But it would have been an injustice had United snatched a point and Fowler made sure they didn't when Ferguson's men left themselves exposed in their search for an equaliser near the end.

League Record

| | Home | | | | | | Away | | | | |
	P	W	D	L	F	A	W	D	L	F	A
95/96 FAPL	18	6	3	0	20	8	4	2	3	15	11
All time FAPL	144	50	18	4	139	39	37	20	15	119	77
FL/FAPL	3700	1086	428	336	3690	1823	569	482	799	2625	3131

	Home	Away	Total
FAPL Attendances	327,434	295,640	623,074

Leeds United   (2) 3
Manchester United   (1) 1

Sunday, 24th December 1995, Elland Road   Att: 39,801

LEEDS UNITED

13	Mark	BEENEY
2	Gary	KELLY
6	David	WETHERALL
16	Richard	JOBSON
3	Tony	DORIGO
4	Carlton	PALMER
18	Thomas	BROLIN
10	Gary	McALLISTER
11	Gary	SPEED
21	Tony	YEBOAH *86
9	Brian	DEANE (Y)

Subs

15	Nigel	WORTHINGTON
8	Rod	WALLACE *
5	Lucas	RADEBE

MANCHESTER UNITED

1	Peter	SCHMEICHEL
20	Gary	NEVILLE
2	Paul	PARKER *74
4	Steve	BRUCE **79
3	Denis	IRWIN
19	Nicky	BUTT
9	Brian	McCLAIR
16	Roy	KEANE
24	David	BECKHAM (Y) +74
17	Andy	COLE
7	Eric	CANTONA

12	David	MAY *
22	Paul	SCHOLES +
23	Phil	NEVILLE **

Match Facts

- First time since November 1992 that United had lost two FAPL games in succession.
- Just three points for United from their last five games.
- Leeds were equally out of form and had taken only one point from their previous four games.
- Only second time in last 16 meetings of the the two clubs that Leeds had won.

Score Sheet

G. McALLISTER 5 mins (pen) — 1-0

A. COLE 29 mins — 1-1

T. YEBOAH 35 mins — 2-1

B. DEANE 65 mins — 3-1

Referee

Mr D.Gallagher (Banbury)

FA Carling Premiership

		P	W	D	L	F	A	Pts
1	Newcastle United	19	14	3	2	40	16	45
2	**Manchester United**	19	10	5	4	36	22	35
3	Liverpool	19	10	4	5	34	16	34
9	**Leeds United**	18	8	4	6	26	25	28

No Christmas Crackers for the Reds

The meeting of two of the top teams of the past couple of decades had a strange look about it as far as form was concerned. United had secured just three points from their previous four matches whilst Leeds went in to the game straight from a 6-2 thrashing by Sheffield Wednesday and a worse record than United with only one point from their last four fixtures. Alex Ferguson suffered a double whammy just prior to kick off when Ryan Giggs failed a fitness test and his obvious replacement, Lee Sharpe, was sent home suffering from 'flu. Roy Keane was back from injury and suspension and was joined by Nicky Butt after his suspension whilst Paul Parker also featured, with David May demoted to the subs bench.

Leeds took an early lead when Butt jumped with his arms in the air and paid the penalty when the ball struck him leaving Mr Gallagher pointing to the spot. McAllister's piledriver beat Schmeichel high to the 'keeper's left and the Yorkshire side almost doubled their lead four minutes later when the slowness of Bruce combined with Parker's rustiness to allow Yeboah to slip through. Schmeichel narrowed the angle but Yeboah's chip easily beat the Dane only for the crossbar to save the day. An awful clearance by Schmeichel from a pass back almost gifted Leeds another goal but Deane's effort from ten yards outside the penalty area was as woeful as the United keeper's clearance and the Reds stayed in the game. Indeed, after 29 minutes Butt atoned for his mistake that led to the penalty when he dispossessed Speed on the left flank of Leeds' penalty area and then quickly hit the byeline before pulling the ball back accurately for Cole to sweep home the equaliser from about ten yards. United, however, were not on level terms for long because six minutes later a dreadful mistake by Parker again let in Yeboah and this time there was no woodwork available to save Schmeichel.

After the interval, United took the game to Leeds but, as they did so, the Reds left themselves exposed at the back. Yeboah again skipped past Parker to set up a good chance for Brolin but the Swede's header was straight at Schmeichel who was promptly fouled by Deane which earned the game's first booking for the striker. The United 'keeper then had to be alert to keep out another Yeboah effort before a clash of heads saw United lose Cantona for running repairs to a head injury received in a collision with Wetherall. With the Reds down to ten men whilst Cantona had six stitches inserted in his head wound, Leeds pressed home their advantage. A run down the Leeds' right by Carlton Palmer did the initial damage and his pull back to Brolin was cleverly chipped into the area from where Deane headed home from the edge of the six yard box. Ferguson now rang the changes with all three substitutes introduced but Leeds shut up shop for the day and Beeney, making his first appearance since February '94, was barely tested as United stretched their run without a win to five games.

League Record

| | Home | | | | | | Away | | | | |
	P	W	D	L	F	A	W	D	L	F	A
95/96 FAPL	19	6	3	0	20	8	4	2	4	16	14
All time FAPL	145	50	18	4	139	39	37	20	16	120	80
FL/FAPL	3701	1086	428	336	3690	1823	569	482	800	2626	3134

	Home	Away	Total
FAPL Attendances	327,434	335,441	662,875

Manchester United   (1) 2
Newcastle United   (0) 0

27th December 1995, Old Trafford   Att: 42,024

MANCHESTER UNITED

1	Peter	SCHMEICHEL
3	Denis	IRWIN (Y)
20	Gary	NEVILLE
12	David	MAY *45
23	Phil	NEVILLE
16	Roy	KEANE
24	David	BECKHAM
19	Nicky	BUTT
11	Ryan	GIGGS
17	Andy	COLE
7	Eric	CANTONA

Subs

22	Paul	SCHOLES
21	Pat	McGIBBON
9	Brian	McCLAIR *

NEWCASTLE UNITED

1	Pavel	SRNICEK
2	Warren	BARTON (Y)
6	Steve	HOWEY
4	Darren	PEACOCK
3	John	BERESFORD (Y)
18	Keith	GILLESPIE *13
8	Peter	BEARDSLEY
19	Lee	CLARK +75
14	David	GINOLA
9	Les	FERDINAND
7	Robert	LEE

19	Steve	WATSON *
28	Paul	KITSON +
26	Robbie	ELLIOTT

Match Facts

- Newcastle still to beat United in the FAPL.
- No win for Newcastle at Old Trafford since Feb 1972 and only one league win at the ground since December 1950.
- Only two league wins for Newcastle, home or away, over the Reds in 23 years.
- Cantona captains United for first time in a competitive match.

Score Sheet

Andy COLE 6 mins — 1-0
Roy KEANE 53 mins — 2-0

Referee:

Mr P.Alcock (Bristol)

FA Carling Premiership

		P	W	D	L	F	A	Pts
1	Newcastle United	20	14	3	3	40	18	45
2	Manchester United	20	11	5	4	38	22	38
3	Spurs	20	9	8	3	26	19	35
4	Liverpool	19	10	4	5	34	16	34
5	Arsenal	20	9	7	4	27	15	34

The Circus Comes to Town

United went into this clash of the Titans in the knowledge that they had to win. Victory for Newcastle would have given the Geordies a massive 13 point lead but the Reds boss Alex Ferguson must have feared the worst when all three of his central defenders, Pallister, Bruce and Parker were ruled out. Day long efforts to get French triallist William Prunier cleared to play failed and United turned to the totally untried partnership of Gary Neville and David May to stop the Newcastle bandwagon that had seen them become the FAPL's top goalscorers.

It was a desperately cold night with the temperature at minus four but the feast of football put on kept everybody warm with United giving their best display of a roller coaster season. The Reds took an early lead and never looked back once Giggs had carried the ball forward from his own half on the six minute mark before delivering a raking thirty yard defence splitting pass into the path of Cole who stroked it first time past the helpless Srnicek from sixteen yards. Gillespie's return to Old Trafford was unlucky as the former Red lasted just thirteen minutes before being carried off with a recurrence of the groin strain that he had battled against all week. Barton was booked for dissent and then there was consternation in the Newcastle camp when his lookalike, John Beresford, was also booked and shown the Red card for a second bookable offence. Referee Mr Alcock realised his mistake over the identity, however, and recalled Beresford. There was more trouble though for Beresford when he needed lengthy treatment after being felled by team mate Ferdinand. Just past the half hour mark, Ferdinand forced Schmeichel into his only save of the night and Newcastle were happy to hear the half time whistle without further mishaps.

United themselves, however, were in the wars losing David May just before the break and he failed to reappear for the second period with McClair taking to the field in his place. But there was no holding this rampant United and they doubled their lead eight minutes after the break with another tremendous goal. Young Phil Neville was the provider with a gem of a forty yard pass that picked out Keane who selected his spot and hammered the ball past Srnicek from an angle on the United right. Another class move begun by a long Schmeichel throw almost saw United go three in front when Giggs burst through the centre and beat the Newcastle 'keeper all ends up only for the ball to bounce to safety off the bar as the Reds began to run riot. But there were no more goals despite the constant pressure and, for a game that was so dominated by United, a strange statistic emerged with Newcastle, despite being totally outplayed, actually winning eight corners to United's five! But there was no doubting the winners and even Kevin Keegan admitted as much when he said after the game "We brought our circus to town but we forgot to bring any tigers".

League Record

| | Home | | | | | Away | | | | |
	P	W	D	L	F	A	W	D	L	F	A
95/96 FAPL	20	7	3	0	22	8	4	2	4	16	14
All time FAPL	146	51	18	4	141	39	37	20	16	120	80
FL/FAPL	3702	1087	428	336	3692	1823	569	482	800	2626	3134

	Home	Away	Total
FAPL Attendances	369,458	335,441	704,899

Manchester United (1) 2
Queens Park Rangers (0) 1

30th December 1995, Old Trafford   Att: 41,890

MANCHESTER UNITED

1	Peter	SCHMEICHEL
3	Denis	IRWIN
20	Gary	NEVILLE
31	William	PRUNIER
23	Phil	NEVILLE *55
24	David	BECKHAM **88
19	Nicky	BUTT
16	Roy	KEANE
11	Ryan	GIGGS
17	Andy	COLE +55
7	Eric	CANTONA

Subs

2	Paul	PARKER *
5	Lee	SHARPE **
9	Brian	McCLAIR +

QPR

25	Jurgen	SOMMER
2	David	BARDSLEY +71
3	Rufus	BREVITT
21	Steve	YATES
6	Danny	MADDIX
7	Andrew	IMPEY
8	Ian	HOLLOWAY
19	Nigel	QUASHIE
27	Matthew	BRAZIER
17	Bradley	ALLEN *47
11	Trevor	SINCLAIR

14	Karl	READY +
1	Tony	ROBERTS (G)
9	Daniel	DICHIO *

Match Facts

- United debut for French international, William Prunier.
- Dichio's strike for Rangers was their first away goal in nine games.
- United unbeaten in FAPL by Rangers after seven meetings and only one win in fifteen league visits to Old Trafford for the London outfit.

Score Sheet

A. COLE 45 mins — 1-0

R. GIGGS 52 mins — 2-0

D. DICHIO 68 mins — 2-1

Referee:
Mr R.Hart (Darlington)

FA Carling Premiership

		P	W	D	L	F	A	Pts
1	Newcastle United	20	14	3	3	40	18	45
2	**Manchester United**	**21**	**12**	**5**	**4**	**40**	**23**	**41**
3	Liverpool	20	10	5	5	36	18	35
4	Spurs	21	9	8	4	27	21	35
5	Arsenal	21	9	7	5	28	18	34
18	**Queens Park Rangers**	21	5	3	13	16	31	18

Cole Fire Warms United

A bitterly cold day saw United reduce Newcastle's lead at the top of the FAPL to just four points when, with Kevin Keegan's outfit frozen off at West Ham, a third goal in consecutive matches from Andy Cole helped the Reds to warm their supporters up. With David May joining Steve Bruce and Gary Pallister on the injury list there was a debut for French international central defender William Prunier who was at Old Trafford on trial from Bordeaux. Not to be outdone, former United player Ray Wilkins, now in charge at QPR, gave a FAPL debut to 17 year old Nigel Quashie.

After their superlative performance against Newcastle three days earlier, United were quickly into their stride with a second minute piledriver from Keane bringing a fine save from Sommer. But it was Rangers who came closest to scoring and, after Prunier had already made a timely interception to break up one attack, Bradley Allen thundered a long range effort against the angle of Schmeichel's right-hand post and the crossbar with the Dane well beaten. Almost immediately, Allen flashed another shot from the edge of the penalty area just wide of the other post whilst after ten minutes Trevor Sinclair squandered a great opportunity when he rushed his effort well wide after a slip by Gary Neville had given him a clear sight of goal.

Prunier showed his attacking ability with a 30 yarder that had Sommer scrambling across his goal to hold and just before half-time he unleashed another long range shot that flew just wide. A minute later United won a corner and it looked as if Prunier's attacking instincts would be rewarded with a debut goal when he got in a powerful header from Giggs' flag kick. Sommer, however, somehow got a hand to the ball and palmed it out but only to Cole who gleefully nodded it back into the net past two helpless defenders.

United quickly capitalised in the second period to go two ahead after a sloppy piece of defending by Rangers near their left corner flag. Irwin, playing at right back, overlapped down the United right but looked to be heading nowhere when he was trapped by the corner flag with both Brevett and Holloway covering him. Brevett appeared to hold Irwin and Holloway stopped, presumably thinking the referee would give a free kick. Irwin broke loose to cut in between the two Rangers players along the byeline before cutting the ball back to Giggs who slotted neatly home from about ten yards. Ferguson, thinking the game was won, immediately made a double substitution but an almighty error by Schmeichel let Rangers right back in the hunt. There was absolutely no danger as the Dane dribbled the ball out of his area from a pass back and Dichio's approach looked forlorn until Schmeichel hammered the ball against the tall striker who then calmly lobbed into the unguarded net to ensure the Reds had to fight all the way for their last three points of 1995.

League Record

| | Home | | | | | | Away | | | | |
	P	W	D	L	F	A	W	D	L	F	A
95/96 FAPL	21	8	3	0	24	9	4	2	4	16	14
All time FAPL	147	52	18	4	143	40	37	20	16	120	80
FL/FAPL	3703	1088	428	336	3694	1824	569	482	800	2626	3134

	Home	Away	Total
FAPL Attendances	411,348	335,441	746,789

Tottenham Hotspur (2) 4
Manchester United (1) 1

Monday, 1st January 1996, White Hart Lane   Att: 32,852

TOTTENHAM HOTSPUR

1	Ian	WALKER
2	Dean	AUSTIN (Y)
14	Stuart	NETHERCOTT
5	Colin	CALDERWOOD
3	Justin	EDINBURGH
8	Ilie	DUMITRESCU *80
20	Darren	CASKEY
23	Sol	CAMPBELL
16	Ronnie	ROSENTHAL
11	Chris	ARMSTRONG
10	Terry	SHERINGHAM

Subs

31	Chris	DAY (G)
32	Steve	SLADE
18	Gerry	McMAHON *

MANCHESTER UNITED

1	Peter	SCHMEICHEL *45
2	Paul	PARKER
20	Gary	NEVILLE
31	William	PRUNIER
23	Phil	NEVILLE +68
24	David	BECKHAM
16	Roy	KEANE **68
19	Nicky	BUTT
11	Ryan	GIGGS
7	Eric	CANTONA
17	Andy	COLE

25	Kevin	PILKINGTON (G) *
5	Lee	SHARPE +
9	Brian	McCLAIR **

Match Facts

• The first time that United had conceded four goals in an FAPL game. The last time was also on New Year's Day and against QPR managed by Spurs boss Gerry Francis.
• Andy Cole becomes third United player to score in four consecutive FAPL games behind Mark Hughes and Eric Cantona.
• First win over United for Spurs (FAPL).

Score Sheet

T. SHERINGHAM 35 mins	1-0
Andy COLE 36 mins —	1-1
Sol CAMPBELL 45 mins —	2-1
C. ARMSTRONG 48 mins —	3-1
C. ARMSTRONG 66 mins —	4-1

Referee

Mr G.Ashby (Worcestershire)

FA Carling Premiership

		P	W	D	L	F	A	Pts
1	Newcastle United	20	14	3	3	40	18	45
2	**Manchester United**	22	12	5	5	41	27	41
3	Liverpool	21	11	5	5	40	20	38
4	**Tottenham Hotspur**	22	10	8	4	31	22	38
5	Aston Villa	20	10	5	5	27	15	35

New Year Hangover

The Reds went into this New Year's Day game in the knowledge that a win would reduce the deficit on leaders Newcastle to just one point. But truth is stranger than fiction and the last time United faced a London team on New Year's Day they had lost 4-1. The manager of QPR that game was none other than Gerry Francis who was now managing Spurs. But United had never conceded four goals in a league fixture since that fateful day so surely history could not repeat itself?

Unlike the defeats against Liverpool and Leeds United in their previous two away games when the Reds were abject failures, United at least fought in this match despite the scoreline indicating otherwise. But, with a makeshift back four that included a Frenchman who could speak no English, and hit by a warm-up injury that left Schmeichel a passenger, they simply could not cope with the crosses that came in from both flanks with endless monotony. The writing was on the wall after just five minutes when Sheringham outjumped Prunier only to see his header hit Schmeichel's left-hand post. Five minutes later Armstrong tested United's woodwork again when he powered in a long range effort that beat the disabled Dane but thundered against the bar and it was a case of third time lucky for Spurs when a right wing cross found Sheringham in acres of space right in front of goal and even a fit Schmeichel would have had trouble keeping out the England man from some ten yards. But within seconds the Reds had pulled level with Phil Neville outstripping the Spurs defence down the left to whip in a low cross that Cole slid home. It was the fourth consecutive game that Cole had netted and, for a time, United held their own. But, right on the half time whistle, the Reds failed to clear a Dean Austin cross and Sol Campbell smashed the ball home from near the penalty spot.

Pilkington replaced the struggling Schmeichel but his first task was to fish the ball out of his net after yet another cross, this time from the left, found United exposed at the far post where Rosenthal headed back across goal for Armstrong to nod home from five yards. United gamely tried to respond and both Cole and Cantona had efforts cleared off the line in frantic scrambles but the game was put beyond recall after 66 minutes. Again it was a cross that did the damage as Sheringham, on the right, lifted the ball into the United area for Armstrong to capitalise on the lack of marking to head home unchallenged from the edge of the six yard box. Sharpe and McClair replaced Keane and Phil Neville but nothing was going right for the Reds whose night of woe was complete when a brilliant overhead scissors kick from Cole found the net only to be disallowed for dangerous play. The scoreline remained at 4-1 and history had, indeed, repeated itself.

League Record

| | Home | | | | | | Away | | | | |
	P	W	D	L	F	A	W	D	L	F	A
95/96 FAPL	22	8	3	0	24	9	4	2	5	17	18
All time FAPL	148	52	18	4	143	40	37	20	17	121	84
FL/FAPL	3704	1088	428	336	3694	1824	569	482	801	2627	3138

	Home	Away	Total
FAPL Attendances	411,348	368,293	779,641

Manchester United (1) 2
Sunderland (0) 2

Saturday, 6th January 1996, Old Trafford   Att: 41,563

MANCHESTER UNITED

1	Kevin	PILKINGTON
2	Gary	NEVILLE +66
4	Steve	BRUCE
6	Gary	PALLISTER
3	Denis	IRWIN (Y)
10	David	BECKHAM (Y) *60
5	Roy	KEANE
8	Nicky	BUTT
11	Ryan	GIGGS
9	Andy	COLE
7	Eric	CANTONA

Subs

12	Brian	McCLAIR
14	Lee	SHARPE *
15	Phil	NEVILLE +

SUNDERLAND

1	Alec	CHAMBERLAIN
2	Dariusz	KUBICKI
3	Martin	SCOTT (Y)
4	Paul	BRACEWELL
5	Kevin	BALL *25
6	Andy	MELVILLE
7	Michael	GRAY
8	Richard	ORD
9	Craig	RUSSELL (Y)
10	Phil	GRAY **87
11	David	KELLY +82

12	Lee	HOWEY **
13	Steve	AGNEW * (Y)
14	Martin	SMITH +

Match Facts

- First FA Cup appearances for United by Andy Cole and Kevin Pilkington.
- First FA Cup goal for Nicky Butt.
- Sunderland not beaten United in eleven attempts in FA and Football League Cups.
- Just one defeat in last 15 FA Cup ties for United.

Prominent Results

Liverpool	7	Rochdale	0
Gravesend & N	0	Aston Villa	3
Hereford United	1	Spurs	1
Leicester City	0	Man City	0
Arsenal	1	Sheff United	1
Charlton	2	Sheff Wed	0

Score Sheet

N. BUTT 13 mins — 1-0
S. AGNEW 61 mins — 1-1
C. RUSSELL 64 mins — 1-2
E. CANTONA 80 mins — 2-2

Referee:
Mr M. Reed (Birmingham)

Red Blushes Saved by Cantona

United went into their third cup competition of the season in the knowledge that they had bit the dust at the first hurdle in both their previous attempts in the UEFA and Coca Cola versions of knock out football. That they didn't make it a hat-trick after a lack lustre performance against Sunderland was thanks only to a late equaliser from Eric Cantona when he powered home a match saving header ten minutes from time.

With Gary Pallister back in the line up after injury, Manager Alex Ferguson was able to call on his first choice back four for the first time since November but their ring rustiness showed immediately as Sunderland broke straight from the kick off when Irwin's pass back was short of 'keeper Pilkington. As both Bruce and the stranded 'keeper tried desperately to retrieve the situation, Sunderland's Phil Gray won the race and looked to have given his side a shock lead only for Gary Neville to hack the ball to safety off the line. Beckham floored Martin Scott to earn an early booking after only six minutes and the visitors' good start continued when Bracewell fired a screamer just past Pilkington's post.

The Reds, however, began to dig in and Chamberlain had already been forced to save from Beckham when Butt gave United the lead after 13 minutes. One of those flowing United passing movements seemed to go on endlessly until Cole flicked the ball through to Butt and the youngster, spotting Chamberlain off his line, calmly lobbed home. But it was a flash in the pan with Sunderland hitting the post as Craig Russell's pace caused the home team all sorts of problems and there was little doubt that the Reds were relieved to hear the whistle for half time. But the visitors kept up the pressure after the interval and could have had a penalty when Pallister seemed to have upended Kubicki but Sunderland's vociferous claims for a spot kick were waived away by Mr Reed. Cole got in a rare shot before disaster struck on the hour mark. The balding Agnew, a 25th minute substitute, suddenly found himself in absolutely acres of space some thirty yards out and he drilled his shot just inside Pilkington's left hand post. Worse was to follow when, two minutes later, Russell's speed once again caught United flat footed as he raced onto Agnew's through ball. There was a hint of offside but no flag came and Russell's cross shot was good enough to beat the shell shocked Pilkington.

But, not for the first time, Eric Cantona came to the rescue of the ragged Reds when he grabbed them a lifeline ten minutes from time by heading home Lee Sharpe's right wing cross at the far post. Some 8,000 Wearsiders returned home feeling cheated of the spoils and United, indeed, were very fortunate not to have collected an unwanted hat-trick of cup dismissals.

All-time FA Cup Record

	Home						Away				
P	W	D	L	F	A	W	D	L	F	A
354	102	32	28	345	153	80	54	58	304	271

	Home	Away	Total
FA Cup Attendances	41,563		41,563

Manchester United   (0) 0
Aston Villa   (0) 0

Saturday, 13th January 1996, Old Trafford   Att: 42,667

MANCHESTER UNITED

1	Peter	SCHMEICHEL (Y)
3	Denis	IRWIN (Y)
20	Gary	NEVILLE (Y)
4	Steve	BRUCE
23	Phil	NEVILLE (Y)
11	Ryan	GIGGS
19	Nicky	BUTT
16	Roy	KEANE
5	Lee	SHARPE *77
17	Andy	COLE
7	Eric	CANTONA

ASTON VILLA

1	Mark	BOSNICH
2	Gary	CHARLES
4	Gareth	SOUTHGATE
5	Paul	McGRATH
14	Alan	WRIGHT
16	Ugo	EHIOGU
7	Ian	TAYLOR
11	Andy	TOWNSEND
9	Savo	MILOSEVIC
8	Mark	DRAPER
10	Tommy	JOHNSON *90

Subs

2	Paul	PARKER
9	Brian	McCLAIR
22	Paul	SCHOLES *

13	Nigel	SPINK
17	Franz	CARR
20	Riccardo	SCIMECA *N

Match Facts

- Bookings for Gary and Phil Neville make them the first pair of brothers to be booked in the same game playing for United.
- Villa still to win at Old Trafford in the FAPL.
- Villa not won a league match at Old Trafford since November 1983.

Score Sheet

Referee:

Mr G.Willard (Worthing)

FA Carling Premiership

	P	W	D	L	F	A	Pts
1 Newcastle United	21	15	3	3	42	18	48
2 Manchester United	**23**	**12**	**6**	**5**	**41**	**27**	**42**
3 Spurs	23	11	8	4	32	22	41
4 Liverpool	22	11	6	5	41	21	39
7 Aston Villa	**21**	**10**	**6**	**5**	**27**	**15**	**36**

United Stifled

United were dealt a blow before the game when Gary Pallister withdrew after his brief return from injury against Sunderland in the FA Cup and they were also without David Beckham who was beginning a two match suspension. Villa also had problems and were without their leading goalscorer Dwight Yorke who was on international duty with Trinidad and Tobago.

United started brightly with Giggs raiding down the right and beating three men in a jinking run before being stopped at the expense of a corner but it was from the opposite flank that the first real danger to the Villa goal came when Phil Neville sent over a cross that neither Butt nor Cole could do justice to. Villa could have taken the lead when a Charles cross intended for his forwards was mis-hit and caused Schmeichel all sorts of problems before the Dane tipped it over the bar. But Villa were, by and large, content to pack their midfield to stifle United's open play and the Reds were finding life difficult against the FAPL's meanest defence which had conceded only 15 goals in 20 games. Cantona, however, should have broken the deadlock in the 20th minute from a Giggs corner but his header was straight at Bosnich.

Phil Neville put in another great cross from the left but Cantona couldn't quite make contact and on 28 minutes Cole squandered the best chance of the game after robbing Southgate. He sent Giggs clear and the Welshman linked up with Butt whose cross was steered well wide by Cole. Former United 'keeper Bosnich made a superb save from Giggs in the midst of a spate of bookings as the game became bogged down. The Neville brothers both went into the book followed by Milosevic for a foul on Gary Neville whilst, right on half time, Schmeichel became the fourth player cautioned when he reacted angrily to a challenge by Taylor.

Villa were almost entirely defensive minded and United couldn't find a way through. Phil Neville did his best with a fifty yard crossfield ball that set Giggs away but the Welshman's cross was cut out by former Red Paul McGrath and then appeals for a penalty were turned down after Keane's cross hit Southgate on the arm. Irwin went into the book and then Cole blazed wildly over from a good position after being put through by Butt. Tiring of Cole's misses, the crowd began to chant for leading scorer Scholes to be introduced but, by the time they got their wish, there was just thirteen minutes left. Scholes immediately created half a chance for himself but fired wide and Cole, Cantona and Keane all fired over from distance as the Reds began to run out of ideas. After the game, Ferguson was scathing of the Villa's defensive tactics saying "They were dour, uncompromising and had no interest in entertaining. It was very frustrating". And that was just about everybody's view.

League Record

| | Home | | | | | | Away | | | | |
	P	W	D	L	F	A	W	D	L	F	A
95/96 FAPL	23	8	4	0	24	9	4	2	5	17	18
All time FAPL	149	52	19	4	143	40	37	20	17	121	84
FL/FAPL	3705	1088	429	336	3694	1824	569	482	801	2627	3138

	Home	Away	Total
FAPL Attendances	454,015	368,293	822,308

Sunderland
Manchester United

(1) 1
(0) 2

Tuesday, 16th January 1996, Roker Park   Att: 21,378

SUNDERLAND

1	Alec	CHAMBERLAIN
2	Dariusz	KUBICKI
3	Martin	SCOTT (Y)
4	Paul	BRACEWELL
5	Steve	AGNEW +74
6	Andy	MELVILLE
7	Michael	GRAY
8	Richard	ORD
9	Craig	RUSSELL
10	Phil	GRAY
11	Martin	SMITH *51

Subs

12	Martin	GRAY +
13	John	MULLIN *
14	Lee	HOWEY

MANCHESTER UNITED

1	Peter	SCHMEICHEL
3	Denis	IRWIN
2	Paul	PARKER (Y) *45
4	Steve	BRUCE
5	Gary	NEVILLE
6	Phil	NEVILLE (Y)
9	Nicky	BUTT +62
10	Roy	KEANE
11	Ryan	GIGGS
7	Eric	CANTONA
8	Andy	COLE

12	Brian	McCLAIR
14	Lee	SHARPE *
15	Paul	SCHOLES +

Match Facts

• First time United had ever won a cup-tie at Roker Park.

• Sunderland still to beat United in any cup competition after twelve attempts.

• First FA Cup goal for Scholes and first FA Cup goal in United colours for Andy Cole.

Significant 3rd Round Replay results:

Blackburn Rovers	0 Ipswich Town	1
Sheff United	1 Arsenal	0
Newcastle	2 Chelsea	2
(Chelsea won on penalties)		
Stockport County	2 Everton	3
Man City	5 Leicester City	0

Score Sheet

P. GRAY 24 mins — 1-0

P. SCHOLES 70 mins — 1-1

A. COLE 89 mins — 1-2

Referee:

Mr M.Reed (Birmingham)

Pocket Sub Turns the Tide

United, having survived by the skin of their teeth in the first game at Old Trafford, travelled to the North East in the knowledge that they had never won a cup-tie at Roker Park. On the other hand, Sunderland had never beaten United in eleven previous attempts in cup competitions so, with the game going to penalties if necessary, something had to give. And, until the introduction of pocket size sub Paul Scholes in the 62nd minute, it looked as though it would be the Old Trafford outfit's record that was going to fall by the way side.

A brilliant run by Giggs set up half a chance for Cole but his reactions were unusually slow and his shot was deflected to Phil Neville whose effort was worse than Cole's. Sunderland began to get on top and were playing the better football when they took a deserved lead just past the twenty minute mark. Bruce's headed clearance only found Agnew who split the defence with a through ball that enabled Phil Gray to cut in from the right and slot home between Schmeichel's legs. Five minutes later the big Dane kept his side in the game with a super save to thwart the goalscorer from adding to his laurels after a tricky run. Cole appeared to have wasted a great opportunity to level matters with a hopeless miss from five yards but he was spared any blushes by a linesman's flag, although he didn't know it at the time of the effort. The home side responded with a slick passing move that left Agnew in the clear and again it was Schmeichel who made a distinctly second best United. Parker was then extremely lucky to stay on when, after already having been booked, he committed an atrocious late tackle and Alex Ferguson would have been relieved to hear the half time whistle without further mishap.

Parker, who had had a poor game, was removed from the fray at the interval in favour of Sharpe and United began to exert a great deal of pressure on Sunderland. But, despite increasing the tempo, United rarely troubled Chamberlain until they threw on Scholes with just under thirty minutes left. Scholes immediately looked to have created a chance of a shot for himself but had the ball whipped off his toes by Cole who was having a stinker. Just when it was beginning to seem that all their possession would count for nothing, Scholes jinked his way through to a position some twenty yards out from where he thundered a daisy cutter past Chamberlain's right hand and just inside the post. It was a superb strike and in the last minute Cole atoned for his earlier poor form when he rose gloriously to head home an inviting left wing cross from Sharpe. All of which added to the woe of former World Mile record holder Steve Cram who had jetted in from America to see the tie. After his long haul flight, Cram was fogbound in London and only arrived at half time after the Sunderland goal but in time to see United's two!

All-time FA Cup Record

	Home					Away				
P	W	D	L	F	A	W	D	L	F	A
355	102	32	28	345	153	81	54	58	306	272

	Home	Away	Total
FA Cup Attendances	41,563	21,378	62,941

West Ham United   (0) 0
Manchester United   (1) 1

Monday, 22nd January 1996, Upton Park   Att: 24,197

WEST HAM UNITED

1	Ludek	MIKLOSKO
15	Kenny	BROWN
8	Marc	RIEPER
4	Steve	POTTS
3	Julian	DICKS
20	Gary	WILLIAMSON
7	Ian	BISHOP
10	John	MONCUR
19	Robbie	SLATER
14	Iain	DOWIE
9	Tony	COTTEE

Subs

12	Keith	ROWLAND
21	Peter	SHILTON (G)
27	Chris	WHYTE

MANCHESTER UNITED

1	Peter	SCHMEICHEL
3	Denis	IRWIN
20	Gary	NEVILLE (Y)
4	Steve	BRUCE (Y)
23	Phil	NEVILLE
11	Ryan	GIGGS
19	Nicky	BUTT (Y) (Y) (R)
16	Roy	KEANE
5	Lee	SHARPE (Y)
17	Andy	COLE (Y) *76
7	Eric	CANTONA

9	Brian	McCLAIR
22	Paul	SCHOLES
24	David	BECKHAM *

Match Facts

- Only eighth ever United league win at Upton Park.
- First success at Upton Park since 1989 (7 years and one day to be precise).
- Nicky Butt 'celebrates' his 21st Birthday a day late by getting two cards he didn't want!
- Second successive meeting of the two clubs where a player has been dismissed.
- West Ham still to beat United in FAPL.

Score Sheet

E. CANTONA 8 mins — 1-0

Referee:
Mr S.Lodge (Barnsley)

FA Carling Premiership

	P	W	D	L	F	A	Pts
1 Newcastle United	23	17	3	3	45	19	54
2 Manchester United	**24**	**13**	**6**	**5**	**42**	**27**	**45**
3 Liverpool	23	12	6	5	46	21	42
4 Spurs	24	11	8	5	33	24	41
16 West Ham United	**22**	**6**	**5**	**11**	**22**	**33**	**23**

Cantona the Peacemaker

This game, just three days short of the first anniversary of Eric Cantona's infamous *kung-fu* attack at Crystal Palace, produced the exact opposite from the Frenchman when he acted as peacemaker to save Andy Cole from being dismissed after the record signing had been the victim of an outrageous two footed tackle from Julian Dicks which the referee allowed to go unpunished some five seconds before Nicky Butt was dismissed for a tackle on Dicks that saw the United youngster actually win the ball. Cole saw red and would have undoubtedly seen the red card as well had Cantona not stepped in.

The game itself had started full of action with the Hammers almost taking a third minute lead when a long clearance from Miklosko was headed on by Dowie for Cottee to smack the bar with Schmeichel beaten. But the Reds bounced back in style to take the lead on eight minutes with a super goal. Giggs left Dicks down the right and played the ball in to Cole who promptly fed the ball back to the Welshman to cut in and deliver a cross that eluded everyone. West Ham appeared to have escaped even when Cantona retrieved the ball on the byeline some six yards away from goal but, somehow, the Frenchman curled it into the roof of the net from an impossible angle. The Reds very quickly almost made it two when a dummy from Cantona let the ball run to Sharpe whose effort was kicked off the line by Brown but, in an incredible opening, the Hammers themselves nearly pulled back level when Schmeichel had to save smartly from a Williamson volley.

United had the ball in the net again ten minutes before the break when Cantona slung a forty yard pass out to Giggs on the right and then got himself into the area to meet the cross. Cantona beat Miklosko to the ball only to get a bad bounce off the 'keeper causing the ball to hit the Frenchman's arm before crossing for Sharpe to nod home from point blank range and the referee disallowed the effort. Cantona was in the thick of the action again right on half time but this time was the villain of the piece as he inexplicably completely missed a close range header that would surely have increased United's lead had he connected with Sharpe's centre.

The second period saw West Ham mount a determined fight back but referee Lodge penalised almost every United tackle and the game flared when he allowed Dicks to get away scot-free with a two footed tackle that would surely have caused Cole serious damage had the striker not jumped out of the way. Within seconds Butt tackled Dicks and succeeded in kicking the ball away only for Mr Lodge to dismiss the youngster causing Cole to react violently. Cantona stepped in and the bench immediately substituted their record signing. The ten men then withstood all the Hammers could throw at them but only with the aid of an amazing clearance by Irwin who saved the day when coming from nowhere to clear Bishop's effort off the line in a frantic finish.

League Record

	Home						Away				
	P	W	D	L	F	A	W	D	L	F	A
95/96 FAPL	24	8	4	0	24	9	5	2	5	18	18
All time FAPL	150	52	19	4	143	40	38	20	17	122	84
FAPL/FL	3706	1088	429	336	3694	1824	570	482	801	2628	3138

	Home	Away	Total
FAPL Attendances	454,015	392,490	846,505

Reading
Manchester United

(0) 0
(1) 3

Saturday, 27th January 1996, Elm Park   Att: 14,780

READING			**MANCHESTER UNITED**		
1	Nicky	HAMMOND	1	Peter	SCHMEICHEL (Y)
2	Tom	JONES	3	Denis	IRWIN
3	Mick	GOODING	4	Steve	BRUCE
4	Andy	BERNAL (Y)	20	Gary	NEVILLE
5	Adrian	WILLIAMS	23	Phil	NEVILLE *53
6	Michael	GILKES	19	Nicky	BUTT
7	Jimmy	QUINN **85	16	Roy	KEANE
8	Phil	PARKINSON (Y) *75	5	Lee	SHARPE
9	Trevor	MORLEY	11	Ryan	GIGGS
10	Lee	NOGAN +75	7	Eric	CANTONA
11	Paul	HOLSGROVE	17	Andy	COLE

Subs

12	Stuart	LOVELL **	2	Paul	PARKER * (Y)
13	James	LAMBERT *	9	Brian	McCLAIR
14	Michael	MEAKER +	22	Paul	SCHOLES

Match Facts

- Paul Parker's first FA Cup goal for United and only his second all-told.
- Tenth meeting of the clubs in the FA Cup with just one defeat for United.
- An incredible record for Eric Cantona of scoring in seven consecutive FA Cup ties in which he played. In 1993/94 he scored against Norwich (4th Rd), Wimbledon (5th), Charlton (6th), missed the semi final, scored twice against Chelsea in the Final, scored in his one appearance in 1994/95 against Sheffield United, and then against Sunderland and Reading in 1995/96.

Score Sheet

R. GIGGS 36 mins — 1-0

P. PARKER 56 mins — 2-0

E. CANTONA 89 mins — 3-0

Referee:
Mr J.Winter (Middlesbrough)

Significant Cup Results:

Everton	2	Port Vale	2
Spurs	1	Wolves	1
Keith	1	Glasgow Rgrs	10

(55 games lost to weather)

Cold and Calculated

Reading's Elm Park, acknowledged as one of the worst playing surfaces in the full time game, was one of only four grounds passed fit in English football as snow blanketed out the rest of the day's sport. But if the Berkshire side thought they would catch United out on a frozen pitch they were mistaken. United's biggest problem came before the game when they complained there was no heating in their dressing room and stewards were sent scurrying to find portable heaters on the coldest day of the year. But if the Reds were cold they didn't show it as they put on a calculated display that was too much for their Endsleigh League opponents.

Reading, too, had problems prior to the game particularly in the goalkeeping department where Bulgaria's most capped player, Boris Mihailov, failed to recover from injury to leave chicken pox victim Nicky Hammond having to turn out. Reading, incidentally, had used seven goalkeepers up to this point in the season.

The home side started well enough with joint player-managers Jimmy Quinn and Mick Gooding belying their combined age of 72 years to give commanding displays. Unfortunately for them, the rest of their side didn't match up to their leader's talents and the Reds began to take control. After United had weathered Reading's opening spell and quietened the crowd the first goal duly arrived some ten minutes before half-time when Giggs dispossessed the home side's defence to get Sharpe free inside the area. The England man's shot was well blocked by Hammond but the ball broke to Giggs who drilled it home from ten yards. Cole was again having a poor game and he had twice missed from good positions before Parker was introduced for Phil Neville who was feeling unwell. The substitution was certainly eventful for, before he had touched the ball, Parker was booked inside sixty seconds and within another two minutes had increased United's lead with only his second goal for the club in his five years at Old Trafford.

Not that he meant to score as he picked the ball up on the right flank. Looking up, he aimed what was surely intended as a cross to the far post only to see the ball curve viciously into the net at the near post leaving Hammond stranded. Indeed, it would have probably taken several of those seven Reading 'keepers to keep that one out.

The game was now killed dead and it was only a question of whether the Reds would add to their score. That they failed to do so before Cantona completed the scoring in the final minute from close range was down to Steve Bruce who was guilty of the miss of the season, let alone the game, when he somehow contrived to place the ball over a completely open goal from five yards after Cantona had drawn the 'keeper out and rolled the ball across the edge of the six yard box to his captain.

FA Cup All-time Record

	Home						Away				
P	W	D	L	F	A	W	D	L	F	A
356	102	32	28	345	153	82	54	58	309	272

	Home	Away	Total
FA Cup Attendances	41,563	36,158	77,721

Wimbledon **(0) 2**
Manchester United **(2) 4**

Saturday, 3rd February 1996, Selhurst Park   Att: 25,380

WIMBLEDON

23	Neil	SULLIVAN
2	Kenny	CUNNINGHAM
15	Alan	REEVES
21	Chris	PERRY
3	Alan	KIMBLE
7	Oyvind	LEONHARDSEN
28	Steven	TALBOYS (Y)
18	Neil	ARDLEY
11	Marcus	GAYLE
10	Dean	HOLDSWORTH
22	Andy	CLARKE

Subs

14	Jon	GOODMAN
34	Jason	EUELL
35	Andy	PEARCE

MANCHESTER UNITED

1	Peter	SCHMEICHEL
3	Denis	IRWIN
4	Steve	BRUCE
20	Gary	NEVILLE
23	Phil	NEVILLE
16	Roy	KEANE
19	Nicky	BUTT
5	Lee	SHARPE
11	Ryan	GIGGS
17	Andy	COLE
7	Eric	CANTONA

22	Paul	SCHOLES
24	David	BECKHAM
32	Tony	COTON

Match Facts

- First return to Selhurst Park for Eric Cantona since his *kung fu* attack.
- First appearance on bench for Tony Coton.
- Six wins in last seven league meetings with the 'Dons' for United.

Score Sheet

A. COLE 41 mins — 0-1

C. PERRY og 45 mins — 0-2

M. GAYLE 68 mins — 1-2

E. CANTONA 70 mins — 1-3

J. EUELL 76 mins — 2-3

E. CANTONA 81 mins — 2-4

Referee:

Mr P.Durkin (Portland)

FA Carling Premiership

	P	W	D	L	F	A	Pts
1 Newcastle United	24	18	3	3	47	19	57
2 Manchester United	**25**	**14**	**6**	**5**	**46**	**29**	**48**
3 Liverpool	25	13	7	5	48	21	46
4 Aston Villa	24	12	6	6	32	18	42
16 Wimbledon	**25**	**6**	**6**	**13**	**35**	**50**	**24**

Many Happy Returns

United caught Wimbledon on a day when the London club's meagre resources were fully stretched with Mick Harford, Efan Ekoku and Robbie Earle all out suspended, 'keepers Hans Segers and Paul Heald both injured whilst hard man Vinnie Jones was at loggerheads with the manager, Joe Kinnear, over a proposed move to Birmingham. The pre-match hype, however, was not about Wimbledon's woes but how Eric Cantona would react on his first return to the scene of his 'kung fu' attack on a spectator the previous January and it turned out to be a case of 'Many Happy Returns' as the Frenchman scored twice to seal a 4-2 victory.

The home side were first to attack with a snap shot from Clarke not that far away in the first minute and an injury to Steve Bruce in the 11th minute didn't improve United's early lack lustre start. Bruce was carried away to have fourteen stitches in a horrific head wound after being caught by Holdsworth's elbow. With Keane dropping into the back four and Beckham coming on into midfield, United's rhythm was not as sharp as normal and, although they launched wave after wave of attacks, they were only lapping gently up on to the Wimbledon beach. That is until the 41st minute when Irwin got in a cross which seemed destined for the same fate as two defenders climbed either side of Cole. But somehow, United's big signing got plenty of head on the ball to score a good goal from the edge of the six yard box. Bruce's injury then gave United a two goal cushion for it was in the time added on for the stoppage that the Reds somewhat luckily found the net again with anyone of three players able to claim it. A Beckham free kick thundered down off the bar and appeared to cross the line before spinning up and out. Perry, the one player who didn't want to claim it, looked like he would head it over his own bar but Keane came barging in to his back leaving the Wimbledon player unable to direct the ball anywhere other than into his own net with Keane trying to claim he had had the last touch. It was a goal that should not have stood.

Sloppy defending in the second period twice let Wimbledon back into the game with Gayle striking from the edge of the six yard box as the United defence stood and watched a Kimble cross from the right travel a long way and then Keane's header back to Schmeichel fell well short of the Dane to allow substitute Euell to nip in and score with ease. In between the two Wimbledon goals Cantona had crowned his return to the Palace with a neat strike when he played a delightful one two at the edge of the Wimbledon area and then quickly made ground to the six yard box where he stooped to head home Beckham's cross. With ten minutes left Cantona restored United's two goal advantage when he converted a spot kick awarded when Cunningham stopped a Giggs jink inside with his hand. It had, indeed, been a happy return for the reformed French maverick.

League Record

| | Home | | | | | | Away | | | | |
	P	W	D	L	F	A	W	D	L	F	A
95/96 FAPL	25	8	4	0	24	9	6	2	5	22	20
All time FAPL	151	52	19	4	143	40	39	20	17	126	86
FL/FAPL	3707	1088	429	336	3694	1824	571	482	801	2632	3140

	Home	Away	Total
FAPL Attendances	454,015	417,870	871,885

Manchester United (1) 1
Blackburn Rovers (0) 0

Saturday, 10th February 1996, Old Trafford   Att: 42,681

MANCHESTER UNITED		
1	Peter	SCHMEICHEL
3	Denis	IRWIN
12	David	MAY
6	Gary	PALLISTER
23	Phil	NEVILLE
24	David	BECKHAM
16	Roy	KEANE (Y)
5	Lee	SHARPE
11	Ryan	GIGGS
17	Andy	COLE
7	Eric	CANTONA

Subs

2	Paul	PARKER
9	Brian	McCLAIR
22	Paul	SCHOLES

BLACKBURN ROVERS		
1	Tim	FLOWERS
20	Henning	BERG
2	Chris	COLEMAN **83
5	Colin	HENDRY
3	Jeff	KENNA
11	Jason	WILCOX +73
4	Tim	SHERWOOD
17	Billy	McKINLAY
10	Mike	NEWALL (Y) *66
9	Alan	SHEARER (Y)
8	Kevin	GALLACHER

12	Nicky	MARKER **
14	Graham	FENTON *(Y)
18	Niklas	GUDMUNDSSON +

Match Facts

• United complete the double over Rovers for the second successive season.
• No win for Blackburn at Old Trafford since October 1962.
• Alan Shearer has never scored at the Old Trafford in the FAPL.
• Sharpe's first League goal in five months.

Score Sheet

L. SHARPE 14mins — 1-0

Referee:
Mr K.Burge (Tonypandy)

FA Carling Premiership

	P	W	D	L	F	A	Pts
1 Newcastle United	25	19	3	3	49	20	60
2 Manchester United	26	15	6	5	47	29	51
3 Liverpool	25	13	7	5	48	21	46
4 Aston Villa	25	13	6	6	34	18	45
5 Spurs	25	11	9	5	33	24	42
6 Blackburn Rovers	26	12	5	9	40	28	41

Shearer Loses Temper

Blackburn came to Old Trafford in the knowledge that they had not won at the ground for over thirty years whilst leading goalscorer Alan Shearer was aware that he had never found the net at United's famous stadium for the Rovers despite all his goals elsewhere. With Steve Bruce out injured and Gary Neville suspended, Alex Ferguson turned to yet another new defensive partnership to combat the Shearer threat when he elected to play Pallister and former Blackburn defender May. It was Pallister's first league game in almost two and a half months due to a back problem and May's first outing for six weeks since being injured against Newcastle. So well did they play, however, that Shearer not only failed to score but was extremely fortunate to finish the game when his frustration got the better of him on the hour mark. Schmeichel had long since claimed the ball when Shearer followed right through with studs showing to catch the Dane right across the thigh in a dreadful challenge that earned only a yellow card when many referees in the present climate would surely have produced a red.

United had taken an early lead with much of the credit going to Cole who had played a delightful one-two with Cantona to get himself goalside of Hendry. His cross shot beat Flowers but not the post and it was left to Sharpe to score his first goal for five months from the rebound as he lashed the awkwardly bouncing ball into the net past a defender on the goal line for a finish that was a lot more difficult than many people gave him credit for. The goal stung Blackburn and three minutes later Newall was booked for throwing Schmeichel to the ground but on the half hour Keane levelled matters when he was also cautioned after whipping Shearer's legs from under him on the halfway line as the match became a scrappy affair for two sides who had finished first and second the previous season.

Irwin lifted the hopes of United fans just before the break with a long range shot that brought the best out of Flowers as the former England 'keeper tipped it over but the second period was not a great deal better than the first. Fenton took just three minutes to get himself booked after coming on and fouling Phil Neville but the substitution almost paid dividends when McKinlay set Fenton free only for the newcomer to blast over from a good position. The Reds almost paid dearly, too, when another substitute, Gundersson, thundered an effort narrowly over the bar from a corner that United failed to clear close to time. United hung on until the final whistle but they would surely have regretted keeping Scholes on the bench for the complete ninety minutes had Rovers grabbed an equaliser. The goal apart, Sharpe and Cole had contributed little and the youngster, who always looks good for goals, must surely have gone home wondering what life is all about.

League Record

| | Home | | | | | Away | | | | |
	P	W	D	L	F	A	W	D	L	F	A
95/96 FAPL	26	9	4	0	25	9	6	2	5	22	20
All time FAPL	152	53	19	4	144	40	39	20	17	126	86
FL/FAPL	3708	1089	429	336	3695	1824	571	482	801	2632	3140

	Home	Away	Total
FAPL Attendances	496,696	417,870	914,566

111

Manchester United (1) 2
Manchester City (1) 1

Sunday, 18th February 1996, Old Trafford   Att: 42,962

MANCHESTER UNITED

1	Peter	SCHMEICHEL
3	Denis	IRWIN (Y)
4	Steve	BRUCE
6	Gary	PALLISTER (Y)
23	Phil	NEVILLE
11	Ryan	GIGGS
16	Roy	KEANE (Y)
19	Nicky	BUTT
5	Lee	SHARPE
17	Andy	COLE (Y)
7	Eric	CANTONA

Subs

12	David	MAY
22	Paul	SCHOLES
32	Tony	COTON (G)

MANCHESTER CITY

21	Eike	IMMEL
16	Nicky	SUMMERBEE
5	Keith	CURLE (Y)
14	Kit	SYMONS
3	Michael	FRONTZECK
4	Steve	LOMAS
18	Nigel	CLOUGH
17	Michael	BROWN (Y)
7	Georgi	KINKLADZE
28	Uwe	ROSLER
9	Niall	QUINN *79

8	Gerry	CREANEY *
13	Martyn	MARGETSON (G)
34	Eduard	ABAZAJ

Match Facts

- Just one 'derby' defeat for Alex Ferguson in sixteen confrontations.
- City not won at Old Trafford since '74.
- Cantona continues to be the scourge of City. He has scored against them in all five starts he has made, netting seven goals in the process. In addition the Frenchman scores for the eighth cup tie in succession in which he has played.

Significant Fifth Round results:

Huddersfield Town	2	Wimbledon	2
Swindon Town	1	Southampton	1
Leeds United	0	Port Vale	0
Grimsby Town	0	Chelsea	0
Shrewsbury Town	0	Liverpool	4

Score Sheet

U. ROSLER 11 mins — 0-1

E. CANTONA 38 mins(pen) — 1-1

L. SHARPE 77 mins — 2-1

Referee:

Mr A.Wilkie (Co. Durham)

Some Things Never Change

With virtually the whole of the FA Premiership table separating the two teams, United went into this fifth FA Cup meeting with their city rivals as hot favourites but an early City goal unsettled the Reds and they were extremely grateful to referee Mr Wilkie (he who sent off Cantona at Crystal Palace in 1995) for awarding a first half penalty for a foul on the Frenchman that only he saw. Even hardened Reds would be hard pushed to justify the decision and, when Mr Wilkie blew for the foul, Roy Keane waved his arms in disgust thinking a free kick had been given against United!

Prior to kick off, a minute's silence was held in memory of former Liverpool boss Bob Paisley who had passed away a few days earlier and then it was down to business with a third minute booking for Keane after he felled Kinkladze from behind. Seven minutes later Brown trod on Butt to cause a skirmish that looked likely to get out of hand before Curle and Cole went into the book alongside Brown. The incident broke United's concentration and, within sixty minutes, City were in front when Kinkladze set Rosler free from just inside the United half. The German advanced on Schmeichel and, as the 'keeper came out to narrow the angle, Rosler kept his nerve to chip into the empty net. United fought well but couldn't break down a City side who had been lifted by the goal and Irwin was next in the book for a foul on Clough as the Reds at last began to peg City back.

For all their territorial advantage, however, United didn't trouble Immel in the City goal until the 37th minute when a left wing flag kick was headed firmly down towards the bottom right hand side of the City net only for the 'keeper to palm it away for a further corner. The second kick from Giggs appeared to be over hit and drifting to safety when suddenly the whistle went and Mr Wilkie was pointing to the penalty spot. Even television replays later failed to identify any infringement but the referee was adamant that Frontzeck had fouled Cantona. It was an amazing decision but Cantona wasn't to look a gift horse in the mouth and, not for the first time, waited for the 'keeper to commit himself before slotting the ball home in the opposite direction.

A deluge of rain commenced at the interval and threatened to flood the ground as United attacked as incessantly as the rain. Just when it seemed as though the Blues had weathered both storms, United took the lead with a fine goal. Giggs held the ball long enough down the left for Neville to overlap and the young full back pulled his cross back into the path of Sharpe who sent a crashing volley into the net from twelve yards. Some things never change. In Manchester on the 18th February 1996, it rained and United beat City.

All-time FA Cup Record

	Home					Away				
P	W	D	L	F	A	W	D	L	F	A
357	103	32	28	347	154	82	54	58	309	272

	Home	Away	Total
FA Cup Attendances	84,255	36,158	120,413

113

Manchester United (1) 2
Everton (0) 0

Wednesday, 21st February 1996, Old Trafford   Att: 42,459

MANCHESTER UNITED

1	Peter	SCHMEICHEL
3	Denis	IRWIN
4	Steve	BRUCE
6	Gary	PALLISTER
23	Phil	NEVILLE
11	Ryan	GIGGS
16	Roy	KEANE
19	Nicky	BUTT
5	Lee	SHARPE *84
17	Andy	COLE
7	Eric	CANTONA

EVERTON

1	Neville	SOUTHALL
24	Jonathon	O'CONNOR (Y)
4	David	UNSWORTH
5	Dave	WATSON
3	Andy	HINCHCLIFFE
17	Andrei	KANCHELSKIS
14	John	EBBRELL (Y)
10	Barry	HORNE
8	Graham	STUART
20	Tony	GRANT *73
12	Daniel	AMOKACHI

Subs

20	Gary	NEVILLE
22	Paul	SCHOLES
24	David	BECKHAM *

13	Jason	KEARTON (G)
23	Michael	BRANCH *
21	Craig	SHORT

Match Facts

- Steve Bruce's 800th game at senior level since making his debut for Gillingham in 1978.
- By contrast Jonathon O'Connor was making his first appearance for Everton.
- Seventh straight win for United.
- 50th league success over Everton.

Score Sheet

R. KEANE 30 mins — 1-0

R. GIGGS 82 mins — 2-0

Referee:
Mr M.Bodenham (Cornwall)

FA Carling Premiership

	P	W	D	L	F	A	Pts
1 Newcastle United	26	19	3	4	49	22	60
2 Manchester United	**27**	**16**	**6**	**5**	**49**	**29**	**54**
3 Liverpool	26	14	7	5	50	22	49
4 Aston Villa	25	13	6	6	34	18	45
5 Spurs	26	11	9	6	33	25	42
8 Everton	**27**	**11**	**7**	**9**	**39**	**30**	**40**

United Close Gap on Newcastle

With Gary Neville free from suspension, manager Alex Ferguson for the first time in the campaign had a full squad to choose from and the fledgling England international found how hard life is at Old Trafford as he was forced to settle for a place on the bench after being a regular choice all season. Everton boss Joe Royle, had no such luxuries and he was down to the bare bones with Duncan Ferguson, Paul Rideout and Joe Parkinson out injured whilst Anders Limpar was suspended. This gave a debut to Jonathon O'Connor in a game which marked the 800th appearance for Steve Bruce during his time at Gillingham, Norwich and United.

The game itself turned out to be one of stark contrasts with much of the fare on offer being mundane stuff whilst both goals, two of the best seen at Old Trafford all season, deserved to figure in a match of much higher calibre.

Everton may have arrived in disarray with their injuries and following a shock exit at the hands of Port Vale from the FA Cup which they had won nine months earlier at the expense of the Reds but they didn't show any signs of cracking in the first half hour when United's only efforts came from Phil Neville who forced Neville Southall into two splendid saves. But the Everton veteran was helpless when Keane timed his run into the box to perfection to get on the end of a Cantona pass after the Frenchman and Nicky Butt had played a decisive one-two on the 30 minute mark.

But if that goal had class written all over it the second, eight minutes from time, was even better and right out of the top drawer of typical United strikes. The move began in the middle of United's own half where Giggs picked up a short pass from Sharpe. The Welshman slipped the ball to Cantona who, in turn, picked out the unmarked Cole on the left wing. The player much maligned for not scoring goals now turned into goal maker as he sped down the left before cutting the ball back into the path of Giggs who had made some sixty yards at pace to receive the cross and beat Southall from just inside the area.

Prior to that, Everton had been denied an equaliser when Schmeichel pushed over a rising Ebbrell effort and then the Dane had to be alert to deny Amokachi at the near post after a jinking run had threatened danger. If the game ended on a low note for Cole who was surely deprived of a welcome goal when the whistle went just as he was about to beat Southall in a one on one situation, it certainly didn't for United who left the pitch to find they had closed the gap on leaders Newcastle to six points after Kevin Keegan's team had foundered, like the Reds themselves so many times in the past, at West Ham. As Alex Ferguson said afterwards "That was a long night for us but it was a good one".

League Record

| | Home | | | | | Away | | | | |
	P	W	D	L	F	A	W	D	L	F	A
95/96 FAPL	27	10	4	0	27	9	6	2	5	22	20
All time FAPL	153	54	19	4	146	40	39	20	17	126	86
FL/FAPL	3709	1090	429	336	3697	1824	571	482	801	2632	3140

	Home	Away	Total
FAPL Attendances	539,155	417,870	957,025

Bolton Wanderers   (0) 0
Manchester United   (2) 6

Sunday, 25th February 1996, Burnden Park   Att: 21,381

BOLTON WANDERERS

1	Keith	BRANAGAN
2	Scott	GREEN
21	Chris	FAIRCLOUGH
17	Simon	COLEMAN
3	Jimmy	PHILLIPS
7	David	LEE *74
4	Sasa	CURCIC
11	Alan	THOMPSON
12	Scott	SELLARS
20	Nathan	BLAKE
14	Fabian	DE FREITAS

MANCHESTER UNITED

1	Peter	SCHMEICHEL
3	Denis	IRWIN
4	Steve	BRUCE
6	Gary	PALLISTER
23	Phil	NEVILLE
24	David	BECKHAM
16	Roy	KEANE
19	Nicky	BUTT
11	Ryan	GIGGS *57
17	Andy	COLE
7	Eric	CANTONA +73

Subs

6	Alan	STUBBS
9	Mixu	PAATELAINEN
10	John	McGINLAY *

9	Brian	McCLAIR *
20	Gary	NEVILLE
22	Paul	SCHOLES +

Match Facts

- United's first visit to Burnden Park for sixteen years.
- Steve Bruce's first goal of the season.
- United's biggest FAPL away victory.
- Biggest ever victory at Burnden Park.
- Only 12th win for United at Burnden Park in 47 visits.

Score Sheet

D. BECKHAM 5 mins — 0-1

S. BRUCE 15 mins — 0-2

A. COLE 70 mins — 0-3

P. SCHOLES 76 mins — 0-4

P. SCHOLES 79 mins — 0-5

N. BUTT 89 mins — 0-6

FA Carling Premiership

	P	W	D	L	F	A	Pts
1 Newcastle United	27	19	4	4	52	25	61
2 Manchester United	**28**	**17**	**6**	**5**	**55**	**29**	**57**
3 Liverpool	27	15	7	5	53	24	52
4 Aston Villa	26	13	7	6	37	21	46
20 Bolton Wanderers	**28**	**4**	**4**	**20**	**28**	**58**	**16**

Referee:

Mr D.Gallagher
(Banbury)

Bolton Blitzed

United went in to this game without Lee Sharpe who had been the previous week's hero when scoring the FA Cup tie winner against Manchester City. But despite his cry off with a back injury there was still no way back for England international Gary Neville with Sharpe being replaced by Beckham.

In a pulsating start, United forced two corners inside fifty seconds but a minute later could have been a goal down when Curcic forced a superb save from Schmeichel as the Dane tipped over a fierce 25 yarder. Not to be outdone, the Reds immediately returned to the offensive with Giggs breaking down the left before pausing just long enough to bring the ball back over a defender's head before hitting it on the volley from the edge of the area. It was a classic piece of football skill and deserved better than to thump the bar but Beckham followed up to head home from point blank range. The frantic start continued with Cole missing a glorious chance to double United's lead when he didn't head the ball wide enough of Branagan to give the 'keeper a chance to turn the ball round his left hand post but the second goal wasn't delayed for long. The Reds won another corner on the right and Bruce came steaming in unmarked to meet the flag kick with a powerful header from the edge of the six yard box that squeezed past Branagan thanks to the sheer force of the effort. But Bolton were contributing their fair share to a hugely entertaining game and when they won their fifth corner after twenty minutes, the flag kick tally was 5-4 in their favour.

The second period saw manager Alex Ferguson soon withdraw Ryan Giggs to save him for sterner tests ahead and it was his replacement Brian McClair who quickly set up the third goal when heading down for Cole to close in and thunder the ball into the roof of the net from close range. Cantona was also withdrawn on the 73 minute mark but if Dolton breathed a sigh of relief they were soon regretting the move when his replacement, United's leading goalscorer Paul Scholes, almost scored immediately with his first touch only to be denied by Branagan's knees. His second touch, however, moments later was more decisive as Cole set up a half chance that the youngster accepted by jinking past a defender before burying his shot in the corner of the net. His third touch was equally adept when he instinctively stuck out a leg to deflect an attempt from Butt past Branagan and the youngster, within ten minutes of his introduction, was incredibly bracing himself for a hat-trick after not making an appearance since coming on as substitute in the FA Cup replay at Sunderland and scoring the equaliser! Bolton must have realised by now it wasn't their day but if they needed confirmation it came when De Freitas forced the ball home only to have it ruled offside and the final nail in the coffin came during stoppage time when Butt burst through to hammer home the sixth to give United their biggest ever Burnden Park victory.

League Record

		Home					Away				
	P	W	D	L	F	A	W	D	L	F	A
95/96 FAPL	28	10	4	0	27	9	7	2	5	28	20
All time FAPL	154	54	19	4	146	40	40	20	17	132	86
FL/FAPL	3710	1090	429	336	3697	1824	572	482	801	2638	3140

	Home	Away	Total
FAPL Attendances	539,155	439,251	978,406

Newcastle United   (0) 0
Manchester United   (0) 1

Monday, 4th March 1996, St James Park   Att: 36,610

NEWCASTLE UNITED

1	Pavel	SRNICEK
2	Warren	BARTON
27	Philippe	ALBERT
6	Steve	HOWEY
3	John	BERESFORD
7	Robert	LEE (Y)
8	Peter	BEARDSLEY
22	David	BATTY
14	David	GINOLA (Y)
9	Les	FERDINAND
11	Faustino	ASPRILLA

Subs

18	Keith	GILLESPIE
19	Steve	WATSON
10	Lee	CLARK

MANCHESTER UNITED

1	Peter	SCHMEICHEL
3	Denis	IRWIN
4	Steve	BRUCE
20	Gary	NEVILLE
23	Phil	NEVILLE
11	Ryan	GIGGS
16	Roy	KEANE
19	Nicky	BUTT (Y)
5	Lee	SHARPE
17	Andy	COLE
7	Eric	CANTONA

12	David	MAY
22	Paul	SCHOLES
24	David	BECKHAM

Match Facts

- Faustino Asprilla's home debut after his £7.5m move from Parma.
- David Batty's debut for Newcastle.
- United end Newcastle's 100% home record after 14 home FAPL games.
- Newcastle yet to beat United in FAPL.
- One of the rare occasions when neither manager uses a substitute.

Score Sheet

E. CANTONA 51 mins — 0-1

Referee:
Mr D.Elleray (Harrow)

FA Carling Premiership

	P	W	D	L	F	A	Pts
1 Newcastle United	**28**	**19**	**4**	**5**	**52**	**26**	**61**
2 Manchester United	**29**	**18**	**6**	**5**	**56**	**29**	**60**
3 Liverpool	28	16	7	5	56	24	55
4 Aston Villa	28	14	7	7	39	24	49
5 Spurs	28	13	9	6	35	25	48

Newcastle Schmeichel'ed

United went into this game with Alex Ferguson's battle cry ringing in their ears as he declared "This is a game we have to win if we are to take the Championship". But Newcastle were able to give a home debut to Columbian Faustino Asprilla following his £7.5m move from Italy whilst, amazingly, they were also able to include £3.5m new signing David Batty after his transfer from Blackburn Rovers despite him still having to serve, in theory, the last match of a suspension picked up at his former club. The FA, however, ruled that Blackburn's game against Manchester City (played after Batty had moved) counted as the last game of the suspension and that he was therefore free to play against the Reds!

This meeting of the two top teams was expected to be a titanic affair and United appeared to be in danger of being swamped by wave upon wave of Newcastle attacks as the home side went all out for goal from the off. That the United boat did not capsize was down to their Viking custodian Peter Schmeichel who made several saves that were not just brilliant but great. He came to the rescue after only three minutes with a brave dive at the feet of Ferdinand who had been put clear by Asprilla and two minutes later he saved superbly to his left as Ferdinand again raced clear of Bruce. United were on the rack and Schmeichel was again at his best diving to his right this time to thwart Beardsley as Newcastle piled on the pressure. When Butt earned a booking on 20 minutes for a foul on Asprilla, the resulting free kick came as close as anything all night to beating Schmeichel when Albert thumped his shot against the bar and the Geordie fans couldn't believe their eyes when Ferdinand blasted the rebound miles high from eight yards. Ginola then twice went close in as many minutes after cutting in from the left and hitting shots across the face of goal but, after all their pressure, Newcastle nearly went in at half time a goal down when a superb passing movement enabled Giggs to fire in a shot that seemed destined for the net until it hit Albert and deflected for a corner just as the interval beckoned.

The Reds began the second period as they had finished the first and Cantona's cross found Cole but he was at full stretch and couldn't get any power into his strike enabling Srnicek to retrieve the situation. But Cole quickly made up for the weak effort when he held off two tackles at the edge of the area before releasing Phil Neville down the left. The youngster's cross was met at the far post by Cantona and he volleyed home past Srnicek to stun the home crowd into silence. The Frenchman had hardly had a kick all night but had appeared from nowhere to score the all important goal. As Newcastle boss Kevin Keegan said afterwards "In the first half we murdered United 0-0" but it was the Reds who went home with the points thanks to the brilliance of Schmeichel.

League Record

	Home						Away				
	P	W	D	L	F	A	W	D	L	F	A
95/96 FAPL	29	10	4	0	27	9	8	2	5	29	20
All time FAPL	155	54	19	4	146	40	41	20	17	133	86
FL/FAPL	3711	1090	429	336	3697	1824	573	482	801	2639	3140

	Home	Away	Total
FAPL Attendances	539,155	475,861	1,015,016

Manchester United (0) 2
Southampton (0) 0

Monday, 11th March 1996, Old Trafford   Att: 45,446

MANCHESTER UNITED

1	Peter	SCHMEICHEL (Y)
3	Denis	IRWIN
4	Steve	BRUCE
20	Gary	NEVILLE
23	Phil	NEVILLE
5	Lee	SHARPE
16	Roy	KEANE
19	Nicky	BUTT
11	Ryan	GIGGS
17	Andy	COLE
7	Eric	CANTONA

Subs

22	Paul	SCHOLES
12	David	MAY
24	David	BECKHAM

SOUTHAMPTON

13	Dave	BEASANT
2	Jason	DODD
5	Richard	HALL
6	Ken	MONKOU
14	Simon	CHARLTON
27	Matthew	OAKLEY
4	Jim	MAGILTON
12	Tommy	WIDDRINGTON
19	Mark	WALTERS *89
7	Matthew	LE TISSIER
9	Neil	SHIPPERLEY

1	Bruce	GROBBELAAR (G)
16	David	HUGHES
26	Matthew	ROBINSON *

Match Facts

• Twelfth meeting of the two sides in the FA Cup with Southampton only winning once in open play (1976 final). The Saints only other success was on penalties after two drawn games in 1992 which was the last time United lost at home in the FA Cup.

• 10th straight win for the Reds in League and Cup during which time they have conceded only four goals.

• First gate of over 45,000 since Easter '92.

• Just one defeat for United in their last nineteen FA Cup ties.

Score Sheet

E. CANTONA 49 mins – 1-0

L. SHARPE 90 mins – 2-0

Referee

Mr S.Dunn (Bristol)

Other quarter-final results:

Liverpool	3	Leeds United	0
(after 0-0 draw)			

Wimbledon	1	Chelsea	3
(after 2-2 draw)			
Forest	0	Aston Villa	1

Cantona Pulls the Strings

Southampton arrived at Old Trafford as the last side to beat the Reds in a FA Cup tie at the ground having won on penalties after two drawn games in 1992. But they found Eric Cantona once again pulling the FA Cup strings as he scored just after half-time to put United in the lead for the second Monday evening in succession as well as adding to his superb record of never having been on the losing side in an FA Cup tie since joining United. The goal also gave him the distinction of scoring in the last six Rounds of the competition in which he had played.

But, with almost the whole of the Premiership table separating the two teams, Southampton could consider themselves unlucky not to have earned a replay with the Reds somewhat off colour whilst the Saints belied their lowly league position with a battling and, at times, skillful display.

United, having gone three up in nine minutes when Southampton visited Old Trafford for the FAPL fixture in November, again started at speed but for all their attacking had nought to show for it though they should clearly have had a penalty when Andy Cole was manhandled to the ground by Richard Hall. Having thwarted the Reds' early efforts, Southampton began to apply their own pressure with wingers Mark Walters and young Matthew Oakley particularly lively. The Saints began to believe in themselves and seemed to have taken the lead on the stroke of half time when Shipperley headed a Jason Dodds centre past Schmeichel only for the referee to harshly adjudge that Sharpe had been leant on as Shipperley rose for his header.

United accepted their piece of luck and took the lead after 49 minutes with Andy Cole playing a big part in the build up as he slipped a telling pass to Giggs down the left. The Welshman hit the byeline and pulled the ball across the area to give Cantona at the far post an easy tap in. Southampton pushed forward in search of an equaliser and the amount of possession they enjoyed was such that they won twelve corners to United's seven. But, for all their efforts, the Saints couldn't get the ball in the net and, unlike in the first half, they couldn't blame the referee with Le Tissier guilty of the most glaring miss when he put a free header well over from eight yards when it was easier to score with only three minutes remaining.

United accepted their second piece of good fortune to seal a semi final appearance for the third consecutive season with virtually the last kick of the contest. Once again Cole was involved with a searching pass seeking out Cantona on the right. The Frenchman beat Charlton before sliding the ball into the middle where a back heel flick from Butt gave Sharpe the easiest of chances to round off the evening with the second United goal.

United's all time FA Cup Record

	Home					Away				
P	W	D	L	F	A	W	D	L	F	A
358	104	32	28	349	154	82	54	58	309	272

	Home	Away	Total
FA Cup Attendances	129,701	36,158	165,859

Queen's Park Rangers (0) 1
Manchester United (0) 1

Saturday, 16th March 1996, Loftus Road   Att: 18,817

QPR

25	Jurgen	SOMMER
2	David	BARDSLEY
5	Simon	BARKER
6	Alan	McDONALD
3	Rufus	BREVETT
19	Nigel	QUASHIE *45
21	Steve	YATES (Y)
8	Ian	HOLLOWAY
11	Trevor	SINCLAIR
10	Kevin	GALLEN **85
9	Daniel	DICHIO (Y) +81

Subs

7	Andrew	IMPEY *
14	Karl	READY **
26	Mark	HATELEY +

MANCHESTER UNITED

1	Peter	SCHMEICHEL
20	Gary	NEVILLE
12	David	MAY (Y) **74
4	Steve	BRUCE
3	Denis	IRWIN
24	David	BECKHAM +74
16	Roy	KEANE
9	Brian	McCLAIR *58
11	Ryan	GIGGS
17	Andy	COLE (Y)
7	Eric	CANTONA

5	Lee	SHARPE **
19	Nicky	BUTT +
22	Paul	SCHOLES *

Match Facts

- First points dropped to QPR at Loftus Road since formation of FAPL.
- First time United had failed to score three goals at Loftus Road in the FAPL.
- QPR still to beat United in FAPL.
- United stretch their unbeaten run in league and cup to thirteen games.

Score Sheet

D. IRWIN OG 63 mins – 1-0
E. CANTONA 90 mins – 1-1

Referee:
Mr R.Hart (Darlington)

FA Carling Premiership

	P	W	D	L	F	A	Pts
1 Manchester United	30	18	7	5	57	30	61
2 Newcastle Utd	28	19	4	5	52	26	61
3 Liverpool	30	17	8	5	60	26	59
4 Aston Villa	31	16	7	8	46	30	55
5 Arsenal	30	14	9	7	42	27	51
19 QPR	31	6	5	20	27	49	23

Last Gasp Cantona Saves Reds

United travelled to Loftus Road with a 100% FAPL record at the ground and, with QPR next to bottom and without a home victory since December, hopes were high that the Reds would secure the win that would put them two points clear at the top from Newcastle who had no game. Alex Ferguson, however, as he had done in 1991/92 when handing the title to Leeds on a plate, made unforced changes to a winning side when leaving out Phil Neville, Nicky Butt and Lee Sharpe from the team that had just registered ten successive victories and it took a 93rd minute equaliser from Eric Cantona to rescue even a solitary point.

But the first period saw home 'keeper Jurgen Sommer play United almost on his own after a one minute's silence had been held in memory of the children who perished in the Dunblane shooting tragedy. The 'keeper's first save came from Giggs who burst into the box from the left flank after a quick fire move between Keane and Cole. The Welshman hit a powerful shot but Sommer was able to parry it away before being quickly back in the action when racing out to block at the feet of McClair who needed one touch too many when put through by Giggs. The young Welshman was certainly looking very threatening and a brilliant run that took him past two defenders after dispossessing McDonald brought another fine save. Beckham, put clear by Cole, was the next to be thwarted as Sommer got a telescopic leg to the ball but the 'keeper was finally well beaten by a Cole effort only to leave the United fans who stood up to celebrate a goal looking in disbelief as the shot grazed the post. Another block by the 'keeper saw the ball break to Beckham but he snatched his shot high and wide.

The interval saw Rangers replace Quashie, who had been suffering a viral infection all week, with Impey and his first touch brought a fingertip save from Schmeichel as the Londoners came more into the game. May and Sinclair clashed in the 55th minute and there was an immediate flare up with several players involved until the referee restored calm with bookings for May and Dichio. Shortly afterwards Rangers took the lead as Dichio raced into the area from the left to beat Schmeichel with a curling shot that appeared as though it may hit the far post. Irwin, unable to take the chance of leaving it, dived full length towards his own goal in an attempt to head the ball over the bar only to steer it into the roof of the net. Ferguson, belatedly realising the errors of his ways, threw on Butt, Sharpe and Scholes but it all appeared to be to no avail as the ninety minute mark arrived. However, Sommer had been wasting a great deal of time and Referee Robbie Hart added on three minutes for the keeper's efforts. With the clock reading 92mins 35secs, Giggs slung over a cross from the left and Cantona stole clear at the far post to head home an equaliser from three yards. It was enough to put United top on goal difference but Newcastle were happier with the result than United.

League Record

	Home						Away				
	P	W	D	L	F	A	W	D	L	F	A
95/96 FAPL	30	10	4	0	27	9	8	3	5	30	21
All time FAPL	156	54	19	4	146	40	41	21	17	134	87
FL/FAPL	3712	1090	429	336	3697	1824	573	483	801	2640	3141

FAPL Attendances	Home	Away	Total
	539,155	494,678	1,033,833

Manchester United (0) 1
Arsenal (0) 0

Wednesday, 20th March 1996, Old Trafford   Att: 50,028

MANCHESTER UNITED

1	Peter	SCHMEICHEL
20	Gary	NEVILLE
4	Steve	BRUCE
12	David	MAY
23	Phil	NEVILLE
16	Roy	KEANE
19	Nicky	BUTT
5	Lee	SHARPE
11	Ryan	GIGGS
17	Andy	COLE *58
7	Eric	CANTONA

Subs

22	Paul	SCHOLES *
9	Brian	McCLAIR
24	David	BECKHAM

ARSENAL

1	David	SEAMAN
2	Lee	DIXON
14	Martin	KEOWN
5	Andy	LINIGHAN
29	Scott	MARSHALL
3	Nigel	WINTERBURN
7	David	PLATT
9	Paul	MERSON +69
10	Dennis	BERGKAMP *45
8	Ian	WRIGHT
16	John	HARTSON

11	Glenn	HELDER +
18	David	HILLIER *
31	Matthew	ROSE

Match Facts

- First time an FAPL attendance had reached 50,000.
- Arsenal still to score at Old Trafford in the FAPL.
- Fourth consecutive match in which Cantona had scored.
- United's fifth clean sheet in their last six fixtures.

Score Sheet

E. CANTONA 66mins – 1-0

Referee:
Mr G.Willard (Worthing)

FA Carling Premiership

	P	W	D	L	F	A	Pts
1 Newcastle United	29	20	4	5	55	26	64
2 Manchester United	**31**	**19**	**7**	**5**	**58**	**30**	**64**
3 Liverpool	30	17	8	5	60	26	59
4 Aston Villa	32	16	8	8	46	30	56
5 Arsenal	**31**	**14**	**9**	**8**	**42**	**28**	**51**

Cantona On Target Again

Alex Ferguson, having been punished for not playing his strongest team against QPR by the loss of two crucial points in the previous game, returned to his strongest line up with the possible exception of Denis Irwin for the visit of Arsenal. The Gunners were without the heart of their formidable defence with both Tony Adams and Steve Bould missing and this was to prove a telling factor even though the Londoners tried to compensate by playing three central defenders in Martin Keown, Andy Linighan and young Scott Marshall.

Playing five across the back, Arsenal withstood everything United could throw at them in front of the FAPL's first ever 50,000 plus attendance and, when the back five were breached, David Seaman was in top form. On the one occasion he was beaten in the first period, Keane's venomous cross shot from the right hand edge of the penalty area zipped against the far post and rebounded to safety. That, plus some wayward efforts again from Cole, denied the rampant Reds a deserved interval lead that doubtless delighted the man invited to draw the half-time lottery. To a mixed reception of boos and cheers, Newcastle boss Kevin Keegan picked the winning numbers but the second period was to see Eric Cantona pluck a winner of his own right out of the top drawer.

Denis Bergkamp, who had scored the winner against United at Highbury in the first clash of the season, was reportedly so desperate to play at Old Trafford that he had got out of his sick bed to do so but when the teams emerged after the interval, the Dutch international had returned to it leaving the stage to United's Frenchman. The goal, scored after 66 minutes, came very soon after Cole had been replaced by Scholes and was worthy of winning any game. There seemed little danger to Arsenal when Phil Neville's left wing cross looked to be floating gently to Seaman as the 'keeper advanced off his line towards the penalty spot to make an everyday sort of catch. But nobody told stand in central defender Andy Linighan and he made ground to clear with a header. But the ball looped straight to Cantona some 25 yards from goal. The Frenchman jumped to take control of the ball in an instant on his chest, propelling it forward in the same movement. He then hit it on the volley high to Seaman's left giving the England 'keeper no chance whatsoever as the Frenchman scored, even by his standards, a breathtaking goal.

The strike proved to be the winner and left the Reds thankful entirely to the Frenchman for all of their last seven points with Cantona having scored the only United goals against Newcastle, QPR and now Arsenal. It had been a vastly one sided affair and surely nobody would have disputed United's right to all three points. Not even the guy who did the half time lottery draw.

League Record

| | Home | | | | | | Away | | | | |
	P	W	D	L	F	A	W	D	L	F	A
95/96 FAPL	31	11	4	0	28	9	8	3	5	30	21
All time FAPL	157	55	19	4	147	40	41	21	17	134	87
FL/FAPL	3713	1091	429	336	3698	1824	573	483	801	2640	3141

	Home	Away	Total
FAPL Attendances	589,183	494,678	1,083,861

Manchester United (0) 1
Tottenham Hotspur (0) 0

Sunday, 24th March 1996, Old Trafford   Att: 50,157

MANCHESTER UNITED

1	Peter	SCHMEICHEL
20	Gary	NEVILLE
4	Steve	BRUCE
12	David	MAY
23	Phil	NEVILLE *64
11	Ryan	GIGGS
16	Roy	KEANE (Y)
19	Nicky	BUTT (Y)
5	Lee	SHARPE
17	Andy	COLE +73
7	Eric	CANTONA

Subs

9	Brian	McCLAIR +
22	Paul	SCHOLES
24	David	BECKHAM *

TOTTENHAM HOTSPURS

1	Ian	WALKER
2	Dean	AUSTIN
6	Gary	MABBUTT (Y)
4	David	HOWELLS
15	Clive	WILSON
7	Ruel	FOX
12	Jason	DOZZELL
23	Sol	CAMPBELL
27	Andy	SINTON
10	Teddy	SHERINGHAM (Y)
11	Chris	ARMSTRONG

14	Stuart	NETHERCOTT *
3	Justin	EDINBURGH
13	Eric	THORSTVEDT (G

Match Facts

- Fifth consecutive match in which Cantona had scored.
- Extends United's unbeaten run to fifteen games.
- Spurs still to win at Old Trafford in FAPL.
- Spurs won only once in last eighteen visits to United
- Only third away defeat of season for Spurs.

Score Sheet

E. CANTONA 52 mins – 1-0

Referee:
Mr G.Ashby (Worcester)

FA Carling Premiership

	P	W	D	L	F	A	Pts
1 Manchester United	32	20	7	5	59	30	67
2 Newcastle Utd	30	20	4	6	55	28	64
3 Liverpool	31	17	8	6	60	27	59
4 Aston Villa	32	16	8	8	46	30	56
5 Arsenal	32	15	9	8	44	28	54
6 Spurs	31	14	9	8	40	31	51

Yet Another for Cantona

Since Spurs inflicted a New Year's mauling on United, the Reds had gone fourteen games undefeated in league and cup but much of their success in March had been down solely to the goals scored by one man, Eric Cantona. And the Frenchman was to do it again with a goal that not only broke the heart of Spurs' boss Gerry Francis but also his temper as he slated the match officials for their mistake that led directly to United's goal. Strangely, however, he didn't slate his three defenders who Cantona dribbled past before slotting home the only goal of the game and that certainly wasn't down to the referee and linesman!

Denis Irwin was still missing from United's line up through injury as was Gary Pallister and the Londoners, who had only suffered defeat twice on their travels prior to this game, started in confident mood. For long periods of the match they looked more than capable of becoming only the second team, after Chelsea, to inflict a double defeat on the Reds in a FAPL season. Schmeichel tipped over a Howells effort and followed up with saves from both Fox and Sheringham. In United's first attack on the quarter hour mark, Mabbutt was booked for pulling Cole back after he had been left stranded by the striker's skillful turn but the ball was quickly back at the other end where a dreadful misjudgement by Bruce almost gifted the lead to Spurs. The skipper allowed a cross to run past him thinking it would carry to Schmeichel but the ball was never going to reach the 'keeper and Armstrong nipped in looking certain to score. But the Great Dane, as so often before, was equal to the occasion and made a super save to spare Bruce's blushes. United hit back with Giggs looking the most likely source of danger and a brilliant run from the Welshman set up a superb chance for Cole but the sadly out of form record signing's effort resembled more of a pass back than a shot. Giggs took it upon himself the next time he got sight of goal but his shot curled narrowly over with Walker beaten. United were still back pedalling most of the time and Ferguson altered his formation to play five at the back to try to keep Spurs at bay.

A goal early in the second period gave United the lead against the run of play and they had more than a little luck going their way when the referee gave a goal kick to the Reds when it should clearly have been a corner. Cantona picked up Schmeichel's kick some forty yards out, ran past three Spurs' defenders and rifled a shot across Walker and into the net at the 'keeper's left hand post for a truly great strike. But the danger Spurs still showed forced Ferguson to send on McClair for Cole to bolster midfield and it must be many years since a United side played five across the back and four in midfield at home leaving Cantona a lone figure up front! But a win is a win and the result moved the Reds three points clear of Newcastle at the top of the Premiership.

League Record

		Home					Away				
	P	W	D	L	F	A	W	D	L	F	A
95/96 FAPL	32	12	4	0	29	9	8	3	5	30	21
All time FAPL	158	56	19	4	148	40	41	21	17	134	87
FL/FAPL	3714	1092	429	336	3699	1824	573	483	801	2640	3141

	Home	Away	Total
FAPL Attendances	639,340	494,678	1,134,018

Chelsea
Manchester United

(1) 1 Semi-final

(0) 2

Match 42

Sunday, 31st March 1996, Villa Park   Att:38,421

CHELSEA

13	Kevin	HITCHCOCK
2	Steve	CLARKE *38
20	David	LEE **86
15	Andy	MYERS (Y)
25	Terry	PHELAN +64
26	Michael	DUBERRY
12	Craig	BURLEY
11	Denis	WISE
7	John	SPENCER
8	Mark	HUGHES
4	Ruud	GULLIT

Subs

5	Erland	JOHNSEN *
14	Paul	FURLONG **
10	Gavin	PEACOCK +

MANCHESTER UNITED

1	Peter	SCHMEICHEL
23	Phil	NEVILLE
20	Gary	NEVILLE
12	David	MAY
5	Lee	SHARPE
24	David	BECKHAM
19	Nicky	BUTT
16	Roy	KEANE
11	Ryan	GIGGS
7	Eric	CANTONA
17	Andy	COLE

Subs

2	Paul	PARKER
9	Brian	McCLAIR
22	Paul	SCHOLES

Match Facts

• United reach third successive FA Cup Final.

• David Beckham's first FA Cup goal.

• United still to lose an FA Cup semi final at Villa Park.

• Chelsea only beaten United once in an FA Cup tie in six meetings. That was in 1949/50.

• Butt's booking was third time he had been booked by Mr Lodge in the three United games that Mr Lodge had officiated in!

Score Sheet

R. GULLIT 35 mins – 1-0

A. COLE 55 mins – 1-1

D. BECKHAM 58 mins – 1-?

Referee:
Mr S.Lodge (Barnsley)

Other semi-final result:
Liverpool 3   Aston Villa 0
(Played at Old Trafford)

Three on Bounce for Reds

United were dealt a massive blow just hours before their semi final clash with Chelsea which would decide if United could make it three FA Cup appearances on the bounce when captain Steve Bruce declared himself unfit with a thigh strain picked up in training. Already shorn of England central defence man, Gary Pallister, Alex Ferguson's team resembled Wembley minus the twin towers and, with Denis Irwin also still absent due to injury, United's defences looked stretched to the limit. This, however, only added to the thrill a minute stuff that both teams served up as they sought to prove that semi finals do not have to be dour battles. In fact, the match was a classic and defied editing into highlights.

United made all the early running on a pitch that resembled Blackpool beach rather than a venue designated to host several Euro 96 fixtures and after only four minutes Sharpe and Giggs combined down the left to set up a half chance for Beckham whose snap shot cracked against the Hitchcock's right hand post before the 'keeper had time to move. But Chelsea themselves soon hit the woodwork at the other end as the Reds backed off Duberry allowing him to advance to within 25 yards of goal. Still expecting a cross, United and Schmeichel were taken by surprise when Duberry, who earlier in the season had been on loan to Bournemouth, chipped a delightful effort onto the underside of the bar from where it bounced down and out to safety. The game continued end to end and when a goal came it was Chelsea who took the lead. Former Red Mark Hughes flattened Beckham but although a foul should have been given there was no doubting the quality of the finish as Hughes crossed perfectly from the left for Gullit to head home at the far post. Cantona's response was a snap shot from 25 yards that clipped Hitchcock's left hand upright and it looked like being one of those days.

The second period, however, was barely ten minutes old when Chelsea got caught by a Red one two that flattened them mainly due to an injury to Phelan. He pulled up in full flight but amazingly was not substituted and the Londoners paid a harsh penalty for their mistake. A short passing move was turned into a sabre thrust when Beckham released Phil Neville into the space patrolled by Phelan whom the youngster outpaced before tricking Spencer and crossing deep to Cantona whose header back across goal was turned in by Cole from a yard out. Three minutes later and with their concentration broken, Chelsea went behind. Burley had done the hard work by recapturing the ball from Giggs but then tried a pass back from the half way line that was always going to fall short. Beckham saw his chance and easily outstripped the crippled Phelan to turn the ball past Hitchcock and, although Phelan was then soon replaced, the damage was done. Try as they might, Chelsea could not break down a resolute United and the Reds were at Wembley for the third season in a row.

United's All-time FA Cup Record

	Home					Away				
P	W	D	L	F	A	W	D	L	F	A
359	104	32	28	349	154	83	54	58	311	273

	Home	Away	Total
FA Cup Attendances	129,701	74,579	204,280

Manchester City (1) 2
Manchester United (2) 3

Saturday, 6th April 1996, Maine Road — Att: 29,688

MANCHESTER CITY

21	Eike	IMMEL
16	Nicky	SUMMERBEE
5	Keith	CURLE (Y)
12	Ian	BRIGHTWELL
14	Kit	SYMONS
3	Michael	FRONTZEK *45
18	Nigel	CLOUGH
17	Michael	BROWN (Y)
7	Georgi	KINKLADZE
9	Niall	QUINN
32	Mikhail	KAVELASHVILI +68

MANCHESTER UNITED

1	Peter	SCHMEICHEL
23	Phil	NEVILLE
4	Steve	BRUCE *74
20	Gary	NEVILLE (Y)
3	Denis	IRWIN
24	David	BECKHAM
19	Nicky	BUTT
16	Roy	KEANE
11	Ryan	GIGGS
7	Andy	COLE (Y) +74
17	Eric	CANTONA

Subs

28	Uwe	ROSLER +
19	Martin	PHILLIPS *
13	Martyn	MARGETSON (G)

5	Lee	SHARPE +
12	David	MAY *
22	Paul	SCHOLES

Match Facts

- Eric Cantona has now scored in all six 'derby' matches in which he has made the starting line-up.
- City still to beat United in the FAPL.
- City captain Keith Curle booked in all three 'derby' games in 95/96.
- Nicky Butt booked for third game in succession.
- Kavelashvili scores on City debut.

Score Sheet

E. CANTONA (pen) 6 mins – 0-1
M. KAVELASHVILI 39 mins – 1-1
A. COLE 40 mins – 1-2
U. ROSLER 71 mins – 2-2
R. GIGGS 77 mins – 2-3

Referee:
Mr M.Reed (Birmingham)

FA Carling Premiership

	P	W	D	L	F	A	Pts
1 Manchester United	33	21	7	5	62	32	70
2 Newcastle Utd	32	21	4	7	60	33	67
3 Liverpool	33	18	8	7	64	31	62
4 Aston Villa	33	17	8	8	48	31	59
17 Manchester City	34	7	10	17	29	53	31

Gigg's Cracker Wins Derby Thriller

One of the most important 'derby' clashes for years saw both the Reds and Blues desperate for points for opposite reasons and the need for outright victory in both camps produced as thrilling a game as any neutral could wish to see. City gave a debut to their latest foreign import, Georgian international Mikhail Kavelashvili, and the Blues twice came back to equalise only to see United promptly restore their lead on both occasions.

United attacked from the off and after only six minutes their pressure paid off with Irwin's left flank raid earning a penalty when he was chopped down a yard inside the area by a clumsy challenge by Summerbee after being freed by a clever ball from Keane. As always, Cantona waited for the 'keeper to reveal which way he would dive before slotting the ball into the opposite corner. The Frenchman then produced a mercurial pass with the outside of his right foot to set up a chance for Cole but the striker's first touch was not good enough and the chance went begging. City hit back and there was a scare when Quinn beat Bruce to a header only to direct his effort straight at Schmeichel from six yards whilst Cantona, of all people, repeated the miss at the other end when he almost hit the corner flag from close in.

The City equaliser came after Butt felled Brown with Frontzek's cross being headed down by Quinn for Kavelashvili to fire home a debut goal from all of five yards as the Reds went to sleep. But, roused from their slumber, United hit back immediately and straight from the kick off advanced slowly forward with a string of passes until the decisive one from Cantona prised open City's rearguard. It was only a two yard pass but suddenly Cole was free and, although he completely mishit his shot, the ball bobbled home.

City started the second period with young Phillips on for Frontzek and he quickly got Kavelashvili in on Schmeichel who dived bravely at the Georgian's feet to take the full force of the shot in his face leaving the Dane needing treatment. At the other end, a clever header from Cole gave Butt an excellent chance but he waited too long and the opportunity of sealing the points was gone. United paid for the miss with City's second substitution paying immediate dividends as Rosler came on to hit home a super shot just three minutes after being thrown into the fray. As the German advanced down the left, Bruce appeared to jockey him well but Rosler suddenly pressed the trigger and rifled home a shot from the edge of the area that gave Schmeichel no hope. But again United forced themselves back into the lead and if Rosler's goal was a superb strike then Ryan Giggs' was even better. Butt won the ball in midfield to feed Cantona whose pass found Giggs cutting in from the left to smash the ball into Immel's top right hand corner for a thrilling finish to a thrilling game.

League Record

	P	W	D	L	F	A	W	D	L	F	A
			Home						*Away*		
95/96 FAPL	33	12	4	0	29	9	9	3	5	33	23
All time FAPL	159	56	19	4	148	40	42	21	17	137	89
FL/FAPL	3715	1092	429	336	3699	1824	574	483	801	2643	3143

	Home	*Away*	*Total*
FAPL Attendances	639,340	524,366	1,163,706

Manchester United (0) 1
Coventry City (0) 0

Monday, 8th April 1996, Old Trafford   Att: 50,332

MANCHESTER UNITED			**COVENTRY CITY**		
1	Peter	SCHMEICHEL	1	Steve	OGRIZOVIC
3	Denis	IRWIN	30	Liam	DAISH
20	Gary	NEVILLE	12	David	BUSST *2
12	David	MAY	17	Ally	PICKERING
5	Lee	SHARPE	7	Paul	TELFER +70
24	David	BECKHAM	6	Kevin	RICHARDSON
19	Nicky	BUTT	4	Paul	WILLIAMS
9	Brian	McCLAIR	9	Peter	NDLOVU
11	Ryan	GIGGS	10	Dion	DUBLIN
17	Andy	COLE	14	Noel	WHELAN
7	Eric	CANTONA	11	John	SALAKO

Subs

2	Paul	PARKER	16	Eoin	JESS +
4	Steve	BRUCE	22	Willie	BOLAND *
22	Paul	SCHOLES	30	John	FILAN (G)

Match Facts

- Coventry still to score a goal at Old Trafford in the FAPL.
- Coventry still to beat United in the FAPL.
- United not lost to Coventry since April 89 which was also the last occasion they scored at Old Trafford.
- Sixth consecutive league game in which Cantona had scored.

Score Sheet

E. CANTONA 47 mins – 1-0

Referee:
Mr D.Gallagher (Banbury)

FA Carling Premiership

	P	W	D	L	F	A	Pts
1 Manchester United	**34**	**22**	**7**	**5**	**63**	**32**	**73**
2 Newcastle United	33	21	4	8	61	35	67
3 Liverpool	34	19	8	7	66	31	65
4 Aston Villa	34	18	8	8	51	31	62
19 Coventry City	**34**	**6**	**12**	**16**	**39**	**60**	**30**

Flag Day for United

United and their Supporters Association had nominated this fixture to be Flag Day and, although they could never have stage managed it at the time the idea was conceived, the day turned out to be a flag day beyond the club's wildest dreams. The Reds, who not many weeks previous had trailed Newcastle by twelve points, finished the day six points in front of Kevin Keegan's men as well as possessing a superior goal difference. Appropriately, with most of the flags being the French Tricolour, Eric Cantona was once again the man who broke the deadlock to give United the points with the only strike of the match which they had gone into without Steve Bruce, Gary Pallister, Phil Neville and Roy Keane.

The game began with a terrible injury to Coventry's David Busst after only two minutes. A right wing corner was palmed away by Schmeichel after Noel Whelan had got a touch on and Busst lunged for the loose ball with Denis Irwin to whom no blame could be attached. The game was held up for nine minutes as the pitch was watered and sanded to clear the blood deposited by Busst whose compound fracture of the leg had left the bones exposed. The players around were visibly shaken by the damage done, none more so than Schmeichel who reeled away clutching his head in grief. The incident seemed to affect the Reds more than the visitors for whom it perhaps acted as a galvanising element and Schmeichel had to make a good block with his body from Whelan soon after the match restarted. The Dane then thwarted former team mate Dion Dublin again after good work by Whelan.

But United began to stamp their authority on the match and Giggs, Beckham and Cole should all have given the fans the chance to wave their flags in celebration before half time.

But the flags were soon out after the second period got underway with Eric Cantona scoring one of the easiest goals he will ever net. It was hardly a classic but nobody cared with the stakes so high. Giggs did the damage down the left before putting in a cross that failed to match the brilliance of his run. But, for some inexplicable reason Williams, who was facing his own goal, decided to back heel the ball. He succeeded only in diverting it straight to Cole whose attempt at a cross cum shot was partially blocked by Richardson allowing the ball to fall at the feet of the totally unmarked Cantona some five yards out. He simply does not miss from there. Another Giggs left wing cross was just too far for the Frenchman to convert as he put his effort narrowly over whilst at full stretch and then Giggs hit the post but, for all that, United were still glad to hear the final whistle as Coventry finished strongly. The best, however, was yet to come with the news later in the evening that Blackburn, for once, had done United a favour by beating Newcastle with two goals in the last four minutes!

League Record

	P	W	D	L	F	A	W	D	L	F	A
			Home						*Away*		
95/96 FAPL	34	13	4	0	30	9	9	3	5	33	23
All time FAPL	160	57	19	4	149	40	42	21	17	137	89
FL/FAPL	3716	1093	429	336	3700	1824	574	483	801	2643	3143

	Home	Away	Total
FAPL Attendances	689,672	524,366	1,214,038

Southampton (3) 3
Manchester United (0) 1

Saturday, 13th April 1996, The Dell   Att: 15,262

SOUTHAMPTON

13	Dave	BEASANT
2	Jason	DODD
6	Ken	MONKOU
15	Mo	NEILSON
3	Francis	BENALI
4	Jim	MAGILTON
22	Barry	VENISON (Y)
14	Simon	CHARLTON
11	Neil	HEANEY
7	Matthew	LE TISSIER
9	Neil	SHIPPERLEY

Subs

21	Frankie	BENNETT
12	Tommy	WIDDRINGTON
19	Mark	WALTERS

MANCHESTER UNITED

1	Peter	SCHMEICHEL
3	Denis	IRWIN
4	Steve	BRUCE
20	Gary	NEVILLE
5	Lee	SHARPE +54
24	David	BECKHAM (Y)
19	Nicky	BUTT *45
16	Roy	KEANE
11	Ryan	GIGGS
7	Eric	CANTONA
17	Andy	COLE

12	David	MAY +
13	Tony	COTON (G)
22	Paul	SCHOLES *

Match Facts

- First league defeat at the Dell for United in their last seven visits.
- First defeat for the Reds in 19 games since New Year's Day defeat at Spurs.
- United change strip at half time from Grey to Blue. They have never won in the grey.
- Matthew Le Tissier's goal was the first he had scored from open play all season!
- First win over United for Saints in FAPL.

Score Sheet

K. MONKOU 11 mins – 1-0

N. SHIPPERLEY 23 mins – 2-0

M. LE TISSIER 43 mins – 3-0

R. GIGGS 89 mins – 3-1

Referee:
Mr G.Poll (Tring)

FA Carling Premiership

	P	W	D	L	F	A	Pts
1 Manchester United	**35**	**22**	**7**	**6**	**64**	**35**	**73**
2 Newcastle United	33	21	4	8	61	35	67
3 Liverpool	34	19	8	7	66	31	65
4 Aston Villa	34	18	8	8	51	31	62
16 Southampton	**35**	**8**	**10**	**17**	**33**	**51**	**34**

A Grey Day

United travelled to the South coast some six points clear of Newcastle at the top and just four games to play. With two of those games at Old Trafford, a win at the Dell, where Alex Ferguson's side had never lost in the FAPL, would surely clinch the title but, after sensationally going three goals down against relegation threatened Southampton in the first period, United were left to merely change their kit at half time from grey to blue. The United players said they could not see the grey shirts and were therefore unable to play their usual passing game. Certainly in five outings they had failed to win in it and had produced their worst displays of the campaign but, in truth, it was plain poor defending that cost them this game.

The writing was on the wall after less than twenty seconds when a poor pass back by Keane wrong footed Neville and Sharpe leaving Dodd to blast a shot against Schmeichel's body. United hit back when Cole's precision pass set Butt free only for the youngster to fire high and wide despite being helped by Beasant slipping and the visitors were punished for the miss when Le Tissier floated in a free kick from the left that caught out Bruce and Neville. They both moved to mark Shipperley leaving Saints Dutch defender Ken Monkou unmarked and with a free header from only five yards. Schmeichel made a fabulous save to palm the ball out only for Monkou to latch on to it quicker than anybody else and despatch a shot from close in. Barely had United conceded this goal than they were almost two down with Le Tissier smacking Schmeichel's left hand woodwork but there was no let up by the Saints and after 23 minutes they went two up. Giggs was heading back towards his own goal when he was caught in possession and robbed by Neilson who quickly whipped in a cross that was turned home by Shipperley.

Southampton's wonder boy Matt Le Tissier had never scored against United in the FAPL, indeed he had not scored against United since 1989, but he put that all behind him and sent the crowd delirious when he notched the third goal just before half time. Unbelievably, Le Tissier had not scored a goal from open play all season but he was to benefit as Schmeichel proved that he is only human by dropping a straight forward cross for Le Tissier to hit home from close range. The Southampton supporters could scarcely believe it and must have been looking for Jeremy Beadle to appear in the interval especially as United reappeared after the break wearing blue as opposed to the grey they had worn in the first period.

The change of kit brought no change in the scoreline until a minute from time when Giggs sidefooted a consolation effort home from Neville's cross leaving the biggest change of all at the top of the table where Newcastle, 24 hours later, would duly move back to within three points of United with a game in hand.

League Record

		Home				Away				
	P	W	D	L	F	A	W	D	L	F	A
95/96 FAPL	35	13	4	0	30	9	9	3	6	34	26
All time FAPL	161	57	19	4	149	40	42	21	18	138	92
FL/FAPL	3717	1093	429	336	3700	1824	574	483	802	2644	3146

	Home	Away	Total
FAPL Attendances	689,672	539,628	1,229,300

Manchester United (0) 1
Leeds United (0) 0

Wednesday, 17th April 1996, Old Trafford   Att: 48,382

MANCHESTER UNITED

1	Peter	SCHMEICHEL
3	Denis	IRWIN
4	Steve	BRUCE *19
6	Gary	PALLISTER
23	Phil	NEVILLE
24	David	BECKHAM
16	Roy	KEANE (Y)
9	Brian	McCLAIR +45
11	Ryan	GIGGS
17	Andy	COLE **65
7	Eric	CANTONA

Subs

5	Lee	SHARPE **
12	David	MAY *
22	Paul	SCHOLES +

LEEDS UNITED

13	Mark	BEENEY (R)
2	Gary	KELLY
6	David	WETHERALL
4	Carlton	PALMER
10	Gary	McALLISTER
22	Mark	FORD *19
26	Paul	BEESLEY
15	Nigel	WORTHINGTON
11	Gary	SPEED
27	Andy	GRAY +83
9	Brian	DEANE **83

7	Phil	MASINGA **
17	Mark	TINKLER
5	Lucas	RADEBE *

Match Facts

• Leeds yet to score at Old Trafford in the FAPL. United have only found the net themselves three times in what must be the dourest fixture in United's calendar.

• No league victory for Leeds at Old Trafford since February 1981.

• United's 100th FAPL victory.

Score Sheet

R. KEANE 71 mins – 1-0

Referee:
Mr K.Cooper (Pontypridd)

FA Carling Premiership

	P	W	D	L	F	A	Pts
1 Manchester United	**36**	**23**	**7**	**6**	**65**	**35**	**76**
2 Newcastle United	35	23	4	8	63	35	73
3 Liverpool	35	19	9	7	67	32	66
4 Aston Villa	36	18	9	9	52	33	63
13 Leeds United	**35**	**12**	**6**	**17**	**39**	**53**	**42**

Ten Men Leeds Make it Difficult

If anyone thought this would be a classic then they only had to study the previous form guide of visits by Leeds to Old Trafford under Howard Wilkinson to realise he always sets out to achieve a goalless draw and stifle any form of enjoyment in the Theatre of Dreams. With his 'keeper Mark Beeney dismissed after just nineteen minutes for handling the ball outside the area and with no substitute custodian on the bench, Wilkinson's defensive tactics became even more ultra cautious than normal. Fortunately, with the title race between the Reds and Newcastle so close, what would otherwise have been a boring encounter did, in fact, keep everyone on the edge of their seats.

The dismissal of Beeney was somewhat unlucky in that he probably commenced his jump for the ball in the area but landed outside. There was, however, little doubt that he had misjudged the bounce and knew what he was doing for, had he not caught Bruce's long through ball, then certainly Cole would have been left in the clear for an open goal. As well as Beeney's, it was also Bruce's last contribution to the game and whilst the Leeds' goalkeeper was being shown the red card, the United captain was leaving of his own volition thanks to another injury. A third player also departed in the same break with young Mark Ford being the unlucky Leeds player to be sacrificed so that Radebe could be brought on to go in goal. Whilst not a recognised 'keeper, Radebe apparently commenced his career in South Africa as a custodian and had already played 44 minutes of Premiership football in goal with a clean sheet.

As United huffed and puffed without looking particularly like blowing the house down, it began to appear that Radebe would add another seventy or so minutes to that tally. But he was finally beaten, much to the relief of the United fans, in the 71st minute by a shot from the edge of the area from Roy Keane. Scholes, on for Cole who again had a miserable time of it, and Irwin combined down the right and when the Leeds defence blocked the shot from Scholes it rebounded to Cantona. Sensing the rearguard, for once, was slightly disorganised the Frenchman unhinged it slightly further with a deft flick to his left that found Keane. The Irishman's shot from the eighteen yard line had to be precise and his unerring effort was just inside Radebe's right hand post. Minutes later Cantona smashed another effort against the crossbar but earlier, Andy Gray, the son of Frank Gray who caused United much trouble in the Seventies, had also lobbed the ball onto the top of Schmeichel's woodwork. The win, however, had not put any further distance between United and their title rivals, Newcastle, who were also winning 1-0 against Southampton to leave everything exactly as it was prior to play commencing.

League Record

			Home				Away				
	P	W	D	L	F	A	W	D	L	F	A
95/96 FAPL	36	14	4	0	31	9	9	3	6	34	26
All time FAPL	162	58	19	4	151	40	42	21	18	138	92
FL/FAPL	3718	1094	429	336	3701	1825	574	483	802	2644	3146

	Home	Away	Total
FAPL Attendances	738,054	539,628	1,277,682

Manchester United (2) 5
Nottingham Forest (0) 0

Sunday, 28th April 1996, Old Trafford   Att: 53,926

MANCHESTER UNITED

1	Peter	SCHMEICHEL
3	Denis	IRWIN
12	David	MAY
6	Gary	PALLISTER
23	Phil	NEVILLE *83
24	David	BECKHAM
16	Roy	KEANE (Y)
11	Ryan	GIGGS
5	Lee	SHARPE
7	Eric	CANTONA
22	Paul	SCHOLES

Subs

9	Brian	McCLAIR
17	Andy	COLE
20	Gary	NEVILLE *

NOTTINGHAM FOREST

1	Mark	CROSSLEY
18	Alf Inge	HAALAND
4	Colin	COOPER
5	Steve	CHETTLE
3	Stuart	PEARCE (Y)
11	Steve	STONE
8	Scott	GEMMILL (Y)
21	Chris	BART-WILLIAMS
14	Ian	WOAN
12	Jason	LEE
22	Bryan	ROY

2	Des	LYTTLE
19	Steve	HOWE
20	Paul	McGREGOR

Match Facts

- United unbeaten at home in entire 1995/96 FAPL campaign.
- United not conceded a goal at home in FAPL during 1996.
- Attendance sets a new FAPL record.

Score Sheet

P. SCHOLES 41 mins – 1-0
D. BECKHAM 44 mins – 2-0
D. BECKHAM 54 mins – 3-0
R. GIGGS 70 mins – 4-0
E. CANTONA 89 mins – 5-0

Referee:
Mr J.Winter (Stockton)

FA Carling Premiership

	P	W	D	L	F	A	Pts
1 Manchester United	37	24	7	6	70	35	79
2 Newcastle United	35	23	4	8	63	35	73
3 Liverpool	36	20	9	7	68	32	69
4 Aston Villa	37	18	9	10	52	34	63
5 Arsenal	36	16	11	9	47	31	59
9 Forest	36	14	12	10	46	53	54

One Hand on Title

Manager Alex Ferguson made a bold move before the start of this game, which United had to win if they were to keep the pressure on Newcastle in the final sprint to the winning line, by leaving out record signing Andy Cole in favour of local lad Paul Scholes and the move paid big dividends. Ferguson, explaining the switch, said "We know he is a goalscorer, we know he is fresh and we know the crowd are on his side and won't get on his back if he misses one".

But the early stages were far from plain sailing and Scholes had hardly touched the ball in a first forty minutes which were littered with errors, the biggest of which saw Lee Sharpe completely misdirect a diving header from Beckham's cross when it seemed easier to score. But the four minutes prior to the interval changed everything as Scholes, with almost his first touch of the game, steered home Giggs' pin point cross from the left after the Welshman had bamboozled Haaland. Barely had the crowd's relief died away than United had the game wrapped up with a second goal that was somewhat more fortunate than the opener. An indirect free kick, which Crossley could therefore have left to enter the net, was instinctively beaten away by the Forest 'keeper only to drop invitingly for Cantona. But, for once, the Frenchman's radar wasn't functioning at full capacity and his volley fizzed across the goalmouth only to be met by Beckham's head. The power of the inaccurate shot was such that any sort of touch would put the ball in the net and Crossley was completely helpless.

The Reds began the second period as they had ended the first and another goal was very much on the cards. After several close shaves, Forest yielded again in the 55th minute when Cantona hit a forty yard pass from the centre circle to Irwin on the right and his cross was stepped over by Scholes allowing Beckham to score with ease past a wrong footed defence. Fifteen minutes later and a classic United strike made it four with Giggs starting the move midway inside his own half and arriving in the Forest penalty area moments later to finish with aplomb. His ball upfield out of defence found Cantona who waited for the Welshman to track forward into his more familiar left wing role. Taking Cantona's pass in his stride, Giggs cut in and curled the ball past Crossley whose cause was not helped by the off-putting presence of Scholes. A minute from time, United played the numbers game as four became five to give United a six point lead and a goal difference seven better than Newcastle's. The goal was a solo effort from Cantona, who else, as he strode forward from the halfway line with purpose until tackled at the edge of the area by Chettle. The ball spun up off the Forest defender and dropped into the path of Cantona who didn't need a second invitation to ram the ball past a bemused Crossley. If the first forty minutes had been fraught, the last fifty minutes had been a delight as the Reds got one hand on the title.

League Record

		Home					Away				
	P	W	D	L	F	A	W	D	L	F	A
95/96 FAPL	37	15	4	0	36	9	9	3	6	34	26
All time FAPL	163	59	19	4	156	40	42	21	18	138	92
FL/FAPL	3719	1095	429	336	3706	1825	574	483	802	2644	3146

	Home	Away	Total
FAPL Attendances	791,980	539,628	1,331,608

Middlesbrough (0) 0
Manchester United (1) 3

Sunday, 5th May 1996, Riverside Stadium — Att: 29,921

MIDDLESBROUGH

13	Gary	WALSH
2	Neil	COX
4	Steve	VICKERS
5	Nigel	PEARSON
30		BRANCO +72
7	Nicky	BARMBY
8	Jamie	POLLOCK *54
6	Derek	WHYTE
11	Robbie	MUSTOE
25		JUNINHO
9	Jan	FJORTOFT

Subs

20	Phil	STAMP *
12	Alan	MOORE +
15	Phil	WHELAN

MANCHESTER UNITED

1	Peter	SCHMEICHEL
3	Denis	IRWIN (Y)
12	David	MAY
6	Gary	PALLISTER (Y)
23	Phil	NEVILLE
24	David	BECKHAM
16	Roy	KEANE
19	Nicky	BUTT
11	Ryan	GIGGS
7	Eric	CANTONA
22	Paul	SCHOLES *53

17	Andy	COLE *
4	Steve	BRUCE
20	Gary	NEVILLE

Match Facts

- First goal of season for David May.
- United's first ever visit to the Riverside Stadium gives them their third title in four seasons.
- Alex Ferguson becomes the first ever manager to win three titles in Scotland and three in England.

Score Sheet

D. MAY 15 mins – 1-0

A. COLE 54 mins – 2-0

R. GIGGS 80 mins – 3-0

Referee:
Mr P.Durkin (Portland)

FA Carling Premiership

	P	W	D	L	F	A	Pts
1 Manchester United	38	25	7	6	73	35	82
2 Newcastle United	38	24	6	8	66	37	78
3 Liverpool	38	20	11	7	70	34	71
4 Aston Villa	38	18	9	11	52	35	63
5 Arsenal	38	17	12	9	49	32	63
12 Middlesbrough	38	11	10	17	35	50	43

He Thinks It's All Over – It Is Now

After the opening day's drubbing by Aston Villa who would have thought that United would come to the final ninety minutes of the season with the destiny of a third Championship victory in four seasons lying in their own hands? But that was the scenario which faced Alex Ferguson and he produced yet another shock when he changed the side that had trounced Nottingham Forest 5-0 in the previous game. Out of the side, and not even on the bench, went Lee Sharpe in order to accommodate the return from suspension of Nicky Butt whilst Andy Cole remained amongst the substitutes.

Middlesbrough, managed by former Reds Bryan Robson and Viv Anderson, brought back to their side another former United player in Gary Walsh and it was the home side who got off to the better start. Juninho attacked down the left as early as the second minute and when his first cross was blocked, the Brazilian got in a second from a prostrate position on the ground from which Cox looked ideally placed at the near post to score only for his header to fizz wide. United began to slowly claw their way into the match and their reward came after 15 minutes when Cantona freed Butt who Pearson stopped at the expense of a corner. There was, however, no respite for Boro' with the flag kick from Giggs being headed fiercely downwards by May and beyond both Walsh and Branco before bouncing high into the roof of the net. The home team bounced back and put United under a great deal of pressure with Juninho, in particular, cutting through the rearguard and it was a run from the Brazilian that set up a glorious opportunity for Barmby which the England player squandered.

The Champions in waiting, however, weathered the storm and arrived at the minute the title was decided early in the second period. Walsh did well to back pedal and turn the ball over from a deflection in the 53rd minute but before the corner could be taken, Alex Ferguson sent on Andy Cole in place of Paul Scholes. Again Giggs delivered from the flag and when the ball was knocked down to him Cole, with his back to goal, executed the perfect overhead kick to score with his first touch. Simultaneously, news arrived by transistor that Spurs had gone one up at Newcastle and the celebrations began with most of the 2,600 United fans who could get tickets joining in a sunshine conga. There was still another goal to come, however, and it really was the icing on the cake as Giggs strode gracefully forward from midfield before hitting a rasping 25 yarder past a helpless Walsh for a strike that was worthy of a Championship.

As the celebrations gathered pace a banner depicting Newcastle boss Kevin Keegan proclaimed "He thinks its all over – it is now" and indeed it was. A twelve point deficit in January had been overturned to an advantage of four points at the finishing line. A truly great performance.

League Record

		Home					Away				
	P	W	D	L	F	A	W	D	L	F	A
95/96 FAPL	38	15	4	0	36	9	10	3	6	37	26
All time FAPL	164	59	19	4	156	40	43	21	18	141	92
FL/FAPL	3720	1095	429	336	3706	1825	575	483	802	2647	3146

	Home	Away	Total
FAPL Attendances	791,980	569,549	1,361,529

Liverpool (0) 0
Manchester United (0) 1

Saturday, 11th May 1996, Wembley   Att: 79,007

LIVERPOOL

1	David	JAMES
2	Rob	JONES +86
5	Mark	WRIGHT
6	Phil	BABB (Y)
12	John	SCALES
4	Jason	McATEER
15	Jamie	REDKNAPP (Y)
10	John	BARNES
17	Steve	McMANAMAN
8	Stan	COLLYMORE *74
23	Robbie	FOWLER

Subs

26	Anthony	WARNER (G)
16	Michael	THOMAS +
9	Ian	RUSH *

MANCHESTER UNITED

1	Peter	SCHMEICHEL
3	Denis	IRWIN
12	David	MAY
6	Gary	PALLISTER
23	Phil	NEVILLE (Y)
24	David	BECKHAM +89
16	Roy	KEANE
19	Nicky	BUTT
11	Ryan	GIGGS
17	Andy	COLE *63
7	Eric	CANTONA

5	Lee	SHARPE
20	Gary	NEVILLE +
22	Paul	SCHOLES *

Match Facts

• United become first ever club to do the Double twice.

• United's ninth FA Cup victory, one more than next best Spurs.

• United's 14th FA Cup Final appearance – another record.

• In their ten FA Cup Final appearances, Liverpool have only once scored in the first half.

• Fowler's failure to score denies him the honour of scoring in every round of the 1995-96 FA Cup.

Score Sheet

E. CANTONA 86 mins – 1-0

Referee:
Mr D.Gallagher (Banbury)

The Double Double

Manager Alex Ferguson showed no sentiment when selecting his side to go into battle on the last leg of footballing history when omitting his faithful servant of many years, Steve Bruce, and he was unable to find even a place on the bench for the old war horse. Ferguson solved his other dilemma by plumping for Andy Cole up front rather than young Paul Scholes but it was to prove a nightmare for Cole who had what can only be described as a stinker before giving way to the local lad early in the second period.

Before setting off in their quest for the double double, the Reds had another double in the pre match warm up when the schools representing United in the mini six aside competition pulverised Liverpool whilst Alex Stepney, Arthur Albiston, Gordon Hill, Jimmy Nicholl and Brian Greenhoff then beat their Liverpool counterparts in a Golden Oldies penalty shoot out. The main event itself didn't live up to its promise but was surely never as drab a game as many of the critics made out. The fact that Liverpool rarely threatened United was down to excellent defensive play and a performance of Trojan proportions from Roy Keane who was rightly voted Man of the Match. United were also denied two other goals, which would have been as much classics as the eventual winner itself, only by equally superb saves from David James. Had those two goals gone in, the same critics who thought the game was poor would have been describing a breathtaking performance by United. Perhaps much of the critic's views stemmed from the fact that, on the day, Liverpool's big guns Collymore and Fowler were never a factor whilst Cole was worse and it was no surprise when both Collymore and Cole were substituted in the second period.

United controlled midfield, where John Barnes in his white boots looked more like a drum majorette and played like one, from the outset to leave Peter Schmeichel seldom troubled. Not so his opposite number, however, and David James was Liverpool's man of the match. His save in the first period from a David Beckham rocket was top class and the whole stadium stood to acclaim an Eric Cantona goal in the early moments of the second half only to sit down again in disbelief that the 'keeper had somehow got the effort round the post. James also claimed every cross in spectacular fashion that United could throw at him until four minutes from time. A curling Giggs corner left him a long way to come and the 'keeper was also partially blocked by one of his own players. His punch was poor and the ball fell to an off balance Cantona at the edge of the area. It bounced so awkwardly that it was odds against the Frenchman even being able to connect cleanly let alone strike a superb volley through a crowded goalmouth as Fowler, James and Jones were all left helpless when the ball flashed only inches past and beyond them into the net. The double double was United's.

United's All-time FA Cup Record

	Home					Away				
P	W	D	L	F	A	W	D	L	F	A
360	104	32	28	349	154	84	54	58	312	273

	Home	Away	Total
FA Cup Attendances	129,701	153,586	283,287

FINAL TABLE 1995-96

FA Carling Premiership

		HOME					AWAY					
	P	W	D	L	F	A	W	D	L	F	A	Pts
MANCHESTER UNITED ...	38	15	4	0	36	9	10	3	6	37	26	82
Newcastle United	38	17	1	1	38	9	7	5	7	28	28	78
Liverpool	38	14	4	1	46	13	6	7	6	24	21	71
Aston Villa	38	11	5	3	32	15	7	4	8	20	20	63
Arsenal	38	10	7	2	30	16	7	5	7	19	16	63
Everton	38	10	5	4	35	19	7	5	7	29	25	61
Blackburn Rovers	38	14	2	3	44	19	4	5	10	17	28	61
Tottenham Hotspur	38	9	5	5	26	19	7	8	4	24	19	61
Nottingham Forest	38	11	6	2	29	17	4	7	8	21	37	58
West Ham United	38	9	5	5	25	21	5	4	10	18	31	51
Chelsea	38	7	7	5	30	22	5	7	7	16	22	50
Middlesbrough	38	8	3	8	27	27	3	7	9	8	23	43
Leeds United	38	8	3	8	21	21	4	4	11	19	36	43
Wimbledon	38	5	6	8	27	33	5	5	9	28	37	41
Sheffield Wednesday	38	7	5	7	30	31	3	5	11	18	30	40
Coventry City	38	6	7	6	21	23	2	7	10	21	37	38
Southampton	38	7	7	5	21	18	2	4	13	13	34	38
Manchester City	38	7	7	5	21	19	2	4	13	12	39	38
QPR	38	6	5	8	25	26	3	1	15	13	31	33
Bolton Wanderers	38	5	4	10	16	31	3	1	15	23	40	29

Composite Table with Prize Money

	P	W	D	L	F	A	Pts	Prize Money	Psn
MANCHESTER UNITED ...	38	25	7	6	73	35	82	£989,300	1
Newcastle United	38	24	6	8	66	37	78	£934,135	2
Liverpool	38	20	11	7	70	34	71	£884,970	3
Aston Villa	38	18	9	11	52	35	63	£835,805	4
Arsenal	38	17	12	9	49	32	63	£768,640	5
Everton	38	17	10	11	64	44	61	£737,475	6
Blackburn Rovers	38	18	7	13	61	47	61	£688,310	7
Tottenham Hotspur	38	16	13	9	50	38	61	£639,145	8
Nottingham Forest	38	15	13	10	50	54	58	£589,980	9
West Ham United	38	14	9	15	43	52	51	£540,815	10
Chelsea	38	12	14	12	46	44	50	£491,650	11
Middlesbrough	38	11	10	17	35	50	43	£442,485	12
Leeds United	38	12	7	19	40	57	43	£393,320	13
Wimbledon	38	10	11	17	55	70	41	£344,155	14

		P	W	D	L	F	A		
Sheffield Wednesday	38	10	10	18	48	61	40	£294,990	15
Coventry City	38	8	14	16	42	60	38	£245,825	16
Southampton	38	9	11	18	34	52	38	£196,660	17
Manchester City	38	9	11	18	33	58	38	£147,495	18
QPR	38	9	6	23	38	57	33	£98,330	19
Bolton Wanderers	38	8	5	25	39	71	29	£49,165	20

All-time Tables 1992-96

Positions Based on Total Points

Psn		P	W	D	L	F	A	Pts	Yrs
1	MANCHESTER UTD ...	164	102	40	22	297	132	346	4
2	Blackburn Rovers	... 164	90	35	39	272	168	305	4
3	Liverpool	... 164	74	42	48	256	181	264	4
4	Aston Villa	 164	65	47	52	206	181	242	4
5	Arsenal	 164	63	52	49	194	147	241	4
6	Leeds United	... 164	62	51	51	221	196	237	4
7	Newcastle United	... 122	67	26	29	215	125	227	3
8	Tottenham Hotspur	... 164	59	50	55	230	221	227	4
9	QPR	 164	59	39	66	224	232	216	4
10	Wimbledon	 164	57	45	62	215	243	216	4
11	Sheffield Wednesday	... 164	54	52	58	228	223	214	4
12	Chelsea	 164	52	55	57	196	206	211	4
13	Everton	 164	55	43	66	203	213	208	3
14	Coventry City	 164	47	55	62	181	224	196	3
15	Manchester City ...	... 164	45	43	47	147	164	189	4
16	Southampton	 164	46	47	71	198	242	185	4
17	Nottingham Forest	... 122	47	34	41	163	159	175	3
18	Norwich City... ...	... 126	43	39	44	163	180	168	3
19	West Ham United	... 122	40	33	49	134	158	153	3
20	Ipswich Town	 126	28	38	60	121	206	122	3
21	Crystal Palace ...	 84	22	28	34	82	110	94	2
22	Sheffield United	 84	22	28	34	96	113	94	2
23	Oldham Athletic	 84	22	23	39	105	142	89	2
24	Middlesbrough	 80	22	21	37	89	125	87	2
25	Bolton Wanderers	 38	8	5	25	39	71	30	1
26	Swindon Town	 42	5	15	22	47	100	30	1
27	Leicester City	 42	6	11	25	45	80	29	1

Positions Based on Points-Games Average

Psn		P	W	D	L	F	A	Pts	%
1	MANCHESTER UTD ...	164	102	40	22	297	132	346	70.33
2	Newcastle United ...	122	67	26	29	215	125	227	62.02
3	Blackburn Rovers ...	164	90	35	39	272	168	305	61.99
4	Liverpool	164	74	42	48	256	181	264	53.66
5	Aston Villa	164	65	47	52	206	181	242	49.19
6	Arsenal	164	63	52	49	194	147	241	48.98
7	Leeds United	164	62	51	51	221	196	237	48.17
8	Nottingham Forest ...	122	47	34	41	163	159	175	47.81
9	Tottenham Hotspur ...	164	59	50	55	230	221	227	46.14
10	Norwich City...	126	43	39	44	163	180	168	44.44
11	QPR	164	59	39	66	224	232	216	43.90
12	Wimbledon	164	57	45	62	215	243	216	43.90
13	Sheffield Wednesday ...	164	54	52	58	228	223	214	43.50
14	Chelsea	164	52	55	57	196	206	211	42.89
15	Everton	164	55	43	66	203	213	208	42.28
16	West Ham United ...	122	40	33	49	134	158	153	41.80
17	Coventry City	164	47	55	62	181	224	196	39.84
18	Manchester City	164	45	43	47	147	164	189	38.41
19	Southampton	164	46	47	71	198	242	185	37.60
20	Crystal Palace	84	22	28	34	82	110	94	37.30
21	Sheffield United	84	22	28	34	96	113	94	37.30
22	Middlesbrough	80	22	21	37	89	125	87	36.25
23	Oldham Athletic	84	22	23	39	105	142	89	35.32
24	Ipswich Town	126	28	38	60	121	206	122	32.32
25	Bolton Wanderers ...	38	8	5	25	39	71	30	25.64
26	Swindon Town	42	5	15	22	47	100	30	23.81
27	Leicester City	42	6	11	25	45	80	29	23.02

Season's Records 95-96

Attendances by Number – *FA Premier League*

Home			Away		
28/04/96	Nottingham Forest	53,926	17/12/95	Liverpool	40,546
8/04/96	Coventry City	50,332	24/12/95	Leeds United	39,801
25/03/96	Spurs	50,157	9/09/95	Everton	39,496
20/03/96	Arsenal	50,028	4/11/95	Arsenal	38,317
17/04/96	Leeds United	48,382	4/03/96	Newcastle United	36,610
10/02/96	Blackburn Rovers	42,681	19/08/95	Aston Villa	34,655
13/01/96	Aston Villa	42,667	23/09/95	Sheffield Wed'y	34,101
21/02/96	Everton	42,459	1/01/96	Spurs	32,852
27/12/95	Newcastle United	42,024	21/10/95	Chelsea	31,019
2/12/95	Chelsea	42,019	5/05/96	Middlesbrough	29,921
30/12/95	QPR	41,890	28/08/95	Blackburn Rovers	29,843
9/12/95	Sheffield Wednesday	41,849	6/04/96	Manchester City	29,688
18/11/95	Southampton	39,301	27/11/95	Nottingham Forest	29,263
28/10/95	Middlesbrough	36,580	3/02/96	Wimbledon	25,380
14/10/95	Manchester City	35,707	22/01/96	West Ham United	24,197
30/09/95	Liverpool	34,934	24/11/95	Coventry City	23,400
16/09/95	Bolton Wanderers	32,812	25/02/96	Bolton Wanderers	21,381
26/08/95	Wimbledon	32,226	16/03/96	QPR	18,817
23/08/95	West Ham Utd	31,966	13/04/96	Southampton	15,262
	Total	*791,980*		*Total*	*569,549*

Attendances by Number – *FA Cup*

Home			Away		
18/02/96	Manchester City	42,692	16/01/96	Sunderland	21,378
6/01/96	Sunderland	41,563	27/01/96	Reading	14,780
11/03/96	Southampton	45,446	31/03/96	Chelsea (Villa Park)	38,421
			11/05/96	Liverpool (Wem'y)	79,007
	Total	129,701		*Total*	*153,586*

Attendances by Number – *Coca Cola Cup*

Home			Away		
20/09/95	York City	29,049	3/10/95	York City	9,386
	Total	*29,049*		*Total*	*9,386*

Attendances by Number – *UEFA Cup*

	Home			Away	
26/09/95	Rotor Volgograd	29,724	12/09/95	Rotor Volgograd	40,000
	Total	*29,724*		*Total*	*40,000*

Sending Offs

United

Date	Player	Fixture	Referee
28/08/95	Roy KEANE	Blackburn Rovs at Ewood Park in FAPL	D.Elleray
20/09/95	Pat McGIBBON	York City at Old Trafford in CCC	J.Rushton
28/10/95	Roy KEANE	Middlesbrough at Old Trafford in FAPL	S.Lodge
22/01/96	Nicky BUTT	West Ham United at Upton Park in FAPL	S.Lodge

Opposition

Date	Player	Fixture	Referee
23/08/95	Marco BOOGERS	West Ham at Old Trafford in FAPL	D.Gallagher
9/09/95	D. UNSWORTH	Everton at Goodison Park in FAPL	G.Poll
20/09/95	Paul BAKER	York City at Old Trafford in CCC	J.Rushton
21/10/95	Frank SINCLAIR	Chelsea at Stamford Bridge in FAPL	A.Wilkie
17/04/96	Mark BEENEY	Leeds United at Old Trafford in FAPL	K.Cooper

Bookings

Date	Player	Fixture	Referee
19/08/95	Paul SCHOLES	Aston Villa (a) in FAPL	Mr R.Hart
28/08/95	Roy KEANE	Blackburn R(a) in FAPL (twice)	Mr D.Elleray
9/09/95		Everton (a) in FAPL	Mr G.Poll
30/09/95		Liverpool (h) in FAPL	Mr D.Elleray
10/02/96		Blackburn Rovers (h) in FAPL	Mr K.Burge
18/02/96		Manchester City (h) in FAC	Mr A.Wilkie
24/03/96		Spurs (h) in FAPL	Mr G.Ashby
31/03/96		Chelsea (n) in FAC	Mr S.Lodge
17/04/96		Leeds United (h) in FAPL	Mr K.Cooper
28/04/96		Nottingham Forest (h) in FAPL	Mr J.Winter
28/08/95	Nicky BUTT	Blackburn Rovers (a) in FAPL	Mr D.Elleray
9/09/95		Everton (a) in FAPL	Mr G.Poll
21/10/95		Chelsea (a) in FAPL	Mr A.Wilkie
28/10/95		Middlesbrough (h) in FAPL	Mr S.Lodge

18/11/95		Southampton (h) in FAPL	Mr P.Danson
22/01/96		West Ham United (a) in FAPL	Mr S.Lodge
4/03/96		Newcastle United (a) in FAPL	Mr D.Elleray
24/03/96		Spurs (h) in FAPL	Mr G.Ashby
31/03/96		Chelsea (n) in FAC	Mr S.Lodge
6/04/96		Manchester City (a) in FAPL	Mr M.Reed
28/08/95	Gary NEVILLE	Blackburn Rovers (a) in FAPL	Mr D.Elleray
14/10/95		Manchester City (h) in FAPL	Mr R.Dilkes
4/11/95		Arsenal (a) in FAPL	Mr P.Durkin
2/12/95		Chelsea (h) in FAPL	Mr M.Bodenham
13/01/96		Aston Villa (h) in FAPL	Mr G.Willard
22/01/96		West Ham United (a) in FAPL	Mr S.Lodge
6/04/96		Manchester City (a) in FAPL	Mr M.Reed
28/08/95	Andy COLE	Blackburn Rovers (a) in FAPL	Mr D.Elleray
22/01/96		West Ham United (a) in FAPL	Mr S.Lodge
18/02/96		Manchester City (h) in FAC	Mr A.Wilkie
16/03/96		QPR (a) in FAPL	Mr R.Hart
6/04/96		Manchester City (a) in FAPL	Mr M.Reed
9/09/95	Denis IRWIN	Everton (a) in FAPL	Mr G.Poll
27/12/95		Newcastle United (h) in FAPL	Mr P.Alcock
6/01/96		Sunderland (h) in FA Cup	Mr M.Reed
13/01/96		Aston Villa (h) in FAPL	Mr G.Willard
18/02/96		Manchester City (h) in FAC	Mr A.Wilkie
5/05/96		Middlesbrough (a) in FAPL	Mr P.Durkin
9/09/95	Lee SHARPE	Everton (a) in FAPL	Mr G.Poll
17/12/95		Liverpool (a) in FAPL	Mr G.Poll
22/01/96		West Ham United (a) in FAPL	Mr S.Lodge
9/09/95	Gary PALLISTER	Everton (a) in FAPL	Mr G.Poll
27/11/95		Nott'm Forest (a) in FAPL	Mr K.Cooper
18/02/96		Manchester City (h) in FAC	Mr A.Wilkie
5/05/96		Middlesbrough (a) in FAPL	Mr P.Durkin
16/09/95	David BECKHAM	Bolton Wanderers (h) in FAPL	Mr S.Dunn
20/09/95		York City (h) in Coca Cola Cup	Mr J.Rushton
3/10/95		York City (a) in Coca Cola Cup	Mr J.Winter
4/11/95		Arsenal (a) in FAPL	Mr P.Durkin
9/12/95		Sheff Wednesday (h) in FAPL	Mr P.Jones
24/12/95		Leeds United (a) in FAPL	Mr D.Gallagher
6/01/96		Sunderland (h) in FA Cup	Mr M.Reed
13/04/96		Southampton (a) in FAPL	Mr G.Poll
3/10/95	P. SCHMEICHEL	York City (a) in Coca Cola Cup	Mr J.Winter
13/01/96		Aston Villa (h) in FAPL	Mr G.Willard
27/01/96		Reading (a) in FA Cup	Mr J.Winter
11/03/96		Southampton (h) in FA Cup	Mr S.Dunn
28/10/95	Steve BRUCE	Middlesbrough (h) in FAPL	Mr S.Lodge

4/11/95		Arsenal (a) in FAPL	Mr P.Durkin
9/12/95		Sheff Wednesday (h) in FAPL	Mr P.Jones
22/01/96		West Ham United (a) in FAPL	Mr S.Lodge
2/12/95	Eric CANTONA	Chelsea (h) in FAPL	Mr M.Bodenham
17/12/95	Brian McCLAIR	Liverpool (a) in FAPL	Mr G.Poll
13/01/96	Phil NEVILLE	Aston Villa (h) in FAPL	Mr G.Willard
16/01/96		Sunderland (a) in FA Cup	Mr M.Reed
4/03/96		Newcastle United (a) in FAPL	Mr D.Elleray
11/05/96		Liverpool (n) FA Cup Final	Mr D.Gallagher
16/01/96	Paul PARKER	Sunderland (a) in FA Cup	Mr M.Reed
27/01/96		Reading (a) in FA Cup	Mr J.Winter
16/03/96	David MAY	QPR (a) in FAPL	Mr R.Hart

Opposition

(OT) denotes at Old Trafford, (h) denotes on own ground

Date	Player	Fixture	Referee
19/08/95	Gary CHARLES	Aston Villa (h) in FAPL	Mr R.Hart
23/08/95	D. HUTCHINSON	West Ham Utd (OT) in FAPL	Mr D.Gallagher
28/08/95	Tim SHERWOOD	Blackburn Rovers (h) in FAPL	Mr D.Elleray
28/08/95	Graham LE SAUX	Blackburn Rovers (h) in FAPL	Mr D.Elleray
28/08/95	David BATTY	Blackburn Rovers (h) in FAPL	Mr D.Elleray
9/09/95	Gary ABLETT	Everton (h) in FAPL	Mr G.Poll
9/09/95	D. UNSWORTH	Everton (h) in FAPL (Twice)	Mr G.Poll
9/09/95	Dave WATSON	Everton (h) in FAPL	Mr G.Poll
16/09/95	Alan THOMPSON	Bolton Wanderers (OT) in FAPL	Mr S.Dunn
26/09/95	JUENENKO	Rotor Volgograd (OT) in UEFA	Mr B.Heynemann
26/09/95	BERKETOV	Rotor Volgograd (OT) in UEFA	Mr B.Heynemann
26/09/95	NIDERGAUS	Rotor Volgograd (OT) in UEFA	Mr B.Heynemann
30/09/95	Jason McATEER	Liverpool (OT) in FAPL	Mr D.Elleray
30/09/95	Michael THOMAS	Liverpool (OT) in FAPL	Mr D.Elleray
20/09/95	Nigel PEPPER	York City (OT) in Coca Cola Cup	Mr J.Rushton
3/10/95		York City (h) in Coca Cola Cup	Mr J.Winter
3/10/95	Scott JORDAN	York City (h) in Coca Cola Cup	Mr J.Winter
3/10/95	Tony BARRAS	York City (h) in Coca Cola Cup	Mr J.Winter
3/10/95	Nick PEVERILL	York City (h) in Coca Cola Cup	Mr J.Winter
14/10/95	Garry FLITCROFT	Manchester City (OT) in FAPL	Mr R.Dilkes
14/10/95	Keith CURLE	Manchester City (OT) in FAPL	Mr R.Dilkes
18/02/96		Manchester City (OT) in FAC	Mr A.Wilkie
6/04/96		Manchester City (h) in FAPL	Mr M.Reed
14/10/95	Terry PHELAN	Manchester City (OT) in FAPL	Mr R.Dilkes
14/10/95	Steve LOMAS	Manchester City (OT) in FAPL	Mr R.Dilkes
21/10/95	Paul FURLONG	Chelsea (h) in FAPL	Mr A.Wilkie
21/10/95	Steve CLARKE	Chelsea (h) in FAPL	Mr A.Wilkie
28/10/95	Neil COX	Middlesbrough (OT) in FAPL	Mr S.Lodge

28/10/95	Jan FJORTOFT	Middlesbrough (OT) in FAPL	Mr S.Lodge
28/10/95	Phil WHELAN	Middlesbrough (OT) in FAPL	Mr S.Lodge
28/10/95	Jamie POLLOCK	Middlesbrough (OT) in FAPL	Mr S.Lodge
4/11/95	Paul MERSON	Arsenal (h) in FAPL	Mr P.Durkin
18/11/95	Neil HEANEY	Southampton (OT) in FAPL	Mr P.Danson
2/12/95	Eddie NEWTON	Chelsea (OT) in FAPL	Mr M.Bodenham
2/12/95	Gareth HALL	Chelsea (OT) in FAPL	Mr M.Bodenham
17/12/95	Robbie FOWLER	Liverpool (h) in FAPL	Mr G.Poll
17/12/95	S.McMANAMAN	Liverpool (h) in FAPL	Mr G.Poll
24/12/95	Brian DEANE	Leeds United (h) in FAPL	Mr D.Gallagher
27/12/95	Warren BARTON	Newcastle Utd (OT) in FAPL	Mr P.Alcock
27/12/95	John BERESFORD	Newcastle Utd (OT) in FAPL	Mr P.Alcock
1/01/96	Dean AUSTIN	Spurs (h) in FAPL	Mr G.Ashby
6/01/96	Steve AGNEW	Sunderland (OT) in FA Cup	Mr M.Reed
6/01/96	Craig RUSSELL	Sunderland (OT) in FA Cup	Mr M.Reed
6/01/96	Martin SCOTT	Sunderland (OT) in FA Cup	Mr M.Reed
16/01/96		Sunderland (h) in FA Cup	Mr M.Reed
13/01/96	Mark DRAPER	Aston Villa (OT) in FAPL	Mr G.Willard
13/01/96	Savo Milosevic	Aston Villa (OT) in FAPL	Mr G.Willard
27/01/96	Andy BERNAL	Reading (h) in FA Cup	Mr J.Winter
27/01/96	Phil PARKINSON	Reading (h) in FA Cup	Mr J.Winter
3/02/96	Steven TALBOYS	Wimbledon (h) in FAPL	Mr P.Durkin
10/02/96	Mike NEWELL	Blackburn Rovers (OT) in FAPL	Mr K.Burge
10/02/96	Alan SHEARER	Blackburn Rovers (OT) in FAPL	Mr K.Burge
10/02/96	Graham FENTON	Blackburn Rovers (OT) in FAPL	Mr K.Burge
18/02/96	Michael BROWN	Manchester City (OT) in FAC	Mr A.Wilkie
6/04/96		Manchester City (h) in FAPL	Mr M.Reed
21/02/96	Jon O'CONNOR	Everton (OT) in FAPL	Mr M.Bodenham
21/02/96	John EBBRELL	Everton (OT) in FAPL	Mr M.Bodenham
21/02/96	Barry HORNE	Everton (OT) in FAPL	Mr M.Bodenham
4/03/96	Robert LEE	Newcastle United (h) in FAPL	Mr D.Elleray
4/03/96	David GINOLA	Newcastle United (h) in FAPL	Mr D.Elleray
16/03/96	Steve YATES	QPR (h) in FAPL	Mr R.Hart
16/03/96	Daniel DICHIO	QPR (h) in FAPL	Mr R.Hart
24/03/96	Gary MABBUTT	Spurs (OT) in FAPL	Mr G.Ashby
24/03/96	T. SHERINGHAM	Spurs (OT) in FAPL	Mr G.Ashby
31/03/96	Andy MYERS	Chelsea (n) in FAC	Mr S.Lodge
13/04/96	Barry VENISON	Southampton (h) in FAPL	Mr G.Poll
28/04/96	Stuart PEARCE	Nottingham Forest (OT) in FAPL	Mr J.Winter
11/05/96	Jamie REDKNAPP	Liverpool (n) FA Cup Final	Mr D.Gallagher
11/05/96	Phil BABB	Liverpool (n) FA Cup Final	Mr D.Gallagher

Bookings by Referee in FAPL

(Number after referee's name denotes number of United games officiated.)

United		Referee	Opponents	
Home	Away		At Old Trafford	On Own Ground
	3	Mr R.Hart (3)		3
	1	Mr D.Gallagher (4)	1	1
1	7	Mr D.Elleray (3)	2	5
	8	Mr G.Poll (3)		7
1		Mr S.Dunn (1)	1	
	3	Mr P.Durkin (4)	2	2
1		Mr K.Burge (3)	3	
1		Mr R.Dilkes (1)	4	
	1	Mr A.Wilkie (1)		2
2	6	Mr S.Lodge (2)	4	
1		Mr P.Danson (1)	1	
1	1	Mr K.Cooper (2)		
2		Mr M.Bodenham (2)	5	
2		Mr P.Jones (1)		
1		Mr P.Alcock (1)	2	
2		Mr G.Ashby (2)	2	
3		Mr G.Willard (2)	2	1
	3	Mr M.Reed (1)		2
1		Mr J.Winter (1)	1	
19	33	Totals	30	23

Suspensions

Eric	CANTONA	Suspended to 30th September 1995 (carry over from 1994/95)	
Steve	BRUCE	1 match August 1995 (carry over from 1994/95)	
Roy	KEANE	3 matches	September 1995
		4 matches	November 1995
		1 match	April 1996
Pat	McGIBBON	3 matches	Sept/Oct 1995
Nicky	BUTT	3 matches	December 1995
		1 match	February 1996
		2 matches	April 1996
David	BECKHAM	2 matches	January 1996
Gary	NEVILLE	2 matches	February 1996

Penalties

United

Date	Player	Fixture	Comp	Outcome
1/10/95	Eric CANTONA	Liverpool (h)	FAPL	Converted
27/11/95	Eric CANTONA	Nottingham Forest (a)	FAPL	Converted
3/02/96	Eric CANTONA	Wimbledon (a)	FAPL	Converted
18/02/96	Eric CANTONA	Manchester City (h)	FAC	Converted
6/04/96	Eric CANTONA	Manchester City (a)	FAPL	Converted

Opponents

Date	Player	Fixture	Comp	Outcome
19/08/95	Dwight YORKE	Aston Villa at Villa Park	FAPL	Converted
20/09/95	Paul BARNES	York City at Old Trafford	CCC	Converted
24/12/95	Gary McALLISTER	Leeds United at Elland Rd	FAPL	Converted

Summary of Appearances

No.	Player		FAPL	FAC	CCC	UEFA
1	Peter	SCHMEICHEL	36	6	1	2
2	Paul	PARKER	5/1	1/1	1	-/1
3	Denis	IRWIN	31	6	1	1
4	Steve	BRUCE	30	5	1/1	2
5	Lee	SHARPE	21/10	4/2	2	2
6	Gary	PALLISTER	21	3	2	2
7	Eric	CANTONA	30	7	1	-
9	Brian	McCLAIR	12/10	-	1	-
11	Ryan	GIGGS	30/3	7	2	2
12	David	MAY	11/5	2	-	-
16	Roy	KEANE	29	7	-/1	2
17	Andy	COLE	32/2	7	1	1
18	Simon	DAVIES	1/5	-	1	-/1
19	Nicky	BUTT	31/1	7	-	2
20	Gary	NEVILLE	30/1	5/1	1	1
21	Pat	McGIBBON	-	-	1	-
22	Paul	SCHOLES	16/10	-/2	1	1/1
23	Phil	NEVILLE	21/3 6/1	1/1	1	-
24	David	BECKHAM	26/7	3	2	2
25	Kevin	PILKINGTON	2/1	1	1	-
27	Terry	COOKE	1/3	-	1/1	-/1
28	Ben	THORNLEY	-/1	-	-	-
30	John	O'KANE	-/1	-	-	1
31	William	PRUNIER	2	-	-	-

Goalscorers

No.	Player		FAPL	FAC	CCC	UEFA
7	Eric	CANTONA	14	5	-	-
17	Andy	COLE	11	2	-	-
11	Ryan	GIGGS	11	1	-	-
22	Paul	SCHOLES	10	1	2	1
24	David	BECKHAM	7	1	-	-
16	Roy	KEANE	6	-	-	-
5	Lee	SHARPE	4	2	-	-
9	Brian	McCLAIR	3	-	-	-
19	Nicky	BUTT	2	1	-	-
3	Denis	IRWIN	1	-	-	-
4	Steve	BRUCE	1	-	-	-
6	Gary	PALLISTER	1	-	-	-

No.	Player		FAPL	FAC	CCC	UEFA
27	Terry	COOKE	-	-	1	-
2	Paul	PARKER	-	1	-	-
1	Peter	SCHMEICHEL	-	-	-	1
		Own Goal	1	-	-	-

List of Scores by Number (FAPL Games Only)

0-0	1-0	0-1	1-1
Sheff Wed (a)	Man City (h)	Arsenal (a)	Forest (a)
Aston V (h)	West Ham (a)		Chelsea (h)
	Blackburn R (h)		QPR (a)
	Newcastle U (a)		
	Arsenal (h)		
	Spurs (h)		
	Coventry C (h)		
	Leeds Utd (a)		

2-0	0-2	2-1	1-2
Middlesbrough (h)	Liverpool (a)	West Ham Utd (h)	
Newcastle (h)		Blackburn Rovs (a)	
Everton (h)		QPR (h)	

2-2	3-0	0-3	3-1
Liverpool (h)	Bolton W (h)		Wimbledon (h)
Sheff Wed (h)	Middlesbrough (a)		

1-3	3-2	3-3	4-0
Aston Villa (a)	Everton (a)		Coventry C (a)
Leeds Utd (a)	Man City (a)		
Southampton (a)			

4-1	1-4	4-2	5-0
Chelsea (a)	Spurs (a)	Wimbledon (a)	Forest (h)
Southampton (h)			

6-0
Bolton W (a)

League Sequences

Consecutive Wins	6
Consecutive Home Wins	7
Consecutive Away Wins	4
Games Without Defeat	12
Games Without a Win	5

Transfers to Manchester United

Player		Date Bought	From	Fee
Nick	CULKIN	September 1995	York City	£250,000
William	PRUNIER	December 1995	Bordeaux	Loan
Tony	COTON	January 1996	Man City	£400,000

Transfers from Manchester United

Player		Date Sold	To	Fee
Paul	INCE	June 1995	Inter Milan	£7m
Mark	HUGHES	June 1995	Chelsea	£1.5m
David	JOHNSON	July 1995	Bury	Free
Mark	RAWLINSON	July 1995	Bournemouth	Free
Richard	IRVING	July 1995	Nottingham Forest	£75,000
Ashley	WESTWOOD	July 1995	Crewe Alexandra	£40,000
Andrei	KANCHELSKIS	August 1995	Everton	£5m
Gary	WALSH	August 1995	Middlesbrough	£250,000
Ben	THORNLEY	November 1995	Stockport County	Loaned
		February 1996	Huddersfield Town	Loaned
Chris	CASPER	January 1996	Bournemouth	Loaned
Kevin	PILKINGTON	February 1996	Rochdale	Loaned
Terry	COOKE	February 1996	Sunderland	Loaned
Graeme	TOMLINSON	March 1996	Luton Town	Loaned
Graeme	TOMLINSON	March 1996	Luton Town	Loaned
Steve	BRUCE	May 1996	Birmingham City	Free
Paul	PARKER	May 1996		Free

Squad Numbers

1	P.Schmeichel	18	S.Davies
2	P.Parker	19	N.Butt
3	D.Irwin	20	G.Neville
4	S.Bruce	21	P.McGibbon
5	L.Sharpe	22	P.Scholes
6	G.Pallister	23	P.Neville
7	E.Cantona	24	D.Beckham
9	B.McClair	25	K.Pilkington
11	R.Giggs	26	C.Casper
12	D.May	27	T.Cooke
13	T.Coton	28	B.Thornley
15	G.Tomlinson	30	J.O'Kane
16	R.Keane	31	W.Prunier
17	A.Cole		

Appearances – FA Carling Premiership

Player Number	1	2	3	4	5	6	7	9	11	12	15	16	17	18	19	20	21	22	23	24	25	26	27	28	30	31	13
Aston Villa (a)	•	•	•	-	•	•	-	•	•	-	-	-	-	s	•	•	•	•	s	45	-	-	-	-	-	-	-
West Ham Utd (h)	•	•	•	-	•	s	-	•	•	-	-	-	•	•	•	•	s	•	s	s	-	-	-	-	59	-	-
Wimbledon (h)	•	s	•	-	•	•	-	•	77	-	-	-	68	s	•	•	•	•	•	•	-	-	-	28	-	-	-
Blackburn Rovers (a)	•	s	•	-	•	•	-	•	76	-	-	s	s	77	•	•	•	s	•	s	-	-	-	-	-	-	-
Everton (a)	•	s	•	-	•	•	-	•	66	-	-	-	•	76	•	•	•	s	•	•	-	-	-	-	-	-	-
Bolton Wanderers (h)	•	•	•	-	•	•	-	•	•	-	-	•	•	73	•	•	•	•	•	•	-	-	-	-	-	-	-
Sheff Wed (a)	•	s	•	-	-	•	-	•	•	-	-	-	s	74	•	•	s	•	•	s	s	66	s	-	-	-	-
Liverpool (h)	•	s	s	-	•	•	•	76	•	-	-	•	s	s	s	•	•	72	•	45	•	•	-	-	-	-	-
Man City (h)	•	s	-	63	•	•	•	79	•	-	-	•	•	•	•	•	•	s	s	45	•	•	-	-	-	-	-
Chelsea (a)	•	•	-	-	•	s	•	45	•	-	-	s	•	•	•	•	•	s	s	•	•	•	-	-	-	-	-
Middlesbrough (h)	•	s	-	64	•	s	•	79	•	-	-	•	•	•	•	•	s	s	s	64	•	•	-	-	-	-	-
Arsenal (a)	•	•	-	•	•	66	•	50	s	-	-	s	s	•	•	•	s	46	•	•	•	•	-	-	-	-	-
Southampton (h)	•	s	•	63	•	•	•	s	79	-	-	•	•	•	•	•	-	57	•	s	•	•	-	-	-	-	-
Coventry City (a)	•	•	-	81	•	s	•	s	•	-	-	•	•	•	•	•	45	45	s	•	•	•	-	-	-	-	-
Nott'm Forest (a)	•	•	-	-	•	s	s	•	•	-	-	s	s	s	•	•	s	•	•	•	-	75	•	-	-	-	-
Chelsea (h)	•	s	•	-	•	•	•	•	•	-	-	s	51	•	•	•	•	s	•	s	•	82	•	-	-	-	-
Sheff Wed (h)	•	•	s	-	•	•	•	•	74	-	-	s	s	•	•	•	52	s	•	s	•	•	-	-	-	-	-
Liverpool (a)	•	•	-	-	•	s	•	45	s	74	-	•	•	•	•	•	74	86	•	•	•	•	-	-	-	-	-
Leeds Utd (a)	•	s	•	88	•	55	•	55	•	s	-	s	•	•	•	•	s	s	s	•	•	•	-	-	•	•	-
QPR (h)	•	-	-	-	•	-	•	•	•	-	-	s	•	•	•	•	•	•	s	45	•	•	-	-	•	•	-
Spurs (a)	s	-	-	68	•	68	•	•	•	-	-	•	•	•	•	•	•	•	s	•	•	•	-	-	-	-	-

Player Number

	1	2	3	4	5	6	7	9	11	12	15	16	17	18	19	20	21	22	23	24	25	26	27	28	30	31	13
Aston Villa (h)	•	S	•	•	S	•	•	S	•	•	•	•	•	•	•	•	•	•	•	•	•	•	•	•	•	•	•
West Ham Utd (a)	•	S	•	•	•	•	•	•	•	•	•	•	S	•	•	•	77	S	S	76	•	•	•	•	•	•	•
Wimbledon (a)	•	•	S	•	•	•	•	•	•	•	•	•	•	•	•	•	•	S	•	15	•	•	•	•	•	•	S
Blackburn R (h)	S	•	•	•	S	•	•	S	•	•	•	•	•	•	•	•	•	S	•	•	•	•	•	•	•	•	•
Everton (h)	•	•	•	•	•	•	•	•	•	•	•	•	•	•	S	S	•	S	•	84	•	•	•	•	•	•	•
Bolton Wanderers (a)	•	•	•	•	•	•	S	57	s	S	•	•	•	•	•	•	•	73	•	•	•	•	•	•	•	•	•
Newcastle United (a)	•	•	•	•	•	•	•	•	•	•	•	•	•	•	74	•	•	•	•	S	S	•	•	•	•	•	•
QPR (a)	•	•	•	•	74	•	•	s	S	•	•	•	•	S	•	•	51	•	•	S	•	•	•	•	•	•	•
Arsenal (h)	•	•	•	•	•	•	•	S	S	•	•	•	•	S	•	•	58	S	S	•	•	•	•	•	•	•	•
Spurs (h)	•	•	•	•	74	•	•	73	•	74	•	•	•	S	•	•	•	S	•	64	•	•	•	•	•	•	•
Man City (a)	•	•	S	74	S	•	•	•	•	•	•	•	•	•	•	•	•	•	•	•	•	•	•	•	•	S	•
Coventry City (h)	S	•	•	•	S	•	•	•	•	54	•	•	S	•	S	•	•	S	•	•	•	•	•	•	•	•	•
Southampton (a)	•	•	•	•	S	•	•	•	•	19	•	•	S	•	S	•	•	45	•	•	•	•	•	•	•	•	•
Leeds Utd (h)	•	•	•	S	65	•	•	s	S	•	•	•	S	•	•	80	•	45	•	•	•	•	•	•	•	•	•
Nott'm Forest (h)	•	•	•	•	•	•	•	S	•	•	•	•	S	•	•	S	•	•	•	S	•	•	•	•	•	•	•
Middlesbrough (a)	•	•	•	S	•	•	•	•	•	•	•	•	•	53	•	•	•	S	•	•	•	•	•	•	•	•	•

Appearances – UEFA Cup

	1	2	3	4	5	6	7	9	11	12	15	16	17	18	19	20	21	22	23	24	25	26	27	28	30	31	13
Rotor Volgograd (a)	•	71	•	•	•	•	•	•	•	•	•	S	•	- 23	•	•	•	S	S	•	S	-	S	-	-	-	-
Rotor Volgograd (h)	•	-	-	•	•	•	•	S	•	•	-	-	-	-	-	-	26	•	S	S	S	83	•	s	-	-	-

Appearances – Coca Cola Cup

Player Number	1	2	3	4	5	6	7	9	11	12	15	16	17	18	19	20	21	22	23	24	25	26	27	28	30	31	13
York City (h)	•	•	57		•	•	•	•				S		S					67				46	-	-	-	-
York City (a)	•	•		S	•	•	•	S				54		•					67				S	-	-	-	-

Appearances – FA Cup

Player Number	1	2	3	4	5	6	7	9	11	12	15	16	17	18	19	20	21	22	23	24	25	26	27	28	30	31	13
Sunderland (h)	-	-	•		60	•	S	S	•	-	-	-	-	-	•	S	-	66	•	s	•	-	-	-	-	-	-
Sunderland (a)	-	S	•		45	-	S	S	•	-	-	-	-	S	•	-	•	-	S	•	s	-	-	-	-	-	-
Reading (a)	•	•	53		•	-	•	S	-	-	-	-	-	•	•	70	•	•	S	•	-	-	-	-	-	-	-
Man City (h)	•	•	•		•	•	•	•	S	•	-	-	-	•	•	•	S	•	•	S	-	-	-	-	-	-	-
Southampton (h)	•	S	•		•	•	S	•	•	S	-	-	-	•	•	•	S	•	S	•	-	-	-	-	-	-	S
Chelsea (n)	•	S	-		S	•	•	•	•	•	-	-	S	•	•	•	S	•	S	•	-	-	-	-	-	-	S
Liverpool (n)	•	•	-		S	•	•	•	•	•	-	-	S	•	•	89	63	•	•	S	-	-	-	-	-	-	-

Squad Numbers
1 P.Schmeichel, 2 P.Parker, 3 D.Irwin, 4 S.Bruce, 5 L.Sharpe, 6 G.Pallister, 7 E.Cantona, 9 B.McClair, 11 R.Giggs, 12 D.May, 13 T.Coton, 15 G.Tomlinson, 16 R.Keane, 17 A.Cole, 18 S.Davies, 19 N.Butt, 20 G.Neville, 21 P.McGibbon, 22 P.Scholes, 23 P.Neville, 24 D.Beckham, 25 K.Pilkington, 26 C.Casper, 27 T.Cooke, 28 B.Thornley, 30 J.O'Kane, 31 W.Prunier.

S – Sub not used   s – denotes the player substituted

A figure shows the number of minutes played when that player was introduced to the game.

	Arsenal	Aston Villa	Blackburn Rovers	Bolton Wand'	Chelsea	Coventry City	Everton	Leeds United	Liverpool	Manchester City
Arsenal	•	2-0	0-0	2-1	1-1	1-1	1-2	2-1	0-0	3-1
Aston Villa	1-1	•	2-0	1-0	0-1	4-1	1-0	3-0	0-2	0-1
Blackburn Rovers	1-1	1-1	•	3-1	3-0	5-1	0-3	1-0	2-3	2-0
Bolton Wanderers	1-0	0-2	2-1	•	2-1	1-2	1-1	0-2	0-1	1-1
Chelsea	1-0	1-2	2-3	3-2	•	2-2	0-0	4-1	2-2	1-1
Coventry City	0-0	0-3	5-0	0-2	1-0	•	2-1	0-0	0-1	2-1
Everton	0-2	1-0	1-0	1-0	1-1	2-2	•	2-0	1-1	2-0
Leeds United	0-3	2-0	0-0	0-1	1-0	3-1	2-2	•	1-0	0-1
Liverpool	3-1	3-0	3-0	5-2	2-0	0-0	1-2	5-0	•	6-0
Manchester City	0-1	1-0	1-1	1-0	0-1	1-1	0-2	0-0	2-2	•
Manchester United	1-0	0-0	0-0	3-0	1-1	1-0	2-0	1-0	2-2	1-0
Middlesbrough	2-3	0-2	2-0	1-4	2-0	2-1	1-0	1-1	2-1	4-1
Newcastle United	2-0	1-0	1-0	2-1	0-0	3-0	3-2	2-1	2-1	3-1
Nottingham Forest	0-1	1-1	1-5	3-2	0-0	0-0	3-1	1-1	1-0	3-0
QPR	1-1	1-0	0-1	4-2	1-2	1-1	2-5	1-2	1-2	1-0
Sheffield Wednesday	1-0	2-0	2-1	1-0	0-0	4-3	2-2	6-2	1-1	1-1
Southampton	0-0	0-1	1-0	2-2	2-3	1-0	0-0	1-1	1-3	1-1
Tottenham Hotspur	2-1	0-1	2-3	1-0	1-1	3-1	2-1	2-1	1-1	1-1
West Ham United	0-1	1-4	1-1	3-2	1-3	3-2	2-1	1-2	0-0	4-2
Wimbledon	0-3	3-3	1-1		1-1	0-2	2-3	2-4	1-0	3-0

RESULTS 1995-96

	Manchester United	Middlesbrough	Newcastle United	Nottingham Forest	QPR	Sheffield Wednesday	Southampton	Tottenham Hotspur	West Ham United	Wimbledon
Arsenal	1-0	1-1	2-0	1-1	3-0	4-2	4-2	0-0	1-0	1-3
Aston Villa	3-1	0-0	1-1	1-1	4-2	3-2	3-0	2-1	1-1	2-0
Blackburn Rovers	1-2	1-1	2-1	7-0	1-0	3-0	2-1	2-1	4-2	3-2
Bolton Wanderers	0-6	1-1	1-3	1-0	0-1	2-1	0-1	2-3	0-3	1-0
Chelsea	1-4	5-0	1-0	1-0	1-1	0-0	3-0	0-0	1-2	1-2
Coventry City	0-4	0-0	0-1	1-1	1-0	0-1	1-1	2-3	2-2	3-3
Everton	2-3	4-0	1-3	3-0	2-0	2-2	2-0	1-1	3-0	2-4
Leeds United	3-1	0-1	0-1	1-3	1-3	2-0	1-0	1-3	2-0	1-1
Liverpool	2-0	1-0	4-3	4-2	1-0	1-0	1-1	0-0	2-0	2-2
Manchester City	2-3	0-1	3-3	1-1	1-1	2-2	2-1	1-1	2-1	1-0
Manchester United	•	2-0	2-0	5-0	2-1	3-1	4-1	1-0	2-1	3-1
Middlesbrough	0-3	•	1-2	1-0	1-0	2-0	0-0	2-1	4-2	1-2
Newcastle United	0-1	1-0	•	3-1	2-1	1-0	1-0	2-1	3-0	6-1
Nottingham Forest	1-1	1-0	1-1	•	3-0	0-3	1-0	2-3	1-1	4-1
QPR	1-1	1-1	2-3	1-1	•		3-0	1-3	3-0	0-3
Sheffield Wednesday	0-0	0-1	0-2	1-3	0-3	•	2-2	0-0	0-1	2-1
Southampton	3-1	2-1	1-0	3-4	2-0	0-1	•	0-0	0-0	0-0
Tottenham Hotspur	4-1	1-1	1-1	0-1	1-3	1-0	1-0	•	0-1	3-1
West Ham United	0-1	2-0	2-0	1-0	1-0	1-1	2-1	1-1	•	1-1
Wimbledon	2-4	0-0	3-3	1-0	2-1	2-2	1-2	0-1	0-1	•

General Records

Football Alliance

Biggest Home Win:	10-1 *v* Lincoln City	21/11/1891
Biggest Away Win:	6-1 *v* Lincoln City	02/04/1892
Biggest Home Defeat:	1-3 *v* Birmingham St George	14/03/1891
Biggest Away Defeats:	0-7 *v* Grimsby Town	08/02/1890
	2-8 *v* Notts Forest	22/11/1890
Highest Home Attendance:	16,000 *v* Nottingham Forest (1-1)	01/01/1892
Most Appearances:	62 WS Stewart	
Leading Goalscorer:	25 AH Farman	
Most Goals in a Season:	20 R Donaldson	1891/1892
Most Consecutive Wins:	5 31/10/1891 to 12/12/1891	
Most Consecutive Defeats:	5 07/03/1891 to 12/09/1891	
Longest Run Without a Win:	6 21/02/1891 to 12/09/1891	
Longest Unbeaten Run:	15 19/09/1891 to 20/02/1892	

United's longest unbeaten run in the Alliance came immediately after their longest sequence of defeats and their longest run without a win!

Football League

Biggest Home Win:	10-1 *v* Wolverhampton Wanderers	15/10/1892
Biggest Away Win:	7-0 *v* Grimsby Town	26/12/1899
Biggest Home Defeat:	1-7 *v* Newcastle United	10/09/1927
	0-6 *v* Aston Villa	14/03/1914
	v Huddersfield Town	10/09/1930*

* In their next home match on 13th September 1930, United were beaten 7-4 by Newcastle United which made a total of thirteen goals conceded at home in a period of four days! They had also conceded six goals at Chelsea in their previous away game.

Biggest Away Defeat:	0-7 *v* Blackburn Rovers	10/04/1926
	v Aston Villa	27/12/1930
	v Wolverhampton Wanderers	26/12/1931*

* This was United's second consecutive Christmas 7-0 defeat.

Highest Home Attendance:	70,504 *v* Aston Villa (lost 1-3)	27/12/1920
	83,260 *v* Arsenal (1-1)*	17/01/1948

* This game was played at Maine Road and set a record Football League attendance which still stands today

Most Appearances:	604 plus 2 as substitute R Charlton	
Leading Goalscorer:	199	R Charlton
Most Goals in a Season:	32	D Viollet	1959/1960
Most Goals in a Game:	There have been numerous instances of players scoring 4 in a game but nobody has achieved five or more.	
Most Consecutive Wins:	14	15/10/1904 to 03/01/1905
Most Consecutive Defeats:	14	26/04/1930 to 25/10/1930

The 12 consecutive defeats United suffered in this spell from the beginning of the 1930/31 season is still a Football League record for the number of defeats from the opening of a season.

Longest Unbeaten Run:	26	04/02/1956 to 13/10/1956
Longest Run Without a Win:	16	19/04/1930 to 25/10/1930
		03/11/1928 to 09/02/1929

FA Premiership

Biggest Home Win:	9-0 *v* Ipswich Town	4/03/95
Biggest Home Defeat:	0-3 *v* Everton	19/08/93
Biggest Away Win:	6-0 *v* Bolton Wanderers	25/02/96
Biggest Away Defeat:	1-4 *v* Spurs	01/01/96
Highest Home Attendance:	53,926 *v* Nottingham Forest	28/04/96
Lowest Home Attendance:	29,736 *v* Crystal Palace	02/09/92
Most Appearances:	153	D. Irwin
Leading Goalscorer:	53	E. Cantona
Most Goals in a Season:	18	E. Cantona 1993/94
Most Consecutive Wins:	9	05/04/1993 to 18/08/1993
Most Goals in a Game:	5	A. Cole *v* Ipswich Town (h) 4/03/95
Longest Unbeaten Run:	22	19/09/1993 to 26/02/1994
Longest Run without a Win:	7	19/09/1992 to 7/11/1992

Note: In 38 league games between 14/03/1993 and 26/03/1994 United lost once.

FA Cup

Biggest Home Win:	8-0 *v* Yeovil Town – 5th Round	12/02/1949
Biggest Away Win:	8-2 *v* Northampton Town – 5th Round	07/02/1970
Biggest Home Defeat:	2-7 *v* Sheffield Wednesday 4th Round replay	01/02/1961
Biggest Away Defeat:	1-7 *v* Burnley – 1st Rnd replay	13/02/1901
	0-6 *v* Sheffield Wednesday (2nd Round)	20/02/1904

Highest Home Attendance:	82,771 v Bradford Park Avenue 4th Round	
	(at Maine Rd)	29/01/1949
	66,673 v Huddersfield Town 2nd Round	
	(at Old Trafford)	2/02/1924
Most Appearances:	79	R Charlton
Leading Goalscorer:	34	D Law
Most Goals in a Game:	6	G Best v Northampton Town 07/02/1970
Longest Unbeaten Run:	13	10/01/1948 to 26/03/1949
		11/01/94 to 20/05/95
Longest Run Without a Win:	5	12/02/1898 to 28/10/1899
		31/01/1920 to 13/01/1923
		11/01/94 to 20/05/95
		24/01/1931 to 17/01/1934

Between January 1929 and January 1935 United won just one FA Cup tie – a replay against Liverpool. From 18th February 1928 to 16th January 1937 United failed to win a single FA Cup tie at Old Trafford.

Football League Cup

Biggest Home Win:	7-2	v Newcastle United	27/10/1976
Biggest Away Win:	6-2	v Arsenal	28/11/1990
Biggest Home Defeat:	0-3	v Everton	01/12/1976
		v Tottenham Hotspur	25/10/1989
		v York City	20/09/1995
Biggest Away Defeat:	1-5	v Blackpool	14/09/1904

United's team for this game was virtually full strength with nine internationals

Highest Home Attendance:	63,418 v Manchester City (2-2)	17/12/1969
	Semi Final	
Most Appearances:	52	B Robson
Leading Goalscorer:	19	B McClair
Most Goals in a Game:	3	G Hill, M Hughes (twice), B McClair and
		L Sharpe
Longest Unbeaten Run:	10	25/09/1991 to 28/10/1992
Longest Run Without a Win:	5	26/09/1979 to 28/10/1981

UEFA Champions' League (nee Cup)

Biggest Home Win:	10-0 v Anderlecht (at Maine Road)	26/09/1956
Biggest Win at Old Trafford:	7-1 v Waterford	02/10/1968
Biggest Away Win:	6-0 v Shamrock Rovers	25/09/1957

Biggest Home Defeat:	None		
Biggest Away Defeat:	0-4 v A.C. Milan		14/05/58
	0-4 v Barcelona		2/11/94
Highest Home Attendance:	75,598 v Borussia Dortmund (1st Round, 1st		
	Leg) at Maine Road		17/10/1956.
	65,000 v Real Madrid (Semi Final, 2nd Leg)		
	at Old Trafford		25/04/1957
Most Appearances:	35	W Foulkes	
Most Goals:	14	D Law	
Most Goals in a Game:	4	D Viollet v Anderlecht	26/09/56
		D Law v Waterford	02/10/68

Law scored 7 in total during this tie having netted a hat-trick in the First Leg.

Most Consecutive Wins:	6	22/09/1965 to 09/03/1966
Longest Unbeaten Run:	6	22/09/1965 to 09/03/1966
		20/04/1966 to 28/02/1968
		24/01/1968 to 13/11/1969
Longest Run Without a Win:	4	28/09/1994 to 23/11/94

European Cup-Winners' Cup

Biggest Home Win:	6-1 v Willem II	15/10/1963

United set their record score in this competition in their first home game – as they had done in the European Cup.

Biggest Away Win:	3-1 v Legia Warsaw	10/04/1991
Biggest Home Defeat:	None	
Biggest Away Defeat:	0-5 v SC Lisbon	18/03/1964

This result overturned a 4-1 lead that United held from the First Leg.

Biggest Home Attendance:	60,000 v SC Lisbon (won 4-1)		26/02/1964
Most Appearances:	16	M Hughes	
Leading Goalscorer:	6	D Law	
Most Goals in a Game:	3	D Law v Willem II	15/10/1963
		D Law v SC Lisbon	26/02/1964
Most Consecutive Wins:	4	19/09/1990 to 07/11/1990	
Longest Unbeaten Run:	11	19/09/1990 to 02/10/1991	
Longest Run Without a Win:	4	Galatasary (a). Barce;pma (h). barce;pma	
		(a), IFK Gothenburg (a), in Group A 1994/95	

Biggest Home Win: 6-1 v Djurgardens   27/10/1964

This completed United's unusual hat-trick of recording their biggest home win in each of the three major European tournaments in their first home game in each respective competition.

Biggest Away Win:	6-1 v Borussia Dortmund	11/11/1964
Biggest Home Defeat:	None	
Biggest Away Defeat:	0-3 v Juventus	03/11/1976
Highest Home Attendance:	59,000 v Juventus (won 1-0)	20/10/1976
Most Appearances:	11 R Charlton	
Leading Goalscorer:	8 R Charlton	
Most Goals in a Game:	3 D Law v Djurgardens	27/10/1964
	R Charlton v Borussia Dortmund	11/11/1964
Most Consecutive Wins:	3 27/10/1964 to 02/12/1964	
Most Consecutive Defeats:	2 06/06/1965 to 16/06/1965	

Both defeats were by Hungarian side, Ferencvaros who thus became the first and, to date, only team to defeat United in consecutive European matches. The second defeat came in a play-off after the first two matches had failed to produce a winner.

Longest Unbeaten Run:	9 23/09/1964 to 31/05/1965	

These were United's first nine games in the competition.

Longest Run Without a Win:	5 30/11/1976 to 29/09/1982	
	5 20/03/1985 to 26/09/1995	

Pot Pourri Facts

Obituaries

Johnny Carey

Johnny Carey passed away on 23rd August 1995 at the age of 75. One of United's all time greats, ranking alongside the names of Charlton, Law, Edwards and Best, Carey captained the Reds to their 1948 FA Cup Final success and was a member of the first Busby Championship winning side in 1951/52 playing in all but four of their matches that season.

Carey arrived at Old Trafford in 1936 for £250 from Irish club St James Gate and made his league debut in 1937/38 against Southampton in a game that resulted in a 1-2 home defeat that was to bely what glories lay in store for him. He went to make sixteen appearances in that first campaign, scoring three goals, and eventually played in ten different positions, including goal, in a United career that was reduced to 344 games in a United shirt by World War Two.

Away from United, Carey created a record that will surely stand for all time when, in 1946, he played for two different countries. Several other players, of course, have done this but not in the space of three days as was the case with Carey! On 28th September he played for Northern Ireland against England and on the last day of the month he turned out, once more against England, for the Republic of Ireland. In all, Carey won seven caps for Northern Ireland and 29 for the Republic but perhaps his biggest honour was being given the captaincy of The Rest of Europe side that played Great Britain in 1947.

When his playing days were finished, he stayed on initially at Old Trafford as a coach but soon wanted to be his own boss. He left for Blackburn Rovers where he was in charge from 1953 to 1958 before leaving for Everton where he spent three years. He then moved to Leyton Orient (whom he guided to an unlikely presence in the top flight) until taking over at Nottingham Forest in 1963 where, in 1966/67, his side pushed United all the way to finishing line as the Reds won the title that was to take them to European glory the following year.

United Playing Career

	League		Cup		Total	
	App	Gls	App	Gls	App	Gls
1937/38	16	3	3	1	19	4
1938/39	32	6	2	0	34	6
1939/40	2	1	0	0	2	1
1945/46	0	0	4	0	4	0
1946/47	31	0	2	0	33	0
1947/48	37	1	6	0	43	1

1948/49	41	1	7	0	48	1
1949/50	38	1	5	0	43	1
1950/51	39	0	4	0	43	0
1951/52	38	3	1	0	39	3
1952/53	32	1	4	0	36	1
Total	306	17	38	1	344	18

Alan Gibson

The death of Alan Gibson, Vice President of the club, in July 1995 saw Manchester United kick off the season without a member of the Gibson family at the club for the first time in 64 years. His father, James, probably saved the club from extinction in 1931 for the club had struggled to survive since the death four years previously of John Davies who had been United's benefactor for many years.

In December 1931, both the financial and playing sides of the club were at their lowest ebb with the club's bankers, The National Provincial Bank, Spring Gardens, Manchester refusing any further loans. There was no cash to pay the players their wages and Christmas was fast approaching. Mr Gibson Snr stepped in with £2,000 to pay the players and some of the debt.

Alan Gibson was introduced to the Board by his father in 1948 and remained a Director until 1984 when he became Vice President. The club issued a statement saying "He was the most gentle of men and always supportive of the managers. He always found something positive to say and never criticised. Alan Gibson was the perfect ambassador for Manchester United and he will be sorely missed".

The New Intake

Manchester United took on fifteen young hopefuls at the start of 1995/96. The trainees came from all over the country but the bulk of them hailed from United's own doorstep including two from Trafford itself.

To enable the reader to follow their progress, the youngsters from the Manchester area were, in addition to Trafford's Gary Bickerton and Jonathon Phillips, David Brown from Bolton, Jamie Wood (Salford), Danny Higginbotham (Manchester) and Jamie Byers (Tameside). The first four named are all forwards whilst the rest are defenders.

Another defender, Elliot Dickman hails from Hexham whilst the North East contingent is completed by wingers Stuart Brightwell of Easington and North Cleveland's Gavin Naylor.

The Midlands provides goalkeeper Christopher Calderone from Derby, defender John Curtis of Nuneaton for whom a massive future in the game is predicted, and midfielder Ryan Ford (Worksop). The contingent was completed by defender Matthew Wicks, the son of the former Chelsea defender, Steve Wicks, Ross Millard another defender from the Bristol area and Mark Wilson, an attacker from Scunthorpe. Matthew Wicks subsequently left to join Arsenal.

United 1995 Champions

United may not have won any trophies in 1995 but they were the year's Champions!

A table of all league games played by the twenty clubs comprising the FAPL for season 1995/96 (including, where appropriate, the games played by the promoted sides in the Endsleigh League First Division) during the calender year 1995 shows United gained five more points in the year than nearest rivals Newcastle United. The Reds also won more league games in 1995 than any other club, scored more goals and conceded fewer than anybody else whilst only Nottingham Forest could match United's total of six defeats. Not a bad record for a club supposedly below their best.

At the other end of the table, incidentally, were Manchester City with seven fewer points than any other FAPL club!

Club	P	W	D	L	F	A	Pts
Manchester United	41	24	11	6	74	32	83
Newcastle United	41	23	9	9	67	41	78
Nottingham Forest	40	19	15	6	67	47	72
Leeds United	41	20	12	9	58	38	72
Blackburn Rovers	42	21	8	13	49	49	71
Liverpool	40	19	10	11	61	36	68
Middlesbrough	42	18	13	11	51	37	65
Tottenham Hotspurs	41	16	16	9	55	45	64
Aston Villa	39	16	11	12	49	38	59
Arsenal	41	15	12	14	54	42	57
Everton	42	14	15	13	53	44	57
Chelsea	41	12	18	11	42	48	54
QPR	41	15	6	20	43	52	51
Wimbledon	41	12	12	17	51	50	50
West Ham United	39	12	12	15	46	52	48
Bolton Wanderers	42	12	11	19	58	56	47
Southampton	40	10	17	13	55	47	47
Sheffield Wednesday	40	10	12	17	48	57	43
Coventry City	40	10	13	17	50	66	43
Manchester City	42	12	11	19	48	56	36

Maine Men Switch

Tony Coton became only the eleventh Manchester City player to transfer directly to United when he completed his £400,000 move to Old Trafford in January 1996. Seven of these players moved in the first six years of the century with four of them crossing the city after a bribes scandal hit the Blues in 1906.

Before Coton moved, the last City 'keeper to transfer to Old Trafford was Len Langford in 1934 after he appeared for City in the 1933 FA Cup Final.

The full list of players to move from City to United is as follows:

Date	Player	Appearances for United
May 1902	Daniel Hurst	21
June 1902	Fred Williams	10
August 1902	Thomas Read	42
December 1906	James Bannister	61
December 1906	Herberet Burgess	52
December 1906	Billy Meredith	332
December 1906	Sandy Turnbull	245
December 1931	Bill Ridding	44
June 1934	Len Langford	15
September 1972	Wyn Davies	17

Did You Know?

That United's Old Trafford ground has a 55,000 gallon underground water tank which is used to water the pitch? The system it feeds into is so designed that for every 500 gallons of water pumped on to the playing surface, about 450 gallons seep back into the underground reservoir to be used again.

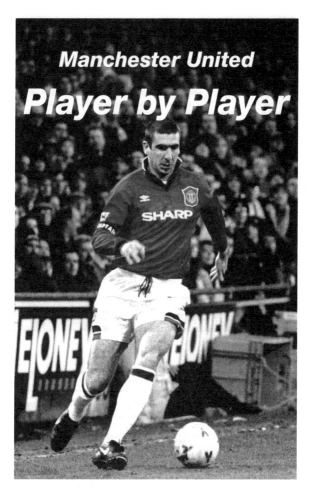

Manchester United

Player by Player

SHARP

David BECKHAM

Date of Birth: 2nd May 1975, Leytonstone, Essex

A London lad whose parents are now amongst the biggest Man United fanatics. Beckham is another of the famed 'Class of 92' that won the FA Youth Cup to make the breakthrough to the big time and it was his first goal in the FA Cup that took United to Wembley in 95/6. Like John O'Kane, Chris Casper, Gary Neville, Nicky Butt and Ben Thornley from the Class of 92, Beckham also played in the following year's FA Youth Cup Final.

He made his first team bow at Brighton in the Second Round, 1st Leg tie of the Coca Cola Cup competition in September 1992 but had to wait another two years for his next taste of action when making the starting line-up for another Second Round, 1st Leg League Cup tie against Port Vale and soon afterwards made his first European start a scoring one when hitting one of United's four goals against Galatasary. Beckham made his first FAPL start against Leeds United in a 0-0 draw at Old Trafford. With the departure of Andrei Kanchelskis to Everton, the opportunity arrived for the youngster to fill in on the right-hand side although Alex Ferguson reckons the player's best position is in a more central role.

Beckham already has international recognition at Under 21, gaining his first cap at that level alongside Phil Neville against Brazil in June 1995, to supplement the caps he won at Under 18.

Appearance Record

	Appearances			Goals		
	Lge	FLC	FAC	Lge	FLC	FAC
94/95	2/2	3	1/1			
95/96	26/7	2	3	7		1

Estimated value: £3,000,000

Nicky BUTT

Date of Birth: 21st January 1975, Manchester

First came to prominence with the Manchester Schoolboys side and his early promise at Youth level was fulfilled when playing in the 'Class of '92' that won the FA Youth Cup. Further Youth honours came his way when he played alongside club mates Chris Casper, Gary Neville and Paul Scholes in the England Under 18 side that participated in the ninth European Under 18 Tournament in 1992/93. After helping England beat France (2-0), Holland (4-1) and Spain (5-1), Butt was unable to play in the Final at Nottingham Forest's City Ground due to injury and had to watch from the stands as his team mates beat Turkey 1-0. Made his first team debut on 21st November 1992 in the home game against Oldham Athletic when he came on as substitute but had to wait almost a further twelve months before making another appearance, again as substitute, in October 1993 against Spurs. His third appearance, also as substitute, was a dream come true for the youngster as it was in the FA Cup semi final at Wembley against Oldham Athletic. 1994/95 saw his graduation with a first full start coming in United's 4-2 win over IFK Gothenburg on 14th September 1994 and his first start in the FAPL coincided with another 4-2 victory, this time at Blackburn Rovers. Strangely, Butt is virtually the same weight as when he first arrived at Old Trafford at the age of fifteen. Although slight of build he is a tigerish tackler but needs to improve on his distribution whilst Youth Coach Eric Harrison professes to his only disappointment regarding Butt as being his difficulty in finding the net at senior level. "He was a regular scorer at Youth and Reserve level and should have had more goals by now in the first team".

Butt, however, needs to spruce up his bad boy image both on and off the pitch. Away from the game he has been in trouble on a couple of occasions with the law whilst on the pitch his disciplinary record for one so young is open to considerable improvement. He is now in very real danger of becoming a victim of his own making in the eyes of referees.

Appearance Record

	Appearances			Goals			
	Lge	FLC	FAC	Lge	FLC	FAC	FAC
92/93	0/1						
93/94	0/1		0/1				
94/95	11/10	3	3/1	1			
95/96	31/1		7	2			1

Estimated value: £3,000,000

Eric CANTONA

Date of Birth: 24th May 1966, Paris

Many critics at the time considered his signing in November 1992 from Leeds United in exchange for £1.2m as confirmation that Alex Ferguson had finally flipped his lid in the frustration of not being able to land the coveted title. The signing of the wayward genius seemed totally out of character for Ferguson who had previously always erred on the side of caution. It was, however, to prove to be the final piece of the jigsaw as United with the talented, but erratic Frenchman, in their side mounted a charge up the table that was to prove unstoppable. The value of Cantona's presence in the side can be gauged by the fact that of his first sixty appearances in United colours, they only lost twice – a remarkable statistic. But

Cantona had equal cause to be thankful to United. At last it seemed, after a nomadic football career, that the Frenchman had found peace of mind, at last playing on a stage he thought worthy of his skills. But after early indications that he had put his disciplinary problems behind him, Cantona was sent off at Galatasary, Swindon and Arsenal in 1993/94 and then at Rangers in a pre-season game at the beginning of the 94/95 campaign.

Then came his moment of infamy at Crystal Palace and a nine month suspension from which he emerged a different character and all the better for it. The final acceptance of his reformed character came from the Football Writer's Association in April 1996 when they voted the Frenchman 'Footballer of the Year'.

He had arrived at Leeds in February 1992 on loan from Nimes via a week's training at Sheffield Wednesday, but the move was soon made permanent in a deal worth £900,000 and with him in their line up, Leeds overtook United to pinch the Championship from under the noses of the Old Trafford faithful. Cantona began his career with Auxerre in 1986 before moving to Marseille during 1988 in a £2.2m deal that was not successful with Cantona making just 40 appearances and spending time on loan at both Montpellier and Bordeaux before moving on to Nimes for £1m in June 1991. Eight months later he was at Leeds and nine months further down the road he was at Old Trafford where it seemed until his sendings off he had found stability for the first time. Even his international career led a chequered existence with him walking out of the French set up at one stage but one thing is for sure, United fans will always have a place in their heart for the man who became the only Frenchman to win English Championship medals with two different clubs

Previous Clubs and Appearance Record

Clubs	Signed	Fee	Appearances			Goals		
			Lge	FLC	FAC	Lge	FLC	FAC
Auxerre			81	23				
Martiques		loan	–	–				
Marseille	1988	£2.2m	55	13				
Bordeaux		loan	11	6				
Montpellier		loan	33	10				
Nimes	1991	£1m	n/k	n/k				
Leeds Utd	2/92	£900,000	16			3		
FA Premier League Record								
Leeds Utd			13	1		6		
Man Utd	11/92	£1.2m	21/1			9		
	93/94		34	5	5	18	1	4
	94/95		21		1	12		1
	95/96		30	1	7	14		5

Because of his unpredictable nature it is difficult to assess how much a club would be prepared to risk on someone who could walk out after a few weeks. Without this side of his nature Cantona would be in the £10m class but anybody buying him from Old Trafford would almost certainly only want to pay a down payment and then so much per game.

Cantona's Crime Sheet

The uproar which followed Eric Cantona's attack on the Crystal Palace spectator in January was not, of course, the first time that controversy had stalked the Frenchman. His full catalogue of disputes reads as follows:

1987	Fined heavily by Auxerre for punching his own goalkeeper Bruno Martini, giving him a black eye in the process.
1988	Banned for a year by the French Football Federation after calling the former international team coach Henri Michel a "shitbag".
1989	Suspended indefinitely by Marseille after kicking the ball into the crowd, throwing his shirt at the referee and storming off the pitch. Loaned out to Bordeaux and Montpellier.
1990	Smashed his boots into Montpellier team mate Jean Claude Lemoult and was banned for ten days by the club, prompting him to return to Marseille.
1991	Sold to Nimes where he was banned for three games after throwing the ball at the referee. When he appeared at the disciplinary hearing he muttered "Idiots". When asked to repeat himself he walked up to each member of the three man board in turn and shouted "Idiot". The ban was increased to two months and Cantona immediately announced his retirement from the game.
1991	Brought to England by Trevor Francis for a trial at Sheffield Wednesday. Bad weather limited his 'trial' to a six aside game on plastic and when Francis said he wanted to see him play in a eleven a side match under proper conditions Cantona said he was insulted and left for Leeds.
1993	Sent off at the end of United's game against Galatasary in Turkey for accusing referee Kurt Rothlisberger of cheating. Involved in the tunnel in an altercation with the Turkish police. Received a four match European ban.
March 1994	Sent off at Swindon and Arsenal in successive games resulting in a five match ban.
June 1994	Cantona is ejected from the Pasadena Rose Bowl for throwing a punch at an official before the World Cup semi-final between Brazil and Sweden on which he was supposed to be acting as summariser for French TV.
August 1994	Sent off against Glasgow Rangers in a curtain raiser to the season at Ibrox Park. Receives a three match ban for his fourth dismissal in nine months.

January 1995   Is dismissed at Crystal Palace and then becomes embroiled in his infamous punch up. Banned for the rest of the season and fined £20,000. The Football Association later add a further £10,000 fine and extend the ban to 30th September. A Court Hearing then sentences Cantona to two weeks in prison for the attack. Amid uproar, Cantona is freed on bail and later has the sentence reduced to 120 hours community service.

Estimated value: £7,500,000

Andrew COLE

Date of Birth: 19th October 1971, Nottingham

Alex Ferguson and Kevin Keegan surprised everybody when the *Magpies*' boss agreed to sell his leading goalscorer to United in exchange for Keith Gillespie and a cool £6m. Cole first came to prominence in the Nottingham Schools side and in December 1985 became an Associated Schoolboy with Arsenal for whom he made his Football League debut against Sheffield United in December 1990 when he came on as a substitute. In May 1992 he represented England at Under 21 level against Czechoslovakia but just two months later was allowed to join Bristol City for £500,000 still having made only the one substitute appearance for the London club. Prior to his move to Bristol, Cole scored three times in thirteen games whilst on loan to Fulham. But it was at Bristol that his career really began to take off with 20 goals in 41 games prompting interest from Kevin Keegan who wanted some more fire power to see his side's promotion bid sealed. Cole joined the Geordies in March 1993 for £1.75m and promptly picked up a First Division Championship medal. His following campaign proved to be nothing short of sensational as he became the first player to score 40 league goals in a season for Newcastle and he finished the country's leading goalscorer to also land the PFA's Young Player of the Year award. Strange to relate, then, that at the time of his transfer to United Cole had not scored in his last nine outings for Newcastle. On joining the Reds, Cole became the first United player to ever score five times in a league game, a feat he performed against Ipswich Town, and soon secured his first England cap against Uruguay in March.

Cole has, however, still to convince many people that he is worth the money paid for him as he has not scored as many goals for United as he should have done given the service he has been given.

176

Previous Clubs and Appearance Record

Clubs	Signed	Fee	Appearances			Goals		
			Lge	FLC	FAC	Lge	FLC	FAC
Arsenal	10/89	---	0/1	-	-	-	-	-
Fulham	5/91	Loan	13	-	-	3	-	-
Bristol City	7/92	£0.5m	41	-	-	20	-	-
Newcastle Utd	3/93	£1.75m	64/1	5	4	59	6	1
FA Premier League Record								
Newcastle United	93/94		40			34		
	94/95		18	5	1	9	-	-
Man United	1/95	£7m	17/1	-	-	12	-	-
	95/96		32/2	1	7	11	-	2

Estimated value: £7,000,000

Ryan Joseph GIGGS

Date of Birth: 29th November 1973, Cardiff

Although born in Cardiff, Ryan Giggs first came under the eye of United fans when he captained England Schoolboys against Scotland at Old Trafford under the name of Ryan Wilson having been brought up in Manchester when his father, good enough at his chosen sport to play for Great Britain, moved to the area to take up Rugby League after a successful Rugby Union career. The young Wilson was actually first spotted by Manchester City and played for one of their junior sides but it was to United that the gifted youngster turned on leaving school. At about this time his mother changed her name to Giggs and that name is now the one on everybody's lips. Giggs was quickly recognised as something very special and was elevated through the ranks at a surprisingly quick rate. He made his first team debut on 2nd March 1991 at the age of 17 when he came on as substitute against Everton in a 2-0 home defeat. By the following season he was a regular, making 38 league appearances and winning a League Cup medal against Notts Forest, a month before he won a FA Youth Cup winners medal against Crystal Palace. Giggs became the youngest ever Welsh full international when he played against Germany on 16th October 1991 aged 17 years 321 days to complete an unusual quartet of home country *youngest* records for United. Duncan Edwards had become the youngest player to play for England, Northern Ireland's Norman Whiteside was the youngest ever player to appear in the Final stages of the World Cup during his days at Old Trafford and the youngest player ever to turn out for Scotland, Denis Law, also later played for the Reds. Giggs also set another record when he became the first player to win the PFA's Young Player of the Year Award in successive seasons, a feat he achieved in 1992 and 1993. He also won the Barclay's Bank Young Eagle of the Year award in 1992.

Previous Clubs and Appearance Record

Clubs	Signed	Fee	Appearances			Goals		
			Lge	FLC	FAC	Lge	FLC	FAC
Man Utd	12/90		33+7	5+3	1	5	3	
FA Premier League Record								
	92/93		40+1	2	2	9		2
	93/94		32+6	6+2	7	13	3	1
	94/95		29		6+1	1		2
	95/96		30/3	2	7	11		2

No British club could surely afford to prise Giggs away from Old Trafford but Continental clubs would also be looking at the youngster's form towards the end of the season when he didn't really look the finished article. His youth would boost the fee, however, although not to the reported £10m that Italian clubs were said to be prepared to pay.

Estimated value: £13,500,000

Roy KEANE

Date of Birth: 10 August 1971, Cork

Roy Keane set a record for a transfer deal between English clubs when signing for United in the summer of 1993 for a £3.75m fee from Nottingham Forest. It gave Forest a massive profit on their lay out of £25,000 which it had cost them to bring the former amateur boxer over from Republic of Ireland outfit Cobh Ramblers. Manager Alex Ferguson saw his costliest player as the replacement for his ageing midfield general Bryan Robson, but the younger Keane looked far from that in his early games for United. He was quite definitely not match fit and looked positively overweight during the pre match friendlies and people were quick to question the wisdom of the outlay. As the season progressed, however, Keane's importance to the cause became apparent with his ability not only to win the ball but to then do something constructive with it. Equally vital Keane seems to have developed the knack of arriving late from deep positions to score goals, much like Robson. Having brought Keane over from the comparative obscurity of Cobh Ramblers in 1990, Brian Clough quickly pushed him into his first team line up and in his first full season Keane had a FA Cup runners-up medal after Spurs beat Forest 2-1 after extra-time. The following season he had another runners-up medal when Forest were beaten at Wembley in the League Cup Final by United but Forest did win the

Zenith Data Systems Cup that year which led to the honours laden United team nick naming Keane 'ZDS'. He was, of course, to have the last laugh on most of his colleagues when he was one of only three United players to participate in the 1994 World Cup Finals in the USA. Keane, once at Forest, had not taken long to attract the attention of the Republic of Ireland's team boss, Jack Charlton, and he won his first cap against Chile on 22nd May 1991.

Previous Clubs and Appearance Record

Clubs	Signed	Fee	Appearances			Goals		
			Lge	FLC	FAC	Lge	FLC	FAC
Notts Forest	5/90	£25,000	74	12	14	16	5	2
FA Premier League Record								
Notts Forest	92/93		42	5	4	6	1	1
Man Utd	93/94		34/3	6/1	6	5	-	1
	94/95		23/1	1	6/1	2	-	-
	95/96		29	-/1	7	6	-	-

Thought by many to be overpriced when bought for £3.75m but has since proved his worth and would now fetch a price well in advance of that figure.

Estimated value: £8,000,000

Denis Joseph IRWIN

Date of Birth: 31st October 1965, Cork

An established international and an important part of United's set up, he made his start by way of the junior ranks at Leeds United, making his debut against Fulham at Elland Road on 21st January 1984 just three months after signing professional forms. After playing some 80 games for the Yorkshire club he received a free transfer in the summer of 1986 from Leeds to Oldham Athletic and is quick to acknowledge the part played in his career by Oldham's Joe Royle and his assistant Willie Donachie. He became a vital part of the best team Oldham ever had and appeared in their 1990 League Cup Final defeat at the hands of Nottingham Forest. In the same season Oldham had two titanic duels against United in the semi-final of the FA Cup and Irwin impressed the United management throughout that campaign. By the end of the summer Ferguson had landed Irwin and he was to play in United's League Cup Finals in 1991 and 1992 to become the only player to appear in the first three League Cup Finals of the 1990's. He was later to make it four League Cup Finals in five years when playing against Aston Villa. By the time he left Boundary Park he was game short of 200 appearances. He had been signed as a right back, a position he plays in regularly when on international duty, and it was in that position that he made his debut for the Reds in August 1990 when United enjoyed a 2-0 home win over Coventry City. Ferguson, however, was struggling with his left back position with Mal Donaghy, Clayton Blackmore, a young Lee Sharpe, and Lee Martin all trying and failing to hold their place in that position. Paul Parker arrived from QPR, ostensibly as a central defender but he was soon converted to right back with Irwin asked to switch to the problematic left back slot, a position he has held ever since for United despite playing right back for his country! He made his international debut just after his move to Old Trafford on 12th September 1990 in Dublin against Morocco and has been first choice ever since and one of only three players to represent United in the 1994 World Cup Finals. The full caps won by Irwin complete the full set as he had already played for his country at School, Youth and Under 21 levels.

Previous Clubs and Appearance Record

Clubs	Signed	Fee	Appearances			Goals		
			Lge	FLC	FAC	Lge	FLC	FAC
Leeds United	10/83		72	5	3	1		
Oldham Athletic	5/86		167	19	13	4	3	
Man Utd	6/90	£625,000	70/2	14/1	6	4		
FA Premier League Record								
	92/93		40	3	3	5		
	93/94		42	8/1	7	2		2
	94/95		40	2	7	2		4
	95/96		31	6	1	1		

Estimated value: £3,500,000

Brian John McCLAIR

Date of Birth: 8th December 1963, Bellshill

One of the few Scots currently on United's books, McClair joined the Old Trafford set up in 1987 for £850,000 after Celtic had originally been pushing for a fee of £2m. Whilst with Celtic he had netted 99 goals in 145 league appearances after joining the Glasgow club from Motherwell for £100,000 in 1983. Strangely, after dropping out of University to concentrate on making a career in football, McClair had failed to make the grade with his first club, Aston Villa, who were later to beat United in the 1994 Coca Cola Cup Final. After being leading goalscorer in all four seasons he was with Celtic, McClair immediately hit the goal trail at Old Trafford becoming, in his first season at the club, the first Red since George Best to hit twenty League goals in a campaign. However, after the arrival back home of United's prodigal son, Mark Hughes, McClair found goalscoring a lot more difficult and was gradually withdrawn to a more midfield role but still completed a century of goals in the United cause in the last game of the 1991/92 season against

Spurs after making his debut at the Dell in a 2-2 draw. McClair played in all three of United's League Cup appearances in the nineties but his first winners medal with the club was in the 1990 FA Cup Final against Crystal Palace quickly followed by his place in the successful European Cup-winners Cup Final side. He won the first of thirty caps against Luxembourg in 1987 shortly before his move to United and was an ever present in the United side that regained the Championship in 1993. With the emergence of Giggs, the signing of Cantona, and the return from illness of Lee Sharpe, however, his role in 1993/94 was mainly as substitute and, given his list of success, it is a great tribute to his loyalty that he stayed throughout a season where he could have commanded a regular first team spot in almost any other FA Premiership side. Alex Ferguson said of him *"If sides were made up of thirteen players out on the pitch, he would be playing every game"*. McClair was voted Scottish Player of the Year in 1987.

Previous Clubs and Appearance Record

Clubs	Signed	Fee	Appearances			Goals		
			Lge	FLC	FAC	Lge	FLC	FAC
Aston Villa	1980	--	-	-	-	-	-	-
Motherwell	1981	--	39			15		
Celtic	1983	£100,000	145			99		
Man Utd	1987	£850,000	190/3	28	24	70	14	11
FA Premier League Record								
	92/93		41/1	3	3	9		
	93/94		12/14	6/1	1/4	1	4	1
	94/95		34/5	3	6/1	5	1	2
	95/96		12/10	1	-	3	-	-

Estimated value: £850,000

Gary NEVILLE

Date of Birth: 18th February 1975, Bury

The youngster first came to prominence as captain of the successful 'Class of 92' that captured the FA Youth Cup but was destined to be a professional sportsman from a much earlier age. His father, Neville Neville, is Commercial manager at Bury FC where his mother is Club Secretary whilst his sister, Alison, is an England international at Netball. Adding to the family's sporting links is younger brother Phil who played alongside Gary against Sheffield Wednesday to become the first pair of brothers to play in the same United side since the Greenhoffs some twenty years earlier. His Wembley appearance in the FA Cup Final was his first game on the hallowed turf and was followed a week later by his father and mother visiting the world famous stadium with Bury in the Third Division play-offs. Brother Phil had already beaten the three of them to it by playing there for England Schoolboys.

Neville made his FAPL debut for the Reds in the final home game of 93/94 against Coventry City but had already made three brief appearances as substitute in European competition. Injury to Paul Parker in 94/95 gave Neville the opportunity to stake his place for a first team position and he grabbed it to such an extent that by the end of the campaign Terry Venables had included him in his international squad.

The following season saw Neville become a regular in the England set up where he was joined in the squad by younger brother Phil. For the record book, the last pair of brothers from the same club to play together for England was Frank and Fred Forman. The Nottingham Forest players appeared three times together in 1899 against Ireland, Wales and Scotland, enjoying a 100% record. The last pair of brothers to play together for their club in an FA Cup Final and for England were the Heron brothers in 1876.

Like his younger brother Phil, Gary was a talented cricketer in addition to his football skills and only missed out on playing for his country at schoolboy level in the summer sport when he broke a finger in the final trial match whilst captaining the North of England.

Appearance Record

	Appearances			Goals		
	Lge	FLC	FAC	Lge	FLC	FAC
93/94	1	-	-	-	-	-
94/95	16/2	2/1	4	-	-	-
95/96	30/1	5/1	1	-	-	-

Estimated value: £3,000,000

Phil Neville

Date of Birth: 21st January 1977, Bury

Although the beginning of 1995/96 saw England Coach Terry Venables rate Gary Neville the best full back in the country, the progress made by his younger brother Phil suggests that before long, Gary may not be the best full back in the family let alone the country! Like his elder brother, Phil is a talented all round sportsman who has already represented England at both cricket and football and he was offered a contract at the other Old Trafford as a cricketer after captaining England at Under 14 and Under 15 levels. But he was also playing for England Schoolboys at soccer and opted for a career in football which has proved to be the right decision.

The 1994/95 campaign proved to be a big break through for the younger of the Neville's with him captaining United's Youth team to the FA Youth Cup whilst making his first team debut against Wrexham in the FA Cup. He went on to make his league debut in the Derby match at Maine Road but made only one more league appearance that term when he came on as substitute against Sheffield Wednesday. He was, however, being groomed for bigger things and won his first Under 21 cap against Brazil in June 95 alongside team mate David Beckham just weeks after winning the last of his Under 18 caps! He had also won some eleven Under 16 caps. He won his first full cap against China in May 1996 when he and Gary became the first pair of brothers to play together for England since the Charltons some 26 years previously. Due to the numerous injuries to United defenders during the course of 1995/96 Phil was given his chance and has never looked back proving to be a deadly crosser of the ball and looks to have a big future ahead of him.

Appearance Record

| | Appearances | | | Goals | | |
	Lge	FLC	FAC	Lge	FLC	FAC
94/95	1/1	-	1	-	-	-
95/96	21/3	1/1	6/1	-	-	-

Estimated value: £3,000,000

Gary Andrew PALLISTER

Date of Birth: 30th June 1965, Ramsgate

When United signed Gary Pallister in August 1989 the fee of £2.3m was not only a club record but a British record. His early games at Old Trafford suggested to many people that he had been overpriced but once he was settled in and, perhaps even more importantly, the team began winning, Pallister went on to prove that he has been a sound investment. His early days were spent in non-league football with Billingham Town and Middlesbrough were the first full-time club to show interest in him. He joined Middlesbrough in November 1984 making his debut for them in August 1985 at Wimbledon in a 3-0 defeat. The Ayresome Park club, however, were in bad state at that time and were relegated that season to Division Three with Pallister going on loan to Darlington for whom he would have signed had the Feethams outfit been able to afford the £4,000 fee! He returned to Middlesbrough and was a virtual regular as they bounced straight back up with a club record points total of 94 to finish runners-up in 1986/87. By 1988 he had made his international debut against Holland and had also played against Saudi Arabia when United signed him. He made his United debut in a dreadful 2-0 home defeat by Norwich but by the end of his first season in United colours he was the proud owner of a FA Cup winners medal. He was also a member of the United sides that appeared in three League Cup Finals in four years and lifted the European Cup-winners Cup in Rotterdam. After his move to Old Trafford he lost his England place but when his

183

form took an upturn along with United's, he came back into international reckoning with a substitute appearance against Cameroon in 1991 and since 1993 has been a regular member of the England set up to take his number of caps to well into double figures. Pallister was voted the PFA's Player of the Year in 1992.

Previous Clubs and Appearance Record

Clubs	Signed	Fee	Appearances			Goals		
			Lge	FLC	FAC	Lge	FLC	FAC
Middlesbrough	11/84	--	156	10	10	5	1	
Darlington	10/85	loan	7					
Man Utd	8/89	£2.3m	108/3	20	14	4		
FA Premier League Record								
	92/93		42	3	3	1		
	93/94		41	9	7	1		
	94/95		42	2	7	2		2
	95/96		21	2	3	1		

Many said United paid over the odds for Pallister but they have had the best out of him for some time now. Still looking as strong as ever and still has a good number of years service left in him.

Estimated value: £3,800,000

Peter Boleslaw SCHMEICHEL

Date of Birth: 18th November 1963, Gladsaxe, Denmark

With respect to Les Sealey who was United's Number 1 when Alex Ferguson plunged for Peter Schmeichel in August 1991, the arrival of the Great Dane solved what has traditionally been a problem position at Old Trafford. Whilst truly great 'keepers such as Frank Swift and Bert Trautmann had prospered at rivals Manchester City, United had always struggled, by and large, in the custodian stakes. Paddy Roche, Pat Dunne, Dave Gaskell, and Ronnie Briggs are just some names that crop up in discussion about United 'keepers but there can be no arguing about Schmeichel's position as the best United 'keeper ever. When Alex Ferguson signed him in August 1991 for £850,000 Schmeichel was already an established Danish international but his best was still to come. After helping United to win the League Cup against Forest in his first season, Schmeichel was to become one of the stars of the 1992 European Nation's Championships when Denmark were let in by the backdoor just days prior to the start of the Championships. The fighting in Yugoslavia brought about the decision to expel them with the Danes taking their place. He kept a clean sheet against England in the Group matches and against Germany in the Final itself to become the first ever United player to win a

European Nations' medal. He kept clean sheets in his first four games for the Reds and seventeen in the League in his first season, a figure he bettered by one in United's FA Premier Championship success the following campaign. As well as stopping goals, however, he has also set up on more than one occasion, goals with his magnificent throws to beyond the half way line. Indeed, the extrovert character was seen marauding in the opposing penalty area in the last seconds of the Old Trafford game against Blackburn as United desperately sought an equaliser!

Previous Clubs and Appearance Record

Clubs	Signed	Fee	Appearances			Goals		
			Lge	FLC	FAC	Lge	FLC	FAC
Man Utd	8/91	£850,000	40	6	3			
FA Premier League Record								
	92/93		42	3	3			
	93/94		40	7	7			
	94/95		32		7			
	95/96		36	1	6			

Possibly United's best buy in terms of value for money. Now acknowledged as the best in Europe if not the world and only the fact that there are so many good number 1's about would keep his value below £4m.

Estimated value: £5,000,000

Paul SCHOLES

Date of Birth: 16th November 1974, Salford

Paul Scholes was not, as many think, one of the famed 'Class of '92' but actually came to prominence a year later once the likes of Giggs and McKee had become too old for the Youth team. He played in the 1993 FA Youth Cup Final side that was surprisingly beaten 4-1 on aggregate by Leeds United in front of gates totalling over 60,000 and the same year played in the Final of the European Under 18 Championship when England beat Turkey 1-0. Scholes made a sensational first team debut in September 1994 when he scored both goals in a 2-1 Coca Cola victory. The last player to score twice on a debut for United was no less than Bobby Charlton! His first FAPL appearance saw him score within eleven minutes of coming on as substitute in a 3-2 defeat at Ipswich Town and his goalscoring prowess was to net him seven goals in ten full starts and fifteen substitute appearances. But despite his above average strike rate, Youth Coach Eric Harrison reckons his best position is central midfield because "he has such craft, intelligence, vision and awareness".

Despite Harrison's views, it is as a goalscorer that he has made his name and such is his record in the limited number of appearances that have come his way that he is surely unlucky to have featured in so few starts.

Appearance Record

	Appearances			Goals		
	Lge	FLC	FAC	Lge	FLC	FAC
94/95	6/11	3	1/2	5	2	
95/96	16/10	1	-/2	10	2	1

Estimated value: £2,000,000

Lee Stuart SHARPE

Date of Birth: 27th May 1971, Halesowen

Although still not 23 at the end of the 93/94 season, Lee Sharpe's career has been blighted by a series of serious injuries and illnesses. It is testament to his ability that, despite the lengthy set backs he has taken, Sharpe has by still such a young age accumulated so many honours in the game. A native of Halesowen, Sharpe's first chance in football was as a YTS apprentice at Torquay United but United quickly spotted his potential and after only nine full games plus five more as substitute they plunged £185,000 in May 1988 for the unknown 17 year old. Sharpe signed professional forms for Torquay on his seventeenth birthday but within days was signing for United. He had played his first Football League game for Torquay coming on as substitute in the local *derby* against Exeter City at the ripe old age of 16 in October 1987. Strangely, the first time he actually started a game was also against Exeter in the return fixture at Plainmoor the following February. If anybody harboured any thoughts about the new young signing being one to watch for the future they were quickly put in their place by a young man determined to make his way to the top in the shortest time possible. The 1988/89 season was just five games old when Sharpe was put in against West Ham United at Old Trafford where the Reds enjoyed a 2-0 victory and he was to play over twenty games that season. He also won the first of his eight Under 21 caps that season when he played against Greece in Patras on 7th February 1989 and he went on to become the most capped United player at Under 21 level other than former 'keeper Gary Bailey. But whereas Bailey won most of his caps as an 'over age' player, Sharpe had won all his prior to his 20th birthday. He missed the first big chunk of his fledgling career when he was out for the second half of the 1989/90 campaign but by September 1990 he was back and was to play a significant part in getting United to the League Cup Final, scoring against Liverpool, netting a hat-trick against Arsenal at Highbury and two of the three goals by which United beat Leeds in the semi-final. His form had not gone unnoticed at international level and he became the youngest player to represent England since the late Duncan Edwards when he played against the Republic of Ireland on 27/3/91, still two months short of his 20th birthday. Despite missing a further eight months between April 91 and November 91, and a total of six months during the first two FAPL competitions, Sharpe has still managed to total over 150 appearances for United. Sharpe was voted the PFA's *Young Player of the Year* in 1991.

Previous Clubs and Appearance Record

Clubs	Signed	Fee	Appearances			Goals		
			Lge	FLC	FAC	Lge	FLC	FAC
Torquay United	5/88		14			3		
Manchester Utd	5/88	£185,000	59/17	11/4	8/2	3	7	
FA Premier League Record								
	92/93		27		3	1		
	93/94		26/4	2/2	1/2	9	2	3
	94/95		26/2	0/2	6/1	3		1
	95/96		21/10	2	4/2	4		2

Very difficult to estimate his worth on the transfer market due to his history of injury and illness. Any buyer would probably insist on a down payment only with a fee per game thereafter.

Estimated value: £3,000,000

UNITED'S *FAPL* PLAYERS

The following 37 players have appeared for United in the FAPL. All figures relate to the FAPL only. Where players have now left the club, a brief resume of their time at Old Trafford is given.

Player	Season	Apps	Goals
David BECKHAM	1994/95	2/2	0
	1995/96	26/7	7
	Total	28/9	7
Clayton BLACKMORE	1992/93	12/2	0
	Total	12/2	0

A Welsh international who came to the fore in the 1982 FA Youth Cup winning side alongside Mark Hughes and Norman Whiteside. Never made the same impact as those players but was a very useful squad player whose most successful campaign was in 1990/91 when he made 56 first team appearances in all competitions. Moved to Middlesbrough shortly after Bryan Robson went there as Manager in 1994. Featured in United's successful European Cup Winners side of 1991 but was on the losing side in the League Cup Final against Sheffield Wednesday which completed a 'full house' as his other Final appearance was as substitute in the drawn FA Cup Final in 1990 against Crystal Palace.

Steve BRUCE	1992/93	42	5 (2 pens)
	1993/94	41	3
	1994/95	35	2
	1995/96	30	1
	Total	148	11

Signed by United from Norwich City in 1987 for £800,00 and became the rock on which United's defence was based. It was a major shock when he activated a clause in his contract that enabled him to leave on a free transfer for Birmingham City in 1996 when still commanding a regular first team place.

Nicky BUTT	1992/93	0/1	0
	1993/94	0/1	0
	1994/95	11/11	1
	1995/96	31/1	2
	Total	42/14	3
Eric CANTONA	1992/93	21/1	9 (1 pen)
	1993/94	34	18 (2 pens)
	1994/95	21	12 (4 pens)
	1995/96	30	14 (4 pens)

Player	Season	Total Apps	Goals
	Total	106/1	53
Andy COLE	1994/95	17/1	12
	1995/96	32/2	11
	Total	49/3	23
Terry COOKE	1995/96	1/3	0
	Total	1/3	0
Simon DAVIES	1994/95	3/2	0
	1995/96	1/5	0
	Total	4/7	0
Dion DUBLIN	1992/93	3/4	1
	1993/94	1/4	1
	Total	4/8	2

A mystery signing from Cambridge United who was a target man when United had never used such a player since the days of Wyn Davies. Although he would never have had the subtlety demanded of United players, Dublin was as honest as the day was long and suffered cruelly from a broken leg just after arriving at Old Trafford. Still, Alex Ferguson must have known something for the Reds doubled their £1m outlay when they transferred the player to Coventry City in 1994 where, it has to be said, Dublin has excelled.

Darren FERGUSON	1992/93	15	0
	1993/94	1/2	0
	Total	16/2	0

Never had the flair required to be a United player and it was almost unfair of his father to keep him at the club for so long when his son was the butt of nepotism cracks for much of his time at Old Trafford. Sold to Wolves for £500,000 in 1994.

Keith GILLESPIE	1994/95	3/6	1
	Total	3/6	1

Had only just burst on to the first team scene when he was sensationally sold to Newcastle United as part of the Andy Cole deal. Has since figured prominently for the 'Magpies'.

Ryan GIGGS	1992/93	40/1	9
	1993/94	32/6	13
	1994/95	29	1
	1995/96	30/3	11
	Total	131/10	34

Player	Season	Apps	Goals
Mark HUGHES	1992/93	41	15
	1993/94	36	11
	1994/95	33/1	8
	Total	*110/1*	*34*

His transfer to Chelsea in 1995 caused uproar amongst the fans who not only saw Hughes as a United man through and through, but who had also been led to believe by the club that Hughes had signed a new two year deal at Old Trafford. The fans loyalty was probably misplaced as there were clear indications that his usefulness as a goalscorer was on the wane at the time of his move. A fantastic trophy cabinet whilst with the Reds including three FA Cup Final winning appearances in 1985, 1990 and 1994 besides a fourth Final in 1995 when losing to Everton, three League Cup Finals, a European Cup Winners Cup Final dream of both goals in a 2-1 success over his old club Barcelona and two FAPL Championship medals.

Paul INCE	1992/93	41	6
	1993/94	39	8
	1994/95	36	5
	Total	*116*	*19*

Definitely led from the front but his eagerness to get involved in situations that did not concern him was a definite problem. His move to Italy in 1995 was shrouded in a mystery which was never fully explained by either club or player but it seemed that outside 'agents' were definitely at work. United enjoyed most of their recent success whilst Ince was at the club and, in addition to his two Championship medals, Ince also played in the European Cup Winners Cup success over Barcelona, appeared in the FA Cup Finals of 1990, 1994 and 1995 and also featured in three League Cup Finals for the Reds.

Denis IRWIN	1992/93	40	5
	1993/94	42	2
	1994/95	40	2 (1 pen)
	1995/96	31	1
	Total	*153*	*10*

Andrei KANCHELSKIS	1992/93	14/13	3
	1993/94	28/3	6
	1994/95	25/5	14
	Total	*67/21*	*23*

Was very definitely under used by Alex Ferguson and it seems that being made substitute at Everton in February 1995 was the last straw for the Russian. However, there were big financial benefits in a move for Kanchelskis and many people considered it was these, rather than the altercations with the manager, that inspired his insistence on getting away from Old Trafford.

Whilst at Old Trafford Kanchelskis appeared in two League Cup Finals (being dismissed in the second one against Aston Villa to become the second United player to be sent off in a Wembley Cup Final) along with an FA Cup winners medal in 1994.

Roy KEANE	1993/94	34/3	5
	1994/95	23/2	2
	1995/96	29	6
	Total	86/5	13

Lee MARTIN	1993/94	1	0
	Total	1	0

Although he only played one FAPL game for the Reds, Martin will always go down in United history for the amazing fact that the only goal he ever scored for the Old Trafford club won the 1990 FA Cup Final. Not only was the goal the only strike of the replay against Crystal Palace but Martin was the only player in the side not to have cost a fee. His one appearance in the FAPL was in a 1-0 victory over Everton at Goodison Park in October 1993 before being sold to Glasgow Celtic for £350,000.

David MAY	1994/95	15/4	2
	1995/96	11/5	1
	Total	26/9	3

Brian McCLAIR	1992/93	41/1	9
	1993/94	12/14	1
	1994/95	35/5	5
	1995/96	12/10	3
	Total	100/30	18

Colin McKEE	1993/94	1	0
	Total	1	0

Signed as a schoolboy from Scotland, McKee progressed through the junior ranks and played two games on loan for Bury before making his United debut in the last game of the 1993/94 season against Coventry City alongside another debutant, Gary Neville. The following campaign had barely commenced when McKee was suddenly sold to Kilmarnock in a joint deal worth £530,000 that also took Neil Whitworth North of the Border. McKee finished his first season in Scottish football as Killies leading goalscorer, albeit with just six goals in 25 appearances.

Gary NEVILLE	1993/94	1	0
	1994/95	16/2	0
	1995/96	30/1	0
	Total	47/3	0

Player	Season	Apps	Goals
Phil NEVILLE	1994/95	1/1	0
	1995/96	21/3	0
	Total	22/4	0
John O'KANE	1995/96	-/1	0
	Total	-/1	0
Gary PALLISTER	1992/93	42	1
	1993/94	41	1
	1994/95	42	2
	1995/96	21	1
	Total	146	5
Paul PARKER	1992/93	31	1
	1993/94	39/1	0
	1994/95	1/1	0
	1995/96	5/1	0
	Total	76/3	1

Signed by United in August 1991 from QPR for £2m, having been capped at Under 21, B and full international levels by England whilst with the London club. Was a regular for three seasons until injury and the Neville brothers forced him out of the reckoning. Given a free transfer in May 1996.

Player	Season	Apps	Goals
Mike PHELAN	1992/93	5/6	0
	1993/94	1/1	0
	Total	6/7	0

Phelan was a £750,000 buy from Norwich City in 1989 but United fans never really warmed to him. He was another whose talent lay in work rate rather than the skill that United supporters want to see and many United fans considered him lucky to gain England recognition. Nevertheless, Phelan played in two League Cup Finals, an FA Cup Final and the European Cup-winners triumph of 1991 before being given a free transfer to West Bromwich Albion for whom he made twenty league appearances in 1994/95.

Player	Season	Apps	Goals
Kevin PILKINGTON	1994/95	0/1	0
	1995/96	2/1	0
	Total	2/2	0

Player	Season	Apps	Goals
William PRUNIER	1995/96	2	0
	Total	2	0

The Frenchman appeared at Old Trafford on trial just prior to Christmas 1995 after falling out with Bordeaux. Almost immediately, injuries to Gary Pallister, Steve Bruce, David May and Paul Parker thrust Prunier into the side after just one Reserve outing. Unable to speak a word of English, with no knowledge of United's style of play and having only seen FAPL action on television, Ferguson's move in playing the newcomer didn't say a lot about his faith in his Reserve team central defender Pat McGibbon. Prunier walked out on United when they refused to offer him a long term contract after they lost 4-1 to Spurs on New Year's Day. He had won one French cap in 1992 and played over 350 French League games along with over 30 European competition appearances.

Player	Season	Apps	Goals
Bryan ROBSON	1992/93	5/9	1
	1993/94	10/5	1
	Total	15/14	2

What can be said about Robson that has not already been said. It was just a shame that United's Championship successes came too late in his glorious career for him to play any significant part.

Player	Season	Apps	Goals
Peter SCHMEICHEL	1992/93	42	0
	1993/94	40	0
	1994/95	32	0
	1995/96	36	0
	Total	150	0
Paul SCHOLES	1994/95	6/11	5
	1995/96	16/10	10
	Total	22/21	15
Lee SHARPE	1992/93	27	1
	1993/94	26/4	9
	1994/95	26/2	3
	1995/96	21/10	4
	Total	100/16	17
Ben THORNLEY	1993/94	0/1	0
	1994/95	0/0	0
	1995/96	0/1	0
	Total	0/2	0

Player	Season	Apps	Goals
Danny WALLACE	1992/93	0/2	0
	Total	0/2	0

Had made over 250 appearances for Southampton scoring 64 goals when he signed for the Reds in 1989. His debut is best forgotten for it coincided with a 5-1 drubbing by Manchester City. He scored just eleven goals in his four years at Old Trafford and spent most of that time either injured or languishing in the Reserves. He moved to Birmingham City in October 1993 for £170,000 but made only 16 appearances there before moving on to Wycombe where he featured just once as a substitute in 1994/95. Picked up an FA Cup winners medal with United in 1990.

Gary WALSH	1993/94	2/1	0
	1994/95	10	0
	Total	12/1	0

Must be one of the unluckiest players about. He first came to notice when he played brilliantly in both legs of the 1986 FA Youth Cup Final against Manchester City to keep the aggregate score down to 3-1 in favour of a City side that was vastly superior to the young Reds of that particular year. Injuries then played havoc with his progress including a head injury that almost finished his career. After understudying Peter Schmeichel for a full season in 1994/95, Walsh was taken by Bryan Robson to Middlesbrough in August 1995 in exchange for £250,000.

Neil WEBB	1992/93	0/1	0
	Total	0/1	0

A lack of pace and a tendency to play the ball square instead of forward did not endear him to the United fans who had seen the club pay Forest £1.5m for his services. He had, however, an excellent pedigree when he arrived with over 100 goals from midfield in 250 games for Reading and Forest along with eleven England caps. Despite scoring on his United debut in a 3-1 win over Arsenal, his goal ratio dropped dramatically at Old Trafford to about one in ten matches perhaps, because of an Achilles injury that kept him out of football for six months shortly after signing for the Reds. Picked up an FA Cup winners medal with United in 1990 and played in the League Cup Final defeat against Sheffield Wednesday in 1991. Returned to Forest but only featured for them 21 times in 93/94 and not at all in 1994/95.

FA Carling Premiership
Stadium Guide

Arsenal

Arsenal Stadium, Highbury, London N5

Nickname: Gunners　　　　　　　**Colours:** Red/White sleeves, White, Red
All-seater Capacity: 39,497　　　**Pitch:** 110 yds x 71 yds

Directions:

From North: M1, J2 follow sign for the City. After Holloway Road station (c 6 miles) take third left into Drayton Park. Then right into Aubert Park after ¾ mile and 2nd left into Avenell Road.

From South: Signs for Bank of England then Angel from London Bridge. Right at traffic lights towards Highbury roundabout. Follow Holloway Road then third right into Drayton Park, thereafter as above. *From West:* A40(M) to A501 ring road. Left at Angel to Highbury roundabout, then as above.

Rail: Drayton Park/Finsbury Park.　　　Tube (Piccadilly line): Arsenal.

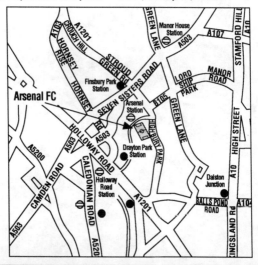

Club: 0171 704 4000 Recorded: 0171 704 4242

Aston Villa

Villa Park, Trinity Rd, Birmingham, B6 6HE

Nickname: The Villains
All-seater Capacity: 40,530

Colours: Claret/Blue, White, Blue/Claret
Pitch: 115 yds x 75 yds

Directions:

M6 J6, follow signs for Birmingham NE. third exit at roundabout then right into Ashton Hall Rd after ¹/₂ mile.
Rail: Witton.

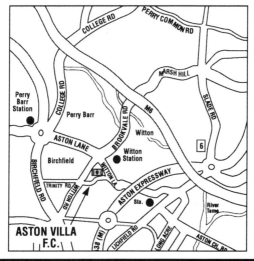

Club: 0121 327 2299 Ticket Info: 0891 121848

Blackburn Rovers

Ewood Park, Blackburn, BB2 4JF

Nickname: Blue and Whites
All-seater Capacity: 30,591

Colours: Blue/White, White, Blue
Pitch: 115yds x 76yds

Directions:

From North, South & West: M6 J31 follow signs for Blackburn then Bolton Road. Turn left after 1½ miles into Kidder Street.
From East: A677 or A679 following signs for Bolton Road, then as above.
Rail: Blackburn Central.

Club: 01254 698888 Ticket Info: 0891 121179

Chelsea

Stamford Bridge, London SW6

Nickname: The Blues **Colours:** Royal Blue, Royal Blue, White
All-seater Capacity: 31,791 (Rising to 41,000) **Pitch:** 110 yds x 72 yds

Directions:

From North & East: A1 or M1 to central London and Hyde Park corner. Follow signs for Guildford (A3) and then Knightsbridge (A4). After a mile turn left into Fulham Road. *From South:* A219 Putney Bridge then follow signs for West End joining A308 and then into Fulham Road. *From West:* M4 then A4 to central London. Follow A3220 to Westminster, after ³/₄ mile right at crossroads into Fulham Road.
Rail/Tube: Fulham Broadway (District line).

Club: 0171 385 5545 Ticket Info: 0891 121011

Coventry City

Highfield Road Stadium, King Richard Street, Coventry, CV2 4FW

Nickname: Sky Blues
All-seater Capacity: 24,021

Colours: All Sky Blue
Pitch: 110 yds x 75 yds

Directions:

From North & West: M6 J3, after 3½ miles turn left into Eagle Street and straight on to Swan Lane. *From South & East:* M1 to M45 then A45 to Ryton-on-Dunsmore where third exit at roundabout is A423. After one mile turn right into B4110. Left at T-junction then right into Swan Lane.
Rail: Coventry.

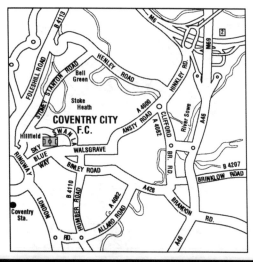

Club: 01203 223535

200

Derby County

The Baseball Ground, Shaftesbury Crescent, Derby, DE23 8NB

Nickname: The Rams
Capacity: 19,500 (15,000 seated)

Colours: White and Black
Pitch: 110yds x 71 yds

Directions:

From South & North – M1 Motorway: M1 J24. At roundabout take 2nd exit
towards Derby – A6. Follow A6 for about 7 miles passing through Shadlow and
Alvaston. Turn onto Ring Road following 'Football Traffic' signs. At next
roundabout – the Spider Bridge roundabout – take 3rd exit (s/p City Centre) into
Osmaston Road (A514). Shaftesbury Crescent about one mile on left.
From North: A38 and continue towards Buxton. A38 becomes Derby Ring Road.
Cross over River Derwent and at next roundabout turn left (s/p Ring Road/M1
South). Continue for about 4 miles to Spider Bridge roundabout. Take 3rd exit (s/p
City Centre) into Osmaston Road (A514). Shaftesbury Crescent one mile on left.

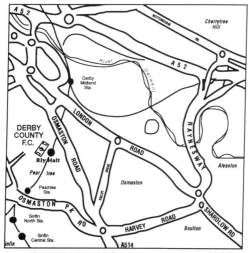

Everton

Goodison Park, Liverpool, L4 4EL

Nickname: The Toffees
All-seater Capacity: 40,160

Colours: Royal Blue, White, Blue
Pitch: 112 yds x 78 yds

Directions:

From North: M6 J8 take A58 to A580 and follow into Walton Hall Avenue.
From South & East: M6 J21A to M62, turn right into Queen's Drive then, after 4 miles, left into Walton Hall Avenue.
From West: M53 through Wallasey Tunnel, follow signs for Preston on A580. Walton Hall Avenue is signposted.
Rail: Liverpool Lime Street

Club: 0151 521 2020 Ticket Info: 0891 121599

Leeds United

Elland Road, Leeds, LS11 0ES

Nickname: United
All-seater Capacity: 39,704

Colours: All White
Pitch: 117 yds x 76 yds

Directions:

From North & East: A58, A61, A63 or A64 into city centre and then onto M621.
Leave motorway after 1½ miles onto A643 and Elland Road.
From West: take M62 to M621 then as above.
From South: M1 then M621 then as above.
Rail: Leeds City.

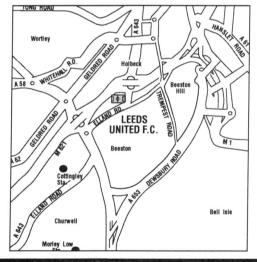

Club: 0113 271 6037 Info: 0891 121180

Leicester City

City Stadium. Filbert Street, Leicester, LE2 7FL

Nickname: Foxes or Fliberts
Capacity: 22,517

Colours: All Blue
Pitch: 112 yds x 75 yds

Directions:

From North: Leave M1 J22, or take A46, A607 to town centre. Towards Rugby via Almond Road, Aylestone Road, and then left into Walnut Street and Filbert Street for the ground. *From South:* M1 or M69 and then A46 to Upperton Road and Filbert Street. *From East:* A47 into town centre, then right along Oxford Street to Aylestone Road and as North. *From West:* M69 and A50 to Aylestone Road, and then as North.
Rail: Leicester

Club: 0115 255 5000 Tickets: 0116 291 5232

Liverpool

Anfield Road, Liverpool 4 0TH

Nickname: Reds or Pool
All-seater Capacity: 41,000

Colours: All Red/White Trim
Pitch: 110 yds x 75 yds

Directions:

From North: M6 J8, follow A58 to Walton Hall Avenue and pass Stanley Park turning left into Anfield Road. *From South/East:* To end of M62 and right into Queens Drive (A5058). After three miles turn left into Utting Avenue and right after one mile into Anfield Road. *From West:* M53 through Wallasey Tunnel, follow signs for Preston then turn into Walton Hall Avenue and right into Anfield Road before Stanley Park. *Rail:* Liverpool Lime Street.

Club: 0151 263 2361 Match: 0151 260 9999

Middlesbrough

Cellnet Riverside Stadium, Middlesbrough, TS3 6RS

Nickname: The Boro

All-seater Capacity: 31,000
(expanding to 34,000 during 1996-97)

Colours: Red with White/Black, White, Red/Black

Pitch: 115 yds x 75 yds

Directions:

From South: Al (M) onto A19. Follow signs to Teesside/Middlesbrough. After approx 31 miles exit onto A66. Keep following signs to Middlesbrough (A66 Middlesbrough By-Pass). At first roundabout (2.5 miles) turn left. New stadium link road off of second roundabout (due for completion by start 1996-97 season).
From North: Take A19 towards Teesside/Middlesbrough. Cross Tees Bridge and join A66 eastbound. Turn left at first roundabout (approx 3 miles). New stadium link road off of second roundabout (due for completion by start 1996-97 season).
Rail: Middlesbrough (600 yards).

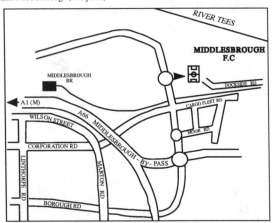

Club: 01642 819659 Tickets: 01642 815996

Newcastle United

St James' Park, Newcastle-upon-Tyne, NE1 4ST

Nickname: Magpies
All-seater Capacity: 36,401

Colours: Black/White, Black, Black
Pitch: 115 yds x 75 yds.

Directions:

From South: Follow A1, A68 then A6127 to cross the Tyne. At roundabout, first exit into Moseley Street. Left into Neville Street, right at end for Clayton Street and then Newgate Street. Left for Leaze Park Road. *From West:* A69 towards city centre. Left into Clayton Street for Newgate Street, left again for Leaze Park Road. *From North:* A1 then follow signs for Hexham until Percy Street. Right into Leaze Park Road.

Rail: Newcastle Central (¹/₂ mile).

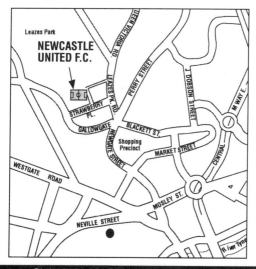

Club: 0191 232 8361 Info: 0891 121190

Nottingham Forest

City Ground, Nottingham, NG2 5FJ

Nickname: The Reds or Forest
All-seater Capacity: 30,539

Colours: Red, White, Red
Pitch: 115 yds x 78 yds

Directions:

From North: Leave the M1 J26 for the A610 and the A606. Left into Radcliffe Road for the ground. *From South:* Leave the M1 J24 to Trent Bridge, turning right into Radcliffe Road. *From East:* A52 to West Bridgeford and right for the ground. *From West:* A52 to A606 and then as for the North.

Rail: Nottingham.

Club: 0115 952 6000 Tickets: 0115 952 6002

Sheffield Wednesday

Hillsborough, Sheffield, S6 1SW

Nickname: The Owls
All-seater Capacity: 36,020

Colours: Blue/White, Blue, Blue
Pitch: 115 yds x 75 yds

Directions:

From North: M1 J34 then A6109 to Sheffield. At roundabout after 1¹/₂ miles take third exit then turn left after three miles into Harries Road.

From South & East: M1 J31 or 33 to A57. At roundabout take Prince of Wales Road exit. A further six miles then turn left into Herries Road South.

From West: A57 to A6101 then turn left after four miles at T junction into Penistone Road.

Rail: Sheffield Midland.

Club: 0114 243 3122 Tickets: 0114 233 7233

Southampton

The Dell, Milton Road, Southampton, SO9 4XX

Nickname: The Saints
All-seater Capacity: 15,288

Colours: Red/White, Black, Black
Pitch: 110 yds x 72 yds

Directions:

From North: A33 into The Avenue then right into Northlands Road. Right at the end into Archer's Road. *From East:* M27 then A334 and signs for Southampton along A3024. Follow signs for the West into Commercial Road, right into Hill Lane then first right into Milton Road.

From West: Take A35 then A3024 towards city centre. Left into Hill Lane and first right into Milton Road.

Rail: Southampton Central.

Club: 01703 220505 Tickets: 01703 228575

Sunderland

Roker Park, Sunderland, SR6 9SW

Nickname: Rokermen
Capacity: 22,657

Colours: Red & White stripes. Black, Red
Pitch: 113 yds x 74 yds

Directions:

From South: A1 J64 towards Washington A195. Follow signs to Tyne Tunnel A182 and Sunderland A1231 onto the Washington Highway. Continue following signs for Sunderland A1231. Once on A1231 follow signs for City Centre. At major junction keep to left and follow signs towards Roker B1289. Enter one-way system following signs to Roker. At Wheatsheaf pub turn left and ground is on left hand side.

From North: From junction of A194M (formerly A19) and A184 follow signs towards Tyne Tunnel A184 and then towards Sunderland A184. Continue through Bolden towards City Centre (A1018). Continue into Newcastle Road. Turn left at traffic lights into Charlton Road towards Roker Park. At next lights turn tight into Fulwell Road. Ground on left hand side.

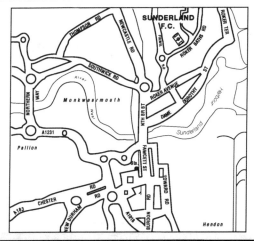

Club: 0191 514 0332

Tottenham Hotspur

748 High Road, Tottenham, London, N17 0AP

Nickname: Spurs
All-seater Capacity: 30,246

Colours: White, Navy Blue, White
Pitch: 110 yds x 73 yds

Directions:

A406 North Circular to Edmonton. At traffic lights follow signs for Tottenham along A1010 then Fore Street for ground.
Rail: White Hart Lane (adjacent).
Tube: Seven Sisters (Victoria Line) or Manor House (Piccadilly Line).

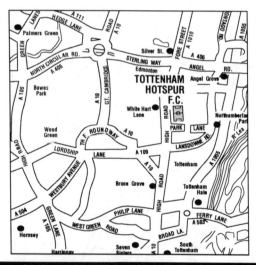

Club: 0181 365 5000 Tickets: 0181 365 5050

West Ham United

Boleyn Ground, Green Street, Upton Park, London E13

Nickname: The Hammers
All-seater Capacity: 24,500

Colours: Claret, White, White
Pitch: 112 yds x 72 yds

Directions:

From North & West: North Circular to East Ham then Barking Rd for 1½ miles until traffic lights. Turn right into Green Street.

From South: Blackwall Tunnel then A13 to Canning Town. Then A124 to East Ham, Green Street on left after two miles.

From East: A13 then A117 and A124. Green Street on right after ¾ miles.

Rail/Tube: Upton Park (¼ mile).

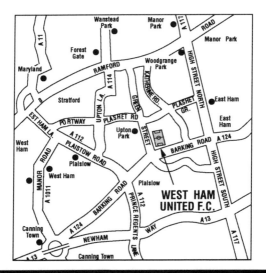

Club: 0181 548 2748 Tickets: 0181 548 2700

Wimbledon

Selhurst Park, South Norwood, London E5

Nickname: The Dons
All-seater Capacity: 26,995

Colours: All Blue with Yellow trim
Pitch: 110 yds x 74 yds

Directions:

From North: M1/A1 to North Circular A406 and Chiswick. Follow South Circular A205 to Wandsworth then A3 and A214 towards Streatham and A23. Then left onto B273 for one mile and turn left at end into High Street and Whitehorse Lane.
From South: On A23 follow signs for Crystal Palace along B266 going through Thornton Heath into Whitehorse Lane. *From East:* A232 Croydon Road to Shirley joining A215, Norwood Road. Turn left after 2½ miles into Whitehorse Lane.
From West: M4 to Chiswick then as above.
Rail: Selhurst, Norwood Junction or Thornton Heath.

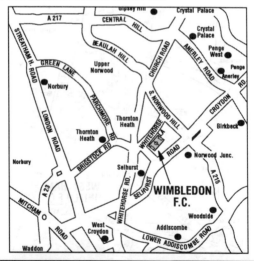

Club: 0181 771 2233 Tickets: 0181 771 8841

All-time Records and Statistics

United Against Other Clubs – *Football Alliance*

Club	Home						Away				
	P	W	D	L	F	A	W	D	L	F	A
Ardwick	2	1	0	0	3	1	0	1	0	2	2
Birmingham St George	6	2	0	1	6	4	1	0	2	5	12
Bootle	6	3	0	0	9	1	0	1	2	2	10
Burton Swifts	2	1	0	0	3	1	0	0	1	2	3
Crewe Alexandra	6	2	0	1	12	8	2	1	0	5	2
Darwen	4	2	0	0	6	3	0	0	2	2	6
Grimsby Town	6	1	1	1	6	5	0	1	2	3	12
Lincoln City	2	1	0	0	10	1	1	0	0	6	1
Long Eaton	2	1	0	0	3	0	1	0	0	3	1
Nottingham Forest	6	0	2	1	2	3	1	0	2	5	12
Sheffield Wednesday	6	0	2	1	3	4	2	0	1	7	6
Small Heath	6	2	1	0	15	5	0	1	2	4	6
Stoke City	2	1	0	0	0	1	0	0	1	1	2
Sunderland Albion	4	1	0	1	5	6	0	0	2	1	4
Walsall Town Swifts	6	2	1	0	10	4	1	0	2	5	7
Total	66	20	7	6	93	47	9	5	19	53	86

United Against Other Clubs – *Football League*

Manchester United met 78 other clubs during their time in the Football League. The following list gives their record against each of those 78 clubs. Where clubs have changed their names, the latest name only is used but the list includes all games against that club under either name (ie Small Heath became Birmingham City, therefore the record shown below in respect of Birmingham City also includes games against Small Heath).

Club	Home						Away				
	P	W	D	L	F	A	W	D	L	F	A
Accrington Stanley	2	0	1	0	3	3	0	1	0	2	2
Arsenal	146	41	20	12	143	70	18	11	44	84	151
Aston Villa	118	37	12	10	127	59	14	15	30	88	128
Barnsley	30	12	2	1	35	7	5	7	3	20	14
Birmingham City	80	23	8	9	60	34	10	15	15	53	62
Blackburn Rovers	62	15	8	8	61	38	10	7	14	55	66
Blackpool	80	26	8	6	83	34	17	9	14	66	60
Bolton Wanderers	92	23	9	14	78	53	11	11	24	52	88

215

Club	Home						Away				
	P	W	D	L	F	A	W	D	L	F	A
Bradford Park Avenue	18	5	0	4	17	12	3	1	5	13	24
Bradford City	42	13	6	2	35	9	5	7	9	26	28
Brentford	10	2	1	2	9	7	2	1	2	10	12
Brighton & Hove Alb	8	3	1	0	7	2	2	1	1	5	2
Bristol City	34	9	3	5	30	18	5	7	5	17	21
Bristol Rovers	2	1	0	0	2	0	0	1	0	1	1
Burnley	102	30	8	13	116	66	17	8	26	64	91
Burton United	24	9	3	0	39	6	5	3	4	22	23
Burton Wanderers	6	1	1	1	5	3	1	0	2	3	7
Bury	38	9	2	8	24	23	10	5	4	34	23
Cardiff City	26	5	6	2	28	19	8	1	4	22	18
Charlton Athletic	41	13	4	3	45	20	8	5	8	27	33
Chelsea	101	21	16	13	81	47	25	12	14	97	75
Chesterfield	20	10	0	0	26	7	3	1	6	15	15
Coventry City	56	15	7	6	49	21	8	8	12	34	37
Crewe Alexandra	4	2	0	0	11	1	2	0	0	4	0
Crystal Palace	24	8	2	2	22	7	5	3	4	21	22
Darwen	12	4	1	1	20	5	2	2	2	7	8
Derby County	76	19	10	9	70	39	9	13	16	58	84
Doncaster Rovers	8	3	1	0	16	0	1	2	1	3	6
Everton	126	32	17	14	107	64	12	16	35	71	140
Fulham	42	17	3	1	44	15	6	7	8	34	32
Gainsborough Trinity	20	8	2	0	26	7	5	3	2	10	7
Glossop North End	14	6	1	0	20	5	5	1	1	14	5
Grimsby Town	37	13	2	4	42	26	4	4	10	26	37
Huddersfield Town	42	11	9	1	46	21	7	6	8	32	39
Hull City	16	7	1	0	22	4	2	2	4	8	13
Ipswich Town	40	13	2	5	31	13	6	4	10	26	40
Leeds City	2	0	0	1	0	3	1	0	0	3	1
Leeds United	68	13	13	8	51	32	11	12	11	41	40
Leicester City	96	32	11	5	115	51	12	11	25	72	90
Leyton Orient	12	3	3	0	13	5	3	1	2	5	3
Lincoln City	28	10	3	1	34	12	3	1	10	12	28
Liverpool	118	27	21	11	100	55	13	16	30	62	103
Loughborough Town	10	5	0	0	23	2	2	2	1	6	5
Luton Town	38	18	0	1	58	10	9	7	3	30	16
Manchester City	116	23	21	14	87	74	18	22	18	75	86
Middlesbrough	74	23	6	8	77	47	12	9	16	56	73
Millwall	12	5	1	0	22	3	3	2	1	6	4
Nelson	2	0	0	1	0	1	1	0	0	2	0
New Brighton Town	6	2	0	1	4	3	2	0	1	7	3

Club	Home						Away				
	P	W	D	L	F	A	W	D	L	F	A
Newcastle United	110	33	13	9	125	67	17	12	26	78	111
Northampton Town	2	1	0	0	6	2	0	1	0	1	1
Norwich City	42	13	5	3	34	10	9	6	6	37	28
Nottingham Forest	86	24	11	8	90	54	13	10	20	55	68
Notts County	48	11	9	4	41	27	9	5	10	33	33
Oldham Athletic	32	9	3	4	32	17	5	6	5	31	23
Oxford United	8	4	0	0	13	3	2	0	2	5	4
Plymouth Argyle	12	4	1	1	12	7	2	1	3	8	13
Port Vale	36	16	1	1	52	10	5	4	9	24	27
Portsmouth	44	13	3	6	38	21	5	9	8	23	30
Preston North End	66	15	11	7	51	35	11	9	13	56	55
Queen's Park Rangers	30	12	2	1	33	11	4	6	5	18	22
Rotherham United	6	3	0	0	9	2	1	1	1	5	5
Sheffield United	82	26	4	11	83	47	11	9	21	49	74
Sheffield Wednesday	96	30	12	6	91	46	11	9	28	62	89
Southshields	6	2	1	0	5	1	2	0	1	5	2
Southampton	64	18	7	7	56	35	9	12	11	38	37
Stockport County	18	7	2	0	21	7	2	0	7	8	11
Stoke City	70	17	13	5	63	29	9	11	15	40	60
Sunderland	96	25	12	11	96	60	12	11	25	61	104
Swansea City	16	6	2	0	18	6	0	2	6	6	14
Tottenham Hotspurs	110	34	11	10	104	58	13	20	22	67	99
Walsall	12	5	1	0	24	1	2	3	1	7	7
Watford	12	4	2	0	13	4	2	2	2	4	7
West Bromwich Alb	100	26	13	11	102	65	13	11	26	72	98
West Ham United	80	24	6	10	91	48	7	10	23	49	70
Wimbledon	12	3	2	1	5	3	2	2	2	9	8
Wolverhampton Wndrs	80	26	5	9	80	44	10	9	21	55	81
York City	2	1	0	0	2	1	1	0	0	1	0
Total	3556		410		3550		532		784		3057
		1036		332		1784		462		2406	

United Against Other Clubs – *FA Premiership*

Club		Home						Away			
	P	W	D	L	F	A	W	D	L	F	A
Arsenal	8	3	1	0	5	0	1	2	1	3	3
Aston Villa	8	2	2	0	5	2	2	0	2	5	6
Blackburn Rovers	8	3	1	0	6	2	2	1	1	6	5
Bolton Wanderers	2	1	0	0	3	0	1	0	0	6	0
Chelsea	8	1	2	1	4	2	2	1	1	8	5
Coventry City	8	3	1	0	8	0	4	0	0	9	2
Crystal Palace	4	2	0	0	4	0	1	1	0	3	1
Everton	8	2	0	1	5	3	3	0	1	6	3
Ipswich Town	6	1	2	0	10	1	1	0	2	5	6
Leeds United	8	2	2	0	3	0	1	1	2	4	5
Leicester City	2	0	1	0	1	1	1	0	0	4	0
Liverpool	8	2	2	0	7	4	1	1	2	5	8
Manchester City	8	4	0	0	10	1	3	1	0	10	5
Middlesbrough	4	2	0	0	5	0	1	1	0	4	1
Newcastle United	6	2	1	0	5	1	1	2	0	3	2
Norwich City	6	2	1	0	4	2	3	0	0	7	1
Nottingham Forest	6	2	0	1	8	2	1	2	0	4	2
Oldham Athletic	4	2	0	0	6	2	1	0	1	5	3
QPR	8	3	1	0	6	2	3	1	0	10	6
Sheffield United	4	2	0	0	5	1	1	0	1	4	2
Sheffield Wedn'y	8	3	1	0	10	3	1	2	1	6	6
Southampton	8	4	0	0	10	3	2	1	1	7	6
Swindon Town	2	1	0	0	4	2	0	1	0	2	2
Tottenham Hotspur	8	3	1	0	7	2	2	1	1	4	5
West Ham United	6	3	0	0	6	1	1	2	0	4	3
Wimbledon	8	3	0	1	9	3	3	0	1	7	4
Total	164	59	19	4	156	40	43	21	18	141	92

United's Full League Record

Year			Home				Away					
	P	W	D	L	F	A	W	D	L	F	A	Pts Pos
Football Alliance												
1889/90	22	7	0	4	27	11	2	2	7	13	34	20 8th
1890/91	22	5	3	3	25	22	2	0	9	12	31	17 9th
1891/92	22	7	4	0	41	14	5	3	3	28	19	31 2nd
Football League – First Division												
1892/93	30	6	3	6	39	35	0	3	12	11	50	18 16th
1893/94	30	5	2	8	29	33	1	0	14	7	39	14 16th
Second Division												
1894/95	30	9	6	0	52	18	6	2	7	26	26	38 3rd
1895/96	30	12	2	1	48	15	3	1	11	18	42	33 6th
1896/97	30	11	4	0	37	10	6	1	8	19	24	39 2nd
1897/98	30	11	2	2	42	10	5	4	6	22	25	38 4th
1898/99	34	12	4	1	51	14	7	1	9	16	29	43 4th
1899/1900	34	15	1	1	44	11	5	3	9	19	16	44 4th
1900/01	34	11	3	3	31	9	3	1	13	11	29	32 10th
1901/02	34	10	2	5	27	12	1	4	12	11	41	28 15th
1902/03	34	9	4	4	32	15	6	4	7	21	23	38 5th
1903/04	34	14	2	1	42	14	6	6	5	23	19	48 3rd
1904/05	34	16	0	1	60	10	8	5	4	21	20	53 3rd
1905/06	38	15	3	1	55	13	13	3	3	35	15	62 2nd
First Division												
1906/07	38	10	6	3	33	15	7	2	10	20	41	42 8th
1907/08	38	15	1	3	43	19	8	5	6	38	29	52 1st
1908/09	38	10	3	6	37	33	5	4	10	21	35	37 13th
1909/10	38	14	2	3	41	20	5	5	9	28	41	45 5th
1910/11	38	14	4	1	47	18	8	4	7	25	22	52 1st
1911/12	38	9	5	5	29	19	4	6	9	16	41	37 13th
1912/13	38	13	3	3	41	14	6	5	8	28	29	46 4th
1913/14	38	8	4	7	27	23	7	2	10	25	39	36 14th
1914/15	38	8	6	5	27	19	1	6	12	19	43	30 18th
1919/20	42	6	8	7	20	17	7	6	8	34	33	40 12th
1920/21	42	9	4	8	34	26	6	6	9	30	42	40 13th
1921/22	42	7	7	7	25	26	1	5	15	16	47	28 22nd
Second Division												
1922/23	42	10	6	5	25	17	7	8	6	26	19	48 4th
1923/24	42	10	7	4	37	15	3	7	11	15	29	40 14th
1924/25	42	17	3	1	40	6	6	8	7	17	17	57 2nd

Year				Home			Away					
	P	W	D	L	F	A	W	D	L	F	A	Pts	Pos

First Division

Year	P	W	D	L	F	A	W	D	L	F	A	Pts	Pos
1925/26	42	12	4	5	40	26	7	2	12	26	47	44	9th
1926/27	42	9	8	4	29	19	4	6	11	23	45	40	15th
1927/28	42	12	6	3	51	27	4	1	16	21	53	39	18th
1928/29	42	8	8	5	32	23	6	5	10	34	53	41	12th
1929/30	42	11	4	6	39	34	4	4	13	28	54	38	17th
1930/31	42	6	6	9	30	37	1	2	18	23	78	22	22nd

Second Division

Year	P	W	D	L	F	A	W	D	L	F	A	Pts	Pos
1931/32	42	12	3	6	44	31	5	5	11	27	41	42	12th
1932/33	42	11	5	5	40	24	4	8	9	31	44	43	6th
1933/34	42	9	3	9	29	33	5	3	13	30	52	34	20th
1934/35	42	16	2	3	50	21	7	2	12	26	34	50	5th
1935/36	42	16	3	2	55	16	6	9	6	30	27	56	1st

First Division

Year	P	W	D	L	F	A	W	D	L	F	A	Pts	Pos
1936/37	42	8	9	4	29	26	2	3	16	26	52	32	21st

Second Division

Year	P	W	D	L	F	A	W	D	L	F	A	Pts	Pos
1937/38	42	15	3	3	50	18	7	6	8	32	32	53	2nd

First Division

Year	P	W	D	L	F	A	W	D	L	F	A	Pts	Pos
1938/39	42	7	9	5	30	20	4	7	10	27	45	38	14th
1946/47	42	17	3	1	61	19	5	9	7	34	35	56	2nd
1947/48	42	11	7	3	50	27	8	7	6	31	21	52	2nd
1948/49	42	11	7	3	40	20	10	4	7	37	24	53	2nd
1949/50	42	11	5	5	42	20	7	9	5	27	24	50	4th
1950/51	42	14	4	3	42	16	10	4	7	32	24	56	2nd
1951/52	42	15	3	3	55	21	8	8	5	40	31	57	1st
1952/53	42	11	5	5	35	30	7	5	9	34	42	46	8th
1953/54	42	11	6	4	41	27	7	6	8	32	31	48	4th
1954/55	42	12	4	5	44	30	8	3	10	40	44	47	5th
1955/56	42	18	3	0	51	20	7	7	7	32	31	60	1st
1956/57	42	14	4	3	55	25	14	4	3	48	29	64	1st
1957/58	42	10	4	7	45	31	6	7	8	40	44	43	9th
1958/59	42	14	4	3	58	27	10	3	8	45	39	55	2nd
1959/60	42	13	3	5	53	30	6	4	11	49	50	45	7th
1960/61	42	14	5	2	58	20	4	4	13	30	56	45	7th
1961/62	42	10	3	8	44	31	5	6	10	28	44	39	15th
1962/63	42	6	6	9	36	38	6	4	11	31	43	34	19th
1963/64	42	15	3	3	54	19	8	4	9	36	43	53	2nd
1964/65	42	16	4	1	52	13	10	5	6	37	26	61	1st
1965/66	42	12	8	1	50	20	6	7	8	34	39	51	4th
1966/67	42	17	4	0	51	13	7	8	6	33	32	60	1st

Year		Home					Away					Pts	Pos
	P	W	D	L	F	A	W	D	L	F	A		
1967/68	42	15	2	4	49	21	9	6	6	40	34	56	2nd
1968/69	42	13	5	3	38	18	2	7	12	19	35	42	11th
1969/70	42	8	9	4	37	27	6	8	7	29	34	45	8th
1970/71	42	9	6	6	29	24	7	5	9	36	42	43	8th
1971/72	42	13	2	6	39	26	6	8	7	30	35	48	8th
1972/73	42	9	7	5	24	19	3	6	12	20	41	37	18th
1973/74	42	7	7	7	23	20	3	5	13	15	28	32	21st
Second Division													
1974/75	42	17	3	1	45	12	9	6	6	21	18	61	1st
First Division													
1975/76	42	16	4	1	40	13	7	6	8	28	29	56	3rd
1976/77	42	12	6	3	41	22	6	5	10	30	40	47	6th
1977/78	42	9	6	6	32	23	7	4	10	35	40	42	10th
1978/79	42	9	7	5	29	25	6	8	7	31	38	45	9th
1979/80	42	17	3	1	43	8	7	7	7	22	27	58	2nd
1980/81	42	9	11	1	30	14	6	7	8	21	22	48	8th
1981/82	42	12	6	3	27	9	10	6	5	32	20	78	3rd
1982/83	42	14	7	0	39	10	5	6	10	17	28	70	3rd
1983/84	42	14	3	4	43	18	6	11	4	28	23	74	4th
1984/85	42	13	6	2	47	13	9	4	8	30	34	76	4th
1985/86	42	12	5	4	35	12	10	5	6	35	24	76	4th
1986/87	42	13	3	5	38	18	1	11	9	14	27	56	11th
1987/88	40	14	5	1	41	17	9	7	4	30	21	81	2nd
1988/89	38	10	5	4	27	13	3	7	9	18	22	51	11th
1989/90	38	8	6	5	26	14	5	3	11	20	33	48	13th
1990/91	38	11	4	4	34	17	5	8	6	24	28	59	6th
1991/92	42	12	7	2	34	13	9	8	4	29	20	78	2nd
FA Premier League													
1992/93	42	14	5	2	39	14	10	7	4	28	17	84	1st
1993/94	42	14	6	1	39	13	13	5	3	41	25	92	1st
1994/95	42	16	4	1	42	4	10	6	5	35	24	88	2nd
1995/96	38	15	4	0	36	9	10	3	6	37	26	82	1st

United in Europe – Country by Country

The following table is a country by country break down of United's performances
in European competition based on the Reds' results against that nation's clubs. For
the purpose of the table, German clubs are shown as either East or West as they
were at the time of meeting. Where percentages are the same, the country against
whose clubs United have played more often is given the higher status.

		P	W	D	L	F	A	%
1	Republic of Ireland	4	4	0	0	19	4	100
2	Finland	2	2	0	0	9	2	100
3	Wales	2	2	0	0	5	0	100
4	Bulgaria	2	2	0	0	4	1	100
5	West Germany	4	3	1	0	13	3	87.5
6	East Germany	4	3	1	0	12	3	87.5
7	France	6	3	3	0	11	2	75
8	Belgium	4	3	0	1	16	3	75
9	Malta	2	1	1	0	4	0	75
10	Austria	2	1	1	0	3	0	75
11	Greece	2	1	1	0	2	0	75
12	Scotland	2	1	1	0	5	4	75
13	Portugal	7	5	0	2	21	16	71.4
14	Hungary	11	7	1	3	18	11	68.2
15	Holland	6	3	2	1	10	3	66.7
16	Yugoslavia	6	3	2	1	8	7	66.7
17	Poland	6	2	3	1	7	4	62.5
18	Turkey	4	1	3	0	7	3	62.5
19	England	4	2	1	1	7	5	62.5
20	Czechoslavakia	4	1	2	1	6	4	50
21	Sweden	2	1	0	1	5	5	50
22	Russia	4	0	4	0	2	2	50
23	Italy	8	3	1	4	6	13	43.7
24	Spain	15	4	5	6	22	28	43.3
	Totals	*113*	*58*	*33*	*22*	*222*	*123*	*66.2*

United Goalscorers in Europe

28	D.Law	4	D.Pegg
22	R.Charlton	3	J.Berry
14	D.Herd		S.Coppell
13	D.Viollett		R.Keane
11	G.Best		B.Kidd
	J.Connolly		A.Muhren
	T.Taylor		D.Sadler
9	M.Hughes		L.Sharpe
8	B.Robson	2	C.Blackmore
7	Own Goals		E.Cantona
6	S.Bruce		W.Foulkes
5	B.McClair		R.Giggs
	F.Stapleton		G.Hill
	L.Whelan		S.McIlroy

	N.Stiles		W.Morgan
	G.Strachan		J.Nicholl
1	J.Aston		G.Pallister
	D.Beckham		Stuart Pearson
	A.Brazil		M.Robins
	F.Burns		C.Sartori
	P.Chisnall		P.Schmeichel
	E.Colman		P.Scholes
	P.Crerand		M.Setters
	A.Davies		E.Taylor
	S.Davies		N.Webb
	A.Graham		C.Webster
	A.Kanchelskis		N.Whiteside
	L.Macari		R.Wilkins

United Goalscorers in the League Cup

19	B.McClair		W.Morgan
16	M.Hughes		D.Wallace
10	L.Macari	2	P.Barnes
9	G.Best		B.Greenhoff
	S.Coppell		S.Houston
	L.Sharpe		P.Ince
	N.Whiteside		J.Jordan
7	R.Charlton		P.McGrath
	B.Kidd		K.Moran
6	S.Bruce		A.Quixall
	R.Giggs		M.Robins
	S.McIlroy		M.Thomas
	F.Stapleton	1	A.Albiston
5	Stuart Pearson		V.Anderson
	B.Robson		E.Cantona
4	G.Daly		T.Cooke
	P.Davenport		A.Dawson
	G.Hill		D.Dublin
	G.McQueen		P.Edwards
	R.Moses		J.Fitzpatrick
	P.Scholes		J.Giles
	Own Goals		A.Gowling
3	C.Blackmore		D.Graham
	A.Brazil		J.Greenhoff
	A.Kanchelskis		D.Herd
	D.Law		D.McCreery

D.May		I.Storey-Moore	
A.Muhren		G.Strachan	
J.Nicholl		D.Viollett	
J.Olsen		N.Webb	
M.Pearson		R.Wilkins	
D.Sadler			

United Leading Goalscorers in the FA Cup

34	D.Law	14	B.McClair
26	J.Rowley	11	C.Mitten
21	G.Best	10	R.Donaldson
	Stan Pearson		B.Robson
19	R.Charlton		J.Spence
17	M.Hughes		A.Turnbull
15	D.Herd		N.Whiteside

United Leading Goalscorers in League/FAPL

199	R.Charlton	74	B.Robson
182	J.Rowley	72	E.West
171	D.Law	63	T.Reid
159	D.Viollett	60	F.Stapleton
158	J.Spence	57	S.McIlroy
137	G.Best	55	Stuart Pearson
128	Stan Pearson		H.Rowley
120	M.Hughes	54	S.Coppell
114	D.Herd	53	T.Bamford
112	T.Taylor		E.Cantona
90	J.Cassidy	52	B.Kidd
	A.Turnbull		J.Peddie
89	G.Wall	50	A.Lochhead
88	B.McClair		C.Mitten
78	L.Macari		A.Quixall
76	R.Donaldson		

Hat-trick Heroes

The following is a complete list of players who have scored hat-tricks (or better) in competitive matches for United.

Four Timers in the Football League

3	D.Law	T.Manley
	J.Rowley	C.Mitten
2	JW.Spence	JB.Picken
1	T.Bamford	R.Smith
	N.Dewar	T.Taylor
	EH.Goldthorpe	A.Turnbull
	A.Gowling	J.Turnbull
	D.Herd	

Hat-tricks in the Football League

9	J.Rowley	WG.Boyd
7	D.Viollett	W.Bryant
6	R.Charlton	KJ.Bullock**
	D.Law	J.Coupar
5	J.Cassidy	G.Daly
	T.Reid	R.Duckworth
4	D.Herd	M.Gillespie
	Stan Pearson	J.Greenhoff
3	G.Best	J.Hanlon
	H.Boyd	W.Henderson
	A.Dawson	C.Jenkyns
	R.Donaldson*	WJ.Kennedy
	J.Peddie	N.Lawton
	JW.Spence	B.McClair
2	T.Bamford	S.McIlroy
	A.Farman	L.Macari
	M.Hughes	W.Morgan
	FC.McPherson	J.Morris
	A.Quixall	G.Mutch
	A.Ritchie	J.Olsen
	C.Sagar	Stuart Pearson
	C.Taylor	E.Pegg
	T.Taylor	J.Peters
	A.Turnbull	JB.Picken
		WE.Rawlings
	G.Wall	C.Rennox
	L.Whelan	A.Scanlon
1	JT.Allan	F.Stapleton
	G.Anderson	WS.Stewart
	D.Bain	C.Webster
	JH.Beddow	E.West

* Donaldson also scored three trebles for United in the Football Alliance prior to the club being accepted into the Football League.

** These were the only goals that Bullock ever scored for United!

Five Timers in the FA Premier League

1	Andy Cole

Hat-tricks in the FA Premier League

1	A.Kanchelskis

Six Timers in FA Cup

1	G.Best

Five Timers in FA Cup

1	J.Rowley

Four Timers in FA Cup

1	J.Hanson

Hat-tricks in FA Cup

4	D.Law	T.Reid
2	Stan Pearson	A.Turnbull
1	J.H. Beddow	J.Turnbull
	W.Bryant	D.Viollet
	A.Dawson	N.Whiteside
	E.Pegg	F.Williams
	JB.Picken	

Hat-tricks in Football League Cup

2	M.Hughes	B.McClair
1	L.Sharpe	G.Hill

Four Timers in Europe

1	D.Viollet
	D.Law

Hat-tricks in Europe

4	D.Law
1	T.Taylor
	J.Connolly
	D.Herd
	R.Charlton

Player													

Players' Career Records

NB League appearances/goals entries include games played in the Football Alliance but not in the FA Premier League which has its own column. Where an asterisk * appears in the European column this denotes the number of 'Test Match' appearances made in the early days of the Football League's promotion and relegation method, not European games. The chart does not include wartime games when innumerable players turned out for whichever club they were stationed closest to at the time.

Player	FAPL App	FAPL Goals	League App	League Goals	FACup App	FACup Goals	LgeCup App	LgeCup Goals	Europe App	Europe Goals	Totals App	Totals Goals
A Ainsworth (1933)	–	–	2	–	–	–	–	–	–	–	2	–
J Aitken (1895)	–	–	2	1	–	–	–	–	–	–	2	1
G Albison (1920)	–	–	1	–	–	–	–	–	–	–	1	–
AR Albiston (1974/88)	–	–	364/15	6	36	1	38/2	1	26/1	–	464/18	7
JT Allan (1904/06)	–	–	35	21	1	1	–	–	–	–	36	22
RA Allen (1950/52)	–	–	75	5	5	–	–	–	–	–	80	–
A Allman (1914)	–	–	12	–	–	–	–	–	–	–	12	–
A Ambler (1899/1900)	–	–	10	1	–	–	–	–	–	–	10	1
G Anderson (1911/14)	–	–	80	37	6	2	–	–	–	–	86	39
J Anderson (1947/48)	–	–	33	1	6	1	–	–	–	–	39	2
T Anderson (1972/73)	–	–	13/6	2	–	–	–	–	–	–	13/6	2
VA Anderson (1987/91)	–	–	50/4	2	7	1	6/1	1	–	–	64/5	4
WJ Anderson (1963/66)	–	–	7/2	–	2	–	–	–	1	–	10/2	–
TA Arkesden (1902/05)	–	–	70	28	9	5	–	–	–	–	79	33
B Asquith (1939)	–	–	1	–	–	–	–	–	–	–	1	–
JE Astley (1925/26)	–	–	2	–	–	–	–	–	–	–	2	–
J Aston snr (1946/53)	–	–	253	29	29	1	–	–	–	–	282	30
J Aston jnr (1964/71)	–	–	139/16	25	5/2	1	12/3	–	8	1	164/21	27
GR Bailey (1978/87)	–	–	294	–	31	–	28	–	20	–	373	–

Player	FAPL App	FAPL Goals	League App	League Goals	FACup App	FACup Goals	LgeCup App	LgeCup Goals	Europe App	Europe Goals	Totals App	Totals Goals
D Bain (1922/23)	—	—	22	9	1	—	—	—	—	—	23	9
J Bain (1899)	—	—	2	1	—	—	—	—	—	—	2	1
J Bain (1924/27)	—	—	4	—	—	—	—	—	—	—	4	—
W Bainbridge (1945)	—	—	—	—	1	1	—	—	—	—	1	1
HC Baird (1936/37)	—	—	49	15	4	3	—	—	—	—	53	18
T Baldwin (1974)	—	—	2	—	—	—	—	—	—	—	2	—
J Ball (1947/49)	—	—	22	—	1	—	—	—	—	—	23	—
JT Ball (1929/34)	—	—	47	17	3	1	—	—	—	—	50	18
WH Ball (1902)	—	—	4	—	—	—	—	—	—	—	4	—
T Bamford (1934/37)	—	—	98	53	11	4	—	—	—	—	109	57
J Banks (1901/02)	—	—	40	—	4	1	—	—	—	—	44	1
J Bannister (1906/09)	—	—	57	7	4	1	—	—	—	—	61	8
J Barber (1922/23)	—	—	3	1	1	1	—	—	—	—	4	2
C Barlow (1919/21)	—	—	29	1	1	—	—	—	—	—	30	1
PS Barnes (1985/87)	—	—	15/1	2	—	—	5	2	4*	—	24/1	4
F Barrett (1896/97)	—	—	118	—	18	—	—	—	—	—	136	—
F Barson (1922/27)	—	—	140	4	12	—	—	—	—	—	152	4
A Beardsworth (1902)	—	—	9	1	3	1	—	—	—	—	12	2
RH Beale (1912/14)	—	—	105	—	7	—	—	—	—	—	112	—
PA Beardley (1982)	—	—	—	—	—	—	1	—	—	—	1	—
RP Beardsmore (1988/92)	—	—	30/26	4	4/4	—	3/1	—	1/2	—	38/33	4
T Beckett (1886)	—	—	—	—	1	—	—	—	—	—	1	—
D Beckham (1992/)	28/9	7	—	—	4/1	1	5/1	—	3/1	1	40/12	9
JH Beddow (1904/06)	—	—	33	12	1	3	—	—	—	—	34	15
W Behan (1933)	—	—	1	—	—	—	—	—	—	—	1	—

Player	FAPL App	FAPL Goals	League App	League Goals	FACup App	FACup Goals	LgeCup App	LgeCup Goals	Europe App	Europe Goals	Totals App	Totals Goals
A Bell (1902/12)	–	–	278	10	28	–	–	–	–	–	306	10
SR Bennion (1921/32)	–	–	286	2	15	1	–	–	–	–	301	3
G Bent (1954/56)	–	–	12	–	–	–	–	–	–	–	12	–
JJ Berry (1951/57)	–	–	247	37	15	4	–	–	11	3	273	44
W Berry (1906/08)	–	–	13	1	1	–	–	–	–	–	14	1
G Best (1963/73)	–	–	361	137	46	21	25	9	34	11	466	178
PA Bielby (1973)	–	–	2/2	–	–	–	–	–	–	–	2/2	–
B Birch (1949/51)	–	–	11	4	4	1	–	–	–	–	15	5
H Birchenough (1902)	–	–	25	–	5	–	–	–	–	–	30	–
C Birkett (1950)	–	–	9	2	4	–	–	–	–	–	13	2
G Birtles (1980/82)	–	–	57/1	11	4	1	2	–	–	–	63/1	12
G Bissett (1919/21)	–	–	40	10	2	–	–	–	–	–	42	10
R Black (1931/33)	–	–	8	3	–	–	–	–	–	–	8	3
CG Blackmore (1983/94)	12/2	–	138/34	19	15/6	1	23/2	3	12	2	200/44	25
P Blackmore (1899)	–	–	1	–	1	–	–	–	–	–	2	–
T Blackstock (1903/06)	–	–	34	–	4	–	–	–	–	–	38	–
J Blanchflower (1951/57)	–	–	105	26	6	1	–	–	5	–	116	27
WH Blew (1905)	–	–	1	–	–	–	–	–	–	–	1	–
SP Blott (1909/12)	–	–	19	2	–	–	–	–	–	–	19	2
T Bogan (1949/50)	–	–	29	7	4	–	–	–	–	–	33	7
JE Bond (1951/52)	–	–	20	4	1	–	–	–	–	–	21	4
RP Bonthron (1903/06)	–	–	119	3	15	–	–	–	–	–	134	3
W Booth (1900)	–	–	2	–	–	–	–	–	–	–	2	–
M Bosnich (1989/91)	–	–	3	–	–	–	–	–	–	–	3	–
H Boyd (:896/98)	–	–	52	32	7	1	–	–	3*	2	62	35

Player	FAPL App	FAPL Goals	League App	League Goals	FACup App	FACup Goals	LgeCup App	LgeCup Goals	Europe App	Europe Goals	Totals App	Totals Goals
WG Boyd (1934)	–	–	6	4	–	–	–	–	–	–	6	4
TW Boyle (1928/29)	–	–	16	6	1	–	–	–	–	–	17	6
L Bradbury (1938)	–	–	2	1	–	–	–	–	–	–	2	1
W Bradley (1958/61)	–	–	63	20	3	1	–	–	–	–	66	21
H Bratt (1960)	–	–	–	–	–	–	1	–	–	–	1	–
AB Brazil (1984/85)	–	–	18/13	8	–/1	–	4/3	3	2	1	27/17	12
DM Brazil (1988/92)	–	–	–/2	–	–	–	–	–	–	–	–/2	–
J Breedon (1935/39)	–	–	38	–	–	–	–	–	–	–	38	–
T Breen (1936/38)	–	–	65	–	6	–	–	–	–	–	71	–
SA Brennan (1957/69)	–	–	291/1	3	36	3	4	–	24	–	355/1	6
FB Brett (1921)	–	–	10	–	–	–	–	–	–	–	10	–
WR Briggs (1960/61)	–	–	9	–	2	–	–	–	–	–	11	–
WH Brooks (1898)	–	–	3	3	–	–	–	–	–	–	3	3
AH Broome (1922)	–	–	1	–	–	–	–	–	–	–	1	–
H Broomfield (1907)	–	–	9	–	–	–	–	–	–	–	9	–
J Brown (1932/33)	–	–	40	17	1	–	–	–	–	–	41	17
J Brown (1935/38)	–	–	102	1	8	–	–	–	–	–	110	1
RB Brown (1947/48)	–	–	4	–	–	–	–	–	–	–	4	–
W Brown (1892)	–	–	7	–	–	–	–	–	–	–	7	–
W Brown (1896)	–	–	7	2	–	–	–	–	–	–	7	2
SR Bruce (1987/96)	148	11	162	26	41	4	32	6	21/1	6	404/3	53
W Bryant (1896/99)	–	–	109	27	14	6	–	–	4*	–	127	33
W Bryant (1934/39)	–	–	151	44	9	–	–	–	–	–	160	44
G Buchan (1973)	–	–	–/3	–	–	–	–/1	–	–	–	–/4	–
MM Buchan (1971/82)	–	–	376	4	39	–	30	–	10	–	455	4

Player	FAPL		League		FACup		LgeCup		Europe		Totals	
	App	Goals	App	Goals	App	Goals	App	Goals	App	Goals	App	Goals
EW Buckle (1946/49)	-	-	20	6	4	1	-	-	-	-	24	7
FC Buckley (1906)	-	-	3	-	-	-	-	-	-	-	3	-
KJ Bullock (1930)	-	-	10	3	-	-	-	-	-	-	10	3
W Bunce (1902)	-	-	2	-	-	-	-	-	-	-	2	-
H Burgess (1906/09)	-	-	49	-	3	-	-	-	-	-	52	-
RS Burke (1946/48)	-	-	28	16	6	6	-	-	-	-	34	22
T Burke (1886)	-	-	5	-	1	-	-	-	-	-	6	-
FS Burns (1967/71)	-	-	111/10	6	11/1	-	10/1	-	10/1	1	142/13	7
N Butt (1992/)	42/14	3	-	-	10/2	-	3	-	7/1	-	62/17	4
D Byrne (1933)	-	-	4	3	-	-	-	-	-	-	4	3
RW Byrne (1951/57)	-	-	245	17	18	2	-	-	14	-	277	19
J Cairns (1894/98)	-	-	2	-	-	-	-	-	-	-	2	-
WC Campbell (1893)	-	-	5	1	-	-	-	-	-	-	5	1
E Cantona (1992/)	106/1	53	-	-	14	10	6	1	6	2	132/1	66
N Cantwell (1960/66)	-	-	123	6	14	2	-	-	7	-	144	8
JP Cape (1933/36)	-	-	59	18	1	-	-	-	-	-	60	18
A Capper (1911)	-	-	1	-	-	-	-	-	-	-	1	-
JJ Carey (1937/52)	-	-	306	17	38	1	-	-	-	-	344	18
J Carman (1897)	-	-	3	1	-	-	-	-	-	-	3	1
JF Carolan (1958/60)	-	-	66	-	4	-	1	-	-	-	71	-
A Carson (1892)	-	-	13	3	-	-	-	-	-	-	13	3
HR Cartman (1922)	-	-	3	-	-	-	-	-	-	-	3	-
WG Cartwright (1895/1903)	-	-	228	8	27	-	-	-	2*	-	257	8
AA Cashmore (1913)	-	-	3	-	-	-	-	-	-	-	3	-
C Casper (1994	-	-	-	-	-	-	1	-	-	-	1	-

Player	FAPL		League		FACup		LgeCup		Europe		Totals	
	App	Goals	App	Goals	App	Goals	App	Goals	App	Goals	App	Goals
J Cassidy (1892/99)	–	–	152	90	15	9	–	–	7*	1	174	100
L Cassidy (1947/51)	–	–	4	–	–	–	–	–	–	–	4	–
WS Chalmers (1932/33)	–	–	34	1	1	–	–	–	–	–	35	1
W Chapman (1926/27)	–	–	26	–	–	–	–	–	–	–	26	–
R Charlton (1956/72)	–	–	604/2	199	79	19	24	7	45	22	752/2	247
RA Chester (1935)	–	–	13	1	–	–	–	–	–	–	13	1
A Chesters (1929/31)	–	–	9	–	–	–	–	–	–	–	9	–
AC Chilton (1939/54)	–	–	353	3	37	–	–	–	–	–	390	3
JP Chisnall (1961/63)	–	–	35	8	8	1	–	–	4	1	47	10
T Chorlton (1913)	–	–	4	–	–	–	–	–	–	–	4	–
D Christie (1908)	–	–	2	–	–	–	–	–	–	–	2	–
J Christie (1902)	–	–	1	–	–	–	–	–	–	–	1	–
J Clark (1899)	–	–	9	–	–	–	–	–	–	–	9	–
J Clark (1976/77)	–	–	0/1	–	–	–	–	–	2*	–	0/1	–
J Clarkin (1893/95)	–	–	67	23	5	–	–	–	–	–	74	23
G Clayton (1956)	–	–	2	–	–	–	–	–	–	–	2	–
H Cleaver (1902)	–	–	1	–	–	–	–	–	–	–	1	–
JE Clements (1891/93)	–	–	72	–	4	–	–	–	2*	–	78	–
F Clempson (1949/52)	–	–	15	2	–	–	–	–	–	–	15	2
H Cockburn (1946/54)	–	–	243	4	32	–	–	–	–	–	275	4
A Cole (1995/)	49/3	23	–	–	7	2	1	–	1	–	58/3	25
C Collinson (1946)	–	–	7	–	–	–	–	–	–	–	7	–
J Collinson (1895/1900)	–	–	62	16	9	1	–	–	–	–	71	17
E Colman (1955/57)	–	–	85	1	9	–	–	–	13	1	107	2
J Colville (1892)	–	–	9	1	1	–	–	–	–	–	10	1

Player	FAPL App	FAPL Goals	League App	League Goals	FACup App	FACup Goals	LgeCup App	LgeCup Goals	Europe App	Europe Goals	Totals App	Totals Goals
J Connachan (1898)	–	–	4	–	–	–	–	–	–	–	4	–
JP Connaughton (1971)	–	–	3	–	–	–	–	–	–	–	3	–
TE Connell (1978)	–	–	2	–	–	–	–	–	–	–	2	–
JM Connelly (1964/66)	–	–	79/1	22	13	2	1	–	19	11	112/1	35
E Connor (1909/10)	–/3	–	15	2	–	–	–	–	–/1	–	15	2
T Cooke (1995/	1/3	–	–	–	–	–	1/1	1	–/1	–	2/5	1
SP Cookson (1914)	–	–	12	–	1	–	–	–	–	–	13	–
R Cope (1956/60)	–	–	93	2	10	–	1	–	2	–	106	2
SJ Coppell (1974/82)	–	–	320/2	54	36	4	25	9	11/1	3	392/3	70
J Coupar (1892/1901)	–	–	32	9	–	–	–	–	2*	1	34	10
PD Coyne (1975)	–	–	1/1	1	–	–	–	–	–	–	1/1	1
T Craig (1889/90)	–	–	25	5	2	1	–	–	–	–	27	6
C Craven (1938)	–	–	11	2	–	–	–	–	–	–	11	2
PT Crerand (1962/70)	–	–	304	10	43	4	4	–	41	1	392	15
J Crompton (1945/56)	–	–	191	–	20	–	–	–	–	–	211	–
GA Crooks (1983)	–	–	6/1	2	–	–	–	–	–	–	6/1	2
S Crowther (1957/58)	–	–	13	–	5	–	–	–	2	–	20	–
J Cunningham (1898)	–	–	15	–	2	–	–	–	–	–	17	–
LP Cunningham (1982)	–	–	3/2	1	–	–	–	–	–	–	3/2	1
JJ Curry (1908/10)	–	–	13	–	1	–	–	–	–	–	14	–
A Dale (1890)	–	–	–	–	1	–	–	–	–	–	1	–
J Dale (1947)	–	–	2	–	–	–	–	–	–	–	2	–
W Dale (1928/31)	–	–	64	–	4	–	–	–	–	–	68	–
E Dalton (1907)	–	–	1	–	–	–	–	–	–	–	1	–
GA Daly (1973/76)	–	–	107/4	23	9/1	5	17	4	4	–	137/5	32

Player	FAPL		League		FACup		LgeCup		Europe		Totals	
	App	Goals	App	Goals	App	Goals	App	Goals	App	Goals	App	Goals
P Davenport (1985/89)	–	–	72/19	22	2/2	–	8/2	4	1*	–	83/23	26
WR Davidson (1893/94)	–	–	40	2	3	–	–	–	1	1	44	2
A Davies (1981/83)	–	–	6/1	–	2	–	–	–	–/1	1	8/2	1
JE Davies (1886/89)	–	–	21	2	2	–	–	–	–	–	23	2
J Davies (1892)	–	–	10	–	1	–	–	–	2*	–	13	–
L Davies (1886)	–	–	–	–	–	–	–	–	–	–	1	–
RT Davies (1974)	4/7	–	–/8	–	–/2	–	–	–	–	–	–/10	–
S Davies (1994)	–	–	–	–	1	–	4	–	2/1	1	10/8	1
WR Davies (1972)	–	–	15/1	4	1	–	–	–	–	–	16/1	4
AD Dawson (1956/71)	–	–	80	45	10	8	3	1	–	–	93	54
H Dean (1931)	–	–	2	–	–	–	–	–	–	–	2	–
J Delaney (1946/50)	–	–	164	25	19	3	–	–	–/1	–	183	28
MJ Dempsey (1983/86)	–	–	1	–	–	–	–	–	–	–	1/1	–
J Denman (1891)	–	–	6	–	1	–	–	–	–	–	7	–
W Dennis (1923)	–	–	3	–	–	–	–	–	–	–	3	–
N Dewar (1932/33)	–	–	36	14	–	–	–	–	–	–	36	14
J Doherty (1952/57)	–	–	25	7	1	–	–	–	–	–	26	7
B Donaghy (1905)	–	–	3	–	–	–	–	–	–	–	3	–
MM Donaghy (1988/92)	–	–	76/13	–	10	–	10/4	–	2/3	–	98/20	–
IR Donald (1972)	–	–	4	–	–	–	2	–	–	–	6	–
R Donaldson (1892/97)	–	–	153	76	16	10	–	–	8*	–	177	86
J Donnelly (1890)	–	–	1	–	–	–	–	–	–	–	1	–
A Donnelly (1908/12)	–	–	34	–	–	3	–	–	–	–	37	–
T Dougan (1938)	–	–	4	–	–	–	–	–	–	–	4	–
J Doughty (1886/91)	–	–	26	11	3	3	–	–	–	–	29	14

Player	FAPL App	FAPL Goals	League App	League Goals	FACup App	FACup Goals	LgeCup App	LgeCup Goals	Europe App	Europe Goals	Totals App	Totals Goals
R Doughty (1891/96)	–	–	56	3	5	1	–	–	3*	–	64	4
W Douglas (1893/95)	–	–	55	–	1	–	–	–	1*	–	57	–
JM Dow (1893/95)	–	–	48	6	1	–	–	–	1*	–	50	6
ALB Downie (1902/09)	–	–	172	12	19	2	–	–	–	–	191	14
JD Downie (1948/52)	–	–	110	35	5	1	–	–	–	–	115	36
WL Draycott (1896/98)	–	–	81	6	10	–	–	–	4*	–	95	6
D Dublin (1992/94)	4/8	2	–	–	1/1	–	1/1	1	-/1	–	6/11	3
R Duckworth (1903/12)	–	–	225	11	26	–	–	–	–	–	251	11
W Dunn (1897)	–	–	10	–	2	–	–	–	–	–	12	–
AP Dunne (1960/72)	–	–	414	2	54/1	1	21	–	40	–	529/1	2
PAJ Dunne (1964/65)	–	–	45	–	7	–	1	–	13	–	66	–
M Duxbury (1980/90)	–	–	274/25	6	20/5	1	32/2	–	17/1	–	343/33	7
JA Dyer (1905)	–	–	1	–	–	–	–	–	–	–	1	–
J Earp (1886)	–	–	–	–	1	–	–	–	–	–	1	–
A Edge (1891)	–	–	19	6	3	3	–	–	–	–	22	9
H Edmonds (1910/11)	–	–	43	–	7	–	–	–	–	–	50	–
D Edwards (1952/57)	–	–	151	20	12	1	–	–	12	–	175	21
PF Edwards (1969/72)	–	–	52/2	–	10	–	4	1	–	–	66/2	1
D Ellis (1923)	–	–	11	–	–	–	–	–	–	–	11	–
FC Erentz (1892/1901)	–	–	280	9	23	–	–	–	7*	–	310	9
H Erentz (1897)	–	–	6	–	3	–	–	–	–	–	9	–
G Evans (1890)	–	–	12	5	1	1	–	–	–	–	13	6
S Evans (1923)	–	–	6	2	–	–	–	–	–	–	6	2
JW Fall (1893)	–	–	23	–	3	–	–	–	1*	–	27	–
AH Farman (1889/94)	–	–	111	43	7	6	–	–	3*	4	121	53

Player	FAPL		League		FACup		LgeCup		Europe		Totals	
	App	Goals	App	Goals	App	Goals	App	Goals	App	Goals	App	Goals
I Feeman (1949)	–	–	12	–	2	–	–	–	–	–	14	–
G Felton (1890)	–	–	8	–	1	–	–	–	–	–	9	–
D Ferguson (1927)	–	–	4	–	–	–	–	–	–	–	4	–
D Ferguson (1990/94)	16/2	–	4/5	–	1	–	1/1	–	–	–	22/8	1
J Ferguson (1931)	–	–	8	1	–	–	–	–	–	–	8	1
RJ Ferrier (1935/37)	–	–	18	4	1	–	–	–	–	–	19	4
WJ Fielding (1946)	–	–	6	–	1	–	–	–	–	–	7	–
J Fisher (1900/01)	–	–	42	2	4	1	–	–	–	–	46	3
J Fitchett (1902/04)	–	–	16	1	2	–	–	–	–	–	18	1
GA Fitton (1931/32)	–	–	12	2	–	–	–	–	–	–	12	2
JH Fitzpatrick (1964/72)	–	–	111/6	8	11	1	12	1	7	–	141/6	10
D Fitzsimmons (1895/99)	–	–	28	–	3	–	–	–	–	–	31	–
T Fitzsimmons (1892/93)	–	–	27	6	1	–	–	–	2*	–	30	6
P Fletcher (1972/73)	–	–	2/5	–	–	–	–	–	–	–	2/5	–
A Foggan (1976)	–	–	–/3	–	–	–	–	–	–	–	–/3	–
G Foley (1899)	–	–	7	1	–	–	–	–	–	–	7	1
JB Ford (1908/09)	–	–	5	–	–	–	–	–	–	–	5	–
T Forster (1919/21)	–	–	35	1	1	–	–	–	–	–	36	1
A Forsyth (1972/77)	–	–	99/2	4	10	1	7	–	–/1	–	116/3	5
W.A Foulkes (1952/69)	–	–	563/3	7	61	–	–	–	52	2	679/3	9
W Fox (1914)	–	–	–	–	1	–	–	–	–	–	1	–
T Frame (1932/33)	–	–	51	4	1	–	–	–	–	–	52	4
SH Gallimore (1930/33)	–	–	72	19	4	1	–	–	–	–	76	20
CR Gardner (1935/36)	–	–	16	1	2	–	–	–	–	–	18	1
WF Garton (1984/88)	–	–	39/2	–	3	–	5/1	–	–/1	–	47/4	–

Player	FAPL App	FAPL Goals	League App	League Goals	FACup App	FACup Goals	LgeCup App	LgeCup Goals	Europe App	Europe Goals	Totals App	Totals Goals
J Garvey (1900)	–	–	6	–	–	–	–	–	–	–	6	–
JD Gaskell (1957/66)	–	–	96	–	–	–	1	–	5	–	118	–
R Gaudie (1903)	–	–	7	–	–	–	–	–	–	–	8	–
CJ Gibson (1985/91)	–	–	74/5	9	8/1	–	7	–	–	–	89/6	9
R Gibson (1921)	–	–	11	–	1	–	–	–	–	–	12	–
TB Gibson (1985/87)	–	–	14/9	1	1/1	–	-/2	–	–	–	15/12	1
TRD Gibson (1950/54)	–	–	108	–	6	–	–	–	–	–	114	–
J Gidman (1981/86)	–	–	94/1	4	9	–	5	–	7/2	–	115/3	4
R Giggs (1990/)	131/10	34	33/7	5	24/2	6	15/5	6	11	2	214/24	53
MJ Giles (1959/62)	–	–	99	10	13	2	2		–	–	114	13
AGD Gill (1986/88)	3/6	1	5/5	1	2/2	–	–	–	–	–	7/7	2
K Gillespie (1992/1995)	–	–	–	–	1	–	3	–	4*	–	7/6	2
M Gillespie (1896/90)	–	–	74	17	11	–	–	–	–	–	89	21
T Gipps (1912/14)	–	–	23	–	–	–	–	–	–	–	23	–
DJ Givens (1969)	–	–	4/4	1	–	–	1	–	–	–	5/4	1
GWE Gladwin (1936/38)	–	–	27	–	1	–	–	–	–	–	28	–
G Godsmark (1899)	–	–	9	4	–	–	–	–	–	–	9	4
EH Goldthorpe (1922/24)	–	–	27	15	3	–	–	–	–	–	30	16
FJ Goodwin (1954/59)	–	–	95	7	8	–	–	–	3	–	106	8
W Goodwin (1920/21)	–	–	7	–	–	–	–	–	–	–	7	–
J Gotheridge (1886)	–	–	5	–	1	–	–	–	–	–	6	–
J Gourlay (1898)	–	–	1	–	–	–	–	–	–	–	1	–
AE Gowling (1967/71)	–	–	64/7	18	6/2	2	7/1	1	–	–	77/10	21
A Graham (1983/84)	–	–	33/4	5	1	–	6	1	6/1	1	46/5	7
DWT Graham (1987)	–	–	1/1	–	0/1	–	0/1	–	–	–	1/3	1

Player	FAPL		League		FACup		LgeCup		Europe		Totals	
	App	Goals	App	Goals	App	Goals	App	Goals	App	Goals	App	Goals
G Graham (1972/74)	–	–	41/2	2	2	–	1	–	–	–	44/2	2
J Graham (1893)	–	–	4	–	–	–	–	–	–	–	4	–
W Grassam (1903/04)	–	–	29	13	8	1	–	–	–	–	37	14
ID Greaves (1954/59)	–	–	67	4	6	–	2	–	–	–	75	4
RE Green (1933)	–	–	9	4	–	–	–	–	–	–	9	4
B Greenhoff (1973/79)	–	–	218/3	13	24	2	19	2	6	–	267/3	17
J Greenhoff (1976/80)	–	–	94/3	26	18/1	9	4	1	2	–	118/4	36
W Greenwood (1900)	–	–	3	–	–	–	–	–	–	–	3	–
H Gregg (1957/66)	–	–	210	–	24	–	2	–	11	–	247	–
CL Griffiths (1973)	–	–	7	–	–	–	–	–	–	–	7	–
J Griffiths (1933/39)	–	–	168	1	8	–	–	–	–	–	176	1
W Griffiths (1898/1904)	–	–	157	27	18	3	–	–	–	–	175	30
AA Grimes (1977/82)	–	–	62/28	10	5	1	6	–	4/2	–	77/30	11
A Grimshaw (1975)	–	–	–/1	–	–	–	–/1	–	–	–	–/2	–
JB Grimwood (1919/26)	–	–	196	8	9	–	–	–	–	–	205	8
J Grundy (1899/1900)	–	–	11	3	–	–	–	–	–	–	11	3
H Gyves (1890)	–	–	–	–	1	–	–	–	–	–	1	–
J Hacking (1933/34)	–	–	32	–	2	–	–	–	–	–	34	–
J Hall (1933/35)	–	–	67	–	6	–	–	–	–	–	73	–
J Hall (1925)	–	–	3	–	–	–	–	–	–	–	3	–
P Hall (1903)	–	–	8	2	–	–	–	–	–	–	8	2
HJ Halse (1907/11)	–	–	109	41	15	9	–	–	–	–	124	50
RL Halton (1936)	–	–	4	1	–	–	–	–	–	–	4	1
M Hamill (1911/13)	–	–	57	2	2	–	–	–	–	–	59	2
JJ Hanlon (1938/48)	–	–	64	20	6	2	–	–	–	–	70	22

Player	FAPL		League		FACup		LgeCup		Europe		Totals	
	App	Goals	App	Goals	App	Goals	App	Goals	App	Goals	App	Goals
C Hannaford (1925/26)	–	–	11	–	1	–	–	–	–	–	12	–
J Hanson (1924/29)	–	–	138	47	9	5	–	–	–	–	147	52
HP Hardman (1908)	–	–	4	–	–	–	–	–	–	–	4	–
FE Harris (1919/21)	–	–	46	2	3	–	–	–	–	–	49	2
T Harris (1926)	–	–	4	1	–	–	–	–	–	–	4	1
C Harrison (1889)	–	–	9	–	1	–	–	–	–	–	10	–
WE Harrison (1920/21)	–	–	44	5	2	–	–	–	–	–	46	5
RW Harrop (1957/58)	–	–	10	5	1	–	–	–	–	–	11	5
W Hartwell (1903/04)	–	–	3	–	1	–	–	–	–	–	4	–
G Haslam (1921/27)	–	–	25	–	2	–	–	–	–	–	27	–
R Haworth (1926)	–	–	2	–	–	–	–	–	–	–	2	–
A Hawksworth (1956)	–	–	1	–	–	–	–	–	–	–	1	–
T Hay (1889)	–	–	15	–	1	–	–	–	–	–	16	–
F Haydock (1960/62)	–	–	6	–	–	–	–	–	–	–	6	–
JV Hayes (1900/10)	–	–	115	–	13	–	–	–	–	–	128	–
H Haywood (1932/33)	–	–	4	2	–	–	–	–	–	–	4	2
JF Haywood (1913/14)	–	–	26	2	–	–	–	–	–	–	26	2
J Heathcote (1899/1900)	–	–	7	–	1	–	–	–	–	–	8	–
W Henderson (1921/24)	–	–	34	17	2	–	–	–	–	–	36	17
J Hendry (1892)	–	–	2	1	–	–	–	–	–	–	2	1
A Henrys (1891/92)	–	–	23	–	3	–	–	–	–	–	26	–
DG Herd (1961/67)	–	–	201/1	114	35	15	1	1	25	14	262/1	144
FTR Heron (1957/60)	–	–	3	–	–	–	–	–	–	–	3	–
W Higgins (1901)	–	–	10	–	–	–	–	–	–	–	10	–
MN Higgins (1985/87)	–	–	6	–	2	–	–	–	–	–	8	–

Player	FAPL App	FAPL Goals	League App	League Goals	FACup App	FACup Goals	LgeCup App	LgeCup Goals	Europe App	Europe Goals	Totals App	Totals Goals
J Higson (1901)	–	–	5	1	–	–	–	–	–	–	5	1
CG Hilditch (1919/31)	–	–	301	7	21	–	–	–	–	–	322	7
GA Hill (1975/77)	–	–	100/1	39	17	6	7	4	8	2	132/1	51
CE Hillam (1933)	–	–	8	–	–	–	–	–	–	–	8	–
EW Hine (1932/34)	–	–	51	12	2	–	–	–	–	–	53	12
J Hodge (1910/19)	–	–	79	2	7	–	–	–	–	–	86	2
J Hodge (1913/14)	–	–	30	–	–	–	–	–	–	–	30	–
FC Hodges (1919/20)	–	–	20	4	–	–	–	–	–	–	20	4
L Hofton (1910/20)	–	–	17	–	1	–	–	–	–	–	18	–
GJ Hogg (1983/87)	–	–	82/1	1	8	–	7/1	–	10	–	107/2	1
RH Holdren (1904/12)	–	–	106	1	11	–	–	–	–	–	117	1
J Holt (1899)	–	–	1	–	–	–	–	–	–	–	1	–
JA Holton (1972/74)	–	–	63	5	2	–	4	–	–	–	69	5
TP Homer (1909/11)	–	–	25	14	–	–	–	–	–	–	25	14
W Hood (1892/93)	–	–	48	11	3	–	–	–	2*	–	53	11
AH Hooper (1909/13)	–	–	7	1	–	–	–	–	–	–	7	1
F Hopkin (1919/20)	–	–	70	8	4	–	–	–	–	–	74	8
J Hopkins (1898)	–	–	1	–	–	–	–	–	–	–	1	–
S Hopkinson (1930/33)	–	–	51	10	2	2	–	–	–	–	53	12
SM Houston (1973/79)	–	–	204/1	13	22	1	16	2	6/1	–	248/2	16
JT Howarth (1921)	–	–	4	–	–	–	–	–	–	–	4	–
E Howells (1886)	–	–	–	–	1	–	–	–	–	–	1	–
EK Hudson (1913/14)	–	–	11	–	–	–	–	–	–	–	11	–
M Hughes (1983/1995)	110/1	35	227/8	85	45/1	17	37/1	16	30/3	9	449/14	162
A Hulme (1907/08)	–	–	4	–	–	–	–	–	–	–	4	–

Player	FAPL		League		FACup		LgeCup		Europe		Totals	
	App	Goals	App	Goals	App	Goals	App	Goals	App	Goals	App	Goals
GH Hunter (1913/14)	–	–	22	2	1	–	–	–	–	–	23	2
RJ Hunter (1958)	–	–	1	–	–	–	–	–	–	–	1	–
W Hunter (1912)	–	–	3	2	–	–	–	–	–	–	3	2
DJ Hurst (1902)	–	–	16	4	5	–	–	–	–	–	21	4
R Iddon (1925/26)	–	–	2	–	–	–	–	–	–	–	2	–
PEC Ince (1989/1995)	116	19	87/2	6	25/1	1	24/1	2	19	–	271/4	28
WW Inglis (1925/28)	–	–	14	1	–	–	–	–	–	–	14	1
D Irwin (1990/)	153	10	70/2	4	29	6	28/2	–	13	–	293/4	20
TA Jackson (1975/76)	–	–	18/1	–	–	–	4	–	–	–	22/1	–
W Jackson (1899/1900)	–	–	61	12	3	2	–	–	–	–	64	14
SR James (1968/74)	–	–	129	4	12	–	17/1	–	2	–	160/1	4
CAL Jenkyns (1896/97)	–	–	35	5	8	–	–	–	4*	1	47	6
WR John (1936)	–	–	15	–	–	–	–	–	–	–	15	–
SC Johnson (1900)	–	–	1	–	–	–	–	–	–	–	1	–
WG Johnston (1927/31)	–	–	71	24	6	3	–	–	–	–	77	27
D Jones (1937)	–	–	1	–	–	–	–	–	–	–	1	–
EP Jones (1957)	–	–	1	–	–	–	–	–	–	–	1	–
M Jones (1950/57)	–	–	103	1	7	–	–	–	10	–	120	1
OJ Jones (1898)	–	–	2	–	–	–	–	–	–	–	2	–
T Jones (1924/36)	–	–	189	–	11	–	–	–	–	–	200	–
TJ Jones (1934)	–	–	20	4	2	–	–	–	–	–	22	4
J Jordan (1977/80)	–	–	109	37	11/1	2	4	2	1	–	125/1	41
N Jovanovich (1979/80)	–	–	20/1	4	1	–	2	–	2	–	25/1	4
A Kanchelskis (1990/95)	67/21	23	29/6	5	14/1	5	12	2	7	1	129/28	36
R Keane (1993/)	86/4	13	–	–	19/1	1	7/2	–	9	3	121/7	17

Player	FAPL App	FAPL Goals	League App	League Goals	FACup App	FACup Goals	LgeCup App	LgeCup Goals	Europe App	Europe Goals	Totals App	Totals Goals
JW Kelly (1975)	–	–	–/1	–	–	–	–	–	–	–	–/1	–
F Kennedy (1923/24)	–	–	17	4	1	–	–	–	–	–	18	4
PA Kennedy (1954)	–	–	1	–	–	–	–	–	–	–	1	–
WJ Kennedy (1895/96)	–	–	30	11	3	1	–	–	–	–	33	12
H Kerr (1903)	–	–	2	–	–	–	–	–	–	–	2	–
B Kidd (1967/73)	–	–	195/8	52	24/1	8	20	7	16	3	255/9	70
J Kinloch (1892)	–	–	1	–	1	1	–	–	–	–	1	1
AJ Kinsey (1964)	–	–	1	1	–	–	–	–	–	–	1	1
F Knowles (1911/14)	–	–	46	1	1	–	–	–	1	–	47	1
F Kopel (1967/68)	–	–	8/2	–	1	–	1	–	–	–	10/2	1
JG Lancaster (1949)	–	–	2	–	2	–	–	–	–	–	4	–
T Lang (1935/36)	–	–	12	1	1	–	–	–	–	–	13	1
L Langford (1934/35)	–	–	15	–	–	–	–	–	–	–	15	–
HH Lappin (1900/02)	–	–	27	4	–	–	–	–	–	–	27	4
D Law (1961/72)	–	–	305/4	171	44/2	34	11	3	33	28	393/6	236
RR Lawson (1900)	–	–	3	–	–	–	–	–	–	–	3	–
N Lawton (1959/62)	–	–	36	6	7	–	1	–	–	–	44	6
E Lee (1898/99)	–	–	11	5	–	–	–	–	–	–	11	5
T Leigh (1899/1900)	–	–	43	15	3	–	–	–	–	–	46	15
J Leighton (1988/91)	–	–	73	–	14	–	7	–	–	–	94	–
HD Leonard (1920)	–	–	10	5	–	–	–	–	–	–	10	5
E Lewis (1952/55)	–	–	20	9	4	2	–	–	–	–	24	11
L Lievesley (1931)	–	–	2	–	1	–	–	–	–	–	3	–
W Lievesley (1922)	–	–	2	–	–	–	–	–	–	–	2	–
OHS Linkson (1908/12)	–	–	55	–	4	–	–	–	–	–	59	–

Player	FAPL		League		FACup		LgeCup		Europe		Totals	
	App	Goals	App	Goals	App	Goals	App	Goals	App	Goals	App	Goals
GT Livingstone (1908/13)	–	–	43	4	3	–	–	–	–	–	46	4
AW Lochhead (1921/25)	–	–	147	50	6	–	–	–	–	–	153	50
W Longair (1894)	–	–	1	–	–	–	–	–	–	–	1	–
W Longton (1886)	–	–	–	–	1	–	–	–	–	–	1	–
T Lowrie (1947/49)	–	–	13	–	1	–	–	–	–	–	14	–
G Lydon (1930/31)	–	–	3	–	–	–	–	–	–	–	3	–
D Lyner (1922)	–	–	3	–	–	–	–	–	–	–	3	–
S Lynn (1947/49)	–	–	13	–	–	–	–	–	–	–	13	–
G Lyons (1903/05)	–	–	4	–	1	–	–	–	–	–	5	–
L Macari (1972/83)	–	–	311/18	78	31/3	8	22/5	10	9/1	1	373/27	97
N McBain (1921/22)	–	–	42	2	1	–	–	–	–	–	43	2
J McCalliog (1973/74)	–	–	31	7	1	–	5/1	–	–	–	37/1	7
P McCarthy (1911)	–	–	1	–	–	–	–	–	–	–	1	–
W McCartney (1903)	–	–	13	1	–	–	–	–	–	–	13	1
WJ McCartney (1894)	–	–	18	1	–	–	–	–	1*	–	20	1
BJ McClair (1987)	100/30	18	190/3	70	34/5	14	41/1	19	17	5	382/39	126
J McClelland (1936)	–	–	5	1	–	–	–	–	–	–	5	1
JJ McCrae (1925)	–	–	9	–	4	–	–	–	–	–	13	–
D McCreery (1974/78)	–	–	48/39	7	1/6	–	4/4	1	4/3	–	57/52	8
K MacDonald (1922/23)	–	–	9	2	–	–	–	–	–	–	9	2
W McDonald (1931/33)	–	–	27	4	–	–	–	–	–	–	27	4
EJ MacDougall (1972)	–	–	18	5	–	–	–	–	–	–	18	5
NW McFarlane (1953)	–	–	1	–	–	–	–	–	–	–	1	–
R McFarlane (1891)	–	–	18	1	3	–	–	–	–	–	21	1
D McFetteridge (1894)	–	–	1	–	–	–	–	–	–	–	1	–

243

Player	FAPL		League		FACup		LgeCup		Europe		Totals	
	App	Goals	App	Goals	App	Goals	App	Goals	App	Goals	App	Goals
ST McGarvey (1891/92)	–	–	13/12	3	–	–	–	–	–	–	13/12	3
P McGibbon (1995/)	–	–	1	–	–	–	–	–	–	–	1	–
C McGillivray (1933)	–	–	8	–	1	–	–	–	–	–	9	–
J McGillivray (1907/08)	–	–	3	–	1	–	–	–	–	–	4	–
W McGlen (1946/51)	–	–	110	2	12	–	–	–	–	–	122	2
P McGrath (1982/89)	–	–	159/4	12	15/3	2	13	2	4	–	191/7	16
W McGuinness (1955/59)	–	–	81	2	2	–	2	–	–	–	85	2
SB McIlroy (1971/81)	–	–	320/22	57	35/3	6	25/3	6	10	2	390/28	71
E McIlvenny (1950)	–	–	2	–	–	–	–	–	–	–	2	–
W McKay (1933/39)	–	–	171	15	13	–	–	–	–	–	184	15
C McKee (1994)	1	–	–	–	–	–	–	–	–	–	1	–
C Mackie (1904)	–	–	5	3	2	1	–	–	–	–	7	4
GH McLachlan (1929/32)	–	–	110	4	6	–	–	–	–	–	116	4
H McLenahan (1929/32)	–	–	112	11	4	1	–	–	–	–	116	12
A Macmillan (1890)	–	–	2	–	–	–	–	–	–	–	2	–
ST McMillan (1961/62)	–	–	15	–	–	–	–	–	–	–	15	–
WS McMillen (1933/34)	–	–	27	2	2	–	–	–	–	–	29	2
JR McNaught (1893/97)	–	–	140	12	17	–	–	–	5*	–	162	12
T McNulty (1949/53)	–	–	57	–	2	–	–	–	–	–	59	–
FC McPherson (1923/27)	–	–	159	45	16	7	–	–	–	–	175	52
G McQueen (1977/84)	–	–	184	20	21	2	16	4	7	–	228	26
H McShane (1950/53)	–	–	56	8	1	–	–	–	–	–	57	8
G Maiorana (1988/)	–	–	2/5	–	–	–	–/1	–	–	–	2/6	–
T Manley (1931/38)	–	–	188	40	7	1	–	–	–	–	195	41
FD Mann (1922/29)	–	–	180	5	17	–	–	–	–	–	197	5

Player	FAPL App	FAPL Goals	League App	League Goals	FACup App	FACup Goals	LgeCup App	LgeCup Goals	Europe App	Europe Goals	Totals App	Totals Goals
H Mann (1931)	–	–	13	2	–	–	–	–	–	–	13	2
T Manns (1933)	–	–	2	–	–	–	–	–	–	–	2	–
AE Marshall (1902)	–	–	6	–	–	–	–	–	–	–	6	–
LA Martin (1987/1993)	1	–	55/17	1	13/1	1	8/2	–	6/5	–	83/25	2
MP Martin (1972/74)	–	–	33/7	2	2	–	1	–	–	–	36/7	2
D May (1994/)	26/9	3	–	–	3	–	2	1	4	–	35/9	4
W Mathieson (1892/93)	–	–	13	–	–	–	–	–	–	–	13	–
T Meehan (1919/20)	–	–	51	3	2	–	–	–	–	–	53	3
J Mellor (1930/36)	–	–	116	6	6	–	–	–	–	–	122	6
AW Menzies (1906/07)	–	–	23	4	2	–	–	–	–	–	25	4
WH Meredith (1906/20)	–	–	303	35	29	–	–	–	–	–	332	35
JW Mew (1912/25)	–	–	186	–	13	–	–	–	–	–	199	–
R Milarvie (1890)	–	–	22	4	1	–	–	–	–	–	23	4
G Millar (1894)	–	–	6	5	1	–	–	–	–	–	7	5
J Miller (1923)	–	–	4	1	–	–	–	–	–	–	4	1
T Miller (1920)	–	–	25	7	2	1	–	–	–	–	27	8
R Milne (1988/91)	–	–	19/4	3	7	–	–	–	–	–	26/4	3
A Mitchell (1886/93)	–	–	90	–	7	–	–	–	3*	–	90	–
A Mitchell (1932)	–	–	–	–	–	–	1	–	–	–	1	–
C Mitten (1946/49)	–	–	142	50	19	11	–	–	–	–	161	61
HH Moger (1903/11)	–	–	242	–	22	–	–	–	–	–	264	–
I Moir (1960/64)	–	–	45	5	–	–	–	–	–	–	45	5
A Montgomery (1905)	–	–	3	–	–	–	–	–	–	–	3	–
J Montgomery (1914/20)	–	–	27	1	1	–	–	–	–	–	27	1
J Moody (1931/32)	–	–	50	–	1	–	–	–	–	–	51	–

Player	FAPL		League		FACup		LgeCup		Europe		Totals	
	App	Goals	App	Goals	App	Goals	App	Goals	App	Goals	App	Goals
CW Moore (1919/29)	–	–	309	–	19	–	–	–	–	–	328	–
G Moore (1963)	–	–	18	4	1	1	–	–	–	–	19	5
KR Moran (1978/88)	–	–	228/3	21	18	1	24/1	2	13/1	–	283/5	24
H Morgan (1900)	–	–	20	4	3	–	–	–	–	–	23	4
W Morgan (1896/1902)	–	–	143	6	9	1	–	–	–	–	152	7
W Morgan (1968/75)	–	–	236/2	25	27	4	24/1	3	4	1	291/3	33
KG Morgans (1957/60)	–	–	17	–	2	–	–	–	4	–	23	–
J Morris (1946/48)	–	–	83	32	9	3	–	–	–	–	92	35
T Morrison (1902/03)	–	–	29	7	7	1	–	–	–	–	36	8
BW Morton (1935)	–	–	1	–	–	–	–	–	–	–	1	–
RM Moses (1981/88)	–	–	143/7	7	11	1	22/2	4	12/1	–	188/10	12
AJH Muhren (1982/84)	–	–	65/5	13	8	1	11	1	8	3	92/5	18
RD Murray (1937)	–	–	4	–	–	–	–	–	–	–	4	–
G Mutch (1934/37)	–	–	112	46	8	3	–	–	–	–	120	49
J Myerscough (1920/22)	–	–	33	8	1	–	–	–	–	–	34	8
G Neville (1992/)	47/3	–	–	–	9/1	–	3/1	–	2/4	–	61/9	–
P Neville (1995/)	22/4	–	–	–	7/1	–	1/1	–	1	–	31/6	–
GW Nevin (1933)	–	–	4	–	1	–	–	–	–	–	5	–
P Newton (1933)	–	–	2	–	–	–	–	–	–	–	2	–
JM Nicholl (1974/81)	–	–	188/9	3	22/4	1	14	1	10	1	234/13	6
JJ Nicholson (1960/65)	–	–	58	5	7	1	3	–	–	–	68	6
G Nichol (1927/28)	–	–	6	2	1	–	–	–	–	–	7	2
R Noble (1965/66)	–	–	31	–	2	–	–	–	–	–	33	–
JP Norton (1913/14)	–	–	37	3	–	–	–	–	–	–	37	3
TA Nuttall (1911/12)	–	–	16	4	–	–	–	–	–	–	16	4

Player	FAPL App	FAPL Goals	League App	League Goals	FACup App	FACup Goals	LgeCup App	LgeCup Goals	Europe App	Europe Goals	Totals App	Totals Goals
LF O'Brien (1986/88)	–	–	16/15	2	-/2	–	1/2	–	–	–	17/19	2
W O'Brien (1901)	–	–	1	–	–	–	–	–	–	–	1	–
P O'Connell (1914)	–	–	34	2	1	–	–	–	–	–	35	2
J O'Kane (1994/)	-/1	–	–	–	1	–	1/1	–	1	–	3/2	–
RL Olive (1952)	–	–	2	–	–	–	–	–	–	–	2	–
J Olsen (1984/89)	–	–	119/20	21	13/3	2	10/3	1	6/1	–	148/27	24
TP O'Neil (1970/72)	–	–	54	–	7	–	7	–	–	–	68	–
W O'Shaughnessey (1890)	–	–	–	–	1	–	–	–	–	–	1	–
A Owen (1898)	–	–	1	–	–	–	–	–	–	–	1	–
G Owen (1889)	–	–	12	2	–	–	–	–	–	–	12	2
J Owen (1889/91)	–	–	52	3	6	–	–	–	–	–	58	3
W Owen (1934/35)	–	–	17	1	–	–	–	–	–	–	17	1
LA Page (1931/32)	–	–	12	–	–	–	–	–	–	–	12	–
GA Pallister (1989/	146	5	108/3	4	34	2	36	–	25/1	1	349/4	12
AA Pape (1924/25)	–	–	18	5	–	–	–	–	–	–	18	5
B Parker (1893)	–	–	11	–	1	–	–	–	–	–	12	–
P Parker (1991/96)	76/3	1	24	–	14/1	1	15	–	16/5	–	145/11	2
TA Parker (1930/31)	–	–	17	–	–	–	–	–	–	–	17	–
R Parkinson (1899)	–	–	15	7	–	–	–	–	–	–	15	7
AE Partridge (1920/28)	–	–	148	16	12	2	–	–	–	–	160	18
SW Paterson (1976/79)	–	–	3/3	–	–	–	2	–	-/2	–	5/5	–
E Payne (1908)	–	–	2	1	–	–	–	–	–	–	2	1
S Pears (1984)	–	–	4	–	1	–	–	–	–	–	5	–
M Pearson (1957/62)	–	–	68	12	7	1	3	1	2	–	80	14
SC Pearson (1937/53)	–	–	315	128	30	21	–	–	–	–	345	149

Player	FAPL		League		FACup		LgeCup		Europe		Totals	
	App	Goals	App	Goals	App	Goals	App	Goals	App	Goals	App	Goals
JS Pearson (1974/77)	–	–	138/1	55	22	5	12	5	6	1	178/1	66
JH Peddie (1902/06)	–	–	112	52	9	6	–	–	–	–	121	58
J Peden (1893)	–	–	28	7	3	1	–	–	1*	–	32	8
J Pedley (1889)	–	–	1	–	–	–	–	–	–	–	1	–
D Pegg (1952/57)	–	–	127	24	9	–	–	–	12	4	148	28
E Pegg (1902/03)	–	–	41	13	10	7	–	–	–	–	51	20
JK Pegg (1947)	–	–	2	–	–	–	–	–	–	–	2	–
F Pepper (1898)	–	–	7	1	1	–	–	–	–	–	8	1
G Perrins (1892/95)	–	–	92	–	6	–	–	–	4*	–	102	–
J Peters (1894/95)	–	–	46	13	4	1	–	–	1*	–	51	14
M Phasey (1891)	–	–	1	–	–	–	–	–	–	–	1	–
MC Phelan (1989/1994)	5/7	1	82/7	2	10	1	14/2	–	14/3	–	125/19	4
JB Picken (1905/10)	–	–	113	39	8	7	–	–	–	–	121	46
K Pilkington (1994/	2/2	–	–	–	1	–	1	–	–	–	4/2	–
MJ Pinner (1960)	–	–	4	–	–	–	–	–	–	–	4	–
W Porter (1934/37)	–	–	61	5	4	–	–	–	–	–	65	5
AA Potts (1913/19)	–	–	27	5	1	–	–	–	–	–	28	5
J Powell (1886/90)	–	–	21	–	4	–	–	–	–	–	25	–
JH Prentice (1919)	–	–	33	14	1	–	–	–	–	–	34	14
S Preston (1901/02)	–	–	1	–	–	–	–	–	–	–	1	–
AJ Prince (1914)	–	–	2	–	–	–	–	–	–	–	2	–
D Prince (1893)	–	–	2	–	–	–	–	–	–	–	2	–
W Prunier (1995/96)	2	–	–	–	–	–	–	–	–	–	2	–
J Pugh (1921/22)	–	–	2	–	–	–	–	–	–	–	2	–
JI Quinn (1908/09)	–	–	2	–	–	–	–	–	–	–	2	–

Player	FAPL		League		FACup		LgeCup		Europe		Totals	
	App	Goals	App	Goals	App	Goals	App	Goals	App	Goals	App	Goals
A Quixall (1958/63)	–	–	165	50	14	4	1	2	3	–	183	56
G Radcliffe (1898)	–	–	1	–	–	–	–	–	–	–	1	–
C Radford (1920/23)	–	–	91	1	5	–	–	–	–	–	96	1
CW Ramsden (1927/30)	–	–	14	3	2	–	–	–	–	–	16	3
R Ramsey (1890)	–	–	22	5	1	–	–	–	–	–	23	5
P Rattigan (1890)	–	–	–	–	1	–	–	–	–	–	1	–
WE Rawlings (1927/29)	–	–	35	19	1	–	–	–	–	–	36	19
TH Read (1902/03)	–	–	35	–	7	–	–	–	–	–	42	–
W Redman (1950/53)	–	–	36	–	2	–	–	–	–	–	38	–
H Redwood (1935/39)	–	–	89	3	7	1	–	–	–	–	96	4
T Reid (1928/32)	–	–	96	63	5	4	–	–	–	–	101	67
C Rennox (1924/26)	–	–	60	24	8	1	–	–	–	–	68	25
CH Richards (1902)	–	–	8	1	3	1	–	–	–	–	11	2
W Richards (1901)	–	–	9	1	–	–	–	–	–	–	9	1
LH Richardson (1925/28)	–	–	38	–	4	–	–	–	–	–	42	–
W Ridding (1931/33)	–	–	42	14	2	–	–	–	–	–	44	14
JA Ridgway (1895/97)	–	–	14	–	3	–	–	–	–	–	17	–
JJ Rimmer (1967/72)	–	–	34	–	3	–	6	–	2/1	–	45/1	–
AT Ritchie (1977/80)	–	–	26/7	13	3/1	–	3/2	–	–	–	32/10	13
J Roach (1945)	–	–	–	–	2	–	–	–	–	–	2	–
DM Robbie (1935)	–	–	1	–	–	–	–	–	–	–	1	–
B Roberts (1898/99)	–	–	9	2	1	–	–	–	–	–	10	2
C Roberts (1903/12)	–	–	271	22	28	1	–	–	–	–	299	23
RHA Roberts (1913)	–	–	2	–	–	–	–	–	–	–	2	–
A Robertson (1903/05)	–	–	33	1	2	–	–	–	–	–	35	1

Player	FAPL		League		FACup		LgeCup		Europe		Totals	
	App	Goals	App	Goals	App	Goals	App	Goals	App	Goals	App	Goals
A Robertson (1903/04)	–	–	28	10	6	–	–	–	–	–	34	10
T Robertson (1903)	–	–	3	–	–	–	–	–	–	–	3	–
WS Robertson (1933/35)	–	–	47	1	3	–	–	–	–	–	50	1
MG Robins (1988/91)	–	–	19/29	11	4/4	3	–/7	2	4/2	1	27/42	17
JW Robinson (1919/21)	–	–	21	3	–	–	–	–	–	–	21	3
M Robinson (1931)	–	–	10	–	–	–	–	–	–	–	10	–
B Robson (1981/94)	15/14	2	310/5	72	33/1	10	50/2	5	26/1	8	434/23	97
PJ Roche (1974/81)	–	–	46	–	4	–	3	–	–	–	53	–
M Rogers (1977)	–	–	1	–	–	–	–	–	–	–	1	–
C Rothwell (1893/96)	–	–	2	1	1	2	–	–	–	–	3	3
H Rothwell (1902)	–	–	22	–	6	–	–	–	–	–	28	–
WG Roughton (1936/38)	–	–	86	–	6	–	–	–	–	–	92	–
E Round (1909)	–	–	2	–	–	–	–	–	–	–	2	–
J Rowe (1913)	–	–	1	–	–	–	–	–	–	–	1	–
HB Rowley (1928/36)	–	–	173	55	7	–	–	–	–	–	180	55
JF Rowley (1937/54)	–	–	380	182	42	26	–	–	–	–	422	208
EJ Royals (1912/13)	–	–	7	–	–	–	–	–	–	–	7	–
J Ryan (1965/69)	–	–	21/3	4	1	–	22	–	2	–	24/3	4
D Sadler (1963/73)	–	–	266/6	22	22/1	1	22	1	16	3	326/7	27
T Sadler (1890)	–	–	1	–	–	–	–	–	–	–	1	–
C Sagar (1905/06)	–	–	30	20	3	4	–	–	–	–	33	24
GD Sapsford (1919/21)	–	–	52	16	1	1	–	–	–	–	53	17
C Sartori (1968/71)	–	–	26/13	4	9	1	3/2	–	2	1	40/15	6
W Sarvis (1922)	–	–	1	–	–	–	–	–	–	–	1	–
J Saunders (1901/02)	–	–	12	–	1	–	–	–	–	–	13	–

Player	FAPL App	FAPL Goals	League App	League Goals	FACup App	FACup Goals	LgeCup App	LgeCup Goals	Europe App	Europe Goals	Totals App	Totals Goals
RE Savage (1937)	–	–	4	–	1	–	–	–	–	–	5	–
F Sawyer (1899/1900)	–	–	6	–	–	–	–	–	–	–	6	–
AJ Scanlon (1954/60)	–	–	115	34	6	1	3	–	3	–	127	35
P Schmeichel (1991/	150	–	40	–	26	–	17	–	13	1	246	1
A Schofield (1900/06)	–	–	157	30	22	5	–	–	–	–	179	35
GW Schofield (1920)	–	–	1	–	–	–	–	–	–	–	1	–
J Schofield (1903)	–	–	2	–	–	–	–	–	–	–	2	–
P Schofield (1921)	–	–	1	–	–	–	–	–	–	–	1	–
P Scholes (1994/	22/21	15	–	–	1/4	1	4	4	1/3	1	28/28	21
J Scott (1921)	–	–	23	–	1	–	–	–	–	–	24	–
J Scott (1952/56)	–	–	3	–	–	–	–	–	–	–	3	–
LJ Sealey (1989/94)	–	–	33	–	4/1	–	9	–	8	–	54/1	–
ME Setters (1959/64)	–	–	159	12	25	1	2	–	7	1	193	14
LS Sharpe (1988/	100/16	17	59/17	4	22/7	3	15/8	9	15/2	3	211/50	36
WH Sharpe (1890/91)	–	–	25	6	–	–	–	–	–	–	25	6
J Sheldon (1910/12)	–	–	26	1	–	–	–	–	–	–	26	1
A Sidebottom (1972/73)	–	–	16	–	2	–	2	–	–	–	20	–
J Silcock (1919/33)	–	–	423	2	26	–	1	–	–	–	449	2
J Sivebaek (1985/87)	–	–	29/2	1	2	–	1	–	–	–	32/2	1
JF Slater (1890/91)	–	–	41	–	4	–	–	–	–	–	45	–
T Sloan (1978/80)	–	–	4/7	–	–	–	–/1	–	–	–	4/8	–
AC Smith (1926)	–	–	5	1	–	–	–	–	–	–	5	1
J Smith (1937/45)	–	–	37	14	5	1	–	–	–	–	42	15
L Smith (1902)	–	–	8	1	2	–	–	–	–	–	10	1
R Smith (1894/1900)	–	–	93	35	7	2	–	–	1*	–	101	37

Player	FAPL		League		FACup		LgeCup		Europe		Totals	
	App	Goals	App	Goals	App	Goals	App	Goals	App	Goals	App	Goals
TG Smith (1923/26)	–	–	83	12	7	4	–	–	–	–	90	16
W Smith (1901)	–	–	16	–	1	–	–	–	–	–	17	–
J Sneddon (1891)	–	–	21	6	3	1	–	–	–	–	24	7
JW Spence (1919/32)	–	–	481	158	29	10	–	–	–	–	510	168
CW Spencer (1928/29)	–	–	46	–	2	–	–	–	–	–	48	–
W Spratt (1914/19)	–	–	13	–	–	–	–	–	–	–	13	–
G Stacey (1907/14)	–	–	241	9	26	–	–	–	–	–	267	9
H Stafford (1895/1902)	–	–	183	–	17	1	–	–	–	–	200	1
FA Stapleton (1981/87)	–	–	204/19	60	21	7	26/1	6	14/1	5	265/21	78
R Stephenson (1895)	–	–	1	1	–	–	–	–	–	–	1	1
AC Stepney (1966/77)	–	–	433	2	44	–	35	–	23	–	535	2
A Steward (1920/31)	–	–	309	–	17	–	–	–	–	–	326	–
W Stewart (1932/33)	–	–	46	7	3	–	–	–	–	–	49	7
WS Stewart (1890/94)	–	–	138	23	9	–	–	–	2*	–	149	23
NP Stiles (1960/70)	–	–	311	17	38	–	7	–	36	2	392	19
H Stone (1893/94)	–	–	6	–	–	–	–	–	1*	–	7	–
I Storey-Moore (1971/73)	–	–	39	11	–	–	4	1	–	–	43	12
GD Strachan (1984/89)	–	–	155/5	33	22	2	12/1	1	6	2	195/6	38
E Street (1902)	–	–	1	–	2	–	–	–	–	–	3	–
JW Sutcliffe (1903)	–	–	21	–	7	–	–	–	–	–	28	–
EE Sweeney (1925/29)	–	–	27	6	5	1	–	–	–	–	32	7
T Tait (1889/90)	–	–	7	1	–	–	–	–	–	–	7	1
NH Tapken (1938)	–	–	14	–	2	–	–	–	–	–	16	–
C Taylor (1924/29)	–	–	28	6	2	1	–	–	–	–	30	7
E Taylor (1957/58)	–	–	22	2	6	1	–	–	2	1	30	4

Player	FAPL App	FAPL Goals	League App	League Goals	FACup App	FACup Goals	LgeCup App	LgeCup Goals	Europe App	Europe Goals	Totals App	Totals Goals
T Taylor (1952/57)	-	-	166	112	9	5	-	-	14	11	189	128
W Taylor (1921)	-	-	1	-	-	-	-	-	-	-	1	-
H Thomas (1921/29)	-	-	128	12	7	1	-	-	-	-	135	13
MR Thomas (1978/80)	-	-	90	11	13	2	5	2	2	-	110	15
A Thomson (1929/30)	-	-	3	-	2	1	-	-	-	-	5	1
E Thomson (1907/08)	-	-	4	1	-	-	-	-	-	-	4	1
J Thompson (1913)	-	-	6	1	-	-	-	-	-	-	6	1
JE Thompson (1936/37)	-	-	3	1	-	-	-	-	-	-	3	1
W Thompson (1893)	-	-	3	-	-	-	-	-	-	-	3	-
B Thornley (1994/)	-/2	-	-	-	-	-	-	-	-	-	-/2	-
G Tomlinson (1994/)	-	-	-	-	-	-	-/2	-	-	-	-/2	-
WE Toms (1919/20)	-	-	13	3	1	1	-	-	-	-	14	4
HW Topping (1932/34)	-	-	12	1	-	-	-	-	-	-	12	1
WJ Tranter (1963)	-	-	1	-	-	-	-	-	-	-	1	-
GE Travers (1913/14)	-	-	21	4	-	-	-	-	-	-	21	4
A Turnbull (1906/14)	-	-	220	90	25	10	-	-	-	-	245	100
JM Turnbull (1907/09)	-	-	67	36	9	6	-	-	-	-	76	42
B Turner (1890)	-	-	-	-	1	-	-	-	-	-	1	-
CR Turner (1985/88)	-	-	64	-	8	-	7	-	-	-	79	-
J Turner (1898/1902)	-	-	3	-	1	-	-	-	-	-	4	-
R Turner (1898)	-	-	2	-	-	-	-	-	-	-	2	-
S Tyler (1923)	-	-	1	-	-	-	-	-	-	-	1	-
IF Ure (1969/70)	-	-	47	1	8	-	10	-	-	-	65	1
R Valentine (1904/05)	-	-	10	-	-	-	-	-	-	-	10	-
J Vance (1895/96)	-	-	11	1	-	-	-	-	-	-	11	1

Player	FAPL		League		FACup		LgeCup		Europe		Totals	
	App	Goals	App	Goals	App	Goals	App	Goals	App	Goals	App	Goals
E Vincent (1931/33)	–	–	64	1	1	–	–	–	–	–	65	1
DS Viollet (1952/61)	–	–	259	159	18	5	2	1	12	13	291	178
G Vose (1933/39)	–	–	197	1	14	–	–	–	–	–	211	1
C Waldron (1976)	–	–	3	–	–	–	1	–	–	–	4	–
DA Walker (1962)	–	–	1	–	–	–	–	–	–	–	1	–
R Walker (1898)	–	–	2	–	–	–	–	–	–	–	2	–
G Wall (1905/14)	–	–	287	89	29	9	–	–	–	–	316	98
DL Wallace (1989/93)	f2	–	36/9	6	7/2	2	4/3	3	5/2	–	52/18	11
G Walsh (1986/95)	12/1	–	37	–	–	–	7	–	6	–	62/1	–
JA Walton (1951)	–	–	2	–	–	–	–	–	–	–	2	–
JW Walton (1945/47)	–	–	21	–	2	–	–	–	–	–	23	–
A Warburton (1929/33)	–	–	35	10	4	–	–	–	–	–	39	10
J Warner (1892)	–	–	22	–	–	–	–	–	–	–	22	–
J Warner (1938/47)	–	–	105	1	13	1	–	–	–	–	118	2
JV Wassall (1935/39)	–	–	46	6	2	–	–	–	–	–	48	6
W Watson (1970/72)	–	–	11	–	–	–	3	–	–	–	14	–
JA Wealands (1982/83)	/1	–	7	–	–	–	1	–	–	–	8	–
NJ Webb (1989/92)	/1	–	70/4	8	9	1	14	1	11	1	104/5	11
C Webster (1953/58)	–	–	65	26	9	4	1	–	5	1	79	31
FE Wedge (1897)	–	–	2	2	–	–	–	–	–	–	2	2
EJ West (1910/14)	–	–	166	72	15	8	–	–	–	–	181	80
J Wetherell (1896)	–	–	2	–	–	–	–	–	–	–	2	–
A Whalley (1909/19)	–	–	97	6	9	–	–	–	–	–	106	6
H Whalley (1935/46)	–	–	33	–	6	–	–	–	–	–	39	–
AG Whelan (1980)	–	–	–/1	–	–	–	–	–	–	–	–/1	–

Player	FAPL		League		FACup		LgeCup		Europe		Totals	
	App	Goals	App	Goals	App	Goals	App	Goals	App	Goals	App	Goals
LA Whelan (1954/57)	–	–	79	43	6	4	–	–	11	5	96	52
J Whitefoot (1949/55)	–	–	93	–	2	–	–	–	–	–	95	–
J Whitehouse (1900/02)	–	–	59	–	5	–	–	–	–	–	64	–
W Whitehurst (1955)	–	–	1	–	–	–	–	–	–	–	1	–
KD Whiteside (1907)	–	–	1	–	–	–	–	–	–	–	1	–
N Whiteside (1981/89)	–	–	193/13	47	24	10	26/3	9	11/2	1	254/18	67
J Whitney (1895/1900)	–	–	3	–	–	–	–	–	–	–	3	–
W Whittaker (1895)	–	–	3	–	–	–	–	–	–	–	3	–
J Whittle (1931)	–	–	1	–	–	–	–	–	–	–	1	–
N Whitworth (1990/94)	–	–	1	–	–	–	–	–	–	–	1	–
TWJ Wilcox (1908)	–	–	2	–	–	–	–	–	–	–	2	–
RC Wilkins (1979/83)	–	–	158/2	7	10	1	14/1	1	8	1	190/3	10
H Wilkinson (1903)	–	–	8	–	1	–	–	–	–	–	9	–
IM Wilkinson (1991)	–	–	–	–	–	–	1	–	–	–	1	–
DR Williams (1927/28)	–	–	31	2	4	–	–	–	–	–	35	2
F Williams (1902)	–	–	8	–	2	4	–	–	–	–	10	4
H Williams (1930)	–	–	3	–	–	–	–	–	–	–	3	–
H Williams (1922)	–	–	5	2	–	–	–	–	–	–	5	2
H Williams (1904/05)	–	–	33	7	4	1	–	–	–	–	37	8
J Williams (1906)	–	–	3	1	–	–	–	–	–	–	3	1
W Williams (1901)	–	–	4	–	–	–	–	–	–	–	4	–
J Williamson (1919)	–	–	2	–	–	–	–	–	–	–	2	–

Player	FAPL App	FAPL Goals	League App	League Goals	FACup App	FACup Goals	LgeCup App	LgeCup Goals	Europe App	Europe Goals	Totals App	Totals Goals
DG Wilson (1988)	–	–	/4	–	/2	–	–	–	–	–	/6	–
E Wilson (1889)	–	–	19	6	1	–	–	–	–	–	20	6
JT Wilson (1926/31)	–	–	130	3	10	–	–	–	–	–	140	3
T Wilson (1907)	–	–	1	–	–	–	–	–	–	–	1	–
W Winterbottom (1936/37)	–	–	25	–	2	–	–	–	–	–	27	–
R Wombwell (1904/06)	–	–	47	3	4	–	–	–	–	–	51	3
J Wood (1922)	–	–	15	1	1	–	–	–	–	–	16	1
NA Wood (1985/86)	–	–	2/1	–	–	–	/1	–	–	–	2/2	–
RE Wood (1949/58)	–	–	178	–	15	1	–	–	12	–	205	–
W Woodcock (1913/19)	–	–	58	20	3	1	–	–	–	–	61	21
H Worrall (1946/47)	–	–	6	–	–	–	–	–	–	–	6	–
P Wratten (1990/91)	–	–	/2	–	–	–	–	–	–	–	/2	–
W Wrigglesworth (1936/46)	–	–	30	8	7	2	–	–	–	–	37	10
W Yates (1906)	–	–	3	–	–	–	–	–	–	–	3	–
J Young (1906)	–	–	2	–	–	–	–	–	–	–	2	–
TA Young (1970/75)	–	–	69/14	1	5	–	5/4	–	–	–	79/18	1

Players' International Appearances Whilst with United*

England

VA Anderson	– 1987 W Germany, 1988 Hungary, Columbia (3)
J Aston	– 1948 Denmark, Wales, Switzerland; 1949 Scotland, Sweden, Norway, France, Rep of Ireland, Wales, N Ireland, Italy; 1950 Scotland, Portugal, Belgium, Chile, USA, N Ireland(17)
GR Bailey	– 1985 Rep of Ireland, Mexico (2)
JJ Berry	– 1953 Argentina, Chile, Uruguay; 1956 Sweden (4)
W Bradley	– 1959 Italy, Mexico, USA (3)
RW Byrne	– 1954 Scotland, Yugoslavia, Hungary, Belgium, Switzerland, Uruguay, N Ireland, Wales, West Germany; 1955 Scotland, France, Spain, Portugal, Denmark, Wales, N Ireland, Spain; 1956 Scotland, Sweden, Brazil, Finland, West Germany, N Ireland, Wales, Yugoslavia, Denmark; 1957 Scotland, Rep of Ireland, Denmark, Rep of Ireland, Wales, N Ireland, France(33)
R Charlton	– 1958 Scotland, Portugal, Yugoslavia, N Ireland, USSR, Wales; 1959 Scotland, Italy, Brazil, Peru, Mexico, USA, Wales, Sweden; 1960 Scotland, Yugoslavia, Spain, Hungary, N Ireland, Luxembourg, Spain, Wales; 1961 Scotland, Mexico, Portugal, Italy, Austria, Luxembourg, Wales, Portugal, N Ireland; 1962 Austria, Scotland, Switzerland, Peru, Hungary, Argentina, Bulgaria, Brazil; 1963 France, Scotland, Brazil, Czechoslovakia, East Germany, Switzerland, Wales, Rest of World, N Ireland; 1964 Scotland, Uruguay, Portugal, Rep of Ireland, USA, Brazil, Argentina, N Ireland, Holland; 1965 Scotland, Wales, Austria, N Ireland, Spain; 1966 West Germany, Scotland, Yugoslavia, Finland, Norway, Poland, Uruguay, Mexico, France, Argentina, Portugal, West Germany, N Ireland, Czechoslovakia, Wales; 1967 Scotland, Wales, N Ireland, USSR; 1968 Scotland, Spain, Spain, Sweden, Yugoslavia, USSR, Romania, Bulgaria; 1969 Romania, N Ireland, Wales, Scotland, Mexico, Brazil, Holland, Portugal; 1970 Holland, Wales, N Ireland, Colombia, Ecuador, Romania, Brazil, Czechoslovakia, West Germany (106)
AC Chilton	– 1950 N Ireland; 1951 France (2)
H Cockburn	– 1946 N Ireland, Rep of Ireland, Wales; 1948 Scotland, Italy, Denmark, N Ireland, Switzerland; 1949 Scotland, Sweden; 1951 Argentina, Portugal, France (13)
A Cole	– 1995 Uruguay (1)
JM Connelly	– 1965 Hungary, Yugoslavia, Sweden, Wales, Austria, N Ireland; 1966 Scotland, Norway, Denmark, Uruguay (10)
SJ Coppell	– 1977 Italy; 1978 West Germany, Brazil, Wales, N Ireland,

	Scotland, Hungary, Denmark, Rep of Ireland, Czechoslovakia; 1979 N Ireland (twice), Wales, Scotland, Bulgaria, Austria, Denmark, N Ireland; 1980 Rep of Ireland, Spain, Argentina, Wales, Scotland, Belgium, Italy, Romania, Switzerland; 1981 Romania, Brazil, Wales, Scotland, Switzerland, Hungary (twice); 1982 Finland, France, Czechoslovakia, Kuwait, West Germany, Luxembourg; 1983 Greece (42)
M Duxbury	– 1983 Luxembourg; 1984, France, Wales, Scotland, USSR, Brazil, Uruguay, Chile, East Germany, Finland (10)
D Edwards	– 1955 Scotland, France, Spain, Portugal; 1956 Scotland, Brazil, Sweden, Finland, West Germany, N Ireland, Denmark; 1957 Scotland, Rep of Ireland, Denmark, Rep of Ireland, Wales, N Ireland, France (18)
WA Foulkes	– 1954 N Ireland (1)
B Greenhoff	– 1976 Wales, N Ireland, Rep of Ireland, Finland, Italy; 1977 Holland, N Ireland, Wales, Scotland, Brazil, Argentina, Uruguay; 1978 Brazil, Wales, N Ireland, Scotland, Hungary (17)
HJ Halse	– 1909 Austria (1)
GA Hill	– 1976 Italy, Rep of Ireland, Finland; 1977 Luxembourg, Switzerland, Luxembourg (6)
P Ince	– 1992 Spain, Norway, Turkey; 1993 Turkey, Holland, Poland, USA, Brazil, Germany; 1994 Poland, Holland, San Marino, Norway, Denmark, Romania; 1995 Eire (16)
B Kidd	– 1970 N Ireland, Ecuador (2)
W McGuinness	– 1958 N Ireland; 1959 Mexico (2)
JW Mew	– 1920 Ireland (1)
G.Neville	– 1995 Japan, Brazil, Columbia, Norway, Switzerland, Portugal, 1996 Bulgaria, Croatia, Hungary, China (10)
P.Neville	– 1996 China (1)
GA Pallister	– 1991 Cameroon, Turkey, Germany; 1993 Norway, USA, Brazil, Germany; 1994 Poland, Holland, San Marino, Denmark, USA, Romania; 1995 Eire, Uruguay, Sweden, Norway, Switzerland (18)
P Parker	– 1991 Germany; 1994 Holland, Denmark (3)
JS Pearson	– 1976 Wales, N Ireland, Scotland, Brazil, Finland, Rep of Ireland; 1977 Holland, Wales, Scotland, Brazil, Argentina, Uruguay, Italy; 1978 West Germany, N Ireland (15)
SC Pearson	– 1948 Scotland, N Ireland; 1949 Scotland, N Ireland, Italy; 1951 Portugal; 1952 Scotland, Italy (8)
D Pegg	– 1957 Rep of Ireland (1)
MC Phelan	– 1989 Italy (1)

C Roberts	– 1905 Ireland, Wales, Scotland (3)
B Robson	– 1981 Hungary; 1982 N Ireland, Wales, Holland, Scotland, Finland, France, Czechoslovakia, West Germany, Spain, Denmark, Greece, Luxembourg; 1983 Scotland, Hungary, Luxembourg; 1984 France, N Ireland, Scotland, USSR, Brazil, Uruguay, Chile, East Germany, Finland, Turkey; 1985 Rep of Ireland, Romania, Finland, Scotland, Italy, Mexico, West Germany, USA, Romania, Turkey; 1986 Israel, Mexico, Portugal, Morocco, N Ireland; 1987 Spain, N Ireland, Turkey, Brazil, Scotland, Turkey, Yugoslavia; 1988 Holland, Hungary, Scotland, Columbia, Switzerland, Rep of Ireland, Holland, USSR, Denmark, Sweden, Saudi Arabia; 1989 Greece, Albania, Albania, Chile, Scotland, Poland, Denmark, Poland, Italy, Yugoslavia; 1990 Czechoslovakia, Uruguay, Tunisia, Rep of Ireland, Holland; 1991 Cameroon, Rep of Ireland, Turkey (77)
JF Rowley	– 1948 Switzerland; 1949 Sweden, France, N Ireland, Italy; 1952 Scotland (6)
D Sadler	– 1967 N Ireland, USSR; 1970 Ecuador, East Germany (4)
LS Sharpe	– 1991 Rep of Ireland; 1993 Turkey, Norway, USA, Brazil, Germany; 1994 Poland (7)
J Silcock	– 1921 Wales, Scotland; 1923 Sweden (3)
JW Spence	– 1926 Belgium, N Ireland (2)
AC Stepney	– 1968 Sweden
NP Stiles	– 1965 Scotland, Hungary, Yugoslavia, Sweden, Wales, Austria, N Ireland, Spain; 1966 Poland, West Germany, Scotland, Norway, Denmark, Poland, Uruguay, Mexico, France, Argentina, Portugal, West Germany, N Ireland, Czechoslovakia, Wales; 1967 Scotland; 1968 USSR; 1969 Romania; 1970 N Ireland, Scotland (28)
T Taylor	– 1953 Argentina, Chile, Uruguay; 1954 Belgium, Switzerland; 1956 Scotland, Brazil, Sweden, Finland, West Germany, N Ireland, Yugoslavia, Denmark; 1957 Rep of Ireland, Denmark, Rep of Ireland, Wales, N Ireland, France (19)
DS Viollet	– 1960 Hungary; 1961 Luxembourg (2)
G Wall	– 1907 Wales; 1908 Ireland; 1909 Scotland; 1910 Wales, Scotland; 1912 Scotland; 1913 Ireland (7)
NJ Webb	– 1989 Sweden; 1990 Italy; 1992 France, Hungary, Brazil (5)
RG Wilkins	– 1979 Denmark, N Ireland, Bulgaria; 1980 Spain, Argentina, Wales, N Ireland, Scotland, Belgium, Italy, Spain; 1981 Spain, Romania, Brazil, Wales, Scotland, Switzerland, Hungary; 1982 N Ireland, Wales, Holland, Scotland, Finland, France, Czechoslovakia, Kuwait, West Germany, Spain, Denmark, West

	Germany; 1983 Denmark; 1984 N Ireland, Wales, Scotland, USSR, Brazil, Uruguay, Chile (38)
RE Wood	– 1954 N Ireland, Wales; 1956 Finland (3)

Northern Ireland (and Ireland prior to 1924)

T Anderson	– 1973 Cyprus, England, Scotland, Wales, Bulgaria, Portugal (6)
G Best	– 1964 Wales, Uruguay, England, Switzerland, Switzerland, Scotland; 1965 Holland, Holland, Albania, Scotland, England, Albania; 1966 England; 1967 Scotland; 1968 Turkey; 1969 England, Scotland, Wales, USSR; 1970 Scotland, England, Wales, Spain; 1971 Cyprus, Cyprus, England, Scotland, Wales, USSR; 1972 Spain, Bulgaria; 1973 Portugal (32)
J Blanchflower	– 1954 Wales, England, Scotland; 1955 Scotland; 1956 Wales, England, Scotland; 1957 Portugal, Scotland, England, Italy; 1958 Italy (12)
T Breen	– 1937 Wales, England, Scotland; 1938 Scotland; 1939 Wales (5)
WR Briggs	– Wales (1)
JJ Carey	– 1946 England, Scotland; 1947 Wales, England; 1948 England, Scotland; 1949 Wales (7)
W Crooks	– 1922 Wales (1)
MM Donaghy	– 1988 Spain; 1989 Spain, Malta, Chile, Rep of Ireland; 1990 Norway, Yugoslavia, Denmark, Austria; 1991 Poland, Yugoslavia, Faroe Islands, Faroe Islands, Austria, Denmark; 1992 Scotland, Lithuania (18)
K. Gillespie	– Portugal, Austria, Rep of Ireland (3)
H Gregg	– 1958 Wales, Czechoslovakia, Argentina, West Germany, France, England; 1959 Wales, Scotland, England; 1960 Wales, England, Scotland; 1961 Scotland, Greece; 1963 Scotland, England (16)
M Hamill	– 1912 England; 1914 England, Scotland (3)
TA Jackson	– 1975 Sweden, Norway, Yugoslavia; 1976 Holland, Belgium; 1977 West Germany, England, Scotland, Wales, Iceland (10)
D Lyner	– 1922 England (1)
D McCreery	– 1976 Scotland, England, Wales, Holland, Belgium; 1977 West Germany, England, Scotland, Wales, Iceland, Iceland, Holland, Belgium; 1978 Scotland, England, Wales, Rep of Ireland, Denmark, Bulgaria; 1979 England, Bulgaria, Wales, Denmark (23)
P McGibbon	– 1995 Canada, Chile, Latvia, Lichenstein (5)
RC McGrath	– 1976 Belgium; 1977 West Germany, England, Scotland, Wales, Iceland, Iceland, Holland, Belgium; 1978 Scotland, England, Wales, Bulgaria; 1979 England, England (15)

SB McIlroy	– 1972 Spain, Scotland; 1974 Scotland, England, Wales, Norway, Sweden; 1975 Yugoslavia, England, Scotland, Wales, Sweden, Norway, Yugoslavia; 1976 Scotland, England, Wales, Holland, Belgium; 1977 England, Scotland, Wales, Iceland, Iceland, Holland, Belgium; 1978 Scotland, England, Wales, Rep of Ireland, Denmark; 1979 England, Bulgaria, England, Scotland, Wales, Denmark, England, Rep of Ireland; 1980 Israel, Scotland, England, Wales, Australia, Australia, Australia, Sweden, Portugal; 1981 Scotland, Portugal, Scotland, Sweden, Scotland, Israel (52)
ST McMillan	– 1962 England, Scotland (2)
WS McMillen	– 1933 England; 1934 Scotland; 1936 Scotland (3)
JM Nicholl	– 1976 Israel, Wales, Holland, Belgium; 1977 England, Scotland, Wales, Iceland, Iceland, Holland, Belgium; 1978 Scotland, England, Wales, Rep of Ireland, Denmark, Bulgaria; 1979 England, Bulgaria, England, Scotland, Wales, Denmark, England, Rep of Ireland; 1980 Israel, Scotland, England, Wales, Sweden, Australia, Australia, Australia, Sweden, Portugal; 1981 Scotland, Portugal, Scotland, Sweden, Scotland, Israel; 1982 England (41)
JJ Nicholson	– 1960 Scotland; 1961 Wales, Greece, England; 1962 Wales, Holland, Poland, England, Scotland, Poland (10)
T Sloan	– 1979 Scotland, Wales, Denmark (3)
N Whiteside	– 1982 Yugoslavia, Honduras, Spain, Austria, France, West Germany, Albania; 1983 Turkey, Austria, Turkey, West Germany, Scotland; 1984 England, Wales, Finland, Romania, Israel, Finland; 1985 England, Spain, Turkey, Romania, England; 1986 France, Denmark, Morocco, Algeria, Spain,Brazil, England; 1987 Israel, England, Yugoslavia, Turkey; 1988 Poland, France (36)

Scotland

A Albiston	– 1982 N Ireland; 1983 Uruguay, Belgium, East Germany; 1984 Wales, England, Yugoslavia, Iceland, Spain; 1985 Spain, Wales, East Germany; 1986 Holland, Uruguay (14)
A Bell	– 1912 Ireland (1)
MM Buchan	– 1972 Wales, Yugoslavia, Czechoslovakia, Brazil, Denmark, Denmark; 1973 England; 1974 West Germany, N Ireland, Wales, Norway, Brazil, Yugoslavia, East Germany; 1975 Spain, Portugal, Denmark, Romania; 1976 Finland, Czechoslovakia; 1977 Chile, Argentina, Brazil, East Germany, Wales; 1978 N Ireland, Peru, Iran, Holland, Austria, Norway, Portugal(32)
FS Burns	– 1969 Austria (1)

PT Crerand	– 1963 N Ireland; 1965 England, Poland, Finland, Poland (5)
J Delaney	– 1947 England, N Ireland, Wales; 1948 England (4)
A Forsyth	– 1973 England; 1974 East Germany, Spain; 1975 N Ireland, Romania, Denmark (6)
G Graham	– 1973 England, Wales, N Ireland, Switzerland, Brazil (5)
JA Holton	– 1973 Wales, N Ireland, England, Switzerland, Brazil, Czechoslovakia, West Germany; 1974 N ireland, Wales, England, Norway, Zaire, Brazil, Yugoslavia, East Germany (15)
SM Houston	– 1975 Denmark (1)
J Jordan	– 1978 Bulgaria, N Ireland, England, Peru, Iran, Holland, Austria, Portugal; 1979 Wales, N Ireland, England, Norway, Belgium; 1980 N Ireland, Wales, England, Poland; 1981 Israel, Wales, England (20)
D Law	– 1962 Wales, N Ireland; 1963 England, Austria, Norway, Rep of Ireland, Spain, Norway, Wales; 1964 England, West Germany, Wales, Finland, N Ireland; 1965 England, Spain, Poland, Finland, N Ireland, Poland; 1966 England, Wales; 1967 England, USSR, N Ireland; 1968 Austria; 1969 West Germany, N Ireland; 1972 Peru, N Ireland, Wales, England, Yugoslavia, Czechoslovakia, Brazil (35)
J Leighton	– 1988 Colombia, England, Norway; 1989 Cyprus, France, Cyprus, England, Chile, Yugoslavia, France, Norway; 1990 Argentina, Malta, Costa Rica, Sweden, Brazil (16)
N McBain	– 1922 England (1)
BJ McClair	– 1987 Bulgaria; 1988 Malta, Spain, Norway, Yugoslavia, Italy; 1989 Cyprus, France, Norway; 1990 Argentina, Bulgaria; 1991 Bulgaria, San Marino, Switzerland, Romania; 1992 Northern Ireland, USA, Canada (18)
G McQueen	– 1978 Bulgaria, N Ircland, Wales, Austria, Norway, Portugal; 1979 N Ireland, England, Norway, Peru, Austria, Belgium; 1981 Wales (13)
L Macari	– 1973 England, Wales, N Ireland, England; 1975 Sweden, Portugal, Wales, England, Romania; 1977 N Ireland, England, Chile, Argentina, East Germany, Wales; 1978 Bulgaria, Peru, Iran (18)
T Miller	– 1921 Ireland, England (2)
W Morgan	– 1972 Peru, Yugoslavia, Czechoslovakia, Brazil, Denmark, Denmark; 1973 England, Wales, N Ireland, England, Switzerland, Brazil, Czechoslovakia, Czechoslovakia, West Germany; 1974 West Germany, N Ireland, Belgium, Brazil, Yugoslavia (20)
GD Strachan	– 1985 Spain, England, Iceland, Wales, Australia; 1986 Romania, Denmark, West Germany, Uruguay, Bulgaria, Rep of Ireland; 1987 Rep of Ireland, Hungary; 1989 France (14)

SR Bennison	– 1925 Scotland; 1926 Scotland; 1927 Scotland, England; 1928 N Ireland, Scotland, England; 1929 N Ireland, Scotland; 1931 N Ireland (10)
CG Blackmore	– 1985 Norway, Scotland, Hungary; 1986 Saudi Arabia, Rep of Ireland, Uruguay, Finland; 1987 USSR, Finland, Czechoslovakia, Denmark, Denmark, Czechoslovakia; 1988 Yugoslavia, Sweden, Malta, Italy, Holland, Finland; 1989 Israel, West Germany, Finland, Holland, West Germany; 1990 Costa Rica, Belgium, Luxembourg; 1992 Rep of Ireland, Austria, Romania, Holland, Argentina, Japan; 1993 Faroe Islands, Cyprus, Belgium, Czechoslovakia; 1994 Sweden (38)
T Burke	– 1887 England, Scotland, 1888 Scotland (3)
A Davies	– 1983 N Ireland, Brazil; 1984 England, N Ireland, Iceland, Iceland; 1985 Norway (7)
J Davies	– 1888 England, Ireland, Scotland; 1889 Scotland; 1890 England (5)
R W Davies	– 1972 England; 1973 Scotland, N Ireland (3)
J Doughty	– 1887 Ireland, Scotland; 1888 England, Ireland, Scotland; 1889 Scotland; 1890 England (7)
R Doughty	– 1888 Ireland, Scotland (2)
RJ Giggs	– 1991 Germany, Luxembourg; 1992 Romania, Faroe Islands, Belgium; 1993 Czechoslovakia, Belgium, Faroe Islands; 1994 Czechoslovakia, Cyprus, Romania, Albania; 1995 Bulgaria, Germany, Albania (15)
LM Hughes	– 1984 England, N Ireland, Iceland, Spain, Iceland; 1985 Norway, Scotland, Spain, Norway, Scotland, Hungary; 1986 Uruguay; 1988 Holland, Finland; 1989 Israel, Sweden, West Germany, Finland, West Germany; 1990 Costa Rica, Denmark, Belgium, Luxembourg; 1991 Belgium, Iceland, Poland, Germany, Brazil, Germany, Luxembourg; 1992 Rep of Ireland, Romania, Holland, Argentina, Japan; 1993 Faroe Islands, Belgium, Czechoslovakia. Cyprus, Eire, Belgium, Faroe Islands; 1994 Norway; 1994 Czechoslovakia, Cyprus, Georgia, Bulgaria, Germany, Georgia (49)
CAL Jenkyns	– 1897 Ireland (1)
T Jones	– 1926 N Ireland; 1927 England, N Ireland; 1930 N Ireland (4)
WH Meredith	– 1907 Ireland, Scotland, England; 1908 England, Ireland; 1909 Scotland, England, Ireland; 1910 Scotland, England, Ireland; 1911 Ireland, Scotland, England; 1912 Scotland, England, Ireland; 1913 Ireland, Scotland, England; 1914 Ireland, Scotland, England; 1920 Ireland, Scotland, England (26)

G Moore	– 1963 Scotland; 1964 N Ireland (2)
G Owen	– 1889 Scotland, Ireland (2)
J Owen	– 1892 England (1)
W Owen	– 1888 England; 1889 England, Scotland, Ireland (4)
J Powell	– 1887 England, Scotland; 1888 England, Ireland, Scotland (5)
H Thomas	– 1927 England
MR Thomas	– 1978 Turkey; 1979 West Germany, Malta, Rep of Ireland, West Germany, Turkey; 1980 England, Scotland, N Ireland, Czechoslovakia; 1981 Scotland, England, USSR (13)
J Warner	– 1939 France (1)
C Webster	– 1957 Czechoslovakia; 1958 Hungary, Mexico, Brazil (4)
DR Williams	– 1928 Scotland, England (2)

Republic of Ireland

T Breen	– 1937 Switzerland, France (2)
SA Brennan	– 1965 Spain, Spain; 1966 Austria, Belgium, Spain, Turkey, Spain; 1969 Czechoslovakia, Denmark, Hungary, Scotland, Czechoslovakia, Denmark, Hungary; 1970 Poland, West Germany (16)
N Cantwell	– 1961 Scotland, Scotland, Czechoslovakia, Czechoslovakia; 1962 Austria, Iceland, Iceland; 1963 Scotland, Austria; 1964 Spain, England, Poland; 1965 Spain, Spain, Spain; 1966 Austria, Belgium, Spain; 1967 Turkey (19)
B Carey	– 1992 USA, 1993 Wales (2)
JJ Carey	– 1937 Norway; 1938 Czechoslovakia, Poland, Switzerland, Poland; 1939 Hungary, Hungary, Germany; 1946 Portugal, Spain, England; 1947 Spain, Portugal; 1948 Portugal, Spain, Switzerland; 1949 Belgium, Portugal, Sweden, Spain, Finland, England, Finland, Sweden; 1950 Norway; 1951 Argentina, Norway; 1952 France; 1953 Austria (29)
JE Carolan	– 1959 Sweden; 1960 Chile (2)
GA Daly	– 1973 Poland, Norway; 1974 Brazil, Uruguay; 1975 West Germany, Switzerland; 1976 England, Turkey, France (9)
AP Dunne	– 1962 Austria, Iceland; 1963 Scotland, Austria; 1964 Spain, Norway, England, Norway, England, Poland; 1965 Spain, Spain, Spain; 1966 Austria, Belgium, Spain, Turkey, Spain; 1968 Poland, Denmark; 1969 Hungary, Hungary; 1970 Sweden; 1971 Italy, Austria (24)
PAJ Dunne	– 1965 Spain, Spain, Spain; 1966 West Germany, Turkey (5)
MJ Giles	– 1959 Sweden; 1960 Chile, Wales, Norway; 1961 Scotland, Scotland, Czechoslovakia, Czechoslovakia; 1962 Austria, Iceland; 1963 Scotland (11)

DJ Givens	– 1969 Denmark, Hungary, Scotland, Czechoslovakia, Denmark, Hungary (6)
AA Grimes	– 1978 Turkey, Poland, Norway, England; 1979 Bulgaria, USA, N Ireland; 1980 England, Cyprus; 1981 Czechoslovakia, West Germany, Poland; 1982 Algeria, Spain; 1983 Spain (15)
DJ Irwin	– 1990 Morocco, Turkey; 1991 Wales, England, Poland, USA, Hungary, Poland; 1992 Wales, USA, Albania, USA, Italy; 1993 Latvia, Denmark, Spain, N. Ireland, Denmark, Albania, Latvia, Lithuania; 1994 Lithuania, Spain, N. Ireland, Bolivia, Germany, Italy, Mexico, Latvia, N. Ireland; 1995 England, N.Ireland, Portugal, Lichenstein, Lichenstein, Austria, Austria,Portugal, Holland, Czechoslavakia (40)
R Keane	– 1994 Lithuania, Spain, N.Ireland, Bolivia, Germany, Czechoslovakia, Italy, Mexico, Norway, Holland, N.Ireland; 1995 N. Ireland, Latvia, Austria; 1996 Russia (15)
P McGrath	– 1985 Italy, Israel, England, Norway, Switzerland, Switzerland, Denmark; 1986 Wales, Iceland, Czechoslovakia, Belgium, Scotland, Poland; 1987 Scotland, Bulgaria, Belgium, Brazil, Luxembourg, Luxembourg, Bulgaria; 1988 Yugoslavia, Poland, Norway, England, Holland, N Ireland; 1989 France, Hungary, Spain, Malta, Hungary (31)
MP Martin	– 1973 USSR, Poland, France, Norway, Poland; 1974 Brazil, Uruguay, Chile, USSR, Turkey; 1975 West Germany, Switzerland, USSR, Switzerland (14)
KR Moran	– 1980 Switzerland, Argentina, Belgium, France, Cyprus; 1981 Wales, Belgium, Czechoslovakia, West Germany, Poland, France; 1982 Algeria, Iceland, Holland, Malta; 1984 Israel, Mexico; 1985 Denmark, Iceland, Czechoslovakia, Belgium, Scotland, Poland; 1987 Scotland, Bulgaria, Belgium, Brazil, Luxembourg, Luxembourg, Bulgaria, Israel; 1988 Romania, Yugoslavia, Poland, Norway, England, USSR, Holland (38)
LF O'Brien	– 1987 Brazil, Israel; 1988 Romania, Yugoslavia, Poland, Tunisia (6)
PJ Roche	– 1974 USSR, Turkey; 1975 West Germany, Switzerland, USSR, Switzerland, Turkey (7)
FA Stapleton	– 1981 Holland, France; 1982 Algeria, Holland, Iceland, Spain; 1983 Malta, Spain, Iceland, Holland, Malta; 1984 Israel, Poland, China, Norway, Denmark; 1985 Italy, Israel, England, Norway, Switzerland, Switzerland, USSR, Denmark; 1986 Uruguay, Iceland, Czechoslovakia, Belgium, Scotland, Poland; 1987 Scotland, Bulgaria, Belgium, Luxembourg (34)
L A Whelan	– 1956 Holland, Denmark; 1957 England, England (4)

France

E Cantona — 1993 Finland, Israel, Sweden, Sweden, Finland, Israel, Bulgaria; 1994 Italy, Slovakia, Romania, Poland, Azerbajan, Holland (13)

Denmark

J Olsen — 1984 Austria, Norway, Switzerland; 1985 East Germany, USSR, Rep of Ireland; 1986 N Ireland, Bulgaria, Poland, Paraguay, Scotland, Uruguay, West Germany, Spain, East Germany, West Germany, Czechoslovakia; 1987 Czechoslovakia, Sweden, West Germany, Wales; 1988 Austria, Hungary, Czechoslovakia, Belgium (25)

P Schmeichel — 1991 Italy, Sweden, Faroe Islands, Austria, N Ireland; 1992 England, Sweden, France, Holland, Germany; 1994 England, 1992 Latvia, Lithuania, Eire, N. Ireland; 1993 Spain, Latvia, Eire, Albania, Lithuania, Albania, N.Ireland, Spain; 1994 Macedonia, Belgium, Spain 1995 Cyprus, Macedonia, Cyprus, Belgium, Spain, Armenia; 1996 Spain, Macedonia, Scotland (34)

J Sivebaek — 1986 N Ireland, Bulgaria, Norway, Poland, Scotland, West Germany, East Germany, Finland, West Germany; 1987 Finland, Czechoslovakia (11)

USSR/Russia

A Kanchelskis — 1991 Hungary, England, Argentina, Cyprus, Sweden, Italy, Norway, Hungary, Italy, Cyprus; 1992 Spain, England; 1994 Germany, San Marino, Scotland; 1995 Slovakia, Scotland, Finland (18)

Yugoslavia

N Jovanovic — 1980 Luxembourg, Denmark; 1982 N Ireland, Spain, Honduras (5)

Rest of the World

D Law — 1963 England (1)

Rest of Europe

JJ Carey — 1947 Great Britain (1)
R Charlton — 1964 Scandinavia (1)
D Law — 1964 Scandinavia (1)

Full Record in Domestic Cup Competitions – *FA Cup*

1886/87

1st Round	v Fleetwood Rangers	(a)	2-2	Doughty 2

(tie awarded to Fleetwood as Newton Heath refused to play extra-time)

1889/90

1st Round	v Preston North End	(a)	1-6	Craig

1890/91

1st Qual Round	v Higher Walton	(h)	2-0	Farman, Evans
2nd Qual Round	v Bootle Reserves	(a)	0-1	

(both teams fielded virtual Reserve teams)

1891/92

1st Qual Round	v Ardwick	(h)	5-1	Farman 2, Doughty, Sneddon, Edge
2nd Qual Round	v Heywood		(Heywood withdrew)	
3rd Qual Round	v South Shore	(a)	2-0	Farman, Doughty,
4th Qual Round	v Blackpool	(h)	3-4	Farman, Edge 2

1892/93

1st Round	v Blackburn Rovers	(a)	0-4	

1893/94

1st Round	v Middlesbrough	(h)	4-0	Farman, Pedden Donaldson 2,
2nd Round	v Blackburn Rovers	(h)	0-0†	
Replay	v Blackburn Rovers	(a)	1-5	Donaldson

1894/95

1st Round	v Stoke City	(h)	2-3	Smith, Peters

1895/96

1st Round	v Kettering Town	(h)	2-1	Donaldson, Smith
2nd Round	v Derby County	(h)	1-1	Kennedy
Replay	v Derby County	(a)	1-5	Donaldson

1896/97

3rd Qual Round	v West Manchester	(h)	7-0	Cassidy 2, Gillespie 2, Rothwell 2, Bryant
4th Qual Round	v Nelson	(h)	3-0	Cassidy, Donaldson, Gillespie
5th Qual Round	v Blackpool	(h)	2-2	Gillespie, Donaldson
Replay	v Blackpool	(a)	2-1	Boyd, Cassidy
1st Round	v Kettering Town	(h)	5-1	Cassidy, Donaldson
2nd Round	v Southampton	(a)	1-1	Donaldson
Replay	v Southampton	(h)	3-1	Bryant 2, Cassidy
3rd Round	v Derby County	(a)	0-2	

† Extra time

1897/98

1st Round	v Walsall	(h)	1-0	Own Goal
2nd Round	v Liverpool	(h)	0-0	
Replay	v Liverpool	(a)	1-2	Collinson

1898/99

1st Round	v Tottenham Hotspur	(a)	1-1	Cassidy
Replay	v Tottenham Hotspur	(h)	3-5	Bryant 3

1899/00

3rd Qual Round	v South Shore	(a)	1-3	Jackson

1900/01

Prelim Round	v Portsmouth	(h)	3-0	Griffiths, Jackson, Stafford
1st Round	v Burnley	(h)	0-0	
Replay	v Burnley	(a)	1-7	Schofield

1901/02

Prelim Round	v Lincoln City	(h)	1-2	Fisher

1902/03

3rd Qual Round	v Accrington Stanley	(h)	7-0	Williams 3, Peddie, Richards, Pegg, Morgan
4th Qual Round	v Oswaldtwistle Rovers	(h)	3-2	Pegg, Beardsworth, Williams
5th Qual Round	v Southport Central	(h)	4-1	Pegg 3, Banks
6th Qual Round	v Burton United	(h)	1-1	Griffiths
Replay	v Burton United	(h)	3-1	Schofield, Pegg, Peddie
1st Round	v Liverpool	(h)	2-1	Peddie 2
2nd Round	v Everton	(a)	1-3	Griffiths

1903/04

Prelim Round	v Small Heath	(h)	1-1	Schofield
Replay	v Small Heath	(a)	1-1†	Arkesden
2nd Replay	v Small Heath	(n)	1-1†	Schofield
3rd Replay	v Small Heath	(n)	3-1	Arkesden 2, Grassam
1st Round	v Notts County	(a)	3-3	Downie, Schofield, Arkesden
Replay	v Notts County	(h)	2-1	Morrison, Pegg
2nd Round	v Sheffield Wednesday	(a)	0-6	

1904/05

Prelim Round	v Fulham	(h)	2-2	Mackie, Arkesden
Replay	v Fulham	(a)	0-0†	
2nd Replay	v Fulham	(n)	0-1	

1905/06

1st Round	v Staple Hill	(h)	7-2	Beddow 3, Picken 2, Allen, Williams

2nd Round	v Norwich City	(h)	3-0	Downie, Peddie, Sagar
3rd Round	v Aston Villa	(h)	5-1	Picken 3, Sagar 2
4th Round	v Woolwich Arsenal	(h)	2-3	Peddie, Sagar
1906/07				
1st Round	v Portsmouth	(a)	2-2	Picken, Wall
Replay	v Portsmouth	(h)	1-2	Wall
1907/08				
1st Round	v Blackpool	(h)	3-1	Wall 2, Bannister
2nd Round	v Chelsea	(h)	1-0	A.Turnbull
3rd Round	v Aston Villa	(a)	2-0	A.Turnbull, Wall
4th Round	v Fulham	(a)	1-2	J.Turnbull
1908/09				
1st Round	v Brighton & H.A	(h)	1-0	Halse
2nd Round	v Everton	(h)	1-0	Halse
3rd Round	v Blackburn Rovers	(h)	6-1	A.Turnbull 3, J.Turnbull 3
4th Round	v Burnley	(a)	3-2	J Turnbull 2, Halse
Semi Final	v Newcastle United	(n)	1-0	Halse
Final	v Bristol City	(n)	1-0	A.Turnbull
1909/10				
1st Round	v Burnley	(a)	0-2	
1910/11				
1st Round	v Blackpool	(a)	2-1	Picken, West
2nd Round	v Aston Villa	(h)	2-1	Halse, Wall
3rd Round	v West Ham United	(a)	1-2	A.Turnbull
1911/12				
1st Round	v Huddersfield Town	(h)	3-1	West 2, Halse
2nd Round	v Coventry City	(a)	5-1	Halse 2, West, Turnbull, Wall
3rd Round	v Reading	(a)	1-1	West
Replay	v Reading	(h)	3-0	A.Turnbull 2, Halse
4th Round	v Blackburn Rovers	(h)	1-1	Own Goal
Replay	v Blackburn Rovers	(a)	2-4†	West 2
1912/13				
1st Round	v Coventry City	(h)	1-1	Wall
Replay	v Coventry City	(a)	2-1	Anderson, Roberts
2nd Round	v Plymouth Argyle	(a)	2-0	Anderson, Wall
3rd Round	v Oldham Athletic	(a)	0-0	
Replay	v Oldham Athletic	(h)	1-2	West
1913/14				
1st Round	v Swindon Town	(a)	0-1	
1914/15				
1st Round	v Sheffield Wednesday	(a)	0-1	

1919/20

1st Round	v Port Vale	(a)	1-0	Toms
2nd Round	v Aston Villa	(h)	1-2	Woodcock

1920/21

1st Round	v Liverpool	(a)	1-1	Miller
Replay	v Liverpool	(h)	1-2	Partridge

1921/22

1st Round	v Cardiff City	(h)	1-4	Sapsford

1922/23

1st Round	v Bradford City	(a)	1-1	Partridge
Replay	v Bradford City	(h)	2-0	Barber, Goldthorpe
2nd Round	v Tottenham Hotspurs	(a)	0-4	

1923/24

1st Round	v Plymouth Argyle	(h)	1-0	McPherson
2nd Round	v Huddersfield Town	(h)	0-3	

1925/25

1st Round	v Sheffield Wednesday	(a)	0-2	

1925/26

3rd Round	v Port Vale	(a)	3-2	Spence 2, McPherson
4th Round	v Tottenham Hotspurs	(a)	2-2	Spence, Thomas
Replay	v Tottenham Hotspurs	(h)	2-0	Spence, Rennox
5th Round	v Sunderland	(a)	3-3	Smith 2, McPherson
Replay	v Sunderland	(h)	2-1	Smith, McPherson
6th Round	v Fulham	(a)	2-1	Smith, McPherson
Semi Final	v Manchester City	(n)	0-3	

1926/27

3rd Round	v Reading	(a)	1-1	Bennion
Replay	v Reading	(h)	2-2	Spence, Sweeney
2nd Replay	v Reading	(n)	1-2	McPherson

1927/28

3rd Round	v Brentford	(h)	7-1	Hanson 4, Spence, McPherson, Johnston
4th Round	v Bury	(a)	1-1	Johnston
Replay	v Bury	(h)	1-0	Spence
5th Round	v Birmingham	(h)	1-0	Johnston
6th Round	v Blackburn Rovers	(a)	0-2	

1928/29

3rd Round	v Port Vale	(a)	3-0	Spence, Hanson, Taylor
4th Round	v Bury	(h)	0-1	

1929/30

3rd Round	v Swindon Town	(h)	0-2	

1930/31

3rd Round	v Stoke City	(a)	3-3	Reid 3
Replay	v Stoke City	(h)	0-0†	
2nd Replay	v Stoke City	(n)	4-2	Hopkinson 2, Spence, Gallimore
4th Round	v Grimsby Town	(a)	0-1	

1931/32

3rd Round	v Plymouth Argyle	(a)	1-4	Reid

1932/33

3rd Round	v Middlesbrough	(h)	1-4	Spence

1933/34

3rd Round	v Portsmouth	(h)	1-1	McLenahan
Replay	v Portsmouth	(a)	1-4	Ball

1934/35

3rd Round	v Bristol Rovers	(a)	3-1	Bamford 2, Mutch
4th Round	v Nottingham Forest	(a)	0-0	
Replay	v Nottingham Forest	(h)	0-3	

1935/36

3rd Round	v Reading	(a)	3-1	Mutch 2, Manley
4th Round	v Stoke City	(a)	0-0	
Replay	v Stoke City	(h)	0-2	

1936/37

3rd Round	v Reading	(h)	1-0	Bamford
4th Round	v Arsenal	(a)	0-5	

1937/38

3rd Round	v Yeovil Town	(h)	3-0	Baird, Bamford, Pearson
4th Round	v Barnsley	(a)	2-2	Baird, Carey
Replay	v Barnsley	(h)	1-0	Baird
5th Round	v Brentford	(a)	0-2	

1938/39

3rd Round	v West Bromwich Alb	(a)	0-0	
Replay	v West Bromwich Alb	(h)	1-5	Redwood

1945/46

3rd Round(leg1)	v Accrington Stanley	(a)	2-2	Smith, Wrigglesworth
3rd Round(leg2)	v Accrington Stanley	(h)	5-1(7-3)	Rowley 2, Bainbridge, Wrigglesworth, Own goal
4th Round(leg1)	v Preston North End	(h)	1-0	Hanlon
4th Round(leg2)	v Preston North End	(a)	1-3(2-3)	Hanlon

1946/47

3rd Round	v Bradford	(a)	3-0	Rowley 2, Buckle
4th Round	v Nottingham Forest	(h)	0-2	

1947/48

3rd Round	v Aston Villa	(a)	6-4	Pearson 2, Morris 2, Delaney, Rowley
4th Round	v Liverpool	(h)	3-0	Morris, Rowley, Mitten
5th Round	v Charlton Athletic	(h)	2-0	Warner, Mitten
6th Round	v Preston North End	(h)	4-1	Pearson 2, Rowley, Mitten
Semi Final	v Derby County	(n)	3-1	Pearson 3
Final	v Blackpool	(n)	4-2	Rowley 2, Pearson, Anderson

1948/49

3rd Round	v Bournemouth	(h)	6-0	Burke 2, Rowley 2, Pearson, Mitten
4th Round	v Bradford	(h)	1-1	Mitten
Replay	v Bradford	(a)	1-1†	Mitten
2nd Replay	v Bradford	(h)	5-0	Burke 2, Rowley 2, Pearson
5th Round	v Yeovil Town	(h)	8-0	Rowley 5, Burke 2, Mitten
6th Round	v Hull City	(a)	1-0	Pearson
Semi Final	v Wolves	(n)	1-1†	Mitten
Replay	v Wolves	(n)	0-1	

1949/50

3rd Round	v Weymouth	(h)	4-0	Rowley 2, Pearson, Delaney
4th Round	v Watford	(a)	1-0	Rowley
5th Round	v Portsmouth	(h)	3-3	Mitten 2, Pearson
Replay	v Portsmouth	(a)	3-1	Delaney, Downie, Mitten
Round 6	v Chelsea	(a)	0-2	

1950/51

3rd Round	v Oldham Athletic	(h)	4-1	Pearson, Aston, Birch, Whyte og
4th Round	v Leeds United	(h)	4-0	Pearson 3, Rowley
5th Round	v Arsenal	(h)	1-0	Pearson
6th Round	v Birmingham City	(a)	0-1	

1951/52

3rd Round	v Hull City	(h)	0-2	

1952/53

3rd Round	v Millwall	(a)	1-0	Pearson
4th Round	v Walthamstow Avenue	(h)	1-1	Lewis

Replay	v Walthamstow Avenue	(n)	5-2	Rowley, Byrne, Lewis, Pearson
5th Round	v Everton	(a)	1-2	Rowley

1953/54

3rd Round	v Burnley	(a)	3-5	Blanchflower, Taylor, Viollet

1954/55

3rd Round	v Reading	(a)	1-1	Webster
Replay	v Reading	(h)	4-1	Webster 2, Viollet, Rowley
4th Round	v Manchester City	(a)	0-2	

1955/56

3rd Round	v Bristol Rovers	(a)	0-4	

1956/57

3rd Round	v Hartlepool United	(a)	4-3	Whelan 2, Berry, Taylor
4th Round	v Wrexham	(a)	5-0	Whelan 2, Taylor 2, Byrne
5th Round	v Everton	(h)	1-0	Edwards
6th Round	v Bournemouth	(a)	2-1	Berry 2
Semi Final	v Birmingham City	(n)	2-0	Berry, Charlton
Final	v Aston Villa	(n)	1-2	Taylor

1957/58

3rd Round	v Workington	(a)	3-1	Viollet 3
4th Round	v Ipswich Town	(h)	2-0	Charlton 2
5th Round	v Sheffield Wednesday	(h)	3-0	Brennan 2, Dawson
6th Round	v West Bromwich Alb	(a)	2-2	E.Taylor, Dawson
Replay	v West Bromwich Alb	(h)	1-0	Webster
Semi Final	v Fulham	(n)	2-2	Charlton 2
Replay	v Fulham	(n)	5-3	Dawson 3, Charlton, Brennan
Final	v Bolton Wanderers	(n)	0-2	

1958/59

3rd Round	v Norwich City	(a)	0-3	

1959/60

3rd Round	v Derby County	(a)	4-2	Goodwin, Charlton, Scanlon, Own goal
4th Round	v Liverpool	(a)	3-1	Charlton 2, Bradley
5th Round	v Sheffield Wednesday	(h)	0-1	

1960/61

3rd Round	v Middlesbrough	(h)	3-0	Dawson 2, Cantwell
4th Round	v Sheffield Wednesday	(a)	1-1	Cantwell
Replay	v Sheffield Wednesday	(h)	2-7	Dawson, Pearson

1961/62

Round	Opponent		Score	Scorers
3rd Round	v Bolton Wanderers	(h)	2-1	Nicholson, Herd
4th Round	v Arsenal	(h)	1-0	Setters
5th Round	v Sheffield Wednesday	(h)	0-0	
Replay	v Sheffield Wednesday	(a)	2-0	Charlton, Giles
6th Round	v Preston North End	(a)	0-0	
Replay	v Preston North End	(h)	2-1	Herd, Charlton
Semi Final	v Tottenham Hotspurs	(n)	1-3	Herd

1962/63

Round	Opponent		Score	Scorers
3rd Round	v Huddersfield Town	(h)	5-0	Law 3, Giles, Quixall
4th Round	v Aston Villa	(h)	1-0	Quixall
5th Round	v Chelsea	(h)	2-1	Quixall, Law
6th Round	v Coventry City	(a)	3-1	Charlton 2, Quixall
Semi Final	v Southampton	(n)	1-0	Law
Final	v Leicester City	(n)	3-1	Herd 2, Law

1963/64

Round	Opponent		Score	Scorers
3rd Round	v Southampton	(a)	3-2	Crerand, Moore, Herd
4th Round	v Bristol City	(h)	4-1	Law 3, Herd
5th Round	v Barnsley	(a)	4-0	Law 2, Best, Herd
6th Round	v Sunderland	(h)	3-3	Charlton, Best, Own goal
Replay	v Sunderland	(a)	2-2†	Charlton, Law
2nd Replay	v Sunderland	(n)	5-1	Law 3, Chisnall, Herd
Semi Final	v West Ham United	(n)	1-3	Law

1964/65

Round	Opponent		Score	Scorers
3rd Round	v Chester	(h)	2-1	Kinsey, Best
4th Round	v Stoke City	(a)	0-0	
Replay	v Stoke City	(h)	1-0	Herd
5th Round	v Burnley	(h)	2-1	Crerand, Law
6th Round	v Wolves	(a)	5-3	Law 2, Crerand, Herd, Best
Semi-Final	v Leeds United	(n)	0-0	
Replay	v Leeds United	(n)	0-1	

1965/66

Round	Opponent		Score	Scorers
3rd Round	v Derby County	(a)	5-2	Best 2, Law 2, Herd
4th Round	v Rotherham United	(h)	0-0	
Replay	v Rotherham United	(a)	1-0†	Connelly
5th Round	v Wolves	(a)	4-2	Law 2, Herd, Best
6th Round	v Preston North End	(a)	1-1	Herd
Replay	v Preston North End	(h)	3-1	Law 2, Connelly
Semi Final	v Everton	(n)	0-1	

1966/67

Round	Opponent		Score	Scorers
3rd Round	v Stoke City	(h)	2-0	Law, Herd

4th Round	*v* Norwich City	(h)	1-2	Law

1967/68

3rd Round	*v* Tottenham Hotspurs	(h)	2-2	Best, Charlton
Replay	*v* Tottenham Hotspurs	(a)	0-1†	

1968/69

3rd Round	*v* Exeter City	(a)	3-1	Fitzpatrick, Kidd, Own goal
4th Round	*v* Watford	(h)	1-1	Law
Replay	*v* Watford	(a)	2-0	Law 2
5th Round	*v* Birmingham City	(a)	2-2	Law, Best
Replay	*v* Birmingham City	(h)	6-2	Law 3, Kidd, Morgan, Crerand
6th Round	*v* Everton	(h)	0-1	

1969/70

3rd Round	*v* Ipswich Town	(a)	1-0	Own goal
4th Round	*v* Manchester City	(h)	3-0	Kidd 2, Morgan
5th Round	*v* Northampton Town	(a)	8-2	Best 6, Kidd 2
6th Round	*v* Middlesbrough	(a)	1-1	Sartori
Replay	*v* Middlesbrough	(h)	2-1	Charlton, Morgan
Semi Final	*v* Leeds United	(n)	0-0	
Replay	*v* Leeds United	(n)	0-0†	
2nd Replay	*v* Leeds United	(n)	0-1	
3rd Place p/o	*v* Watford	(n)	2-0	Kidd 2

1970/71

3rd Round	*v* Middlesbrough	(h)	0-0	
Replay	*v* Middlesbrough	(a)	1-2	Best

1971/72

3rd Round	*v* Southampton	(a)	1-1	Charlton
Replay	*v* Southampton	(h)	4-1†	Best 2, Sadler, Aston
4th Round	*v* Preston North End	(a)	2-0	Gowling 2
5th Round	*v* Middlesbrough	(h)	0-0	
Replay	*v* Middlesbrough	(a)	3-0	Morgan, Charlton, Best
6th Round	*v* Stoke City	(h)	1-1	Best
Replay	*v* Stoke City	(a)	1-2†	Best

1972/73

3rd Round	*v* Wolves	(a)	0-1	

1973/74

3rd Round	*v* Plymouth Argyle	(h)	1-0	Macari
4th Round	*v* Ipswich Town	(h)	0-1	

1974/75

3rd Round	*v* Walsall	(h)	0-0	
Replay	*v* Walsall	(a)	2-3†	McIlroy, Daly

1975/76

3rd Round	v Oxford United	(h)	2-1	Daly 2
4th Round	v Peterborough United	(h)	3-1	Forsyth, McIlroy, Hill
5th Round	v Leicester City	(a)	2-1	Daly, Macari
6th Round	v Wolves	(h)	1-1	Daly
Replay	v Wolves	(a)	3-2†	B.Greenhoff, McIlroy, Pearson
Semi Final	v Derby County	(n)	2-0	Hill 2
Final	v Southampton	(n)	0-1	

1976/77

3rd Round	v Walsall	(h)	1-0	Hill
4th Round	v Queens Park Rangers	(h)	1-0	Macari
5th Round	v Southampton	(a)	2-2	Macari, Hill
Replay	v Southampton	(h)	2-1	J.Greenhoff 2
6th Round	v Aston Villa	(h)	2-1	Houston, Macari
Semi Final	v Leeds United	(n)	2-1	Coppell, J.Greenhoff
Final	v Liverpool	(n)	2-1	Pearson, J.Greenhoff

1977/78

3rd Round	v Carlisle United	(a)	1-1	Macari
Replay	v Carlisle United	(h)	4-2	Pearson 2, Macari 2
4th Round	v West Bromwich Alb	(h)	1-1	Coppell
Replay	v West Bromwich Alb	(a)	2-3	Pearson, Hill

1978/79

3rd Round	v Chelsea	(h)	3-0	Coppell, J.Greenhoff, Grimes
4th Round	v Fulham	(a)	1-1	J.Greenhoff
Replay	v Fulham	(h)	1-0	J.Greenhoff
5th Round	v Colchester United	(a)	1-0	J.Greenhoff
6th Round	v Tottenham Hotspurs	(a)	1-1	Thomas
Replay	v Tottenham Hotspurs	(h)	2-0	McIlroy, Jordan
Semi Final	v Liverpool	(n)	2-2	Jordan, B.Greenhoff
Replay	v Liverpool	(n)	1-0	J.Greenhoff
Final	v Arsenal	(n)	2-3	McQueen, McIlroy

1979/80

3rd Round	v Tottenham Hotspurs	(a)	1-1	McIlroy
Replay	v Tottenham Hotspurs	(h)	0-1†	

1980/81

3rd Round	v Brighton & Hove Alb	(h)	2-2	Duxbury, Thomas
Replay	v Brighton & Hove Alb	(a)	2-0	Nicholl, Birtles
4th Round	v Nottingham Forest	(a)	0-1	

1981/82

3rd Round	v Watford	(a)	0-1	

1982/83

3rd Round	v West Ham United	(h)	2-0	Stapleton, Coppell
4th Round	v Luton Town	(a)	2-0	Moses, Moran
5th Round	v Derby County	(a)	1-0	Whiteside
6th Round	v Everton	(h)	1-0	Stapleton
Semi Final	v Arsenal	(n)	2-1	Robson, Whiteside
Final	v Brighton & Hove Alb	(n)	2-2†	Stapleton, Wilkins
Replay	v Brighton & Hove Alb	(n)	4-0	Robson 2, Muhren, Whiteside

1983/84

3rd Round	v AFC Bournemouth	(a)	0-2	

1984/85

3rd Round	v AFC Bournemouth	(h)	3-0	Strachan, McQueen, Stapleton
4th Round	v Coventry City	(h)	2-1	Hughes, McGrath
5th Round	v Blackburn Rovers	(a)	2-0	Strachan, McGrath
6th Round	v West Ham United	(h)	4-2	Whiteside 3, Hughes
Semi Final	v Liverpool	(n)	2-2†	Robson, Stapleton
Replay	v Liverpool	(n)	2-1	Robson, Hughes
Final	v Everton	(n)	1-0†	Whiteside

1985/86

3rd Round	v Rochdale	(h)	2-0	Stapleton, Hughes
4th Round	v Sunderland	(a)	0-0	
Replay	v Sunderland	(h)	3-0	Olsen 2, Whiteside
5th Round	v West Ham United	(a)	1-1	Stapleton
Replay	v West Ham United	(h)	0-2	

1986/87

3rd Round	v Manchester City	(h)	1-0	Whiteside
4th Round	v Coventry City	(h)	0-1	

1987/88

3rd Round	v Ipswich Town	(a)	2-1	Own goal, Anderson
4th Round	v Chelsea	(h)	2-0	Whiteside, McClair
5th Round	v Arsenal	(a)	1-2	McClair

1988/89

3rd Round	v Queens Park Rangers	(h)	0-0	
Replay	v Queens Park Rangers	(a)	2-2†	Gill, Graham
2nd Replay	v Queens Park Rangers	(h)	3-0	McClair 2(1pen), Robson
4th Round	v Oxford United	(h)	4-0	Hughes, Bruce, Own goal, Robson
5th Round	v AFC Bournemouth	(a)	1-1	Hughes
Replay	v AFC Bournemouth	(h)	1-0	McClair
6th Round	v Nottingham Forest	(h)	0-1	

1989/90

3rd Round	v Nottingham Forest	(a)	1-0	Robins
4th Round	v Hereford United	(a)	1-0	Blackmore
5th Round	v Newcastle United	(a)	3-2	Robins, Wallace, McClair
6th Round	v Sheffield United	(a)	1-0	McClair
Semi Final	v Oldham Athletic	(n)	3-3aet	Robson, Webb, Wallace
Replay	v Oldham Athletic	(n)	2-1aet	McClair, Robins
Final	v Crystal Palace	(n)	3-3aet	Hughes 2, Robson
Replay	v Crystal Palace	(n)	1-0	Martin

1990/91

3rd Round	v Queens Park Rangers	(h)	2-1	Hughes, McClair
4th Round	v Bolton Wanderers	(h)	1-0	Hughes
5th Round	v Norwich City	(a)	1-2	McClair

1991/92

3rd Round	v Leeds United	(a)	1-0	Hughes
4th Round	v Southampton	(a)	0-0	
Replay	v Southampton	(h)	2-2	Kanchelskis, McClair

(Southampton won 4-2 on penalties)

1992/93

3rd Round	v Bury	(h)	2-0	Gillespie, Phelan
4th Round	v Brighton & Hove Alb	(h)	1-0	Giggs
5th Round	v Sheffield United	(a)	1-3	Giggs

1993/94

3rd Round	v Sheffield United	(a)	1-0	Hughes
4th Round	v Norwich City	(a)	2-0	Keane, Cantona
5th Round	v Wimbledon	(a)	3-0	Cantona, Bruce, Irwin
6th Round	v Charlton Athletic	(h)	3-1	Hughes, Kanchelskis 2
S/F	v Oldham Athletic	(n)	1-1	Hughes
S/F	v Oldham Athletic	(n)	4-1	Ince, Kanchelskis, Robson, Giggs
Final	v Chelsea	(n)	4-0	Cantona 2pen Hughes, McClair

1994/95

3rd Round	v Sheffield United	(a)	2-0	Hughes, Cantona
4th Round	v Wrexham	(h)	5-2	Irwin 2, Giggs, McClair, og
5th Round	v Leeds United	(h)	3-1	Bruce, McClair, Hughes
6th Round	v Queens Park Rangers	(h)	2-0	Sharpe, Irwin

S/F	*v* Crystal Palace	(n)	2-2	Irwin, Pallister
Replay	*v* Crystal Palace	(n)	2-0	Bruce, Pallister
Final	*v* Everton	(n)	0-1	

1995/96

3rd Round	*v* Sunderland	(h)	2-2	Butt, Cantona
3rd Round Replay	*v* Sunderland	(a)	2-1	Scholes, Cole
4th Round	*v* Reading	(a)	3-0	Giggs, Parker, Cantona
5th Round	*v* Manchester City	(h)	2-1	Cantona, Scholes
6th Round	*v* Southampton	(h)	2-0	Cantona, Sharpe
Semi Final	*v* Chelsea	(n)	2-1	Cole, Beckham
Final	*v* Liverpool	(n)	1-0	Cantona

Full record in Domestic Cup Competitions – *League Cup*

1960/61

1st Round	*v* Exeter City	(a)	1-1	Dawson
Replay	*v* Exeter City	(h)	4-1	Quixall 2(1pen), Giles, Pearson
2nd Round	*v* Bradford City	(a)	1-2	Viollet

1966/67

| 2nd Round | *v* Blackpool | (a) | 1-5 | Herd |

1969/70

2nd Round	*v* Middlesbrough	(h)	1-0	Sadler
3rd Round	*v* Wrexham	(h)	2-0	Kidd, Best
4th Round	*v* Burnley	(a)	0-0	
Replay	*v* Burnley	(h)	1-0	Best
5th Round	*v* Derby County	(a)	0-0	
Replay	*v* Derby County	(h)	1-0	Kidd
Semi Final(leg1)	*v* Manchester City	(a)	1-2	Charlton
Semi Final(leg2)	*v* Manchester City	(h)	2-2 (3-4)	Edwards, Law

1970/71

2nd Round	*v* Aldershot	(a)	3-1	Law, Kidd, Best
3rd Round	*v* Portsmouth	(h)	1-0	Charlton
4th Round	*v* Chelsea	(h)	2-1	Best, Charlton
5th Round	*v* Crystal Palace	(h)	4-2	Kidd 2, Charlton, Fitzpatrick
Semi Final(leg1)	*v* Aston Villa	(h)	1-1	Kidd
Semi Final(leg2)	*v* Aston Villa	(a)	1-2 (2-3)	Kidd

1971/72

2nd Round	*v* Ipswich Town	(a)	3-1	Best 2, Morgan
3rd Round	*v* Burnley	(h)	1-1	Charlton
Replay	*v* Burnley	(a)	1-0	Charlton
4th Round	*v* Stoke City	(h)	1-1	Gowling
Replay	*v* Stoke City	(a)	0-0†	

2nd Replay	v Stoke City	(a)	1-2	Best

1972/73

2nd Round	v Oxford United	(a)	2-2	Charlton, Law
Replay	v Oxford United	(h)	3-1	Best 2, Storey-Moore
3rd Round	v Bristol Rovers	(a)	1-1	Morgan
Replay	v Bristol Rovers	(h)	1-2	McIlroy

1973/74

2nd Round	v Middlesbrough	(h)	0-1	

1974/75

2nd Round	v Charlton Athletic	(h)	5-1	Macari 2, Houston, McIlroy, Own goal
3rd Round	v Manchester City	(h)	1-0	Daly
4th Round	v Burnley	(h)	3-2	Macari 2, Morgan
5th Round	v Middlesbrough	(a)	0-0	
Replay	v Middlesbrough	(h)	3-0	McIlroy, Pearson, Macari
Semi Final(leg1)	v Norwich City	(h)	2-2	Macari 2
Semi Final(leg2)	v Norwich City	(a)	0-1(2-3)	

1975/76

2nd Round	v Brentford	(h)	2-1	McIlroy, Macari
3rd Round	v Aston Villa	(a)	2-1	Coppell, Macari
4th Round	v Manchester City	(a)	0-4	

1976/77

2nd Round	v Tranmere Rovers	(h)	5-0	Daly 2, Pearson, Macari, Hill
3rd Round	v Sunderland	(h)	2-2	Pearson, Own goal
Replay	v Sunderland	(a)	2-2†	Daly, B.Greenhoff
2nd Replay	v Sunderland	(h)	1-0	B.Greenhoff
4th Round	v Newcastle United	(h)	7-2	Hill 3, Nicholl, Houston, Coppell, Pearson
5th Round	v Everton	(h)	0-3	

1977/78

2nd Round	v Arsenal	(a)	2-3	McCreery, Pearson

1978/79

2nd Round	v Stockport County	(a)	3-2	McIlroy, J.Greenhoff, Jordan
3rd Round	v Watford	(h)	1-2	Jordan

1979/80

2nd Round(leg1)	v Tottenham Hotspurs	(a)	1-2	Thomas
2nd Round (leg2)	v Tottenham Hotspurs	(h)	3-1(4-3)	Coppell, Thomas, OG
3rd Round	v Norwich City	(a)	1-4	McIlroy

1980/81

2nd Round (leg1)	*v* Coventry City	(h)	0-1	
2nd Round (leg2)	*v* Coventry City	(a)	0-1(0-2)	

1981/82

2nd Round (leg1)	*v* Tottenham Hotspurs	(a)	0-1	
2nd Round (leg2)	*v* Tottenham Hotspurs	(h)	0-1(0-2)	

1982/83

2nd Round (leg1)	*v* AFC Bournemouth	(h)	2-0	Own goal, Stapleton
2nd Round (leg2)	*v* AFC Bournemouth	(a)	2-2	Muhren, Coppell
3rd Round	*v* Bradford City	(a)	0-0	
Replay	*v* Bradford City	(h)	4-1	Moses, Albiston, Moran, Coppell
4th Round	*v* Southampton	(h)	2-0	McQueen, Whiteside
5th Round	*v* Nottingham Forest	(h)	4-0	McQueen 2, Coppell, Robson
Semi Final (leg1)	*v* Arsenal	(a)	4-2	Coppell 2, Whiteside, Stapleton
Semi Final (leg2)	*v* Arsenal	(h)	2-1(6-3)	Coppell, Moran
Final	*v* Liverpool	(n)	1-2†	Whiteside

1983/84

2nd Round (leg1)	*v* Port Vale	(a)	1-0	Stapleton
2nd Round (leg2)	*v* Port Vale	(h)	2-0(3-0)	Whiteside, Wilkins
3rd Round	*v* Colchester United	(a)	2-0	McQueen, Moses
4th Round	*v* Oxford United	(a)	1-1	Hughes
Replay	*v* Oxford United	(h)	1-1†	Stapleton
2nd Replay	*v* Oxford United	(a)	1-2aet	Graham

1984/85

2nd Round (leg1)	*v* Burnley	(h)	4-0	Hughes 3, Robson
2nd Round (leg2)	*v* Burnley	(a)	3-0 (7-0)	Brazil 2, Olsen
3rd Round	*v* Everton	(h)	1-2	Brazil

1985/86

2nd Round (leg1)	*v* Crystal Palace	(a)	1-0	Barnes
2nd Round (leg2)	*v* Crystal Palace	(h)	1-0 (2-0)	Whiteside
3rd Round	*v* West Ham United	(h)	1-0	Whiteside
4th Round	*v* Liverpool	(a)	1-2	McGrath

1986/87

2nd Round (leg1)	*v* Port Vale	(h)	2-0	Stapleton, Whiteside
2nd Round (leg2)	*v* Port Vale	(a)	5-2 (7-2)	Moses 2, Stapleton, Barnes, Davenport
3rd Round	*v* Southampton	(h)	0-0	
Replay	*v* Southampton	(a)	1-4	Davenport

1987/88

2nd Round (leg1)	v Hull City	(h)	5-0	McGrath, Davenport, Whiteside, Strachan, McClair
2nd Round (leg2)	v Hull City	(a)	1-0 (6-0)	McClair
3rd Round	v Crystal Palace	(h)	2-1	McClair 2
4th Round	v Bury	(a)	2-1	Whiteside, McClair
5th Round	v Oxford United	(a)	0-2	

1988/89

2nd Round (leg1)	v Rotherham United	(a)	1-0	Davenport
2nd Round (leg2)	v Rotherham United	(h)	5-0 (6-0)	McClair 3, Robson, Bruce
3rd Round	v Wimbledon	(a)	1-2	Robson

1989/90

2nd Round (leg1)	v Portsmouth	(a)	3-2	Ince 2, Wallace
2nd Round (leg2)	v Portsmouth	(h)	0-0 (3-2)	
3rd Round	v Tottenham Hotspurs	(h)	0-3	

1990/91

2nd Round (leg1)	v Halifax Town	(a)	3-1	Blackmore, McClair, Webb
2nd Round (leg2)	v Halifax Town	(h)	2-1 (5-2)	Bruce, Anderson
3rd Round	v Liverpool	(h)	3-1	Bruce, Hughes, Sharpe
4th Round	v Arsenal	(a)	6-2	Sharpe 3, Blackmore, Hughes, Wallace
5th Round	v Southampton	(a)	1-1	Hughes
Replay	v Southampton	(h)	3-2	Hughes 3
Semi Final (leg1)	v Leeds United	(h)	2-1	Sharpe, McClair
Semi Final (leg2)	v Leeds United	(a)	1-0 (3-1)	Sharpe
Final	v Sheffield Wednesday	(n)	0-1	

1991/92

2nd Round (leg1)	v Cambridge United	(h)	3-0	Giggs, McClair, Bruce
2nd Round (leg2)	v Cambridge United	(a)	1-1 (4-1)	McClair
3rd Round	v Portsmouth	(h)	3-1	Robins 2, Robson
4th Round	v Oldham Athletic	(h)	2-0	McClair, Kanchelskis
5th Round	v Leeds United	(a)	3-1	Blackmore, Kanchelskis, Giggs
Semi Final (leg1)	v Middlesbrough	(a)	0-0	
Semi Final (leg2)	v Middlesbrough	(h)	2-1 (2-1)	Sharpe, Giggs
Final	v Nottingham Forest	(n)	1-0	McClair

1992/93

2nd Round (leg1)	v Brighton & Hove Alb	(h)	1-1	Hughes
2nd Round (leg2)	v Brighton & Hove Alb	(a)	1-0	Wallace
3rd Round	v Aston Villa	(a)	0-1	

1993/94

2nd Round (leg1)	v Stoke City	(a)	1-2	Dublin
2nd Round (leg2)	v Stoke City	(h)	2-0	Sharpe, McClair
3rd Round	v Leicester City	(h)	5-1	Bruce 2, McClair, Sharpe, Hughes
4th Round	v Everton	(a)	2-0	Hughes, Giggs
5th Round	v Portsmouth	(h)	2-2	Giggs, Cantona
Replay	v Portsmouth	(a)	1-0	McClair
Semi Final (leg1)	v Sheffield Wednesday	(h)	1-0	Giggs
Semi Final (leg2)	v Sheffield Wednesday	(a)	4-1	Hughes 2, McClair, Kanchelskis
Final	v Aston Villa	(n)	1-3	Hughes

1994/95

2nd Round (leg 1)	v Port Vale	(a)	2-1	Scholes 2,
2nd Round (leg2)	v Port Vale	(h)	2-0	McClair, May
3rd Round	v Newcastle Utd	(a)	0-2	

1995/96

2nd Round (leg 1)	v York City	(h)	0-3	
2nd Round (leg 2)	v York City	(a)	3-1	Scholes 2, Cooke

Cup Final Squads – *FA Cup*

Date	Opponents	Venue	Score	Att.
24/4/09	v Bristol City	The Crystal Palace	Won 1-0	71,401

Team: Moger, Stacey, Hayes, Duckworth, Roberts, Bell, Meredith, Halse, Turnbull, **A Turnbull**, Wall

24/4/48	v Blackpool	Wembley	Won 4-2	100,000

Team: Crompton, Carey, Aston, **Anderson**, Chilton, Cockburn, Delaney, Morris, **Rowley (2)**, **Pearson**, Mitten

5/5/57	v Aston Villa	Wembley	Lost 1-2	100,000

Team: Wood, Foulkes, Byrne, Colman, Blanchflower, Edwards, Berry, Whelan, T **Taylor**, Charlton, Pegg

3/5/58	v Bolton Wanderers	Wembley	Lost 0-2	100,000

Team: Gregg, Foulkes, Greaves, Goodwin, Cope, Crowther, Webster, E Taylor, Dawson, Charlton, Brennan

Stan Crowther having played for Aston Villa twelve months earlier thus played against and for United in consecutive FA Cup Finals.

25/5/63	v Leicester City	Wembley	Won 3-1	100,000

Team: Gaskell, Dunne, Cantwell, Crerand, Foulkes, Setters, Giles, Stiles, Quixall, **Herd (2)**, **Law**, Charlton

1/5/76   v Southampton   Wembley   Lost 0-1   100,000
Team: Stepney, Forsyth, Houston, Daly, B Greenhoff, Buchan, Coppell, McIlroy, Pearson, Macari, Hill (McCreery)

21/5/77   v Liverpool   Wembley   Won 2-1   100,000
Team: Stepney, Nicholl, Albiston, McIlroy, B Greenhoff, Buchan, Coppell, **J Greenhoff, Pearson**, Macari, Hill (McCreery)
This was Arthur Albiston's FA Cup debut. Martin Buchan became the first player ever to captain both an English and a Scottish Cup winning side.

12/5/79   v Arsenal   Wembley   Lost 2-3   100,000
Team: Bailey, Nicholl, Albiston, **McIlroy, McQueen**, Buchan, Coppell, J.Greenhoff, Jordan, Macari, Thomas

21/5/83   v Brighton & Hove Albion   Wembley   Drew 2-2 aet 100,000
Team: Bailey, Duxbury, Albiston, **Wilkins**, Moran, McQueen, Robson, Muhren, **Stapleton**, Whiteside, Davies
Like Albiston seven years earlier, this was Alan Davies' FA Cup debut.

26/5/83   v Brighton & Hove Albion   Wembley   Won 4-0   92,000
Team: Bailey, Duxbury, Albiston, Wilkins, Moran, McQueen, **Robson (2), Muhren**, Stapleton, **Whiteside**, Davies
In this game Davies created the unusual career record of only ever playing two FA Cup ties for United, both of which were FA Cup Finals. He compounded this record further 12 months later when he made his only European appearance. He certainly knew how to pick his games for he came on as substitute against Juventus in the semi-final of the Cup-winners Cup and scored United's equaliser in a 1-1 draw! Norman Whiteside also set the record in this game of becoming the youngest ever player to score in the Finals of both League Cup and FA Cup.

18/5/85   v Everton   Wembley   Won 1-0 aet 100,000
Team: Bailey, Gidman, Albiston (Duxbury), **Whiteside**, McGrath, Moran, Robson, Strachan, Hughes, Stapleton, Olsen
Kevin Moran was the first player ever to be dismissed in a FA Cup Final.

12/5/90   v Crystal Palace   Wembley   Drew 3-3 at 80,000
Team: Leighton, Ince, Martin (Blackmore), Bruce, Phelan, Pallister (Robins), **Robson**, Webb, McClair, **Hughes (2)**, Wallace

17/5/90   v Crystal Palace   Wembley   Won 1-0   80,000
Team: Sealey, Ince, **Martin**, Bruce, Phelan, Pallister, Robson, Webb, McClair, Hughes, Wallace
This FA Cup winning goal was the only goal Martin ever scored in the competition.

14/5/94   v Chelsea   Wembley   Won 4-0   80,000
Team: Schmeichel, Parker, Irwin (Sharpe), Bruce, Pallister, Ince, Keane, **Cantona (2)**, Kanchelskis (**McClair**), **Hughes**, Giggs

20/05/95   v Everton   Wembley   Lost 0-1   79,592
Team: Schmeichel, G. Neville, Bruce (Giggs), Pallister, Irwin, Butt, Keane, Ince, Sharpe (Scholes), Hughes, McClair. Sub Walsh (G)

11/05/96   v Liverpool   Wembley   Won 1-0   79,007
Team: Schmeichel, Irwin, May, Pallister, P.Neville, Beckham (G.Neville), Keane, Butt, Giggs, Cole (Scholes), **Cantona**

Cup Final Squads – *League Cup*

Date	Opponents	Venue	Score	Att.
26/3/83	*v* Liverpool	Wembley	Lost 1-2 aet	100,000

Team: Bailey, Duxbury, Albiston, Moses, Moran (Macari), McQueen, Wilkins, Muhren, Stapleton, **Whiteside**, Coppell

Date	Opponents	Venue	Score	Att.
21/4/91	*v* Sheffield Wednesday	Wembley	Lost 0-1	80,000

Team: Sealey, Irwin, Blackmore, Bruce, Webb (Phelan), Pallister, Robson, Ince, McClair, Hughes, Sharpe

Date	Opponents	Venue	Score	Att.
12/4/92	*v* Nottingham Forest	Wembley	Won 1-0	76,810

Team: Schmeichel, Parker, Irwin, Bruce, Phelan, Pallister, Kanchelskis (Sharpe), Ince, **McClair**, Hughes, Giggs

Date	Opponents	Venue	Score	Att.
27/3/94	*v* Aston Villa	Wembley	Lost 1-3	77,231

Team: Sealey, Parker, Irwin, Bruce (McClair), Pallister, Cantona, Ince, **Hughes**, Giggs (Sharpe), Kanchelskis, Keane

Cup Final Squads – *European Champions' Cup*

Date	Opponents	Venue	Score	Att.
29/5/68	*v* Benfica	Wembley	Won 4-1 aet	100,000

Team: Stepney, Dunne, Burns, Crerand, Foulkes, Stiles, **Best**, **Kidd**, **Charlton (2)**, Sadler, Aston

Cup Final Squads – *European Cup-Winners' Cup*

Date	Opponents	Venue	Score	Att.
15/5/91	*v* Barcelona	Rotterdam	Won 2-1	45,000

Team: Schmeichel, Irwin, Blackmore, Bruce, Phelan, Pallister, Robson, Ince, McClair, **Hughes (2)**, Sharpe

United in Europe – *European Champions' Cup*

1956/57

Prelim (1)	*v* Anderlecht	(a)	2-0	Viollet, Taylor
Prelim (2)	*v* Anderlecht	(h)	10-0	Viollet 4, Taylor 3, Whelan 2, Berry
Round 1(1)	*v* Borussia Dortmund	(h)	3-2	Viollet 2, Pegg
Round 1(2)	*v* Borussia Dortmund	(a)	0-0	
Q Final(1)	*v* Athletic Bilbao	(a)	3-5	Taylor, Viollet, Whelan
Q Final(2)	*v* Athletic Bilbao	(h)	3-0	Viollet, Taylor, Berry
S Final(1)	*v* Real Madrid	(a)	1-3	Taylor

S Final(2)	v Real Madrid	(h)	2-2	Taylor, Charlton

1957/58

Prelim (1)	v Shamrock Rovers	(a)	6-0	Taylor 2, Whelan 2, Pegg, Berry
Prelim (2)	v Shamrock Rovers	(h)	3-2	Viollet 2, Pegg
Round 1(1)	v Dukla Prague	(h)	3-0	Webster, Taylor, Pegg
Round 1(2)	v Dukla Prague	(a)	0-1	
Q Final(1)	v Red Star Belgrade	(h)	2-1	Colman, Charlton
Q Final(2)	v Red Star Belgrade	(a)	3-3	Charlton 2, Viollet
S Final(1)	v AC Milan	(h)	2-1	Taylor(pen), Viollet
S Final(2)	v AC Milan	(a)	0-4	

1965/66

Prelim (1)	v HJK Helsinki	(a)	3-2	Connelly, Herd, Law
Prelim (2)	v HJK Helsinki	(h)	6-0	Connelly 3, Best 2, Charlton
Round 1(1)	v ASK Vorwaerts	(a)	2-0	Law, Connelly
Round 1(2)	v ASK Vorwaerts	(h)	3-1	Herd 3
Q Final(1)	v Benfica	(h)	3-2	Herd, Law, Foulkes
Q Final(2)	v Benfica	(a)	5-1	Best 2, Charlton, Connelly, Crerand.
S Final(1)	v FK Partizan Belgrade	(a)	0-2	
S Final(2)	v FK Partizan Belgrade	(h)	1-0	Stiles

1967/68

Round 1(1)	v Hibernians (Malta)	(h)	4-0	Sadler 2, Law 2
Round 1(2)	v Hibernians (Malta)	(a)	0-0	
Round 2(1)	v FK Sarajevo	(a)	0-0	
Round 2(2)	v FK Sarajevo	(h)	2-1	Best, Aston
Q Final(1)	v Gornik Zabre	(h)	2-0	Kidd, own goal
Q Final(2)	v Gornik Zabre	(a)	0-1	
S Final(1)	v Real Madrid	(h)	1-0	Best
S Final(2)	v Real Madrid	(a)	3-3	Foulkes, Sadler, Own goal
Final	v Benfica	(n)	4-1	Charlton 2, Best, Kidd

1968/69

Round 1(1)	v Waterford	(a)	3-1	Law 3
Round 1(2)	v Waterford	(h)	7-1	Law 4, Stiles, Burns, Charlton
Round 2(1)	v RSC Anderlecht	(h)	3-0	Law 2, Kidd
Round 2(2)	v RSC Anderlecht	(a)	1-3	Sartori
Q Final(1)	v Rapid Vienna	(h)	3-0	Best 2, Morgan
Q Final(2)	v Rapid Vienna	(a)	0-0	
S Final(1)	v AC Milan	(a)	0-2	
S Final(2)	v AC Milan	(h)	1-0	Charlton

1993/94

Round 1(1)	v Honved	(a)	3-2	Keane 2, Cantona
Round 1(2)	v Honved	(h)	2-1	Bruce 2
Round 2(1)	v Galatasary	(h)	3-3	Robson, own goal, Cantona
Round 2(2)	v Galatasary	(a)	0-0	

1994/95

Group A	v IFK Gothenburg	(h)	4-2	Giggs 2, Kanchelskis, Sharpe
Group A	v Galatasary	(a)	0-0	
Group A	v Barcelona	(h)	2-2	Hughes, Sharpe
Group A	v Barcelona	(a)	0-4	
Group A	v IFK Gothenburg	(a)	1-3	Hughes
Group A	v Galatasary	(h)	4-0	Davies, Beckham, Keane, OG

United in Europe – *European Cup-Winners' Cup*

1963/64

Round 1(1)	v Willem II	(a)	1-1	Herd
Round 1(2)	v Willem II	(h)	6-1	Law 3, Charlton, Chisnall, Setters
Round 2(1)	v Tottenham Hotspurs	(a)	0-2	
Round 2(2)	v Tottenham Hotspurs	(h)	4-1	Charlton 2, Herd 2
Q Final(1)	v Sporting Club Lisbon	(h)	4-1	Law 3, Charlton
Q Final(2)	v Sporting Club Lisbon	(a)	0-5	

1977/78

Round 1(1)	v AS Saint-Etienne	(a)	1-1	Hill
Round 1(2)	v AS Saint-Etienne	(h)	2-0	Coppell, Pearson
Round 2(1)	v FC Porto	(a)	0-4	
Round 2(2)	v FC Porto	(h)	5-2	Coppell 2, Nicholl, 2 own goals

1983/84

Round 1(1)	v Dukla Prague	(h)	1-1	Wilkins
Round 1(2)	v Dukla Prague	(a)	2-2	Robson, Stapleton
Round 2(1)	v Spartak Varna	(a)	2-1	Robson, Graham
Round 2(2)	v Spartak Varna	(h)	2-0	Stapleton 2
Q Final(1)	v FC Barcelona	(a)	0-2	
Q Final(2)	v FC Barcelona	(h)	3-0	Robson 2, Stapleton
S Final(1)	v Juventus	(h)	1-1	Davies
S Final(2)	v Juventus	(a)	1-2	Whiteside

1990/91

Round 1(1)	v Pecsi Munkas	(h)	2-0	Blackmore, Webb
Round 1(2)	v Pecsi Munkas	(a)	1-0	McClair
Round 2(1)	v Wrexham	(h)	3-0	McClair, Bruce, Pallister

Round 2(2)	v Wrexham	(a)	2-0	Robins, Bruce
Q Final(1)	v Montpellier	(h)	1-1	McClair
Q Final(2)	v Montpellier	(a)	2-0	Blackmore, Bruce
S Final(1)	v Legia Warsaw	(a)	3-1	McClair, Hughes, Bruce
S Final(2)	v Legia Warsaw	(h)	1-1	Sharpe
Final	v Barcelona	(n)	2-1	Hughes 2

1991/92

Round 1(1)	v Panathinaikos	(a)	0-0	
Round 1(2)	v Panathinaikos	(h)	2-0	Hughes, McClair
Round 2(1)	v Athletico Madrid	(a)	0-3	
Round 2(2)	v Athletico Madrid	(h)	1-1	Hughes

United in Europe – *Inter-Cities Fairs Cup*

1964/65

Round 1(1)	v Djurgardens IF	(a)	1-1	Herd
Round 1(2)	v Djurgardens IF	(h)	6-1	Law 3, Charlton 2, Best
Round 2(1)	v Borussia Dortmund	(a)	6-1	Charlton 3, Herd, Law, Best
Round 2(2)	v Borussia Dortmund	(h)	4-0	Charlton 2, Connelly, Law
Round 3(1)	v Everton	(h)	1-1	Connelly
Round 3(2)	v Everton	(a)	2-1	Connelly, Herd
Q Final(1)	v RC Strasbourg	(a)	5-0	Law 2, Connelly, Charlton,Herd.
Q Final(2)	v RC Strasbourg	(h)	0-0	
S Final(1)	v Ferencvaros	(h)	3-2	Herd 2, Law
S Final(2)	v Ferencvaros	(a)	0-1	
Play Off	v Ferencvaros	(a)	1-2	Connelly

United in Europe – *UEFA Cup*

1976/77

Round 1(1)	v Ajax Amsterdam	(a)	0-1	
Round 1(2)	v Ajax Amsterdam	(h)	2-0	McIlroy, Macari
Round 2(1)	v Juventus	(h)	1-0	Hill
Round 2(2)	v Juventus	(a)	0-3	

1980/81

Round 1(1)	v Widzew Lodz	(h)	1-1	McIlroy
Round 1(2)	v Widzew Lodz	(a)	0-0	

1982/83

Round 1(1)	v Valencia CF	(h)	0-0	
Round 1(2)	v Valencia CF	(a)	1-2	Robson

1984/85

Round 1(1)	v Raba Vasas ETO	(h)	3-0	Robson, Muhren, Hughes
Round 1(2)	v Raba Vasas ETO	(a)	2-2	Brazil, Muhren
Round 2(1)	v PSV Eindhoven	(a)	0-0	
Round 2(2)	v PSV Eindhoven	(h)	1-0	Strachan
Round 3(1)	v Dundee United	(h)	2-2	Strachan, Robson
Round 3(2)	v Dundee United	(a)	3-2	Hughes, Muhren, Own goal
Q Final(1)	v Videoton	(h)	1-0	Stapleton
Q Final(2)	v Videoton	(a)	0-1	
				Lost 5-4 on penalties

1992/93

Round 1(1)	v Moscow Torpedo	(h)	0-0	
Round 1(2)	v Moscow Torpedo	(a)	0-0	
				Lost 4-3 on penalties

1995/96

Round 1(1)	v Rotor Vologrodu	(a)	0-0	
Round 1(2)	v Rotor Vologrodu	(h)	2-2	Scholes, Schmeichel
				Lost on away goals rule

Other Competitions – *World Club Championships*

Date	Round/Leg	Opponents	Venue	Score	Att.
25/9/68	First Leg	v Estudiantes	(a)	lost 0-1	55,000

Team: Stepney, Dunne, Burns, Crerand, Foulkes, Stiles, Morgan, Sadler, Charlton, Law, Best.

16/10/68	Second Leg	v Estudiantes	(h)	drew 1-1	63,500

Team: Stepney, Brennan, Dunne, Crerand, Foulkes, Sadler, **Morgan,** Kidd, Charlton, Law (Sartori), Best.

Other Competitions – *European Super Cup*

Date	Round/Leg	Opponents	Venue	Score	Att.
19/11/91		v Red Star Belgrade		won 1-0	22,110

Team; Schmeichel, Irwin, Martin (Giggs), Bruce, Webb, Pallister, Kanchelskis, Ince, **McClair,** Hughes, Blackmore.

Other Competitions – *Anglo-Italian Cup*

Group 1			
21st February 1973	v Fiorentina (h)	drew 1-1	Att: 23,951
21st March 1973	v Lazio (a)	drew 0-0	Att: 52,834
4th April 1973	v Bari (h)	won 3-1	Att: 14,303

2nd May 1973   v Verona (a)   won 4-1   Att: 8,168
Despite remaining unbeaten United failed to qualify for the semi-final stages.

Other Competitions – *Watney Cup*

Date	Round/Leg	Opponents	Venue	Score	Att.
1970/71	1st Round	v Reading	(a)	Won 3-2	
	Semi-Final	v Hull City	(a)	1-1aet	

Won 4-3 on penalties. This is thought to be the first occasion any first class game in England was decided by penalties.

| | Final | v Derby County | (a) | Lost 1-4 | |

| 1971/72 | 1st Round | v Halifax Town | (a) | Lost 1-2 | |

Of the thirteen United players to take part in this game, eleven – Stepney, Dunne, Crerand, Burns, Sadler, Morgan, Kidd, Charlton, Law and Best – were full internationals whilst Gowling was an Under 23 International.

United in the FA Charity Shield

27/4/08   v Queen's Park Rangers   Stamford Bridge   1-1   6,000
Scorer: Meredith
Team: Moger, Stacey, Burgess, Duckworth, Roberts, Bell, **Meredith**, Bannister, J Turnbull, A Turnbull, Wall

29t/8/08   v Queen's Park Rangers   Stamford Bridge   4-0   6,000
Team: Moger, Stacey, Burgess, Duckworth, Roberts, Bell, Meredith, Bannister, J **Turnbull (3)**, Picken, **Wall**

25t/9/11   v Swindon Town   Stamford Bridge   8-4   10,000
Team: Edmonds, Hofton, Stacey, Duckworth, Roberts, Bell, Meredith, Hamill, **Halse (6), Turnbull, Wall**

6/10/48   v Arsenal   Highbury   3-4   31,000
Team: Crompton, Carey, Aston, Anderson, Chilton, Warner, Delaney, Morris, **Burke, Rowley**, Mitten – **Smith (o.g)**

24/9/52   v Newcastle United   Old Trafford   4-2   11,381
Team: Wood, McNulty, Aston, Carey, Chilton, Gibson, Berry, **Downie, Rowley (2)**, Pearson, **Byrne**

24/10/56   v Manchester City   Maine Road   1-0   30,495
Team: Wood (Gaskell), Foulkes, Byrne, Colman, Jones, Edwards, Berry, Whelan, Taylor, **Viollet**, Peg

22/10/57   v Aston Villa   Old Trafford   4-0   27,923
Team: Wood, Foulkes, Byrne, Goodwin, Blanchflower, Edwards, **Berry,** Whelan, **Taylor (3),** Viollet, Pegg

17/8/63   v Everton   Goodison Park   0-4   54,840
Team: Gaskell, A Dunne, Cantwell, Crerand, Foulkes, Setters, Giles, Quixall, Herd, Law, Charlton

14/8/65   *v* Liverpool   Old Trafford   2-2   48,502
Team: P Dunne, Brennan, A Dunne, Crerand, Cantwell, Stiles, **Best** (Anderson), Charlton, **Herd,** Law, Aston

12/8/67   *v* Tottenham Hotspurs   Old Trafford   3-3   54,106
Team: Stepney, Brennan, A Dunne, Crerand, Foulkes, Stiles, Best, Kidd, **Charlton (2),** Law, Aston

13/8/77   *v* Liverpool   Wembley   0-0   82,000
Team: Stepney, Nicholl, Albiston, McIlroy, B Greenhoff, Buchan, Coppell, J Greenhoff (McCreery), Pearson, Macari, Hill

20/8/83   *v* Liverpool   Wembley   2-0   92,000
Team: Bailey, Duxbury, Albiston, Wilkins, Moran, McQueen, **Robson (2),** Muhren (Gidman), Stapleton, Whiteside, Graham

10/8/85   *v* Everton   Wembley   0-2   82,000
Bailey, Gidman, Albiston, Whiteside, McGrath, Hogg, Robson, Duxbury (Moses), Hughes, Stapleton, Olsen

19/8/90   *v* Liverpool   Wembley   1-1   66,558
Team: Sealey, Irwin, Donaghy, Bruce, Phelan, Pallister, **Blackmore,** Ince, McClair, Hughes, Wallace (Robins)

7/8/93   *v* Arsenal   Wembley   1-1   60,000
                                             United won 5-4 on penalties
Team: Schmeichel, Parker, Irwin, Bruce, Kanchelskis, Pallister, Cantona, Ince, Keane, **Hughes,** Giggs (Robson)

14/08/94   *v* Blackburn Rovers   Wembley   2-0   60,402
Team: Schmeichel, May, Bruce, Pallister, Sharpe, Kanchelskis, McClair, **Ince,** Giggs, **Cantona** (pen), Hughes

United in FA Youth Cup Finals

4/5/53   1st Leg   *v* Wolves   Old Trafford   7-1   20,934
Team: Clayton, Fulton, Kennedy, Colman, Cope, Edwards, **McFarlane (2), Whelan, Lewis (2), Pegg, Scanlon**

9/5/53   2nd Leg   *v* Wolves   Molineux   2-2   14,290
Team: Clayton, Fulton, Kennedy, Colman, Cope, Edwards, McFarlane, **Whelan, Lewis,** Pegg, Scanlon
                                             Aggregate: 9-3

23/4/54   1st Leg   *v* Wolves   Old Trafford   4-4   18,246
Team: Hawksworth, Beswick, Rhodes, Colman, Harrop, McGuinness, Littler, **Edwards (2),** Charlton, **Pegg (2-1 via penalty),** Scanlon

26/4/54   2nd Leg   *v* Wolves   Molineux   1-0   28,651
Team: Hawksworth, Beswick, Rhodes, Colman, Harrop, McGuinness, Littler, Edwards, Charlton, **Pegg (penalty),** Scanlon   *Aggregate: 5-4*

27/4/55   1st Leg   *v* West Brom   Old Trafford   4-1   16,696
Team: Hawksworth, Queenan, Rhodes, **Colman (2),** Jones, McGuinness, **Beckett,** Brennan, Edwards, **Charlton,** Fidler

30/4/55　2nd Leg　*v* West Brom　The Hawthorns　3-0　8,335
Team: Hawksworth, Queenan, Rhodes, Colman, Jones, McGuinness, Beckett, Brennan, **Edwards, Charlton,** Fidler – **Cooke (og)**　　*Aggregate: 7-1*

30/4/56　1st Leg　*v* Chesterfield　Old Trafford　3-2　25,544
Team: Hawksworth, Queenan, Jones, **Carolan,** Holland, McGuinness, Morgans, **Pearson,** Dawson, **Charlton,** Fidler

7/5/56　2nd Leg　*v* Chesterfield　Recreation Grnd　1-1　15,838
Team: Hawksworth, Queenan, Jones, Carolan, Holland, McGuinness, Morgans, Pearson, Dawson, Charlton, **Fidler**　　*Aggregate: 4-3*
Gordon Banks kept goal for Chesterfield in both games

2/5/57　1st Leg　*v* West Ham Utd　Upton Park　3-2　14,000
Team: Gaskell, Smith, Madison, English, Holland, Bratt, Morgans, **Lawton, Dawson,** Pearson, **Hunter**

7/5/57　2nd Leg　*v* West Ham Utd　Old Trafford　5-0　23,349
Team: Gaskell, Smith, Madison, English, Holland, Bratt, **Morgans,** Lawton, Dawson, **Pearson (3), Hunter**　　*Aggregate: 8-2*

27/5/64　1st Leg　*v* Swindon Town　County Ground　1-1　17,000
Team: Rimmer, Duff, Noble, McBride, Farrar, Fitzpatrick, Anderson, **Best,** Sadler, Kinsey, Aston.

30/4/64　2nd Leg　*v* Swindon Town　Old Trafford)　4-1　25,563
Team: Rimmer, Duff, Noble, McBride, Farrar, Fitzpatrick, Anderson, Best, **Sadler (3),** Kinsey, **Aston**　　*Aggregate: 5-2*

26/4/82　1st Leg　*v* Watford　Old Trafford　2-3　7,280
Team: P Hughes, Hill, Scott, Hogg, Garton, **Blackmore,** Pearson, **Dempsey,** Whiteside, M Hughes, Docherty (Woods)

6/5/82　2nd Leg　*v* Watford　Vicarage Road　4-4†　8,000
Team: P Hughes, Hill, Scott, Hogg, Garton, Williams (Wood), Blackmore, **Dempsey, Whiteside, M Hughes (2),** Docherty　　*Aggregate: 6-7*

24/4/86　1st Leg　*v* Manchester City　Old Trafford　1-1　7,602
Team: Walsh, Gill, Martin, Scott, Gardner, Bottomley, Murphy, Todd, Cronin, Wilson (Hopley), **Harvey**

29/5/86　2nd leg　*v* Manchester City　Maine Road　0-2　18,158
Team: Walsh, Gill, Martin, Scott, Gardner, Harvey, Murphy, Todd, Cronin, Bottomley (Hopley), Goddard　　*Aggregate: 1-3*

14/4/92　1st Leg　*v* Crystal Palace　Selhurst Park　3-1　7,825
Team: Pilkington, O'Kane, Switzer, Casper, G Neville, **Beckham, Butt (2),** Davies, McKee, Savage (Roberts), Thornley

15/5/92　2nd Leg　*v* Crystal Palace　Old Trafford　3-2　14,681
Team: Pilkington, O'Kane, Switzer, Casper, G Neville, Beckham, Butt, Davies (Gillespie), McKee, Giggs, Thornley (Savage)　　*Aggregate: 6-3*

N.B. Of the starting line up for this second leg tie, only George Switzer never made a first team appearance. He subsequently went on to play in the Football League for Darlington.

10/4/93   1st Leg   *v* Leeds Utd   Old Trafford   0-2   30,562
Team: Whitmarsh, O'Kane, Riley, Casper, G Neville, Gillespie, Butt, Beckham (Savage), Irving (Murdock), Scholes, Thornley

13/5/93   2nd Leg   *v* Leeds Utd   Elland Road   1-2   31,037
Team: Whitmarsh, P.Neville, Riley, Casper, G Neville, Gillespie, **Scholes** (pen), Beckham, Irving (Murdock), Savage, Thornley   *Aggregate: 1-4*

11/05/95 1st Leg   *v* Tottenham Hotspur   White Hart Lane   1-2   3,000
Team: Gibson, P Neville, Westwood, Clegg, Wallwork, Mulryne (Gordon), Mustoe, Hall, Baker (Crutis), Johnson, **Cooke**, Sub: Maxon (G)

15/05/95 2nd Leg   *v* Tottenham Hotspur   Old Trafford   1-0   20,190
Team: Gibson, Curtis, Westwood, Wallwork, P Neville, Mustoe, Hall (Gardner), Brebner, Mulryne (Hilton), **Cooke**, Baker, Sub: Maxon (G)
(After Extra-Time – Aggregate Score 2-2 , United won 4-3 on penalties)

UNITED'S MATCH BY MATCH RECORD 1946/47-1995/96

Season: 1946/47

No	Date	Opponents	Score	Att	Scorers
1	31/08/46	GRIMSBY TN	2-1	41,025	Mitten, Rowley
2	04/09/46	Chelsea	3-0	27,750	Mitten, Rowley, Pearson
3	07/09/46	Charlton Ath	3-1	44,088	Hanlon, Rowley, og
4	11/09/46	LIVERPOOL	5-0	41,657	Pearson 3, Mitten, Rowley
5	14/09/46	MIDDLESBROUGH	1-0	65,112	Rowley
6	18/09/46	CHELSEA	1-1	30,275	Chilton
7	21/09/46	Stoke City	2-3	41,699	Delaney, Hanlon
8	28/09/46	ARSENAL	5-2	62,718	Hanlon 2, Rowley 2, Wrigglesworth
9	05/10/46	PRESTON N'H END	1-1	55,395	Wrigglesworth
10	12/10/46	Sheffield United	2-2	35,543	Rowley 2
11	19/10/46	Blackpool	1-3	26,307	Delaney
12	26/10/46	SUNDERLAND	0-3	48,385	
13	02/11/46	Aston Villa	0-0	53,668	
14	09/11/46	DERBY COUNTY	4-1	57,340	Pearson 2, Mitten, Rowley
15	16/11/46	Everton	2-2	45,832	Pearson, Rowley
16	23/11/46	HUDDERSFIELD TN	5-2	39,216	Mitten 2, Morris 2, Rowley
17	30/11/46	Wolverhampton Wdrs	2-3	46,704	Hanlon, Delaney
18	07/12/46	BRENTFORD	4-1	31,962	Rowley 3, Mitten
19	14/12/46	Blackburn Rovers	1-2	21,455	Morris
20	25/12/46	Bolton Wanderers	2-2	28,505	Rowley 2
21	26/12/46	BOLTON WDRS	1-0	57,186	Pearson
22	28/12/46	Grimsby Town	0-0	17,183	
23	04/01/47	CHARLTON ATH	4-1	43,406	Burke 2, Buckle, Pearson
24	18/01/47	Middlesbrough	4-2	37,435	Pearson 2, Buckle, Morris
25	01/02/47	Arsenal	2-6	29,415	Morris, Pearson
26	05/02/47	STOKE CITY	1-1	8,456	Buckle
27	22/02/47	BLACKPOOL	3-0	29,993	Rowley 2, Hanlon
28	01/03/47	Sunderland	1-1	25,038	Delaney
29	08/03/47	ASTON VILLA	2-1	36,965	Burke, Pearson
30	15/03/47	Derby County	3-4	19,579	Burke 2, Pearson
31	22/03/47	EVERTON	3-0	43,441	Burke, Delaney, Warner
32	29/03/47	Huddersfield Town	2-2	18,509	Delaney, Pearson
33	05/04/47	WOLVERH'N WDRS	3-1	66,967	Rowley 2, Hanlon
34	07/04/47	LEEDS UTD	3-1	41,772	Burke 2, Delaney
35	08/04/47	Leeds United	2-0	15,528	Burke, McGlen
36	12/04/47	Brentford	0-0	21,714	
37	19/04/47	BLACKBURN RVRS	4-0	46,196	Pearson 2, Rowley, og
38	26/04/47	Portsmouth	1-0	30,623	Delaney
39	03/05/47	Liverpool	0-1	48,800	
40	10/05/47	Preston North End	1-1	23,278	Pearson
41	17/05/47	PORTSMOUTH	3-0	37,614	Mitten, Morris, Rowley
42	26/05/47	SHEFFIELD UTD	6-2	34,059	Rowley 3, Morris 2, Pearson

Season: 1947/48

No	Date	Opponents	Score	Att	Scorers
1	23/08/47	Middlesbrough	2-2	39,554	Rowley 2
2	27/08/47	LIVERPOOL	2-0	52,385	Morris, Pearson
3	30/08/47	CHARLTON ATH	6-2	52,659	Rowley 4, Morris, Pearson
4	03/09/47	Liverpool	2-2	48,081	Mitten, Pearson
5	06/09/47	Arsenal	1-2	64,905	Morris
6	08/09/47	Burnley	0-0	37,517	
7	13/09/47	SHEFFIELD UTD	0-1	49,808	
8	20/09/47	Manchester City	0-0	71,364	
9	27/09/47	Preston North End	1-2	34,372	Morris
10	04/10/47	STOKE CITY	1-1	45,745	Hanlon
11	11/10/47	GRIMSBY TN	3-4	40,035	Mitten, Morris, Rowley
12	18/10/47	Sunderland	0-1	37,148	
13	25/10/47	ASTON VILLA	2-0	47,078	Delaney, Rowley
14	01/11/47	Wolverhampton Wdrs	6-2	44,309	Morris 2, Pearson 2, Delaney, Mitten
15	08/11/47	HUDDERSFIELD TN	4-4	59,772	Rowley 4
16	15/11/47	Derby County	1-1	32,990	Carey
17	22/11/47	EVERTON	2-2	35,509	Cockburn, Morris
18	29/11/47	Chelsea	4-0	43,617	Morris 3, Rowley
19	06/12/47	BLACKPOOL	1-1	63,683	Pearson
20	13/12/47	Blackburn Rovers	1-1	22,784	Morris
21	20/12/47	MIDDLESBROUGH	2-1	46,666	Pearson 2
22	25/12/47	PORTSMOUTH	3-2	42,776	Morris 2, Rowley
23	27/12/47	Portsmouth	3-1	27,674	Morris 2, Delaney
24	01/01/48	BURNLEY	5-0	59,838	Rowley 3, Mitten 2
25	03/01/48	Charlton Ath	2-1	40,484	Morris, Pearson
26	17/01/48	ARSENAL	1-1	81,962	Rowley
27	31/01/48	Sheffield United	1-2	45,189	Rowley
28	14/02/48	PRESTON N'TH END	1-1	61,765	Delaney
29	21/02/48	Stoke City	2-0	36,794	Buckle, Pearson
30	06/03/48	SUNDERLAND	3-1	55,160	Delaney, Mitten, Rowley
31	17/03/48	Grimsby Town	1-1	12,284	Rowley
32	20/03/48	WOLVERH'N WDRS	3-2	50,667	Delaney, Mitten, Morris
33	22/03/48	Aston Villa	1-0	52,366	Pearson
34	26/03/48	BOLTON WDRS	0-2	71,623	
35	27/03/48	Huddersfield Town	2-0	38,266	Burke, Pearson
36	29/03/48	Bolton Wanderers	1-0	44,225	Anderson
37	03/04/48	DERBY COUNTY	1-0	49,609	Pearson
38	07/04/48	MANCHESTER CITY	1-1	71,690	Rowley
39	10/04/48	Everton	0-2	44,198	
40	17/04/48	CHELSEA	5-0	43,225	Pearson 2, Delaney, Mitten, Rowley
41	28/04/48	Blackpool	0-1	32,236	
42	01/05/48	BLACKBURN RVRS	4-1	44,439	Pearson 3, Delaney

Season: 1948/49

No	Date	Opponents	Score	Att	Scorers
1	21/08/48	DERBY COUNTY	1-2	52,620	Pearson
2	23/08/48	Blackpool	3-0	36,880	Rowley 2, Mitten
3	28/08/48	Arsenal	1-0	64,150	Mitten
4	01/09/48	BLACKPOOL	3-1	51,187	Delaney, Mitten, Morris
5	04/09/48	HUDDERSFIELD TN	4-1	57,714	Pearson 2, Delaney, Mitten
6	08/09/48	Wolverhampton Wdrs	2-3	42,617	Morris, Rowley
7	11/09/48	Manchester City	0-0	64,502	
8	15/09/48	WOLVERHA'N WDRS	2-0	33,871	Buckle, Pearson
9	18/09/48	Sheffield United	2-2	36,880	Buckle, Pearson
10	25/09/48	ASTON VILLA	3-1	53,820	Mitten 2, Pearson
11	02/10/48	Sunderland	1-2	54,419	Rowley
12	09/10/48	CHARLTON ATH	1-1	46,964	Burke
13	16/10/48	Stoke City	1-2	45,830	Morris
14	23/10/48	BURNLEY	1-1	47,093	Mitten
15	30/10/48	Preston North End	6-1	37,372	Mitten 2, Pearson 2, Morris, Rowley
16	06/11/48	EVERTON	2-0	42,789	Delaney, Morris
17	13/11/48	Chelsea	1-1	62,542	Rowley
18	20/11/48	BIRMINGHAM CITY	3-0	45,482	Morris, Pearson, Rowley
19	27/11/48	Middlesbrough	4-1	31,331	Rowley 3, Delaney
20	04/12/48	NEWCASTLE UTD	1-1	70,787	Mitten
21	11/12/48	Portsmouth	2-2	29,966	McGlen, Mitten
22	18/12/48	Derby County	3-1	31,498	Burke 2, Pearson
23	25/12/48	LIVERPOOL	0-0	47,788	
24	26/12/48	Liverpool	2-0	53,325	Burke, Pearson
25	01/01/49	ARSENAL	2-0	58,688	Burke, Mitten
26	22/12/49	MANCHESTER CITY	0-0	66,485	
27	19/02/49	Aston Villa	1-2	68,354	Rowley
28	05/03/49	Charlton Ath	3-2	55,291	Pearson 2, Downie
29	12/03/49	STOKE CITY	3-0	55,949	Downie, Mitten, Rowley
30	19/03/49	Birmingham City	0-1	46,819	
31	06/04/49	Huddersfield Town	1-2	17,256	Rowley
32	09/04/49	CHELSEA	1-1	27,304	Mitten
33	15/04/49	Bolton Wanderers	1-0	44,999	Carey
34	16/04/49	Burnley	2-0	37,722	Rowley 2
35	18/04/49	BOLTON WDRS	3-0	47,653	Rowley 2, Mitten
36	21/04/49	SUNDERLAND	1-2	30,640	Mitten
37	23/04/49	PRESTON N'H END	2-2	43,214	Downie 2
38	27/04/49	Everton	0-2	39,106	
39	30/04/49	Newcastle United	1-0	38,266	Burke
40	02/05/49	MIDDLESBROUGH	1-0	20,158	Rowley
41	04/05/49	SHEFFIELD UTD	3-2	20,880	Downie, Mitten, Pearson
42	07/05/49	PORTSMOUTH	3-2	49,808	Rowley 2, Mitten

Season: 1949/50

No	Date	Opponents	Score	Att	Scorers
1	20/08/49	Derby County	1-0	35,687	Rowley
2	24/08/49	BOLTON WDRS	3-0	41,748	Mitten, Rowley, og
3	27/08/49	WEST BROM ALBION	1-1	44,655	Pearson
4	31/08/49	Bolton Wanderers	2-1	36,277	Mitten, Pearson
5	03/09/49	MANCHESTER CITY	2-1	47,760	Pearson 2
6	07/09/49	Liverpool	1-1	51,587	Mitten
7	10/09/49	Chelsea	1-1	61,357	Rowley
8	17/09/49	STOKE CITY	2-2	43,522	Rowley 2
9	24/09/49	Burnley	0-1	41,072	
10	01/10/49	SUNDERLAND	1-3	49,260	Pearson
11	08/10/49	CHARLTON ATH	3-2	43,809	Mitten 2, Rowley
12	15/10/49	Aston Villa	4-0	47,483	Mitten 2, Bogan, Rowley
13	22/10/49	WOLVERH'N WDRS	3-0	51,427	Pearson 2, Bogan
14	29/10/49	Portsmouth	0-0	41,098	
15	05/11/49	HUDDERSFIELD TN	6-0	40,295	Pearson 2, Rowley 2, Delaney, Mitten
16	12/11/49	Everton	0-0	46,672	
17	19/11/49	MIDDLESBROUGH	2-0	42,626	Pearson, Rowley
18	26/11/49	Blackpool	3-3	27,742	Pearson 2, Bogan
19	03/12/49	NEWCASTLE UTD	1-1	30,343	Mitten
20	10/12/49	Fulham	0-1	35,362	
21	17/12/49	DERBY COUNTY	0-1	33,753	
22	24/12/49	West Bromwich Albion	2-1	46,973	Bogan, Rowley
23	26/12/49	ARSENAL	2-3	53,928	Pearson 2
24	27/12/49	Arsenal	0-0	65,133	
25	31/12/49	Manchester City	2-1	63,704	Delaney, Pearson
26	14/01/50	CHELSEA	1-0	46,594	Mitten
27	21/01/50	Stoke City	1-3	38,877	Mitten
28	04/02/50	BURNLEY	3-2	46,702	Rowley 2, Mitten
29	18/02/50	Sunderland	2-2	63,251	Chilton, Rowley
30	25/02/50	Charlton Ath	2-1	44,920	Carey, Rowley
31	08/03/50	ASTON VILLA	7-0	22,149	Mitten 4, Downie 2, Rowley
32	11/03/50	Middlesbrough	3-2	46,702	Downie 2, Rowley
33	15/03/50	LIVERPOOL	0-0	43,456	
34	18/03/50	BLACKPOOL	1-2	53,688	Delaney
35	25/03/50	Huddersfield Town	1-3	34,348	Downie
36	01/04/50	EVERTON	1-1	35,381	Delaney
37	07/04/50	BIRMINGHAM CITY	0-2	47,170	
38	08/04/50	Wolverhampton Wdrs	1-1	54,296	Rowley
39	10/04/50	Birmingham City	0-0	35,863	
40	15/04/50	PORTSMOUTH	0-2	44,908	
41	22/04/50	Newcastle United	1-2	52,203	Downie
42	29/04/50	FULHAM	3-0	11,968	Rowley 2, Cockburn

Season: 1950/51

No	Date	Opponents	Score	Att	Scorers
1	19/08/50	FULHAM	1-0	44,042	Pearson
2	23/08/50	Liverpool	1-2	30,211	Rowley
3	26/08/50	Bolton Wanderers	0-4	40,431	
4	30/08/50	LIVERPOOL	1-0	34,835	Downie
5	02/09/50	BLACKPOOL	1-0	53,260	Bogan
6	04/09/50	Aston Villa	3-1	42,724	Rowley 2, Pearson
7	09/09/50	Tottenham Hotspurs	0-1	60,621	
8	13/09/50	ASTON VILLA	0-0	33,021	
9	16/09/50	CHARLTON ATH	3-0	36,619	Delaney, Pearson, Rowley
10	23/09/50	Middlesbrough	2-1	48,051	Pearson 2
11	30/09/50	Wolverhampton Wdrs	0-0	45,898	
12	07/10/50	SHEFFIELD W'DAY	3-1	40,651	Downie, McShane, Rowley
13	14/10/50	Arsenal	0-3	66,150	
14	21/10/50	PORTSMOUTH	0-0	41,842	
15	28/10/50	Everton	4-1	51,142	Rowley 2, Aston, Pearson
16	04/11/50	BURNLEY	1-1	39,454	McShane
17	11/11/50	Chelsea	0-0	51,882	
18	18/11/50	Stoke City	0-0	30,031	
19	25/11/50	West Bromwich Albion	1-0	28,146	Birch
20	02/12/50	NEWCASTLE UTD	1-2	34,502	Birch
21	09/12/50	Huddersfield Town	3-2	26,713	Aston 2, Birkett
22	16/12/50	Fulham	2-2	19,649	Pearson 2
23	23/12/50	BOLTON WDRS	2-3	35,382	Aston, Pearson
24	25/12/50	Sunderland	1-2	41,125	Aston
25	26/12/50	SUNDERLAND	3-5	35,176	Bogan 2, Aston
26	13/01/51	TOTTENHAM	2-1	43,283	Birch, Rowley
27	20/01/51	Charlton Ath	2-1	31,978	Aston, Birkett
28	03/02/51	MIDDLESBROUGH	1-0	44,633	Pearson
29	17/02/51	WOLVERH'N WDRS	2-1	42,022	Birch, Rowley
30	26/02/51	Sheffield Wednesday	4-0	25,693	McShane, Downie, Pearson, Rowley
31	03/03/51	ARSENAL	3-1	46,202	Aston 2, Downie
32	10/03/51	Portsmouth	0-0	33,148	
33	17/03/51	EVERTON	3-0	29,317	Aston, Downie, Pearson
34	23/03/51	DERBY COUNTY	2-0	42,009	Aston, Downie
35	24/03/51	Burnley	2-1	36,656	Aston, McShane
36	26/03/51	Derby County	4-2	25,860	Aston, Downie, Pearson, Rowley
37	31/03/51	CHELSEA	4-1	25,779	Pearson 3, McShane
38	07/04/51	Stoke City	0-2	25,690	
39	14/04/51	WEST BROM ALBION	3-0	24,764	Downie, Pearson, Rowley
40	21/04/51	Newcastle United	2-0	45,209	Rowley, Pearson
41	28/04/51	HUDDERSFIELD TN	6-0	25,560	Aston 2, McShane 2, Downie, Rowley
42	05/05/51	Blackpool	1-1	22,864	Downie

Season: 1951/52

No	Date	Opponents	Score	Att	Scorers
1	18/08/51	West Bromwich Albion	3-3	27,486	Rowley 3
2	22/08/51	MIDDLESBROUGH	4-2	37,339	Rowley 3, Pearson
3	25/08/51	NEWCASTLE UTD	2-1	51,850	Downie, Rowley
4	29/08/51	Middlesbrough	4-1	44,212	Pearson 2, Rowley 2
5	01/09/51	Bolton Wanderers	0-1	52,239	
6	05/09/51	CHARLTON ATH	3-2	26,773	Rowley 2, Downie
7	08/09/51	STOKE CITY	4-0	43,660	Rowley 3, Pearson
8	12/09/51	Charlton Ath	2-2	28,806	Downie 2
9	15/09/51	Manchester City	1-2	52,571	Berry, McShane
10	22/09/51	Tottenham Hotspurs	0-2	70,882	
11	29/09/51	PRESTON N'TH END	1-2	53,454	Aston
12	06/10/51	DERBY COUNTY	2-1	39,767	Berry, Pearson
13	13/10/51	Aston Villa	5-2	47,795	Pearson 2, Rowley 2, Bond
14	20/10/51	SUNDERLAND	0-1	40,915	
15	27/10/51	Wolverhampton Wdrs	2-0	46,167	Pearson, Rowley
16	03/11/51	HUDDERSFIELD TN	1-1	25,616	Pearson
17	10/11/51	Chelsea	2-4	48,960	Pearson, Rowley
18	17/11/51	PORTSMOUTH	1-3	35,914	Downie
19	24/11/51	Liverpool	0-0	42,378	
20	01/12/51	BLACKPOOL	3-1	34,154	Downie 2, Rowley
21	08/12/51	Arsenal	3-1	55,451	Pearson, Rowley, og
22	15/12/51	WEST BROM ALBION	5-1	27,584	Downie 2, Pearson 2, Berry
23	22/12/51	Newcastle United	2-2	45,414	Bond, Cockburn
24	25/12/51	FULHAM	3-2	33,802	Berry, Bond, Rowley
25	26/12/51	Fulham	3-3	32,671	Bond, Pearson, Rowley
26	29/12/51	BOLTON WDRS	1-0	53,205	Pearson
27	05/01/52	Stoke City	0-0	36,389	
28	19/01/52	MANCHESTER CITY	1-1	54,245	Carey
29	26/01/52	TOTTENHAM	2-0	40,845	Pearson, og
30	09/02/52	Preston North End	2-1	38,792	Aston, Berry
31	16/02/52	Derby County	3-0	27,693	Aston, Pearson, Rowley
32	01/03/52	ASTON VILLA	1-1	39,910	Berry
33	08/03/52	Sunderland	2-1	48,078	Cockburn, Rowley
34	15/03/52	WOLVERH'N WDRS	2-0	45,109	Aston, Clempson
35	22/03/52	Huddersfield Town	2-3	30,316	Clempson, Pearson
36	05/04/52	Portsmouth	0-1	25,522	
37	11/04/52	Burnley	1-1	38,907	Byrne
38	12/04/52	LIVERPOOL	4-0	42,970	Byrne 2, Downie, Rowley
39	14/04/52	BURNLEY	6-1	44,508	Byrne 2, Carey, Downie, Pearson, Rowley
40	19/04/52	Blackpool	2-2	29,118	Byrne, Rowley
41	21/04/52	CHELSEA	3-0	37,436	Carey, Pearson, og
42	26/04/52	ARSENAL	6-1	53,651	Rowley 3, Pearson 2, Byrne

Season: 1952/53

No	Date	Opponents	Score	Att	Scorers
1	23/08/52	CHELSEA	2-0	43,629	Berry, Downie
2	27/08/52	Arsenal	1-2	58,831	Rowley
3	30/08/52	Manchester City	1-2	56,140	Downie
4	03/09/52	ARSENAL	0-0	39,193	
5	06/09/52	Portsmouth	0-2	37,278	
6	10/09/52	Derby County	3-2	20,226	Pearson 3
7	13/09/52	BOLTON WDRS	1-0	40,531	Berry
8	20/09/52	Aston Villa	3-3	43,490	Rowley 2, Downie
9	27/09/52	SUNDERLAND	0-1	28,967	
10	04/10/52	Wolverhampton Wdrs	2-6	40,132	Rowley 2
11	11/10/52	STOKE CITY	0-2	28,968	
12	18/10/52	Preston North End	5-0	33,502	Aston 2, Pearson 2, Rowley
13	25/10/52	BURNLEY	1-3	36,913	Aston
14	01/11/52	Tottenham Hotspurs	2-1	44,300	Berry 2
15	08/11/52	SHEFFIELD W'DAY	1-1	48,571	Pearson
16	15/11/52	Cardiff City	2-1	40,096	Aston, Pearson
17	22/11/52	NEWCASTLE UTD	2-2	33,528	Aston, Pearson
18	29/11/52	West Bromwich Albion	1-3	23,499	Lewis
19	06/12/52	MIDDLESBROUGH	3-2	27,617	Pearson 2, Aston
20	13/12/52	Liverpool	2-1	34,450	Aston, Pearson
21	20/12/52	Chelsea	3-2	23,261	Doherty 2, Aston
22	25/12/52	Blackpool	0-0	27,778	
23	26/12/52	BLACKPOOL	2-1	48,077	Carey, Lewis
24	01/01/53	DERBY CITY	1-0	34,813	Lewis
25	03/01/53	MANCHESTER CITY	1-1	47,883	Pearson
26	17/01/53	PORTSMOUTH	1-0	32,341	Lewis
27	24/01/53	Bolton Wanderers	1-2	43,638	Lewis
28	07/02/53	ASTON VILLA	3-1	34,339	Rowley 2, Lewis
29	18/02/53	Sunderland	2-2	24,263	Lewis, Pegg
30	21/02/53	WOLVERH'N WDRS	0-3	38,269	
31	28/02/53	Stoke City	1-3	30,219	Berry
32	07/03/53	PRESTON N'H END	5-2	52,590	Pegg 2, Taylor 2, Rowley
33	14/03/53	Burnley	1-2	45,682	Byrne
34	25/03/53	TOTTENHAM	3-2	18,384	Pearson 2, Pegg
35	28/03/53	Sheffield Wednesday	0-0	36,509	
36	03/04/53	Charlton Ath	2-2	41,814	Berry, Taylor
37	04/04/53	CARDIFF CITY	1-4	37,163	Byrne
38	06/04/53	CHARLTON ATH	3-2	30,105	Taylor 2, Rowley
39	11/04/53	Newcastle United	2-1	38,970	Taylor
40	18/04/53	WEST BROM ALBION	2-2	31,380	Pearson, Viollet
41	20/04/53	LIVERPOOL	3-1	20,869	Berry, Pearson, Rowley
42	25/04/53	Middlesbrough	0-5	34,344	

Season: 1953/54

No	Date	Opponents	Score	Att	Scorers
1	19/08/53	CHELSEA	1-1	28,936	Pearson
2	22/08/53	Liverpool	4-4	48,422	Byrne, Lewis, Rowley, Taylor
3	26/08/53	WEST BROM ALBION	1-3	31,806	Taylor
4	29/08/53	NEWCASTLE UTD	1-1	27,837	Chilton
5	02/09/53	West Bromwich Albion	0-2	28,892	
6	05/09/53	Manchester City	0-2	53,097	
7	09/09/53	MIDDLESBROUGH	2-2	18,161	Rowley 2
8	12/09/53	Bolton Wanderers	0-0	43,544	
9	16/09/53	Middlesbrough	4-1	23,607	Taylor 2, Byrne, Rowley
10	19/09/53	PRESTON N'H END	1-0	41,171	Byrne
11	26/09/53	Tottenham Hotspurs	1-1	52,837	Rowley
12	03/10/53	BURNLEY	1-2	37,696	Pearson
13	10/10/53	SUNDERLAND	1-0	34,617	Rowley
14	17/10/53	Wolverhampton Wdrs	1-3	40,084	Taylor
15	24/10/53	ASTON VILLA	1-0	32,266	
16	31/10/53	Huddersfield Town	0-0	34,175	
17	07/11/53	ARSENAL	2-2	28,141	Blanchflower, Rowley
18	14/11/53	Cardiff City	6-1	26,844	Viollet 2, Berry, Blanchflower, Rowley, Taylor
19	21/11/53	BLACKPOOL	4-1	49,853	Taylor 3, Viollet
20	28/11/53	Portsmouth	1-1	29,233	Taylor
21	05/12/53	SHEFFIELD UTD	2-2	31,693	Blanchflower 2
22	12/12/53	Chelsea	1-3	37,153	Berry
23	19/12/53	LIVERPOOL	5-1	26,074	Blanchflower 2, Taylor 2, Viollet
24	25/12/53	SHEFFIELD WED'Y	5-2	27,123	Taylor 3, Blanchflower, Viollet
25	26/12/53	Sheffield Wednesday	1-0	44,196	Viollet
26	02/01/54	Newcastle United	2-1	55,780	Blanchflower, Foulkes
27	16/01/54	MANCHESTER CITY	1-1	46,379	Berry
28	23/01/54	BOLTON WDRS	1-5	46,663	Taylor
29	06/02/54	Preston North End	3-1	30,064	Blanchflower, Rowley, Taylor
30	13/02/54	TOTTENHAM	2-0	35,485	Rowley, Taylor
31	20/02/54	Burnley	0-2	29,576	
32	27/02/54	Sunderland	2-0	58,440	Blanchflower, Taylor
33	06/03/54	WOLVERH'N WDRS	1-0	38,939	Berry
34	13/03/54	Aston Villa	2-2	26,023	Taylor 2
35	20/03/54	HUDDERSFIELD TN	3-1	40,181	Blanchflower, Rowley, Viollet
36	27/03/54	Arsenal	1-3	42,753	Taylor
37	03/04/54	CARDIFF CITY	2-3	22,832	Rowley, Viollet
38	10/04/54	Blackpool	0-2	25,996	
39	16/04/54	CHARLTON ATH	2-0	31,876	Aston, Viollet
40	17/04/54	PORTSMOUTH	2-0	29,663	Blanchflower, Viollet
41	19/04/54	Charlton Ath	0-1	19,111	
42	24/04/54	Sheffield United	3-1	29,189	Aston, Blanchflower, Viollet

Season: 1954/55

No	Date	Opponents	Score	Att	Scorers
1	21/08/54	PORTSMOUTH	1-3	38,203	Rowley
2	23/08/54	Sheffield Wednesday	4-2	38,118	Blanchflower 2, Viollet 2
3	28/08/54	Blackpool	4-2	31,855	Webster 2, Blanchflower, Viollet
4	01/09/54	SHEFFIELD W'DAY	2-0	31,371	Viollet 2
5	04/09/54	CHARLTON ATH	3-1	38,105	Rowley 2, Taylor
6	08/09/54	Tottenham Hotspurs	2-0	35,162	Berry, Webster
7	11/09/54	Bolton Wanderers	1-1	44,661	Webster
8	15/09/54	TOTTENHAM	2-1	29,212	Rowley, Viollet
9	18/09/54	HUDDERSFIELD TN	1-1	45,648	Viollet
10	25/09/54	Manchester City	2-3	54,105	Blanchflower, Taylor
11	02/10/54	Wolverhampton Wdrs	2-4	39,617	Rowley, Viollet
12	09/10/54	CARDIFF CITY	5-2	39,378	Taylor 4, Viollet
13	16/10/54	Chelsea	6-5	55,966	Viollet 3, Taylor 2, Blanchflower
14	23/10/54	NEWCASTLE UTD	2-2	29,217	Taylor, og
15	30/10/54	Everton	2-4	63,021	Taylor, Rowley
16	06/11/54	PRESTON N'H END	2-1	30,063	Viollet 2
17	13/11/54	Sheffield United	0-3	26,257	
18	20/11/54	ARSENAL	2-1	33,373	Blanchflower, Taylor
19	27/11/54	West Bromwich Albion	0-2	33,931	
20	04/12/54	LEICESTER CITY	3-1	19,369	Webster, Rowley, Viollet
21	11/12/54	Burnley	4-2	24,977	Webster 3, Viollet
22	18/12/54	Portsmouth	0-0	26,019	
23	27/12/54	ASTON VILLA	0-1	49,136	
24	28/12/54	Aston Villa	1-2	48,718	Taylor
25	01/01/55	BLACKPOOL	4-1	51,918	Blanchflower 2, Edwards, Viollet
26	22/01/55	BOLTON WDRS	1-1	39,873	Taylor
27	05/02/55	Huddersfield Town	3-1	31,408	Berry, Edwards, Pegg
28	12/02/55	MANCHESTER CITY	0-5	47,914	
29	23/02/55	WOLVERH'N WDRS	2-4	15,679	Edwards, Taylor
30	26/02/55	Cardiff City	0-3	16,329	
31	05/03/55	BURNLEY	1-0	31,729	Edwards
32	19/03/55	EVERTON	1-2	32,295	Scanlon
33	26/03/55	Preston North End	2-0	13,327	Byrne, Scanlon
34	02/04/55	SHEFFIELD UTD	5-0	21,158	Taylor 2, Berry, Viollet, Whelan
35	08/04/55	Sunderland	3-4	43,882	Edwards 2, Scanlon
36	09/04/55	Leicester City	0-1	34,362	
37	11/04/55	SUNDERLAND	2-2	36,013	Byrne, Taylor
38	16/04/55	WEST BROM ALBION	3-0	24,765	Taylor 2, Viollet
39	18/04/55	Newcastle United	0-2	35,540	
40	23/04/55	Arsenal	3-2	42,754	Blanchflower 2, og
41	26/04/55	Charlton Ath	1-1	13,149	Viollet
42	30/04/55	CHELSEA	2-1	34,933	

Season: 1955/56

No	Date	Opponents	Score	Att	Scorers
1	20/08/55	Birmingham City	2-2	37,994	Viollet 2
2	24/08/55	TOTTENHAM	2-2	25,406	Berry, Webster
3	27/08/55	WEST BROM ALBION	3-1	31,996	Lewis, Scanlon, Viollet
4	31/08/55	Tottenham Hotspurs	2-1	27,453	Edwards 2
5	03/09/55	Manchester City	0-1	59,162	
6	07/09/55	EVERTON	2-1	27,843	Blanchflower, Edwards
7	10/09/55	Sheffield United	0-1	28,241	
8	14/09/55	Everton	2-4	34,897	Blanchflower, Webster
9	17/09/55	PRESTON N'H END	3-2	33,078	Pegg, Taylor, Viollet
10	24/09/55	Burnley	0-0	26,873	
11	01/10/55	LUTON TN	3-1	34,409	Taylor 2, Webster
12	08/10/55	WOLVER'N WDRS	3-2	48,638	Taylor 2, Doherty, Pegg
13	15/10/55	Aston Villa	4-4	29,478	Pegg 2, Blanchflower, Webster
14	22/10/55	HUDDERSFIELD TN	3-0	34,150	Berry, Pegg, Taylor
15	29/10/55	Cardiff City	1-0	27,795	Taylor
16	05/11/55	ARSENAL	1-1	41,586	Taylor
17	12/11/55	Bolton Wanderers	1-3	38,109	Taylor
18	19/11/55	CHELSEA	3-0	22,192	Taylor 2, Byrne
19	26/11/55	Blackpool	0-0	26,240	
20	03/12/55	SUNDERLAND	2-1	39,901	Doherty, Viollet
21	10/12/55	Portsmouth	2-3	24,594	Pegg, Taylor
22	17/12/55	BIRMINGHAM CITY	2-1	27,704	Jones, Viollet
23	24/12/55	West Bromwich Albion	4-1	25,168	Viollet 3, Taylor
24	26/12/55	CHARLTON ATH	5-1	44,611	Viollet 2, Byrne, Doherty, Taylor
25	27/12/55	Charlton Ath	0-3	42,040	
26	31/12/55	MANCHESTER CITY	2-1	60,956	Taylor, Viollet
27	14/01/56	SHEFFIELD UTD	3-1	30,162	Berry, Pegg, Taylor
28	21/01/56	Preston North End	1-3	28,047	Whelan
29	04/02/56	BURNLEY	2-0	27,342	Taylor, Viollet
30	11/02/56	Luton Town	2-0	16,354	Viollet, Whelan
31	18/02/56	Wolverhampton Wdrs	2-0	40,014	Taylor 2
32	25/02/56	ASTON VILLA	1-0	36,277	Whelan
33	03/03/56	Chelsea	4-2	32,050	Viollet 2, Pegg, Taylor
34	10/03/56	CARDIFF CITY	1-1	44,693	Byrne
35	17/03/56	Arsenal	1-1	50,758	Viollet
36	24/03/56	BOLTON WDRS	1-0	46,114	Taylor
37	30/03/56	NEWCASTLE UTD	5-2	58,994	Viollet 2, Doherty, Pegg, Taylor
38	31/03/56	Huddersfield Town	2-0	37,780	Taylor 2
39	02/04/56	Newcastle United	0-0	37,395	
40	07/04/56	BLACKPOOL	2-1	62,277	Berry, Taylor
41	14/04/56	Sunderland	2-2	19,865	McGuinness, Whelan
42	21/04/56	PORTSMOUTH	1-0	38,417	Viollet

Season: 1955/56

No	Date	Opponents	Score	Att	Scorers
1	20/08/55	Birmingham City	2-2	37,994	Viollet 2
2	24/08/55	TOTTENHAM	2-2	25,406	Berry, Webster
3	27/08/55	WEST BROM ALBION	3-1	31,996	Lewis, Scanlon, Viollet
4	31/08/55	Tottenham Hotspurs	2-1	27,453	Edwards 2
5	03/09/55	Manchester City	0-1	59,162	
6	07/09/55	EVERTON	2-1	27,843	Blanchflower, Edwards
7	10/09/55	Sheffield United	0-1	28,241	
8	14/09/55	Everton	2-4	34,897	Blanchflower, Webster
9	17/09/55	PRESTON N'TH END	3-2	33,078	Pegg, Taylor, Viollet
10	24/09/55	Burnley	0-0	26,873	
11	01/10/55	LUTON TN	3-1	34,409	Taylor 2, Webster
12	08/10/55	WOLVERH'N WDRS	3-2	48,638	Taylor 2, Doherty, Pegg
13	15/10/55	Aston Villa	4-4	29,478	Pegg 2, Blanchflower, Webster
14	22/10/55	HUDDERSFIELD TN	3-0	34,150	Berry, Pegg, Taylor
15	29/10/55	Cardiff City	1-0	27,795	Taylor
16	05/11/55	ARSENAL	1-1	41,586	Taylor
17	12/11/55	Bolton Wanderers	1-3	38,109	Taylor
18	19/11/55	CHELSEA	3-0	22,192	Taylor 2, Byrne
19	26/11/55	Blackpool	0-0	26,240	
20	03/12/55	SUNDERLAND	2-1	39,901	Doherty, Viollet
21	10/12/55	Portsmouth	2-3	24,594	Pegg, Taylor
22	17/12/55	BIRMINGHAM CITY	2-1	27,704	Jones, Viollet
23	24/12/55	West Bromwich Albion	4-1	25,168	Viollet 3, Taylor
24	26/12/55	CHARLTON ATH	5-1	44,611	Viollet 2, Byrne, Doherty, Taylor
25	27/12/55	Charlton Ath	0-3	42,040	
26	31/12/55	MANCHESTER CITY	2-1	60,956	Taylor, Viollet
27	14/01/56	SHEFFIELD UTD	3-1	30,162	Berry, Pegg, Taylor
28	21/01/56	Preston North End	1-3	28,047	Whelan
29	04/02/56	BURNLEY	2-0	27,342	Taylor, Viollet
30	11/02/56	Luton Town	2-0	16,354	Viollet, Whelan
31	18/02/56	Wolverhampton Wdrs	2-0	40,014	Taylor 2
32	25/02/56	ASTON VILLA	1-0	36,277	Whelan
33	03/03/56	Chelsea	4-2	32,050	Viollet 2, Pegg, Taylor
34	10/03/56	CARDIFF CITY	1-1	44,693	Byrne
35	17/03/56	Arsenal	1-1	50,758	Viollet
36	24/03/56	BOLTON WDRS	1-0	46,114	Taylor
37	30/03/56	NEWCASTLE UTD	5-2	58,994	Viollet 2, Doherty, Pegg, Taylor
38	31/03/56	Huddersfield Town	2-0	37,780	Taylor 2
39	02/04/56	Newcastle United	0-0	37,395	
40	07/04/56	BLACKPOOL	2-1	62,277	Berry, Taylor
41	14/04/56	Sunderland	2-2	19,865	McGuinness, Whelan
42	21/04/56	PORTSMOUTH	1-0	38,417	Viollet

Season: 1956/57

No	Date	Opponents	Score	Att	Scorers
1	18/08/56	BIRMINGHAM CITY	2-2	32,752	Viollet 2
2	20/08/56	Preston North End	3-1	32,569	Taylor 2, Whelan
3	25/08/56	West Bromwich Albion	3-2	26,387	Taylor, Viollet, Whelan
4	29/08/56	PRESTON N'TH END	3-2	32,515	Viollet 3
5	01/09/56	PORTSMOUTH	3-0	40,369	Berry, Pegg, Viollet
6	05/09/56	Chelsea	2-1	29,082	Taylor, Whelan
7	08/09/56	Newcastle United	1-1	50,130	Whelan
8	15/09/56	SHEFFIELD W'DAY	4-1	48,078	Berry, Taylor, Viollet
9	22/09/56	MANCHESTER CITY	2-0	53,525	Whelan, Viollet
10	29/09/56	Arsenal	2-1	62,479	Berry, Whelan
11	06/10/56	CHARLTON ATH	4-2	41,439	Charlton 2, Berry, Whelan
12	13/10/56	Sunderland	3-1	49,487	Whelan, Viollet, og
13	20/10/56	EVERTON	2-5	43,451	Charlton, Whelan
14	27/10/56	Blackpool	2-2	32,632	Taylor
15	03/11/56	WOLVERH'N WDRS	3-0	59,835	Pegg, Taylor, Whelan
16	10/11/56	Bolton Wanderers	0-2	39,922	
17	17/11/56	LEEDS UTD	3-2	51,131	Whelan 2, Charlton
18	24/11/56	Tottenham Hotspurs	2-2	57,724	Berry, Colman
19	01/12/56	LUTON TN	3-1	34,736	Edwards, Pegg, Taylor
20	08/12/56	Aston Villa	3-1	42,530	Taylor 2, Viollet
21	15/12/56	Birmingham City	1-3	36,146	Whelan
22	26/12/56	CARDIFF CITY	3-1	28,607	Taylor, Whelan, Viollet
23	29/12/56	Portsmouth	3-1	32,147	Edwards, Pegg, Viollet
24	01/01/57	CHELSEA	3-0	42,116	Taylor 2, Whelan
25	12/01/57	NEWCASTLE UTD	6-1	44,911	Pegg 2, Whelan 2, Viollet 2
26	19/01/57	Sheffield Wednesday	1-2	51,068	Taylor
27	02/02/57	Manchester City	4-2	63,872	Edwards, Taylor, Whelan, Viollet
28	09/02/57	ARSENAL	6-2	60,384	Berry 2, Whelan 2, Edwards, Taylor
29	18/02/57	Charlton Ath	5-1	16,308	Charlton 3, Taylor 2
30	23/02/57	BLACKPOOL	0-2	42,602	
31	06/03/57	Everton	2-1	34,029	Webster 2
32	09/03/57	ASTON VILLA	1-1	55,484	Charlton
33	16/03/57	Wolverhampton Wdrs	1-1	53,228	Charlton
34	25/03/57	BOLTON WDRS	0-2	60,862	
35	30/03/57	Leeds United	2-1	47,216	Berry, Charlton
36	06/04/57	TOTTENHAM	0-0	60,349	
37	13/04/57	Luton Town	2-0	21,227	Taylor 2
38	19/04/57	Burnley	3-1	41,321	Whelan 3
39	20/04/57	SUNDERLAND	4-0	58,725	Whelan 2, Edwards, Taylor
40	22/04/57	BURNLEY	2-0	41,321	Dawson, Webster
41	27/04/57	Cardiff City	3-2	17,708	Scanlon 2, Dawson
42	29/04/57	WEST BROM ALBION	1-1	20,357	Dawson

Season: 1957/58

No	Date	Opponents	Score	Att	Scorers
1	24/08/57	Leicester City	3-0	40,214	Whelan 3
2	28/08/57	EVERTON	3-0	59,103	Taylor, Viollet, og
3	31/08/57	MANCHESTER CITY	4-1	63,347	Berry, Edwards, Taylor, Viollet
4	04/09/57	Everton	3-3	72,077	Berry, Viollet, Whelan
5	07/09/57	LEEDS UTD	5-0	50,842	Berry 2, Taylor 2, Viollet
6	09/09/57	Blackpool	4-1	34,181	Viollet 2, Whelan 2
7	14/09/57	Bolton Wanderers	0-4	48,003	
8	18/09/57	BLACKPOOL	1-2	40,763	Edwards
9	21/09/57	ARSENAL	4-2	47,142	Whelan 2, Pegg, Taylor
10	28/09/57	Wolverhampton Wdrs	1-3	48,825	Doherty
11	05/10/57	ASTON VILLA	4-1	43,102	Taylor 2, Pegg, og
12	12/10/57	Nottingham Forest	2-1	47,654	Viollet, Whelan
13	19/10/57	PORTSMOUTH	0-1	38,253	
14	26/10/57	West Bromwich Albion	3-4	52,160	Taylor 2, Whelan
15	02/11/57	BURNLEY	1-0	49,449	Taylor
16	09/11/57	Preston North End	1-1	39,063	Whelan
17	16/11/57	SHEFFIELD W'DAY	2-1	40,366	Webster 2
18	23/11/57	Newcastle United	2-1	53,890	Edwards, Taylor
19	30/11/57	TOTTENHAM	3-4	43,077	Pegg 2, Whelan
20	07/12/57	Birmingham City	3-3	35,791	Viollet 2, Taylor
21	14/12/57	CHELSEA	0-1	36,853	
22	21/12/57	LEICESTER CITY	4-0	41,631	Viollet 2, Charlton, Scanlon
23	25/12/57	LUTON TN	3-0	39,444	Charlton, Edwards, Taylor
24	26/12/57	Luton Town	2-2	26,458	Scanlon, Taylor
25	28/12/57	Manchester City	2-2	70,483	Charlton, Viollet
26	11/01/58	Leeds United	1-1	39,401	Viollet
27	18/01/58	BOLTON WDRS	7-2	41,141	Charlton 3, Viollet 2, Edwards, Scanlon
28	01/02/58	Arsenal	5-4	63,578	Taylor 2, Charlton, Edwards, Viollet
29	22/02/58	NOTTINGHAM FOR	1-1	66,124	Dawson
30	08/03/58	WEST BROM ALBION	0-4	63,278	
31	15/03/58	Burnley	0-3	37,247	
32	29/03/58	Sheffield Wednesday	0-1	35,608	
33	31/03/58	Aston Villa	2-3	16,631	Dawson, Webster
34	04/04/58	SUNDERLAND	2-2	47,421	Charlton, Dawson
35	05/04/58	PRESTON N'TH END	0-0	47,816	
36	07/04/58	Sunderland	2-1	51,302	Webster 2
37	12/04/58	Tottenham Hotspurs	0-1	59,836	
38	16/04/58	Portsmouth	3-3	39,975	Dawson, E.Taylor, Webster
39	19/04/58	BIRMINGHAM CITY	0-2	38,991	
40	21/04/58	WOLVERH'N WDRS	0-4	33,267	
41	23/04/58	NEWCASTLE UTD	1-1	28,393	Dawson
42	26/04/58	Chelsea	1-2	45,011	E.Taylor

Season: 1958/59

No	Date	Opponents	Score	Att	Scorers
1	23/08/58	CHELSEA	5-2	52,382	Charlton 3, Dawson 2
2	27/08/58	Nottingham Forest	3-0	44,971	Charlton 2, Scanlon
3	30/08/58	Blackpool	1-2	36,719	Viollet
4	03/09/58	NOTT'M FOREST	1-1	51,880	Charlton
5	06/09/58	BLACKBURN RVRS	6-1	65,187	Charlton 2, Viollet 2, Scanlon, Webster
6	08/09/58	West Ham United	2-3	35,672	McGuinness, Webster
7	13/09/58	Newcastle United	1-1	60,670	Charlton
8	17/09/58	WEST HAM UTD	4-1	53,276	Scanlon 3, Webster
9	20/09/58	TOTTENHAM	2-2	62,277	Webster
10	27/09/58	Manchester City	1-1	62,912	Charlton
11	04/10/58	Wolverhampton Wdrs	0-4	36,840	
12	08/10/58	PRESTON N'TH END	0-2	46,163	
13	11/10/58	ARSENAL	1-1	56,148	Viollet
14	18/10/58	Everton	2-3	64,079	Cope 2
15	25/10/58	WEST BROM ALBION	1-2	51,721	Goodwin
16	01/11/58	Leeds United	2-1	48,574	Goodwin, Scanlon
17	08/11/58	BURNLEY	1-3	48,509	Quixall
18	15/11/58	Bolton Wanderers	3-6	33,358	Dawson 2, Charlton
19	22/11/58	LUTON TN	2-1	42,428	Charlton, Viollet
20	29/11/58	Birmingham City	4-0	28,658	Charlton, Bradley, Scanlon
21	06/12/58	LEICESTER CITY	4-1	38,482	Bradley, Charlton, Scanlon, Viollet
22	13/12/58	Preston North End	4-3	26,290	Bradley, Charlton, Scanlon, Viollet
23	20/12/58	Chelsea	3-2	48,550	Charlton, Goodwin, og
24	26/12/58	ASTON VILLA	2-1	63,098	Quixall, Viollet
25	27/12/58	Aston Villa	2-0	56,450	Pearson, Viollet
26	03/12/59	BLACKPOOL	3-1	61,961	Charlton 2, Viollet
27	31/01/59	NEWCASTLE UTD	4-4	49,008	Charlton, Scanlon, Quixall, Viollet
28	07/02/59	Tottenham Hotspurs	3-1	48,401	Charlton 2, Scanlon
29	16/02/59	MANCHESTER CITY	4-1	59,846	Bradley 2, Goodwin, Scanlon
30	21/02/59	WOLVERH'N WDRS	2-1	62,794	Charlton, Viollet
31	28/02/59	Arsenal	2-3	67,162	Bradley, Viollet
32	02/03/59	Blackburn Rovers	3-1	40,401	Bradley 2, Scanlon
33	07/03/59	EVERTON	2-1	51,254	Goodwin, Scanlon
34	14/03/59	West Bromwich Albion	3-1	35,463	Bradley, Scanlon, Viollet
35	21/03/59	LEEDS UTD	4-0	45,473	Viollet 3, Charlton
36	27/03/59	PORTSMOUTH	6-1	52,004	Charlton 2, Viollet 2, Bradley, og
37	28/03/59	Burnley	2-4	44,577	Goodwin, Viollet
38	30/03/59	Portsmouth	3-1	29,359	Charlton, Bradley
39	04/04/59	BOLTON WDRS	3-0	61,528	Charlton, Scanlon, Viollet
40	11/01/59	Luton Town	0-0	27,025	
41	18/04/59	BIRMINGHAM CITY	1-0	43,006	Quixall
42	25/04/59	Leicester City	1-2	38,466	Bradley

Season: 1959/60

No	Date	Opponents	Score	Att	Scorers
1	22/08/59	West Bromwich Albion	2-3	40,076	Viollet 2
2	26/08/59	CHELSEA	0-1	57,674	
3	29/08/59	NEWCASTLE UTD	3-2	53,257	Viollet 2, Charlton
4	02/09/59	Chelsea	6-3	66,579	Bradley 2, Viollet 2, Charlton, Quixall
5	05/09/59	Birmingham City	1-1	38,220	Quixall
6	09/09/59	LEEDS UTD	6-0	48,407	Bradley 2, Charlton 2, Scanlon, Viollet
7	12/09/59	TOTTENHAM	1-5	55,402	Viollet
8	16/09/59	Leeds United	2-2	34,048	Charlton, og
9	19/09/59	Manchester City	0-3	58,300	
10	26/09/59	Preston North End	0-4	35,016	
11	03/10/59	LEICESTER CITY	4-1	41,637	Viollet 2, Charlton, Quixall
12	10/10/59	ARSENAL	4-2	51,626	Charlton, Quixall, Viollet, og
13	17/10/59	Wolverhampton Wdrs	2-3	45,451	Viollet, og
14	24/10/59	SHEFFIELD W'DAY	3-1	39,259	Viollet 2, Bradley
15	31/10/59	Blackburn Rovers	1-1	39,621	Quixall
16	07/11/59	FULHAM	3-3	44,063	Charlton, Scanlon, Viollet
17	14/11/59	Bolton Wanderers	1-1	37,892	Dawson
18	21/11/59	LUTON TN	4-1	40,572	Viollet 2, Goodwin, Quixall
19	28/11/59	Everton	1-2	46,095	Viollet
20	05/12/59	BLACKPOOL	3-1	45,558	Viollet 2, Pearson
21	12/12/59	Nottingham Forest	5-1	31,666	Viollet 3, Dawson, Scanlon
22	19/12/59	WEST BROM ALBION	2-3	33,677	Dawson, Quixall
23	26/12/59	BURNLEY	1-2	62,376	Quixall
24	28/12/59	Burnley	4-1	47,253	Scanlon 2, Viollet 2
25	02/01/60	Newcastle United	3-7	57,200	Quixall 2, Dawson
26	16/01/60	BIRMINGHAM CITY	2-1	47,361	Quixall, Viollet
27	23/01/60	Tottenham Hotspurs	1-2	62,602	Bradley
28	06/02/60	MANCHESTER CITY	0-0	59,450	
29	13/02/60	PRESTON N'TH END	1-1	44,014	Viollet
30	24/02/60	Leicester City	1-3	33,191	Scanlon
31	27/02/60	Blackpool	6-0	23,996	Charlton 3, Viollet 2, Scanlon
32	05/03/60	WOLVERH'N WDRS	0-2	60,560	
33	19/03/60	NOTT'M FOREST	3-1	35,269	Charlton 2, Dawson
34	26/03/60	Fulham	5-0	38,250	Viollet 2, Dawson, Giles, Pearson
35	30/03/60	Sheffield Wednesday	2-4	26,821	Charlton, Viollet
36	02/04/60	BOLTON WDRS	2-0	45,298	Charlton 2
37	09/04/60	Luton Town	3-2	21,242	Dawson 2, Bradley
38	15/04/60	West Ham United	1-2	34,969	Dawson
39	16/04/60	BLACKBURN RVRS	1-0	45,945	Dawson
40	18/04/60	WEST HAM UTD	5-3	34,676	Charlton 2, Dawson 2, Quixall
41	23/04/60	Arsenal	2-5	41,057	Giles, Pearson
42	30/04/60	EVERTON	5-0	43,823	Dawson 3, Bradley, Quixall

Season: 1960/61

No	Date	Opponents	Score	Att	Scorers
1	20/08/60	BLACKBURN RVRS	1-3	47,778	Charlton
2	24/08/60	Everton	0-4	51,602	
3	31/08/60	EVERTON	4-0	51,818	Dawson 2, Charlton, Nicholson
4	03/09/60	Tottenham Hotspurs	1-4	55,445	Viollet
5	05/09/60	West Ham United	1-2	30,506	Quixall
6	10/09/60	LEICESTER CITY	1-1	35,493	Giles
7	14/09/60	WEST HAM UTD	6-1	33,695	Charlton 2, Viollet 2, Quixall, Scanlon
8	17/09/60	Aston Villa	1-3	43,593	Viollet
9	24/09/60	WOLVERH'N WDRS	1-3	44,458	Charlton
10	01/10/60	Bolton Wanderers	1-1	39,197	Giles
11	15/10/60	Burnley	3-5	32,011	Viollet 3
12	22/10/60	NEWCASTLE UTD	3-2	37,516	Dawson, Setters, Stiles
13	24/10/60	NOTT'M FOREST	2-1	23,628	Viollet 2
14	29/10/60	Arsenal	1-2	45,715	Quixall
15	05/11/60	SHEFFIELD W'DAY	0-0	36,855	
16	12/11/60	Birmingham City	1-3	31,549	Charlton
17	19/11/60	WEST BROM ALBION	3-0	32,756	Dawson, Quixall, Viollet
18	26/11/60	Cardiff City	0-3	21,122	
19	03/12/60	PRESTON N'TH END	1-0	24,094	Dawson
20	10/12/60	Fulham	4-4	23,625	Quixall 2, Charlton, Dawson
21	17/12/60	Blackburn Rovers	2-1	17,285	Pearson 2
22	24/12/60	Chelsea	2-1	37,601	Dawson, Charlton
23	26/12/60	CHELSEA	6-0	50,164	Dawson 3, Nicholson 2, Charlton
24	31/12/60	MANCHESTER CITY	5-1	61,213	Dawson 3, Charlton 2
25	14/01/61	TOTTENHAM	2-0	65,295	Pearson, Stiles
26	21/01/61	Leicester City	0-6	31,308	
27	04/02/61	ASTON VILLA	1-1	33,525	Charlton
28	11/02/61	Wolverhampton Wdrs	1-2	38,526	Nicholson
29	18/02/61	BOLTON WDRS	3-1	37,558	Dawson 2, Quixall
30	25/02/61	Nottingham Forest	2-3	26,850	Charlton, Quixall
31	04/03/61	Manchester City	3-1	50,479	Charlton, Dawson, Pearson
32	11/03/61	Newcastle United	1-1	28,870	Charlton
33	18/03/61	ARSENAL	1-1	29,732	Moir
34	25/03/61	Sheffield Wednesday	1-5	35,901	Charlton
35	31/03/61	Blackpool	0-2	30,835	
36	01/04/61	FULHAM	3-1	24,654	Charlton, Quixall, Viollet
37	03/04/61	BLACKPOOL	2-0	39,169	Nicholson, og
38	08/04/61	West Bromwich Albion	1-1	27,750	Pearson
39	12/04/61	BURNLEY	6-0	25,019	Quixall 3, Viollet 3
40	15/04/61	BIRMINGHAM CITY	4-1	28,376	Pearson 2, Quixall, Viollet
41	22/04/61	Preston North End	4-2	21,252	Charlton 2, Setters 2
42	29/04/61	CARDIFF CITY	3-3	30,320	Charlton 2, Setters

Season: 1961/62

No	Date	Opponents	Score	Att	Scorers
1	19/08/61	West Ham United	1-1	32,628	Stiles
2	23/08/61	CHELSEA	3-2	45,847	Herd, Pearson, Viollet
3	26/08/61	BLACKBURN RVRS	6-1	45,302	Herd 2, Quixall 2, Charlton, Setters
4	30/08/61	Chelsea	0-2	42,248	
5	02/09/61	Blackpool	3-2	28,156	Viollet 2, Charlton
6	09/09/61	TOTTENHAM	1-0	57,135	Quixall
7	16/09/61	Cardiff City	2-1	29,251	Dawson, Quixall
8	18/09/61	Aston Villa	1-1	38,837	Stiles
9	23/08/61	MANCHESTER CITY	3-2	56,345	Stiles, Viollet, og
10	30/09/61	WOLVERH'N WDRS	0-2	39,457	
11	07/10/61	West Bromwich Albion	1-1	25,645	Dawson
12	14/10/61	BIRMINGHAM CITY	0-2	30,674	
13	21/10/61	Arsenal	1-5	54,245	Viollet
14	28/10/61	BOLTON WDRS	0-3	31,442	
15	04/11/61	Sheffield Wednesday	1-3	35,998	Viollet
16	11/11/61	LEICESTER CITY	2-2	21,567	Giles, Viollet
17	18/11/61	Ipswich Town	1-4	25,755	McMillan
18	25/11/61	BURNLEY	1-4	41,029	Herd
19	02/12/61	Everton	1-5	48,099	Herd
20	09/12/61	FULHAM	3-0	22,193	Herd 2, Lawton
21	16/12/61	WEST HAM UTD	1-2	29,472	Herd
22	26/12/61	NOTT'M FOREST	6-3	30,822	Lawton 3, Brennan, Charlton, Herd
23	13/01/62	BLACKPOOL	0-1	26,999	
24	15/01/62	ASTON VILLA	2-0	20,807	Charlton, Quixall
25	20/01/62	Tottenham Hotspurs	2-2	55,225	Charlotn, Stiles
26	03/02/62	CARDIFF CITY	3-0	29,200	Giles, Lawton, Stiles
27	10/02/62	Manchester City	2-0	49,959	Chisnall, Herd
28	24/02/62	WEST BROM ALBION	4-1	32,456	Charlton 2, Setters, Quixall
29	28/02/62	Wolverhampton Wdrs	2-2	27,565	Herd, Lawton
30	03/03/62	Birmingham City	1-1	25,817	Herd
31	17/03/62	Bolton Wanderers	0-1	34,366	
32	20/03/62	Nottingham Forest	0-1	27,833	
33	24/03/62	SHEFFIELD W'DAY	1-1	31,322	Charlton
34	04/04/62	Leicester City	3-4	15,318	McMillan 2, Quixall
35	07/04/62	IPSWICH TN	5-0	24,976	Quixall 3, Setters, Stiles
36	10/04/62	Blackburn Rovers	0-3	14,623	
37	14/04/62	Burnley	3-1	36,240	Brennan, Cantwell, Herd
38	16/04/62	ARSENAL	2-3	24,258	Cantwell, McMillan
39	21/04/62	EVERTON	1-1	31,296	Herd
40	23/04/62	SHEFFIELD UTD	0-1	30,073	
41	24/04/62	Sheffield United	3-2	25,324	McMillan 2, Stiles
42	28/04/62	Fulham	0-2	40,113	

Season: 1962/63

No	Date	Opponents	Score	Att	Scorers
1	18/08/62	WEST BROM ALBION	2-2	51,685	Herd, Law
2	22/08/62	Everton	1-3	69,501	Moir
3	25/08/62	Arsenal	3-1	62,308	Herd 2, Chisnall
4	29/08/62	EVERTON	0-1	63,437	
5	01/09/62	BIRMINGHAM CITY	2-0	39,847	Giles, Herd
6	05/09/62	Bolton Wanderers	0-3	44,859	
7	08/09/62	Leyton Orient	0-1	24,901	
8	12/09/62	BOLTON WDRS	3-0	37,721	Herd 2, Cantwell
9	15/09/62	MANCHESTER CITY	2-3	49,193	Law 2
10	22/09/62	BURNLEY	2-5	45,954	Law, Stiles
11	29/09/62	Sheffield Wednesday	0-1	40,520	
12	06/10/62	Blackpool	2-2	33,242	Herd 2
13	13/10/62	BLACKBURN RVRS	0-3	42,252	
14	20/10/62	Tottenham Hotspurs	2-6	51,314	Herd, Quixall
15	27/10/62	WEST HAM UTD	3-1	29,204	Quixall 2, Law
16	03/11/62	Ipswich Town	5-3	18,483	Law 4, Herd
17	10/11/62	LIVERPOOL	3-3	43,810	Giles, Herd, Quixall
18	17/11/62	Wolverhampton Wdrs	3-2	27,305	Law 2, Herd
19	24/11/62	ASTON VILLA	2-2	36,852	Quixall 2
20	01/12/62	Sheffield United	1-1	25,173	Charlton
21	08/12/62	NOTT'HAM FOREST	5-1	27,946	Herd 2, Charlton, Giles, Law
22	15/12/62	West Bromwich Albion	0-3	18,113	
23	26/12/62	Fulham	1-0	23,928	Charlton
24	21/02/63	BLACKPOOL	1-1	43,121	Herd
25	02/03/63	Blackburn Rovers	2-2	27,924	Charlton, Law
26	09/03/63	TOTTENHAM	0-2	53,416	
27	18/03/63	West Ham United	1-3	28,950	Herd
28	23/03/63	IPSWICH TN	0-1	32,792	
29	01/04/63	FULHAM	0-2	28,124	
30	09/04/63	Aston Villa	2-1	26,867	Charlton, Stiles
31	13/04/63	Liverpool	0-1	51,529	
32	15/04/63	LEICESTER CITY	2-2	50,005	Charlton, Herd
33	16/04/63	Leicester City	3-4	37,002	Law 3
34	20/04/63	SHEFFIELD UTD	1-1	31,179	Law
35	22/04/63	WOLVERH'N WDRS	2-1	36,147	Herd, Law
36	01/05/63	SHEFFIELD W'DAY	1-3	31,878	Setters
37	04/05/63	Burnley	1-0	30,266	Law
38	06/05/63	ARSENAL	2-3	35,999	Law 2
39	10/05/63	Birmingham City	1-2	21,814	Law
40	15/05/63	Manchester City	1-1	52,424	Quixall
41	18/05/63	LEYTON ORIENT	3-1	32,759	Charlton, Law, og
42	20/05/63	Nottingham Forest	2-3	16,130	Giles, Herd

Season: 1963/64

No	Date	Opponents	Score	Att	Scorers
1	24/08/63	Sheffield Wednesday	3-3	32,177	Charlton 2, Moir
2	28/08/63	IPSWICH TN	2-0	39,921	Law 2
3	31/08/63	EVERTON	5-1	62,965	Chisnall 2, Law 2, Sadler
4	03/09/63	Ipswich Town	7-2	28,113	Law 3, Chisnall, Moir, Sadler, Setters
5	07/09/63	Birmingham City	1-1	36,874	Chisnall
6	11/09/63	BLACKPOOL	3-0	47,400	Charlton, Law
7	14/09/63	WEST BROM ALBION	1-0	50,453	Sadler
8	16/09/63	Blackpool	0-1	29,806	
9	21/09/63	Arsenal	1-2	56,776	Herd
10	28/09/63	LEICESTER CITY	3-1	41,374	Herd 2, Setters
11	02/10/63	Chelsea	1-1	45,351	Setters
12	05/10/63	Bolton Wanderers	1-0	35,872	Herd
13	19/10/63	Nottingham Forest	2-1	41,426	Chisnall, Quixall
14	26/10/63	WEST HAM UTD	0-1	45,120	
15	28/10/63	BLACKBURN RVRS	2-2	41,169	Quixall 2
16	02/11/63	Wolverhampton Wdrs	0-2	34,159	
17	09/11/63	TOTTENHAM	4-1	57,413	Law 3, Herd
18	16/11/63	Aston Villa	0-4	36,276	
19	23/11/63	LIVERPOOL	0-1	54,654	
20	30/11/63	Sheffield United	2-1	30,615	
21	07/12/63	STOKE CITY	5-2	52,232	Law 4, Herd
22	14/12/63	SHEFFIELD W'DAY	3-1	35,139	Herd 3
23	21/12/63	Everton	0-4	48,027	
24	26/12/63	Burnley	1-6	35,764	Herd
25	28/12/63	BURNLEY	5-1	47,834	Herd 2, Moore 2, Best
26	11/01/64	BIRMINGHAM CITY	1-2	44,695	Sadler
27	18/01/64	West Bromwich Albion	4-1	25,624	Law 2, Best, Charlton
28	01/02/64	ARSENAL	3-1	48,340	Herd, Law, Setters
29	08/02/64	Leicester City	2-3	35,538	Herd, Law
30	19/02/64	BOLTON WDRS	5-0	33,926	Best 2, Herd 2, Charlton
31	22/02/64	Blackburn Rovers	3-1	36,726	Law 2, Chisnall
32	07/03/64	West Ham United	2-0	27,027	Herd, Sadler
33	21/03/64	Tottenham Hotspurs	3-2	56,392	Charlton, Law, Moore
34	23/03/64	CHELSEA	1-1	42,931	Law
35	27/03/64	Fulham	2-2	41,769	Herd, Law
36	28/03/64	WOLVERH'N WDRS	2-2	44,470	Charlton, Law
37	30/03/64	FULHAM	3-0	42,279	Crerand, Foulkes, Herd
38	04/04/64	Liverpool	0-3	52,559	
39	06/04/64	ASTON VILLA	1-0	25,848	Law
40	13/04/64	SHEFFIELD UTD	2-1	27,587	Law, Moir
41	18/04/64	Stoke City	1-3	45,670	Charlton
42	25/04/64	NOTT'HAM FOREST	3-1	31,671	Law 2, Moore

Season: 1964/65

No	Date	Opponents	Score	Att	Scorers
1	22/08/64	WEST BROM ALBION	2-2	52,007	Charlton, Law
2	24/08/64	West Ham United	1-3	37,070	Law
3	29/08/64	Leicester City	2-2	32,373	Law, Sadler
4	02/09/64	WEST HAM UTD	3-1	45,123	Best, Connelly, Law
5	05/09/64	Fulham	1-2	36,291	Connelly
6	08/09/64	Everton	3-3	63,024	Connelly, Herd, Law
7	12/09/64	NOTT'HAM FOREST	3-0	45,012	Herd 2, Connelly
8	16/09/64	EVERTON	2-1	49,968	Best, Law
9	19/09/64	Stoke City	2-1	40,031	Connelly, Herd
10	26/09/64	TOTTENHAM	4-1	53,058	Crerand 2, Law 2
11	30/09/64	Chelsea	2-0	60,769	Best, Law
12	06/10/64	Burnley	0-0	30,761	
13	10/10/64	SUNDERLAND	1-0	48,577	Herd
14	17/10/64	Wolverhampton Wdrs	4-2	26,763	Law 2, Herd, og
15	24/10/64	ASTON VILLA	7-0	35,807	Law 4, Herd 2, Connelly
16	31/10/64	Liverpool	2-0	52,402	Crerand, Herd
17	07/11/64	SHEFFIELD W'DAY	1-0	50,178	Herd
18	14/11/64	Blackpool	2-1	31,129	Connelly, Herd
19	21/11/64	BLACKBURN RVRS	3-0	49,633	Best, Connelly, Herd
20	28/11/64	Arsenal	3-2	59,627	Law 2, Connelly
21	05/12/64	LEEDS UTD	0-1	53,374	
22	12/12/64	West Bromwich Albion	1-1	28,126	Law
23	16/12/64	BIRMINGHAM CITY	1-1	25,721	Charlton
24	26/12/64	Sheffield United	1-0	37,295	Best
25	28/12/64	SHEFFIELD UTD	1-1	42,219	Herd
26	16/01/65	Nottingham Forest	2-2	43,009	Law 2
27	23/01/65	STOKE CITY	1-1	50,392	Law
28	06/02/65	Tottenham Hotspurs	0-1	58,639	
29	13/02/65	BURNLEY	3-2	38,865	Best, Charlton, Herd
30	24/02/65	Sunderland	0-1	51,336	
31	27/02/65	WOLVERH'N WDRS	3-0	37,018	Charlton 2, Connelly
32	13/03/65	CHELSEA	4-0	56,261	Herd 2, Best, Law
33	15/03/65	FULHAM	4-1	45,402	Connelly 2, Herd 2
34	20/03/65	Sheffield Wednesday	0-1	33,549	
35	22/03/65	BLACKPOOL	2-0	42,318	Law 2
36	03/04/65	Blackburn Rovers	5-0	29,363	Charlton 3, Connelly, Herd
37	12/04/65	LEICESTER CITY	1-0	34,114	Herd
38	17/04/65	Leeds United	1-0	52,368	Connelly
39	19/04/65	Birmingham City	4-2	28,907	Best 2, Cantwell, Charlton
40	24/04/65	LIVERPOOL	3-0	55,772	Law 2, Connelly
41	26/04/65	ARSENAL	3-1	51,625	Law 2, Best
42	28/04/65	Aston Villa	1-2	36,081	Charlton

Season: 1965/66

No	Date	Opponents	Score	Att	Scorers
1	21/08/65	SHEFFIELD W'DAY	1-0	37,524	Herd
2	24/08/65	Nottingham Forest	2-4	33,744	Aston, Best
3	28/08/65	Northampton Town	1-1	21,140	Connelly
4	01/09/65	NOTT'HAM FOREST	0-0	38,777	
5	04/09/65	STOKE CITY	1-1	37,603	Herd
6	08/09/65	Newcastle United	2-1	57,380	Herd, Law
7	11/09/65	Burnley	0-3	30,235	
8	15/09/65	NEWCASTLE UTD	1-1	30,401	Stiles
9	18/09/65	CHELSEA	4-1	37,917	Law 3, Charlton
10	25/09/65	Arsenal	2-4	56,757	Aston, Charlton
11	09/10/65	LIVERPOOL	2-0	58,161	Best, Law
12	16/10/65	Tottenham Hotspurs	1-5	58,051	Charlton
13	23/10/65	FULHAM	4-1	32,716	Herd 3, Charlton
14	30/10/65	Blackpool	2-1	24,703	Herd 2
15	06/11/65	BLACKBURN RVRS	2-2	38,823	Charlton, Law
16	13/11/65	Leicester City	5-0	34,551	Herd 2, Best, Charlton, Connelly
17	20/11/65	SHEFFIELD UTD	3-1	37,922	Best 2, Law
18	04/12/65	WEST HAM UTD	0-0	32,924	
19	11/12/65	Sunderland	3-2	37,417	Best 2, Herd
20	15/12/65	EVERTON	3-0	32,624	Best, Charlton, Herd
21	18/12/65	TOTTENHAM	5-1	39,270	Law 2, Charlton, Herd, og
22	27/12/65	WEST BROM ALBION	1-1	54,102	Law
23	01/01/66	Liverpool	1-2	53,790	Law
24	08/01/66	SUNDERLAND	1-1	39,162	Best
25	12/01/66	Leeds United	1-1	49,672	Herd
26	15/01/66	Fulham	1-0	33,018	Charlton
27	29/01/66	Sheffield Wednesday	0-0	39,281	
28	05/02/66	NORTHAMPTON TN	6-2	34,986	Charlton 3, Law 2, Connelly
29	19/02/66	Stoke City	2-2	36,667	Connelly, Herd
30	26/02/66	BURNLEY	4-2	49,892	Herd 3, Charlton
31	12/03/66	Chelsea	0-2	60,269	
32	19/03/66	ARSENAL	2-1	47,246	Law, Stiles
33	06/04/66	Aston Villa	1-1	28,211	Cantwell
34	09/04/66	LEICESTER CITY	1-2	42,593	Connelly
35	16/04/66	Sheffield United	1-3	22,330	Sadler
36	25/04/66	Everton	0-0	50,843	
37	27/04/66	BLACKPOOL	2-1	26,953	Charlton, Law
38	30/04/66	West Ham United	2-3	36,416	Aston, Cantwell
39	04/05/66	West Bromwich Albion	3-3	22,609	Aston, A.Dunne, Herd
40	07/05/66	Blackburn Rovers	4-1	14,513	Herd 2, Charlton, Sadler
41	09/05/66	ASTON VILLA	6-1	23,039	Herd 2, Sadler 2, Charlton, Ryan
42	19/05/66	LEEDS UTD	1-1	35,008	Herd

Season: 1966/67

No	Date	Opponents	Score	Att	Scorers
1	20/08/66	WEST BROM ALBION	5-3	41,343	Law 2, Best, Herd, Stiles
2	23/08/66	Everton	2-1	60,657	Law 2
3	27/08/66	Leeds United	1-3	45,092	Best
4	31/08/66	EVERTON	3-0	61,114	Connelly, Foulkes, Law
5	03/09/66	NEWCASTLE UTD	3-2	44,448	Connelly, Herd, Law
6	07/09/66	Stoke City	0-3	44,337	
7	10/09/66	Tottenham Hotspurs	1-2	56,295	Law
8	17/09/66	MANCHESTER CITY	1-0	62,085	Law
9	24/09/66	BURNLEY	4-1	52,697	Crerand, Herd, Law
10	01/10/66	Nottingham Forest	1-4	41,854	Charlton
11	08/10/66	Blackpool	2-1	33,555	Law 2
12	15/10/66	CHELSEA	1-1	56,789	Law
13	29/10/66	ARSENAL	1-0	45,387	Sadler
14	05/11/66	Chelsea	3-3	55,958	Aston 2, Best
15	12/11/66	SHEFFIELD W'DAY	2-0	46,942	Charlton, Herd
16	19/11/66	Southampton	2-1	29,458	Charlton 2
17	26/11/66	SUNDERLAND	5-0	44,687	Herd 4, Law
18	30/11/66	Leicester City	2-1	39,014	Best, Law
19	03/12/66	Aston Villa	1-2	39,937	Herd
20	10/12/66	LIVERPOOL	2-2	61,768	Best 2
21	17/12/66	West Bromwich Albion	4-3	32,080	Herd 3, Law
22	26/12/66	Sheffield United	1-2	42,752	Herd
23	27/12/66	SHEFFIELD UTD	2-0	59,392	Crerand, Herd
24	31/12/66	LEEDS UTD	0-0	53,486	
25	14/01/67	TOTTENHAM	1-0	57,366	Herd
26	21/01/67	Manchester City	1-1	62,983	Foulkes
27	04/02/67	Burnley	1-1	40,165	Sadler
28	11/02/67	NOTT'HAM FOREST	1-0	62,727	Law
29	25/02/67	BLACKPOOL	4-0	47,158	Charlton 2, Law, Hughes(og)
30	03/03/67	Arsenal	1-1	63,363	Aston
31	11/03/67	Newcastle United	0-0	37,430	
32	18/03/67	LEICESTER CITY	5-2	50,281	Aston, Charlotn, Herd, Law, Sadler
33	25/03/67	Liverpool	0-0	53,813	
34	27/03/67	Fulham	2-2	47,290	Best, Stiles
35	28/03/67	FULHAM	2-1	51,673	Foulkes, Stiles
36	01/04/67	WEST HAM UTD	3-0	61,308	Best, Charlton, Law
37	10/04/67	Sheffield Wednesday	2-2	51,101	Charlton 2
38	18/04/67	SOUTHAMPTON	3-0	54,291	Charlton, Law, Sadler
39	22/04/67	Sunderland	0-0	43,570	
40	29/04/67	ASTON VILLA	3-1	55,782	Aston, Best, Law
41	06/05/67	West Ham United	6-1	38,424	Law 2, Best, Charlton, Crerand, Foulkes
42	13/05/67	STOKE CITY	0-0	61,071	

Season: 1967/68

No	Date	Opponents	Score	Att	Scorers
1	19/08/67	Everton	1-3	61,452	Charlton
2	23/08/67	LEEDS UTD	1-0	53,016	Charlton
3	26/08/67	LEICESTER CITY	1-1	51,256	Foulkes
4	02/09/67	West Ham United	3-1	36,562	Kidd, Ryan, Sadler
5	06/09/67	Sunderland	1-1	51,527	Kidd
6	09/09/67	BURNLEY	2-2	55,809	Burns, Crerand
7	16/09/67	Sheffield Wednesday	1-1	47,274	Best
8	23/09/67	TOTTENHAM	3-1	58,779	Best 2, Law
9	30/09/67	Manchester City	2-1	62,942	Charlton 2
10	07/10/67	Arsenal	1-0	60,197	Aston
11	14/10/67	Sheffield United	3-0	29,170	Aston, Kidd, Law
12	25/10/67	COVENTRY CITY	4-0	54,253	Aston 2, Best, Charlton
13	28/10/67	Nottingham Forest	1-3	49,946	Best
14	04/11/67	STOKE CITY	1-0	51,041	Charlton
15	08/11/67	Leeds United	0-1	43,999	
16	11/11/67	Liverpool	2-1	54,515	Best 2
17	18/11/67	SOUTHAMPTON	3-2	48,732	Aston, Charlton, Kidd
18	25/11/67	Chelsea	1-1	54,712	Kidd
19	02/12/67	WEST BROM ALBION	2-1	52,568	Best 2
20	09/12/67	Newcastle United	2-2	48,639	Dunne, Kidd
21	16/12/67	EVERTON	3-1	60,736	Aston, Law, Sadler
22	23/12/67	Leicester City	2-2	40,104	Charlton, Law
23	26/12/67	WOLVERH'N WDRS	4-0	63,450	Best 2, Charlton, Kidd
24	30/12/67	Wolverhampton Wdrs	3-2	53,940	Aston, Charlton, Kidd
25	06/01/68	WEST HAM UTD	3-1	54,498	Aston, Best, Charlton
26	20/01/68	SHEFFIELD UTD	4-2	55,254	Best 2, Charlton, Kidd
27	03/02/68	Tottenham Hotspurs	2-1	57,790	Best, Charlton
28	17/02/68	Burnley	1-2	31,965	Best
29	24/02/68	Arsenal	2-0	46,417	Best, Storey(og)
30	02/03/68	CHELSEA	1-3	62,978	Kidd
31	16/03/68	Coventry City	0-2	47,110	
32	23/03/68	NOTT'HAM FOREST	3-0	61,978	Herd, Brennan, Burns
33	27/03/68	MANCHESTER CITY	1-3	63,004	Best
34	30/03/68	Stoke City	4-2	30,141	Aston, Best, Gowling, Ryan
35	05/04/68	LIVERPOOL	1-2	63,059	Best
36	12/04/68	Fulham	4-0	40,152	Best 2, Kidd, Law
37	13/04/68	Southampton	2-2	30,079	Best, Charlton
38	15/04/68	FULHAM	3-0	60,465	Aston, Best, Charlton
39	20/04/68	SHEFFIELD UTD	1-0	55,033	Law
40	27/04/68	West Bromwich Albion	3-6	43,412	Kidd 2, Law
41	04/05/68	NEWCASTLE UTD	6-0	59,976	Best 3, Kidd 2, Sadler
42	11/05/68	SUNDERLAND	1-2	62,963	Best

Season: 1968/69

No	Date	Opponents	Score	Att	Scorers
1	10/08/68	EVERTON	2-1	61,311	Best, Charlton
2	14/08/68	West Bromwich Albion	1-3	38,299	Charlton
3	17/08/68	Manchester City	0-0	63,052	
4	21/08/68	COVENTRY CITY	1-0	51,201	Ryan
5	24/08/68	CHELSEA	0-4	55,114	
6	28/08/68	TOTTENHAM	3-1	62,649	Fitzpatrick 2, og
7	31/08/68	Sheffield Wednesday	4-5	50,490	Law 2, Best, Charlton
8	07/09/68	WEST HAM UTD	1-1	63,274	Law
9	14/09/68	Burnley	0-1	32,935	
10	21/09/68	NEWCASTLE UTD	3-1	47,262	Best 2, Law
11	05/10/68	ARSENAL	0-0	61,843	
12	09/10/68	Tottenham Hotspurs	2-2	56,205	Crerand, Law
13	12/10/68	Liverpool	0-2	53,392	
14	19/10/68	SOUTHAMPTON	1-2	46,526	Best
15	26/10/68	Queens Park Rgrs	3-2	31,138	Best 2, Law
16	02/11/68	LEEDS UTD	0-0	53,839	
17	09/11/68	Sunderland	1-1	33,151	og
18	16/11/68	IPSWICH TN	0-0	45,796	
19	23/11/68	Stoke City	0-0	30,562	
20	30/11/68	WOLVERH'N WDRS	2-0	50,165	Best, Law
21	07/12/68	Leicester City	1-2	36,303	Law
22	14/12/68	LIVERPOOL	1-0	55,354	Law
23	21/12/68	Southampton	0-2	26,194	
24	26/12/68	Arsenal	0-3	62,300	
25	11/01/69	Leeds United	1-2	48,145	Charlton
26	18/01/69	SUNDERLAND	4-1	45,670	Law 3, Best
27	01/02/69	Ipswich Town	0-1	30,837	
28	15/02/69	Wolverhampton Wdrs	2-2	44,023	Best, Charlton
29	08/03/69	MANCHESTER CITY	0-1	63,264	
30	10/03/69	Everton	0-0	57,514	
31	15/03/69	Chelsea	2-3	60,436	James, Law
32	19/03/69	QUEENS PARK RGRS	8-1	36,638	Morgan 3, Best 2, Aston, Kidd, Stiles
33	22/03/69	SHEFFIELD W'DAY	1-0	45,527	Best
34	24/03/69	STOKE CITY	1-1	39,931	Aston
35	29/03/69	West Ham United	0-0	41,546	
36	31/03/69	Nottingham Forest	1-0	41,892	Best
37	02/04/69	WEST BROM ALBION	2-1	38,846	Best 2
38	05/04/69	NOTT'HAM FOREST	3-1	51,952	Morgan 2, Best
39	08/04/69	Coventry City	1-2	45,402	Fitzpatrick
40	12/04/69	Newcastle United	0-2	46,379	
41	19/04/69	BURNLEY	2-0	52,626	Best, og
42	17/05/69	LEICESTER CITY	3-2	45,860	Best, Law, Morgan

Season: 1969/70

No	Date	Opponents	Score	Att	Scorers
1	09/08/69	Crystal Palace	2-2	48,610	Charlton, Morgan
2	13/08/69	EVERTON	0-2	57,752	
3	16/08/69	SOUTHAMPTON	1-4	46,328	Morgan
4	19/08/69	Everton	0-3	53,185	
5	23/08/69	Wolverhampton Wdrs	0-0	50,783	
6	27/08/69	NEWCASTLE UTD	0-0	52,774	
7	30/08/69	SUNDERLAND	3-1	50,570	Best, Givens, Kidd
8	06/09/69	Leeds United	2-2	44,271	Best 2
9	13/09/69	LIVERPOOL	1-0	56,509	Morgan
10	17/09/69	Sheffield Wednesday	3-1	39,298	Best 2, Kidd
11	20/09/69	Arsenal	2-2	59,498	Best, Sadler
12	27/09/69	WEST HAM UTD	5-2	58,579	Best 2, Burns, Charlton, Kidd
13	04/10/69	Derby County	0-2	40,724	
14	08/10/69	Southampton	3-0	31,044	Best, Burns, Kidd
15	11/10/69	IPSWICH TN	2-1	52,281	Best, Kidd
16	18/10/69	NOTT'HAM FOREST	1-1	53,702	Best
17	25/10/69	West Bromwich Albion	1-2	45,120	Kidd
18	01/11/69	STOKE CITY	1-1	53,406	Charlton
19	08/11/69	Coventry City	2-1	43,446	Aston, Law
20	15/11/69	Manchester City	0-4	63,013	
21	22/11/69	TOTTENHAM	3-1	50,003	Charlton 2, Burns
22	29/11/69	Burnley	1-1	23,770	Best
23	06/12/69	CHELSEA	0-2	49,344	
24	13/12/69	Liverpool	4-1	47,682	Charlton, Morgan, Ure, og
25	26/12/69	WOLVERH'N WDRS	0-0	50,806	
26	27/12/69	Sunderland	1-1	36,504	Kidd
27	10/01/70	ARSENAL	2-1	41,055	Morgan, Sartori
28	17/01/70	West Ham United	0-0	41,643	
29	26/01/70	LEEDS UTD	2-2	59,879	Kidd, Sadler
30	31/01/70	DERBY COUNTY	1-0	59,315	Charlton
31	10/02/70	Ipswich Town	1-0	29,755	Kidd
32	14/02/70	CRYSTAL PALACE	1-1	54,711	Kidd
33	28/02/70	Stoke City	2-2	38,917	Morgan, Sartori
34	17/03/70	BURNLEY	3-3	38,377	Best, Crerand, Law
35	21/03/70	Chelsea	1-2	61,479	Morgan
36	28/03/70	MANCHESTER CITY	1-2	59,777	Kidd
37	30/03/70	COVENTRY CITY	1-1	38,647	Kidd
38	31/03/70	Nottingham Forest	2-1	39,228	Charlton, Gowling
39	04/04/70	Newcastle United	1-5	43,094	Charlton
40	08/04/70	WEST BROM ALBION	7-0	26,582	Charlton 2, Fitzpatrick 2, Gowling 2, Best
41	13/04/70	Tottenham Hotspurs	1-2	41,808	Fitzpatrick
42	15/04/70	SHEFFIELD W'DAY	2-2	36,649	Best, Charlton

Season: 1970/71

No	Date	Opponents	Score	Att	Scorers
1	15/08/70	LEEDS UTD	0-1	59,365	
2	19/08/70	CHELSEA	0-0	50,979	
3	22/08/70	Arsenal	0-4	54,117	
4	25/08/70	Burnley	2-0	29,385	Law 2
5	29/08/70	WEST HAM UTD	1-1	50,643	Fitzpatrick
6	02/09/70	EVERTON	2-0	51,346	Best, Charlton
7	05/09/70	Liverpool	1-1	52,542	Kidd
8	12/09/70	COVENTRY CITY	2-0	48,939	Best, Charlton
9	19/09/70	Ipswich Town	0-4	27,776	
10	26/09/70	BLACKPOOL	1-1	46,647	Best
11	03/10/70	Wolverhampton Wdrs	2-3	38,629	Gowling, Kidd
12	10/10/70	CRYSTAL PALACE	1-0	42,979	
13	17/10/70	Leeds United	2-2	50,190	Charlton, Fitzpatrick
14	24/10/70	WEST BROM ALBION	2-1	43,278	Kidd, Law
15	31/10/70	Newcastle United	0-1	45,140	
16	07/11/70	STOKE CITY	2-2	47,451	Law, Sadler
17	14/11/70	Nottingham Forest	2-1	36,364	Gowling, Sartori
18	21/11/70	Southampton	0-1	30,202	
19	28/11/70	HUDDERSFIELD TN	1-1	45,306	Best
20	05/12/70	Tottenahm Hotspurs	2-2	55,693	Best, Law
21	12/12/70	MANCHESTER CITY	1-4	52,636	Kidd
22	19/12/70	ARSENAL	1-3	33,182	Sartori
23	26/12/70	Derby County	4-4	34,068	Law 2, Best, Kidd
24	09/01/71	Chelsea	2-1	53,482	Gowling, Morgan
25	16/01/71	BURNLEY	1-1	40,135	Aston
26	30/01/71	Huddersfield Town	2-1	41,464	Aston, Law
27	06/02/71	TOTTENHAM	2-1	48,965	Best, Morgan
28	20/02/71	SOUTHAMPTON	5-1	36,060	Gowling 4, Morgan
29	23/02/71	Everton	0-1	52,544	
30	27/02/71	NEWCASTLE UTD	1-0	41,902	Kidd
31	06/03/71	West Bromwich Albion	3-4	41,112	Aston, Best, Kidd
32	13/03/71	NOTT'M FOREST	2-0	40,473	Best, Law
33	20/03/71	Stoke City	2-1	40,005	Best 2
34	03/04/71	West Ham United	1-2	38,507	Best
35	10/04/71	DERBY COUNTY	1-2	45,691	Law
36	12/04/71	WOLVERH'N WDRS	1-0	41,886	Gowling
37	13/04/71	Coventry City	1-2	33,818	Best
38	17/04/71	Crystal Palace	5-3	39,145	Law 3, Best 2
39	19/04/71	LIVERPOOL	0-2	44,004	
40	24/04/71	IPSWICH TN	3-2	33,566	Charlton, Best, Kidd
41	01/05/71	Blackpool	1-1	29,857	Law
42	05/05/71	Manchester City	4-3	43,626	Best 2, Charlton, Law

Season: 1971/72

No	Date	Opponents	Score	Att	Scorers
1	14/08/71	Derby County	2-2	35,886	Gowling, Law
2	18/08/71	Chelsea	3-2	54,763	Charlton. Kidd, Morgan
3	20/08/71	ARSENAL	3-1	27,649	Charlton, Gowling, Kidd
4	23/08/71	WEST BROM ALBION	3-1	23,146	Best 2, Gowling
5	28/08/71	Wolverhampton Wdrs	1-1	46,471	Best
6	31/08/71	Everton	0-1	52,151	
7	04/09/71	IPSWICH TN	1-0	45,656	Best
8	11/09/71	Crystal Palace	3-1	44,020	Law 2, Kidd
9	18/09/71	WEST HAM UTD	4-2	53,339	Best 3, Charlton
10	25/09/71	Liverpool	2-2	55,634	Charlton, Law
11	02/10/71	SHEFFIELD UTD	2-0	51,735	Best, Gowling
12	09/10/71	Huddersfield Town	3-0	33,458	Best, Charlton, Law
13	16/10/71	DERBY COUNTY	1-0	53,247	Best
14	23/10/71	Newcastle United	1-0	52,411	Best
15	30/10/71	LEEDS UTD	0-1	53,960	
16	06/11/71	Manchester City	3-3	63,326	Gowling, Kidd, McIlroy
17	13/11/71	TOTTENHAM	3-1	54,058	Law 2, McIlroy
18	20/11/71	LEICESTER CITY	3-2	48,757	Law 2, Kidd
19	27/11/71	Southampton	5-2	30,323	Best 3, Kidd, McIlroy
20	04/12/71	NOT'HAM FOREST	3-2	45,411	Kidd 2, Best
21	11/12/71	Stoke City	1-1	33,857	Law
22	18/12/71	Ipswich Town	0-0	29,229	
23	27/12/71	COVENTRY CITY	2-2	52,117	James. Law
24	01/01/72	West Ham United	0-3	41,892	
25	08/01/72	WOLVERH'N WDRS	1-3	46,781	McIlroy
26	22/01/72	CHELSEA	0-1	55,927	
27	29/01/72	West Bromwich Albion	1-2	47,012	Kidd
28	12/02/72	NEWCASTLE UTD	0-2	44,983	
29	19/02/72	Leeds United	1-5	45,399	Burns
30	04/03/72	Tottenham Hotspurs	0-2	54,814	
31	08/03/72	EVERTON	0-0	38.415	
32	11/03/72	HUDDERSFIELD TN	2-0	53,581	Best, Storey-Moore
33	25/03/72	CRYSTAL PALACE	4-0	41,550	Charlton, Gowling, Law, Storey-Moore
34	01/04/72	Coventry City	3-2	37,901	Best, Charlton, Storey-Moore
35	03/04/72	LIVERPOOL	0-3	53,826	
36	04/04/72	Sheffield United	1-1	45,045	Sadler
37	08/04/72	Leicester City	0-2	35,970	
38	12/04/72	MANCHESTER CITY	1-3	56,362	Buchan
39	15/04/72	SOUTHAMPTON	3-2	38,437	Best, Kidd, Storey-Moore
40	22/04/72	Nottingham Forest	0-0	35,063	
41	25/04/72	Arsenal	0-3	49,125	
42	29/04/72	STOKE CITY	3-0	34,959	Best, Charlton, Storey-Moore

Season: 1972/73

No	Date	Opponents	Score	Att	Scorers
1	12/08/72	IPSWICH TN	1-2	51,459	Law
2	15/08/72	Liverpool	0-2	54,799	
3	19/08/72	Everton	0-2	52,348	
4	23/08/72	LEICESTER CITY	1-1	40,067	Best
5	26/08/72	ARSENAL	0-0	48,108	
6	30/08/72	CHELSEA	0-0	44,482	
7	02/09/72	West Ham United	2-2	31,939	Best, Storey-Moore
8	09/09/72	COVENTRY CITY	0-1	37,073	
9	16/09/72	Wolverhampton Wdrs	0-2	34,049	
10	23/09/72	DERBY COUNTY	3-0	48,255	Davies, Morgan, Storey-Moore
11	30/09/72	Sheffield United	0-1	37,347	
12	07/10/72	West Bromwich Albion	2-2	39,209	Best, Storey-Moore
13	14/10/72	BIRMINGHAM CITY	1-0	52,104	MacDougall
14	21/10/72	Newcastle United	1-2	38,170	Charlton
15	28/10/72	TOTTENHAM	1-4	52,497	Charlton
16	04/11/72	Leicester City	2-2	32,575	Best, Davies
17	11/11/72	LIVERPOOL	2-0	53,944	Davies, MacDougall
18	18/11/72	Manchester City	0-3	52,050	
19	25/11/72	SOUTHAMPTON	2-1	36,073	Davies, MacDougall
20	02/12/72	Norwich City	2-0	35,910	MacDougall, Storey-Moore
21	09/12/72	STOKE CITY	0-2	41,347	
22	16/12/72	Crystal Palace	0-5	39,484	
23	23/12/72	LEEDS UTD	1-1	46,382	MacDougall
24	26/12/72	Derby County	1-3	35,098	Storey-Moore
25	06/01/73	Arsenal	1-3	51,194	Kidd
26	20/01/73	WEST HAM UTD	2-2	50,878	Charlton, Macari
27	24/01/73	EVERTON	0-0	58,970	
28	27/01/73	Coventry City	1-1	42,767	Holton
29	10/02/73	WOLVERH'N WDRS	2-1	52,089	Charlton 2
30	17/02/73	Ipswich Town	1-4	31,918	Macari
31	03/03/73	WEST BROM ALBION	2-1	46,735	Kidd, Macari
32	10/03/73	Birmingham City	1-3	51,278	Macari
33	17/03/73	NEWCASTLE UTD	2-1	48,426	Holton, Martin
34	24/03/73	Tottenham Hotspurs	1-1	49,751	Graham
35	31/03/73	Southampton	2-0	23,161	Charlton, Holton
36	07/04/73	NORWICH CITY	1-0	48,593	Martin
37	11/04/73	CRYSTAL PALACE	2-0	46,891	Kidd, Morgan
38	14/04/73	Stoke City	2-2	37,051	Macari, Morgan
39	18/04/73	Leeds United	1-0	45,450	Anderson
40	21/04/73	MANCHESTER CITY	0-0	61,676	
41	23/04/73	SHEFFIELD UTD	1-2	57,280	Kidd
42	28/04/73	Chelsea	0-1	44,184	

Season: 1973/74

No	Date	Opponents	Score	Att	Scorers
1	25/08/73	Arsenal	0-3	51,501	
2	29/08/73	STOKE CITY	1-0	43,614	James
3	01/09/73	QUEENS PARK RGRS	2-1	44,156	Holton, McIlroy
4	05/09/73	Leicester City	0-1	29,152	
5	08/09/73	Ipswich Town	1-2	22,023	Anderson
6	12/09/73	LEICESTER CITY	1-2	40,793	Stepney
7	15/09/73	WEST HAM UTD	3-1	44,757	Kidd 2, Storey-Moore
8	22/09/73	Leeds United	0-0	47,058	
9	29/09/73	LIVERPOOL	0-0	53,882	
10	06/10/73	Wolverhampton Wdrs	1-2	32,962	McIlroy
11	13/10/73	DERBY COUNTY	0-1	43,724	
12	20/10/73	BIRMINGHAM CITY	1-0	48,937	Stepney
13	27/10/73	Burnley	0-0	31,976	
14	03/11/73	CHELSEA	2-2	48,036	Greenhoff, Young
15	10/11/73	Tottenham Hotspurs	1-2	42,756	Best
16	17/11/73	Newcastle United	2-3	41,768	Graham, Macari
17	24/11/73	NORWICH CITY	0-0	36,338	
18	08/12/73	SOUTHAMPTON	0-0	31,648	
19	15/12/73	COVANTRY CITY	2-3	28,589	Best, Morgan
20	22/12/73	Liverpool	0-2	40,420	
21	26/12/73	SHEFFIELD UTD	1-2	38,653	Macari
22	29/12/73	IPSWICH TN	2-0	36,365	Macari, McIlroy
23	01/01/74	Queens Park Rgrs	0-3	32,339	
24	12/01/74	West Ham United	1-2	34,147	McIlroy
25	19/01/74	ARSENAL	1-1	38,589	James
26	02/02/74	Coventry City	0-1	25,313	
27	09/02/74	LEEDS UTD	0-2	60,025	
28	16/02/74	Derby County	2-2	29,987	Greenhoff, Houston
29	23/02/74	WOLVERH'N WDRS	0-0	39,260	
30	02/03/74	Sheffield United	1-0	29,203	Macari
31	13/03/74	Manchester City	0-0	51,331	
32	16/03/74	Birmingham City	0-1	37,768	
33	23/03/74	TOTTENHAM	0-1	36,278	
34	30/03/74	Chelsea	3-1	29,602	Daly, McIlroy, Morgan
35	03/04/74	BURNLEY	3-3	33,336	Forsyth, Holton, McIlroy
36	06/04/74	Norwich City	2-0	28,223	Greenhoff, Macari
37	13/04/74	NEWCASTLE UTD	1-0	44,751	McCalliog
38	15/04/74	EVERTON	3-0	48,424	McCalliog 2, Houston
39	20/04/74	Southampton	1-1	30,789	McCalliog
40	23/04/74	Everton	0-1	46,093	
41	27/04/74	MANCHESTER CITY	0-1	56,996	
42	29/04/74	Stoke City	0-1	27,392	

Season: 1974/75

No	Date	Opponents	Score	Att	Scorers
1	17/08/74	Orient	2-0	17,732	Houston, Morgan
2	24/08/74	MILLWALL	4-0	44,756	Daly 3, Pearson
3	28/08/74	PORTSMOUTH	2-1	42,547	Daly, McIlroy
4	31/08/74	Cardiff City	1-0	22,344	Daly
5	07/09/74	NOTT'HAM FOREST	2-2	40,671	Greenhoff, McIlroy
6	14/09/74	West Bromwich Albion	1-1	23,721	Pearson
7	16/09/74	Millwall	1-0	16,988	Daly
8	21/09/74	BRISTOL RVRS	2-0	42,948	Greenhoff, og
9	25/09/74	BOLTON WDRS	3-0	47,084	Houston, Macari, og
10	28/09/74	Norwich City	0-2	24,586	
11	05/10/74	Fulham	2-1	26,513	Pearson 2
12	12/10/74	NOTTS COUNTY	1-0	46,565	McIlroy
13	15/10/74	Portsmouth	0-0	25,608	
14	19/10/74	Blackpool	3-0	25,370	Forsyth, Macari, McCalliog
15	26/10/74	SOUTHAMPTON	1-0	48,724	Pearson
16	02/11/74	OXFORD UTD	4-0	41,909	Pearson 3 Macari
17	09/11/74	Bristol City	0-1	28,104	
18	16/11/74	ASTON VILLA	2-1	55,615	Daly 2
19	23/11/74	Hull City	0-2	23,287	
20	30/11/74	SUNDERLAND	3-2	60,585	McIlroy, Morgan, Pearson
21	07/12/74	Sheffield Wednesday	4-4	35,230	Macari 2, Houston, Pearson
22	14/12/74	ORIENT	0-0	41,200	
23	21/12/74	York City	1-0	15,567	Pearson
24	26/12/74	WEST BROM ALBION	2-1	51,104	Daly, McIlroy
25	28/12/74	Oldham Ath	0-1	26,384	
26	11/01/75	SHEFFIELD W'DAY	2-0	45,662	McCalliog 2
27	18/01/75	Sunderland	0-0	45,976	
28	01/02/75	BRISTOL CITY	0-1	47,118	
29	08/02/75	Oxford United	0-1	15,959	
30	15/02/75	HULL CITY	2-0	44,712	Houston, Pearson
31	22/02/75	Aston Villa	0-2	39,156	
32	01/03/75	CARDIFF CITY	4-0	43,601	Houston, McIlroy, Macari, Pearson
33	08/03/75	Bolton Wanderers	1-0	38,152	Pearson
34	15/03/75	NORWICH CITY	1-1	56,202	Pearson
35	22/03/75	Nottingham Forest	1-0	21,893	Daly
36	28/03/75	Bristol City	1-1	19,337	Macari
37	29/03/75	YORK CITY	2-1	46,802	Macari, Morgan
38	31/03/75	OLDHAM ATH	3-2	56,618	Coppell, Macari, McIlroy
39	05/04/75	Southampton	1-0	21,866	Macari
40	12/04/75	FULHAM	1-0	52,971	Daly
41	19/04/75	Notts County	2-2	17,320	Greenhoff, Houston
42	26/04/75	BLACKPOOL	4-0	58,769	Pearson 2, Greenhoff, Macari

Season: 1975/76

No	Date	Opponents	Score	Att	Scorers
1	16/08/75	Wolverhampton Wdrs	2-0	32,348	Macari 2
2	19/08/75	Birmingham City	2-0	33,177	McIlroy
3	23/08/75	SHEFFIELD UTD	5-1	55,949	Pearson 2, Daly, McIlroy, og
4	27/08/75	COVENTRY CITY	1-1	52,169	Pearson
5	30/08/75	Stoke City	1-0	33,092	og
6	06/09/75	TOTTENHAM	3-2	51,641	Daly 2, og
7	13/09/75	Queens Park Rgrs	0-1	29,237	
8	20/09/75	IPSWICH TN	1-0	50,513	Houston
9	24/09/75	Derby County	1-2	33,187	Daly
10	27/09/75	Manchester City	2-2	46,931	Macari, McCreery
11	04/10/75	LEICESTER CITY	0-0	47,878	
12	11/10/75	Leeds United	2-1	40,264	McIlroy 2
13	18/10/75	ARSENAL	3-1	53,885	Coppell 2, Pearson
14	25/10/75	West Ham United	1-2	38,528	Macari
15	01/11/75	NORWICH CITY	1-0	50,587	Pearson
16	08/11/75	Liverpool	1-3	49,136	Coppell
17	15/11/75	ASTON VILLA	2-0	51,682	Coppell, McIlroy
18	22/11/75	Arsenal	1-3	40,102	Pearson
19	29/11/75	NEWCASTLE UTD	1-0	52,624	Daly
20	06/11/75	Middlesbrough	0-0	32,454	
21	13/11/75	Sheffield United	4-1	31,741	Pearson 2, Hill, Macari
22	20/11/75	WOLVERH'N WDRS	1-0	44,269	Hill
23	23/11/75	Everton	1-1	41,732	Macari
24	27/11/75	BURNLEY	2-1	59,726	Macari, McIlroy
25	10/01/76	QUEENS PARK RGRS	2-1	58,312	Hill, McIlroy
26	17/01/76	Tottenham Hotspurs	1-1	49,189	Hill
27	31/01/76	BIRMINGHAM CITY	3-1	50,724	Forsyth, Macari, McIlroy
28	07/02/76	Coventry City	1-1	33,922	Macari
29	18/02/76	LIVERPOOL	0-0	59,709	
30	21/02/76	Aston Villa	1-2	50,094	Macari
31	25/02/76	DERBY COUNTY	1-1	59,632	Pearson
32	28/02/76	WEST HAM UTD	4-0	57,220	Forsyth, Macari, McCreery, Pearson
33	13/03/76	LEEDS UTD	3-2	59,429	Daly, Houston, Pearson
34	17/03/76	Norwich City	1-1	27,787	Hill
35	20/03/76	Newcastle United	4-3	45,043	Pearson 2, 2 ogs
36	27/03/76	MIDDLESBROUGH	3-0	58,527	Daly, Hill, McCreery
37	10/04/76	Ipswich Town	0-3	34,886	
38	17/04/76	EVERTON	2-1	61,879	McCreery, og
39	19/04/76	Burnley	1-0	27,418	Macari
40	21/04/76	STOKE CITY	0-1	53,879	
41	24/04/76	Leicester City	1-2	31,053	Coyne
42	04/05/76	MANCHESTER CITY	2-0	59,517	Hill, McIlroy

Season: 1976/77

No	Date	Opponents	Score	Att	Scorers
1	21/08/76	BIRMINGHAM CITY	2-2	58,898	Coppell, Pearson
2	24/08/76	Coventry City	2-0	26,775	Hill, Macari
3	28/08/76	Derby County	0-0	30,054	
4	04/09/76	TOTTENHAM	2-3	60,723	Coppell, Pearson
5	11/09/76	Newcastle United	2-2	39,037	B.Greenhoff, Pearson
6	18/09/76	MIDDLESBROUGH	2-0	56,712	Pearson, og
7	25/09/76	Manchester City	3-1	48,861	Coppell, Daly, McCreery
8	02/10/76	Leeds United	2-0	44,512	Coppell, Daly
9	16/10/76	West Bromwich Albion	0-4	36,615	
10	23/10/76	NORWICH CITY	2-2	54,356	Daly, Hill
11	30/10/76	IPSWICH TN	0-1	57,416	
12	06/11/76	Aston Villa	2-3	44,789	Hill, Pearson
13	10/11/76	SUNDERLAND	3-3	42,685	B.Greenhoff, Hill, Pearson
14	20/11/76	Leicester City	1-1	26,421	Daly
15	27/11/76	WEST HAM UTD	0-2	55,366	
16	18/12/76	Arsenal	1-3	39,572	McIlroy
17	27/12/76	EVERTON	4-0	56,786	J.Greenhoff, Hill, Macari, Pearson
18	01/01/77	ASTON VILLA	2-0	55,446	Pearson 2
19	03/01/77	Ipswich Town	1-2	30,105	Pearson
20	15/01/77	COVENTRY CITY	2-0	46,567	Macari 2
21	19/01/77	BRISTOL CITY	2-1	43,051	B.Greenhoff, Pearson
22	22/01/77	Birmingham City	3-2	35,316	J.Greenhoff, Houston, Pearson
23	05/02/77	DERBY COUNTY	3-1	54,044	Houston, Macari, og
24	12/02/77	Tottenham Hotspurs	3-1	46,946	Hill, Macari, McIlroy
25	16/02/77	LIVERPOOL	0-0	57,487	
26	19/02/77	NEWCASTLE UTD	3-1	51,828	J.Greenhoff 3
27	05/03/77	MANCHESTER CITY	3-1	58,595	Coppell, Hill, Pearson
28	12/03/77	LEEDS UTD	1-0	60,612	og
29	23/03/77	WEST BROM ALBION	2-2	51,053	Coppell, Hill
30	02/04/77	Norwich City	1-2	24,161	og
31	05/04/77	Everton	2-1	38,216	Hill 2
32	09/04/77	STOKE CITY	3-0	53,102	Houston, Macari, Pearson
33	11/04/77	Sunderland	1-2	38,785	Hill
34	16/04/77	LEICESTER CITY	1-1	49,161	J.Greenhoff
35	19/04/77	Queens Park Rgrs	0-4	28,848	
36	26/04/77	Middlesbrough	0-3	21,744	
37	30/04/77	QUEENS PARK RGRS	1-0	50,788	Macari
38	03/05/77	Liverpool	0-1	53,046	
39	07/05/77	Bristol City	1-1	28,864	J.Greenhoff
40	10/05/77	Stoke City	3-3	24,204	Hill 2, McCreery
41	14/05/77	ARSENAL	3-2	53,232	J.Greenhoff, Hill, Macari
42	16/05/77	West Ham United	2-4	29,904	Hill, Pearson

Season: 1977/78

No	Date	Opponents	Score	Att	Scorers
1	20/08/77	Birmingham City	4-1	28,005	Macari 3, Hill
2	24/08/77	COVENTRY CITY	2-1	55,726	Hill, McCreery
3	27/08/77	IPSWICH TN	0-0	57,904	
4	03/09/77	Derby County	1-0	21,279	Macari
5	10/09/77	Manchester City	1-3	50,856	Nicholl
6	17/09/77	CHELSEA	0-1	54,951	
7	24/09/77	Leeds United	1-1	33,517	Hill
8	01/10/77	LIVERPOOL	2-0	55,089	Macari, McIlroy
9	08/10/77	Middlesbrough	1-2	26,822	Coppell
10	15/10/77	NEWCASTLE UTD	3-2	55,056	Coppell, J.Greenhoff, Macari
11	22/10/77	West Bromwich Albion	0-4	27,526	
12	29/10/77	Aston Villa	1-2	39,144	Nicholl
13	05/11/77	ARSENAL	1-2	53,055	Hill
14	12/11/77	Nottingham Forest	1-2	30,183	Pearson
15	19/11/77	NORWICH CITY	1-0	48,729	Pearson
16	26/11/77	Queens Park Rgrs	2-2	25,367	Hill 2
17	03/12/77	WOLVERH'N WDRS	3-1	48,874	J.Greenhoff, McIlroy, Pearson
18	10/12/77	West Ham United	1-2	20,242	McGrath
19	17/12/77	NOTT'HAM FOREST	0-4	54,374	
20	26/12/77	Everton	6-2	48,335	Macari 2, Coppell, J.Greenhoff, Hill, McIlroy
21	27/12/77	LEICESTER CITY	3-1	57,396	Coppell, J.Greenhoff, Hill
22	31/12/77	Coventry City	0-3	24,706	
23	02/01/78	BIRMINGHAM CITY	1-2	53,501	J.Greenhoff
24	14/01/78	Ipswich Town	2-1	23,321	McIlroy, Pearson
25	21/01/78	DERBY COUNTY	4-0	57,115	Hill 2, Buchan, Pearson
26	08/02/78	BRISTOL CITY	1-1	43,457	Hill
27	11/02/78	Chelsea	2-2	32,849	Hill, McIlroy
28	25/02/78	Liverpool	1-3	49,094	McIlroy
29	01/03/78	LEEDS UTD	0-1	49,101	
30	04/03/78	MIDDLESBROUGH	0-0	46,332	
31	11/03/78	Newcastle United	2-2	25,825	Hill, Jordan
32	15/03/78	MANCHESTER CITY	2-2	58,398	Hill 2
33	18/03/78	WEST BROM ALBION	1-1	46,329	McQueen
34	25/03/78	Leicester City	3-2	20,299	J.Greenhoff, Hill, Pearson
35	27/03/78	EVERTON	1-2	55,277	Hill
36	29/03/78	ASTON VILLA	1-1	41,625	McIlroy
37	01/04/78	Arsenal	1-3	40,829	Jordan
38	08/04/78	QUEENS PARK RGRS	3-1	42,677	Pearson 2, Grimes
39	15/04/78	Norwich City	3-1	19,778	Coppell, Jordan, McIlroy
40	22/04/78	WEST HAM UTD	3-0	54,089	Grimes, McIlroy, Pearson
41	25/04/78	Bristol City	1-0	26,035	Pearson
42	29/04/78	Wolverhampton Wdrs	1-2	24,774	B.Greenhoff

Season: 1978/79

No	Date	Opponents	Score	Att	Scorers
1	19/08/78	BIRMINGHAM CITY	1-0	56,139	Jordan
2	23/08/78	Leeds United	3-2	36,845	Macari, McIlroy, McQueen
3	26/08/78	Ipswich Town	0-3	21,802	
4	02/09/78	EVERTON	1-1	53,982	Buchan
5	09/09/78	Queens Park Rgrs	1-1	23,477	J.Greenhoff
6	16/09/78	NOTT'HAM FOREST	1-1	53,039	J.Greenhoff
7	23/09/78	Arsenal	1-1	45,393	Coppell
8	30/09/78	MANCHESTER CITY	1-0	55,301	Jordan
9	07/10/78	MIDDLESBROUGH	3-2	45,402	Macari 2, Jordan
10	14/10/78	Aston Villa	2-2	36,204	Macari, McIlroy
11	21/10/78	BRISTOL CITY	1-3	47,211	J.Greenhoff
12	28/10/78	Wolverhampton Wdrs	4-2	23,141	J.Greenhoff, B.Greenhoff, Jordan
13	04/11/78	SOUTHAMPTON	1-1	46,259	J.Greenhoff
14	11/11/78	Birmingham City	1-5	23,550	Jordan
15	18/11/78	IPSWICH TN	2-0	42,109	Coppell, J.Greenhoff
16	21/11/78	Everton	0-3	42,126	
17	25/11/78	Chelsea	1-0	28,162	J.Greenhoff
18	09/12/78	Derby County	3-1	23,180	Ritchie 2, J.Greenhoff
19	16/12/78	TOTTENHAM	2-0	52,026	McIlroy, Ritchie
20	22/12/78	Bolton Wanderers	0-3	32,390	
21	26/12/78	LIVERPOOL	0-3	54,910	
22	30/12/78	WEST BROM ALBION	3-5	45,091	B.Greenhoff, McIlroy, McQueen
23	03/02/79	ARSENAL	0-2	45,460	
24	10/02/79	Manchester City	3-0	46,151	Coppell 2, Ritchie
25	24/02/79	ASTON VILLA	1-1	44,437	J.Greenhoff
26	28/02/79	QUEENS PARK RGRS	2-0	36,085	Coppell, J.Greenhoff
27	03/03/79	Bristol City	2-1	24,583	McQueen, Ritchie
28	20/03/79	Coventry City	3-4	25,382	Coppell 2, McIlroy
29	24/03/79	LEEDS UTD	4-1	51,191	Ritchie 3, Thomas
30	27/03/79	Middlesbrough	2-2	20,138	Coppell, McQueen
31	07/04/79	Norwich City	2-2	19,382	Macari, McQueen
32	11/04/79	BOLTON WDRS	1-2	49,617	Buchan
33	14/04/79	Liverpool	0-2	46,608	
34	16/04/79	COVENTRY CITY	0-0	43,035	
35	18/04/79	Nottingham Forest	1-1	33,074	Jordan
36	21/04/79	Tottenham Hotspurs	1-1	36,665	McQueen
37	25/04/79	NORWICH CITY	1-0	33,678	Macari
38	28/04/79	DERBY COUNTY	0-0	42,546	
39	30/04/79	Southampton	1-1	21,616	Ritchie
40	05/05/79	West Bromwich Albion	0-1	27,960	
41	07/05/79	WOLVERH'N WDRS	3-2	39,402	Coppell 2, Ritchie
42	16/05/79	CHELSEA	1-1	38,109	Coppell

Season: 1979/80

No	Date	Opponents	Score	Att	Scorers
1	18/08/79	Southampton	1-1	21,768	McQueen
2	22/08/79	WEST BROM ALBION	2-0	53,377	Coppell, McQueen
3	25/08/79	Arsenal	0-0	44,380	
4	01/09/79	MIDDLESBROUGH	2-1	51,015	Macari 2
5	08/09/79	Aston Villa	3-0	34,859	Coppell, Grimes, Thomas
6	15/09/79	DERBY COUNTY	1-0	54,308	Grimes
7	22/09/79	Wolverhampton Wdrs	1-3	35,503	Macari
8	29/09/79	STOKE CITY	4-0	52,596	McQueen 2, McIlroy, Wilkins
9	06/10/79	BRIGHTON & HOVE	2-0	52,641	Coppell, Macari
10	10/10/79	West Bromwich Albion	0-2	27,713	
11	13/10/79	Bristol City	1-1	28,305	Macari
12	20/10/79	IPSWICH TN	1-0	50,826	Grimes
13	27/10/79	Everton	0-0	37,708	
14	03/11/79	SOUTHAMPTON	1-0	50,215	Macari
15	10/11/79	Manchester City	0-2	50,067	
16	17/11/79	CRYSTAL PALACE	1-1	52,800	Jordan
17	24/11/79	NORWICH CITY	5-0	46,540	Jordan 2, Coppell, Macari, Moran
18	01/12/79	Tottenham Hotspurs	2-1	51,389	Coppell, Macari
19	08/12/79	LEEDS UTD	1-1	58,348	Thomas
20	15/12/79	Coventry City	2-1	25,541	Macari, McQueen
21	22/12/79	NOTT'HAM FOREST	3-0	54,607	Jordan 2, McQueen
22	26/12/79	Liverpool	0-2	51,073	
23	29/12/79	ARSENAL	3-0	54,295	Jordan, McIlroy, McQueen
24	12/01/80	Middlesbrough	1-1	30,587	Thomas
25	02/02/80	Derby County	3-1	27,783	McIlroy, Thomas, og
26	09/02/80	WOLVERH'N WDRS	0-1	51,568	
27	16/02/80	Stoke City	1-1	28,389	Coppell
28	23/02/80	BRISTOL CITY	4-0	43,329	Jordan 2, McIlroy, og
29	27/02/80	BOLTON WDRS	2-0	47,546	Coppell, McQueen
30	01/03/80	Ipswich Town	0-6	30,229	
31	12/03/80	EVERTON	0-0	45,515	
32	15/03/80	Brighton & Hove Albion	0-0	29,621	
33	22/03/80	MANCHESTER CITY	1-0	56,387	Thomas
34	29/03/80	Crystal Palace	2-0	33,056	Jordan, Thomas
35	02/04/80	Nottingham Forest	0-2	31,417	
36	05/04/80	LIVERPOOL	2-1	57,342	Greenhoff, Thomas
37	07/04/80	Bolton Wanderers	3-1	31,902	Coppell, McQueen, Thomas
38	12/04/80	TOTTENHAM	4-1	53,151	Ritchie 3, Wilkins
39	19/04/80	Norwich City	2-0	23,274	Jordan 2
40	23/04/80	ASTON VILLA	2-1	45,201	Jordan 2
41	26/04/80	COVENTRY CITY	2-1	52,154	McIlroy 2
42	03/05/80	Leeds United	0-2	39,625	

Season: 1980/81

No	Date	Opponents	Score	Att	Scorers
1	16/08/80	MIDDLESBROUGH	3-0	54,394	Grimes, Macari, Thomas
2	19/08/80	Wolverhampton Wdrs	0-1	31,955	
3	23/08/80	Birmingham City	0-0	28,661	
4	30/08/80	SUNDERLAND	1-1	51,498	Jovanovic
5	06/09/80	Tottenham Hotspurs	0-0	40,995	
6	13/09/80	LEICESTER CITY	5-0	43,229	Jovanovic 2, Coppell, Grimes, Macari
7	20/09/80	Leeds United	0-0	32,539	
8	27/09/80	MANCHESTER CITY	2-2	55,918	Albiston, Coppell
9	04/10/80	Nottingham Forest	2-1	29,801	Coppell, Macari
10	08/10/80	ASTON VILLA	3-3	38,831	McIlroy 2, Coppell
11	11/10/80	ARSENAL	0-0	49,036	
12	18/10/80	Ipswich Town	1-1	28,572	McIlroy
13	22/10/80	Stoke City	2-1	24,534	Jordan, Macari
14	25/10/80	EVERTON	2-0	54,260	Coppell, Jordan
15	01/11/80	Crystal Palace	0-1	31,449	
16	08/11/80	COVENTRY CITY	0-0	42,794	
17	12/11/80	WOLVERH'N WDRS	0-0	37,959	
18	15/11/80	Middlesbrough	1-1	20,606	Jordan
19	22/11/80	Brighton & Hove Albion	4-1	23,293	Jordan 2, Duxbury, McIlroy
20	29/11/80	SOUTHAMPTON	1-1	46,840	Jordan
21	06/12/80	Norwich City	2-2	18,780	Coppell, og
22	13/12/80	STOKE CITY	2-2	39,568	Jordan,Macari
23	20/12/80	Arsenal	1-2	33,730	Macari
24	26/12/80	LIVERPOOL	0-0	57,049	
25	27/12/80	West Bromwich Albion	1-3	30,326	Jovanovic
26	10/01/81	BRIGHTON & HOVE	2-1	42,208	Macari, McQueen
27	28/01/81	Sunderland	0-2	31,910	
28	31/01/81	BIRMINGHAM CITY	2-0	39,081	Jordan, Macari
29	07/02/81	Leicester City	0-1	26,085	
30	17/02/81	TOTTENHAM	0-0	40,642	
31	21/02/81	Manchester City	0-1	50,114	
32	28/02/81	LEEDS UTD	0-1	45,733	
33	07/03/81	Southampton	0-1	22,698	
34	14/03/81	Aston Villa	3-3	42,182	Jordan 2, McIlroy
35	18/03/81	NOTT'HAM FOREST	1-1	38,205	og
36	21/03/81	IPSWICH TN	2-1	46,685	Nicholl, Thomas
37	28/03/81	Everton	1-0	25,856	Jordan
38	04/04/81	CRYSTAL PALACE	1-0	37,954	Duxbury
39	11/04/81	Coventry City	2-0	20,201	Jordan 2
40	14/04/81	Liverpool	1-0	31,276	McQueen
41	18/04/81	WEST BROM ALBION	2-1	44,442	Jordan, Macari
42	25/04/81	NORWICH CITY	1-0	40,165	Jordan

Season: 1981/82

No	Date	Opponents	Score	Att	Scorers
1	29/08/81	Coventry ity	1-2	19,329	Macari
2	31/08/81	NOTT'HAM FOREST	0-0	51,496	
3	05/09/81	IPSWICH TN	1-2	45,555	Stapleton
4	12/09/81	Aston Villa	1-1	37,661	Stapleton
5	19/09/81	SWANSEA CITY	1-0	47,309	Birtles
6	22/09/81	Middlesbrough	2-0	19,895	Birtles, Stapleton
7	26/09/81	Arsenal	0-0	39,795	
8	30/09/81	LEEDS UTD	1-0	47,019	Stapleton
9	03/10/81	WOLVERH'N WDRS	5-0	46,837	McIlroy 3, Birtles, Stapleton
10	10/10/81	Manchester City	0-0	52,037	
11	17/10/81	BIRMINGHAM CITY	1-1	48,800	Coppell
12	21/10/81	MIDDLESBROUGH	1-0	38,342	Moses
13	24/10/81	Liverpool	2-1	41,438	Albiston, Moran
14	31/10/81	NOTTS COUNTY	2-1	45,928	Birtles, Moses
15	07/11/81	Sunderland	5-1	27,070	Stapleton 2, Birtles, Moran, Robson
16	21/11/81	Tottenham Hotspurs	1-3	35,534	Birtles
17	28/11/81	BRIGHTON & HOVE	2-0	41,911	Birtles, Stapleton
18	05/12/81	Southampton	2-3	24,404	Robson, Stapleton
19	06/01/82	EVERTON	1-1	40,451	Stapleton
20	23/01/82	Stoke City	3-0	19,793	Birtles, Coppell, Stapleton
21	27/01/82	WEST HAM UTD	1-0	41,291	Macari
22	30/01/82	Swansea City	0-2	24,115	
23	06/02/82	ASTON VILLA	4-1	43,184	Moran 2, Coppell, Robson
24	13/02/82	Wolverhampton Wdrs	1-0	22,481	Birtles
25	20/02/82	ARSENAL	0-0	43,833	
26	27/02/82	MANCHESTER CITY	1-1	57,830	Moran
27	06/03/82	Birmingham City	1-0	19,637	Birtles
28	17/03/82	COVENTRY CITY	0-1	34,499	
29	20/03/82	Notts County	3-1	17,048	Coppell 2, Stapleton
30	27/03/82	SUNDERLAND	0-0	40,776	
31	03/04/82	Leeds United	0-0	30,953	
32	07/04/82	LIVERPOOL	0-1	48,371	
33	10/04/82	Everton	3-3	29,306	Coppell 2, Grimes
34	12/04/82	WEST BROM ALBION	1-0	38,717	Moran
35	17/04/82	TOTTENHAM	2-0	50,724	Coppell, McGarvey
36	20/04/82	Ipswich Town	1-2	25,744	Gidman
37	24/04/82	Brighton & Hove	1-0	20,750	Wilkins
38	01/05/82	SOUTHAMPTON	1-0	40,038	McGarvey
39	05/05/82	Nottingham Forest	1-0	18,449	Stapleton
40	08/05/82	West Ham United	1-1	26,337	Moran
41	12/05/82	West Bromwich Albion	3-0	19,707	Birtles, Coppell, Robson
42	15/05/82	STOKE CITY	2-0	43,072	Robson, Whiteside

Season: 1982/83

No	Date	Opponents	Score	Att	Scorers
1	28/08/82	BIRMINGHAM CITY	3-0	48,673	Coppell, Moran, Stapleton
2	01/09/82	Nottingham Forest	3-0	23,956	Robson, Whiteside, Wilkins
3	04/09/82	West Bromwich Albion	1-3	24,928	Robson
4	08/09/82	EVERTON	2-1	43,186	Robson, Whiteside
5	11/09/82	IPSWICH TN	3-1	43,140	Whiteside 2, Coppell
6	18/09/82	Southampton	1-0	21,700	Macari
7	25/09/82	ARSENAL	0-0	43,198	
8	02/10/82	Luton Town	1-1	17,009	Grimes
9	09/10/82	STOKE CITY	1-0	43,132	Robson
10	16/10/82	Liverpool	0-0	40,853	
11	11/10/82	MANCHESTER CITY	2-2	57,334	Stapleton 2
12	30/10/82	West Ham United	1-3	31,684	Moran
13	06/11/82	Brighton & Hove Albion	0-1	18,379	
14	13/11/82	TOTTENHAM	1-0	47,869	Muhren
15	20/11/82	Aston Villa	1-2	35,487	Stapleton
16	27/11/82	NORWICH CITY	3-0	34,579	Robson 2, Muhren
17	04/12/82	Watford	1-0	25,669	Whiteside
18	11/12/82	NOTTS COUNTY	4-0	33,618	Duxbury, Robson, Stapleton, Whiteside
19	18/12/82	Swansea City	0-0	15,748	
20	27/12/82	SUNDERLAND	0-0	47,783	
21	28/12/82	Coventry City	0-3	18,945	
22	01/01/83	ASTON VILLA	3-1	41,545	Stapleton 2, Coppell
23	03/01/83	WEST BROM ALBION	0-0	39,123	
24	15/01/83	Birmingham City	2-1	19,333	Robson, Whiteside
25	22/01/83	NOTT'HAM FOREST	2-0	38,615	Coppell, Muhren
26	05/02/83	Ipswich Town	1-1	23,804	Stapleton
27	26/02/83	LIVERPOOL	1-1	57,397	Muhren
28	02/03/83	Stoke City	0-1	21,266	
29	05/03/83	Manchester City	2-1	45,400	Stapleton 2
30	19/03/83	BRIGHTON & HOVE	1-1	36,264	Albiston
31	22/03/83	WEST HAM UTD	2-1	30,227	McGarvey, Stapleton
32	02/04/83	COVENTRY CITY	3-0	36,814	Macari, Stapleton, og
33	04/04/83	Sunderland	0-0	31,486	
34	09/04/83	SOUTHAMPTON	1-1	37,120	Robson
35	19/04/83	Everton	0-2	21,715	
36	23/04/83	WATFORD	2-0	43,048	Cunningham, Grimes
37	30/04/83	Norwich City	1-1	22,233	Whiteside
38	02/05/83	Arsenal	0-3	23,602	
39	07/05/83	SWANSEA CITY	2-1	35,724	Robson, Stapleton
40	09/05/83	LUTON TN	3-0	34,213	McGrath 2, Stapleton
41	11/05/83	Tottenham Hotspurs	0-2	32,803	
42	14/05/83	Notts County	2-3	14,395	McGrath, Muhren

Season: 1983/84

No	Date	Opponents	Score	Att	Scorers
1	27/08/83	QUEENS PARK RGRS	3-1	48,742	Muhren 2, Stapleton
2	29/08/83	NOTT'HAM FOREST	1-2	43,005	Moran
3	03/09/83	Stoke City	1-0	23,704	Muhren
4	06/09/83	Arsenal	3-2	42,703	Moran, Robson, Stapleton
5	10/09/83	LUTON TN	2-0	41,013	Muhren, Albiston
6	17/09/83	Southampton	0-3	20,674	
7	24/09/83	LIVERPOOL	1-0	56,121	Stapleton
8	01/10/83	Norwich City	3-3	19,290	Whiteside 2, Stapleton
9	15/10/83	WEST BROM ALBION	3-0	42,221	Albiston, Graham, Whiteside
10	22/10/83	Sunderland	1-0	26,826	Wilkins
11	29/10/83	WOLVERH'N WDRS	3-0	41,880	Stapleton 2, Robson
12	05/11/83	ASTON VILLA	1-2	45,077	Robson
13	12/11/83	Leicester City	1-1	24,409	Robson
14	19/11/83	WATFORD	4-1	43,111	Stapleton 3, Robson
15	27/11/83	West Ham United	1-1	23,355	Wilkins
16	03/12/83	EVERTON	0-1	43,664	
17	10/12/83	Ipswich Town	2-0	19,779	Crooks, Graham
18	16/12/83	TOTTENHAM	4-2	33,616	Graham 2, Moran 2
19	26/12/83	Coventry City	1-1	21,553	Muhren
20	27/12/83	NOTTS COUNTY	3-3	41,544	Crooks, McQueen, Moran
21	31/12/83	STOKE CITY	1-0	40,164	Graham
22	02/01/84	Liverpool	1-1	44,622	Whiteside
23	13/01/84	Queens Park Rgrs	1-1	16,308	Robson
24	21/01/84	SOUTHAMPTON	3-2	40,371	Muhren, Robson, Stapleton
25	04/02/84	NORWICH CITY	0-0	36,851	
26	07/02/84	Birmingham City	2-2	19,957	Hogg, Whiteside
27	12/02/84	Luton Town	5-0	11,265	Robson 2, Whiteside 2, Stapleton
28	18/02/84	Wolverhampton Wdrs	1-1	20,676	Whiteside
29	25/02/84	SUNDERLAND	2-1	40,615	Moran 2
30	03/03/84	Aston Villa	3-0	32,874	Moses, Robson, Whiteside
31	10/03/84	LEICESTER CITY	2-0	39,473	Hughes, Moses
32	17/03/84	ARSENAL	4-0	48,942	Muhren 2, Robson, Stapleton
33	31/03/84	West Bromwich Albion	0-2	28,104	
34	07/04/84	BIRMINGHAM CITY	1-0	39,896	Robson
35	14/04/84	Notts County	0-1	13,911	
36	17/04/84	Watford	0-0	20,764	
37	21/04/84	COVENTRY CITY	4-1	38,524	Hughes 2, McGrath, Wilkins
38	28/04/84	WEST HAM UTD	0-0	44,124	
39	05/05/84	Everton	1-1	28,802	Stapleton
40	07/05/84	IPSWICH TN	1-2	44,257	Hughes
41	12/05/84	Tottenham Hotspurs	1-1	39,790	Whiteside
42	16/05/84	Nottingham Forest	0-2	23,651	

Season: 1984/85

No	Date	Opponents	Score	Att	Scorers
1	25/08/84	WATFORD	1-1	53,668	Strachan
2	28/08/84	Southampton	0-0	22,183	
3	01/09/84	Ipswich Town	1-1	20,876	Hughes
4	05/09/84	CHELSEA	1-1	48,398	Olsen
5	08/09/84	NEWCASTLE UTD	5-0	54,915	Strachan 2, Hughes, Moses, Olsen
6	15/09/84	Coventry City	3-0	18,312	Whiteside 2, Robson
7	22/09/84	LIVERPOOL	1-1	56,638	Strachan
8	29/09/84	West Bromwich Albion	2-1	26,292	Robson, Strachan
9	06/10/84	Aston Villa	0-3	37,131	
10	13/10/84	WEST HAM UTD	5-1	47,559	Brazil, Hughes, McQueen, Moses, Strachan
11	20/10/84	TOTTENHAM	1-0	54,516	Hughes
12	27/10/84	Everton	0-5	40,742	
13	02/11/84	ARSENAL	4-2	32,279	Strachan 2, Hughes, Robson
14	10/11/84	Leicester City	3-2	23,840	Brazil, Hughes, Strachan
15	17/11/84	LUTON TN	2-0	41,630	Whiteside 2
16	24/11/84	Sunderland	2-3	25,405	Hughes, Robson
17	01/12/84	NORWICH CITY	2-0	36,635	Hughes, Robson
18	08/12/84	Nottingham Forest	2-3	25,902	Strachan 2
19	15/12/84	QUEENS PARK RGRS	3-0	36,134	Brazil, Duxbury, Gidman
20	22/12/84	IPSWICH TN	3-0	35,168	Gidman, Robson, Strachan
21	26/12/84	Stoke City	1-2	20,985	Stapleton
22	29/12/84	Chelsea	3-1	42,197	Hughes, Moses, Stapleton
23	01/01/85	SHEFFIELD W'DAY	1-2	47,625	Hughes
24	12/01/85	COVENTRY CITY	0-1	35,992	
25	02/02/85	WEST BROM ALBION	2-0	36,681	Strachan 2
26	09/02/85	Newcastle United	1-1	32,555	Moran
27	23/02/85	Arsenal	1-0	48,612	Whiteside
28	02/03/85	EVERTON	1-1	51,150	Olsen
29	12/03/85	Tottenham Hotspurs	2-1	42,908	Hughes, Whiteside
30	15/03/85	West Ham United	2-2	16,674	Robson, Stapleton
31	23/03/85	ASTON VILLA	4-0	40,941	Hughes 3, Whiteside
32	31/03/85	Liverpool	1-0	34,886	Stapleton
33	03/04/85	LEICESTER CITY	2-1	35,590	Robson, Stapleton
34	06/04/85	STOKE CITY	5-0	42,940	Hughes 2, Olsen 2, Whiteside
35	09/04/85	Sheffield Wednesday	0-1	39,380	
36	21/04/85	Luton Town	1-2	10,320	Whiteside
37	24/04/85	SOUTHAMPTON	0-0	31,291	
38	27/04/85	SUNDERLAND	2-2	38,979	Moran, Robson
39	04/05/85	Norwich City	1-0	15,502	Moran
40	06/05/85	NOTT'HAM FOREST	2-0	41,775	Gidman, Stapleton
41	11/05/85	Queens Park Rgrs	3-1	20,483	Brazil 2, Strachan
42	13/05/85	Watford	1-5	20,500	Moran

Season: 1985/86

No	Date	Opponents	Score	Att	Scorers
1	17/08/85	ASTON VILLA	4-0	49,743	Hughes 2, Olsen, Whiteside
2	20/08/85	Ipswich Town	1-0	18,777	Robson
3	24/08/85	Arsenal	2-1	37,145	Hughes, McGrath
4	26/08/85	WEST HAM UTD	2-0	50,773	Hughes, Strachan
5	31/08/85	Nottingham Forest	3-1	26,274	Barnes, Hughes, Stapleton
6	04/09/85	NEWCASTLE UTD	3-0	51,102	Stapleton 2, Hughes
7	07/09/85	OXFORD UTD	3-0	51,820	Barnes, Robson, Whiteside
8	14/09/85	Manchester City	3-0	48,773	Albiston, Duxbury, Robson
9	21/09/85	West Bromwich Albion	5-1	25,068	Brazil 2, Blackmore, Stapleton, Strachan
10	28/09/85	SOUHTHAMPTON	1-0	52,449	Hughes
11	05/10/85	Luton Town	1-1	17,454	Hughes
12	12/10/85	QUEENS PARK RGRS	2-0	48,845	Hughes, Olsen
13	19/10/85	LIVERPOOL	1-1	54,492	McGrath
14	26/10/85	Chelsea	2-1	42,485	Hughes, Olsen
15	02/11/85	COVENTRY CITY	2-0	46,748	Olsen 2
16	09/11/85	Sheffield Wednesday	0-1	48,105	
17	16/11/85	TOTTENHAM	0-0	54,575	
18	23/11/85	Leicester City	0-3	22,008	
19	30/11/85	WATFORD	1-1	42,181	Brazil
20	07/12/85	IPSWICH TN	1-0	37,981	Stapleton
21	14/12/85	Aston Villa	3-1	27,626	Blackmore, Hughes, Strachan
22	21/12/85	ARSENAL	0-1	44,386	
23	26/12/85	Everton	1-3	42,551	Stapleton
24	01/01/86	BIRMINGHAM CITY	1-0	43,095	C.Gibson
25	11/01/86	Oxford United	3-1	13,280	C.Gibson, Hughes, Whiteside
26	18/01/86	NOT'HAM FOREST	2-3	46,717	Olsen 2
27	02/02/86	West Ham United	1-2	22,642	robson
28	09/02/86	Liverpool	1-1	35,064	C.Gibson
29	22/02/86	WEST BROM ALBION	3-0	45,193	Olsen 3
30	01/03/86	Southampton	0-1	19,012	
31	15/03/86	Queens Park Rgrs	0-1	23,407	
32	19/03/86	LUTON TN	2-0	33,668	Hughes, McGrath
33	22/03/86	MANCHESTER CITY	2-2	51,274	C.Gibson, Strachan
34	29/03/86	Birmingham City	1-1	22,551	Robson
35	31/03/86	EVERTON	0-0	51,189	
36	05/04/86	Coventry City	3-1	17,160	C.Gibson, Robson, Strachan
37	09/04/86	CHELSEA	1-2	45,355	Olsen
38	13/04/86	SHEFFIELD W'DAY	0-2	32,331	
39	16/04/86	Newcastle United	4-2	31,840	Hughes 2, Robson, Whiteside
40	19/04/86	Tottenham Hotspurs	0-0	32,357	
41	26/04/86	LEICESTER CITY	4-0	38,840	Blackmore, Davenport, Hughes, Stapleton
42	03/05/86	Watford	1-1	18,414	Hughes

Season: 1986/87

No	Date	Opponents	Score	Att	Scorers
1	23/08/86	Arsenal	0-1	41,382	
2	25/08/86	WEST HAM UTD	2-3	43,306	Stapleton, Davenport
3	30/08/86	CHARLTON ATH	0-1	37,544	
4	06/09/86	Leicester City	1-1	16,785	Whiteside
5	13/09/86	SOUTHAMPTON	5-1	40,135	Stapleton 2, Olsen, Davenport, Whiteside
6	16/09/86	Watford	0-1	21,650	
7	21/09/86	Everton	1-3	25,843	Robson
8	28/09/86	CHELSEA	0-1	33,340	
9	04/10/86	Nottingham Forest	1-1	34,828	Robson
10	11/10/86	SHEFFIELD W'DAY	3-1	45,890	Davenport 2, Whiteside
11	18/10/86	LUTON TN	1-0	39,927	Stapleton
12	26/10/86	Manchester City	1-1	32,440	Stapleton
13	01/11/86	COVENTRY CITY	1-1	36,946	Davenport
14	08/11/86	Oxford United	0-2	13,545	
15	15/11/86	Norwich City	0-0	22,684	
16	22/11/86	QUEENS PARK RGRS	1-0	42,235	Sivebaek
17	29/11/86	Wimbledon	0-1	12,112	
18	07/12/86	TOTTENHAM	3-3	35,957	Davenport 2, Whiteside
19	13/12/86	Aston Villa	3-3	29,205	Davenport 2, Whiteside
20	20/12/86	LEICESTER CITY	2-0	34,180	C.Gibson, Stapleton
21	26/12/86	Liverpool	1-0	40,663	Whiteside
22	27/12/86	NORWICH CITY	0-1	44,610	
23	01/01/87	NEWCASTLE UTD	4-1	43,334	Whiteside, Stapleton, Olsen, og
24	03/01/87	Southampton	1-1	20,409	Olsen
25	24/01/87	ARSENAL	2-0	51,367	Strachan, T.Gibson
26	07/02/87	Charlton Ath	0-0	15,482	
27	14/02/87	WATFORD	3-1	35,763	McGrath, Davenport, Strachan
28	21/02/87	Chelsea	1-1	26,516	Davenport
29	28/02/87	EVERTON	0-0	47,421	
30	07/03/87	MANCHESTER CITY	2-0	48,619	Robson, og
31	14/03/87	Luton Town	1-2	12,509	Robson
32	21/03/87	Sheffield Wednesday	0-1	29,888	
33	28/03/87	NOTT'HAM FOREST	2-0	39,182	McGrath, Robson
34	04/04/87	OXFORD UTD	3-2	32,443	Davenport 2, Robson
35	14/04/87	West Ham United	0-0	23,486	
36	18/04/87	Newcastle United	1-2	32,706	Strachan
37	20/04/87	LIVERPOOL	1-0	54,103	Davenport
38	25/04/87	Queens Park Rgrs	1-1	17,414	Strachan
39	02/05/87	WIMBLEDON	0-1	31,686	
40	04/05/87	Tottenham Hotspurs	0-4	36,692	
41	06/05/87	Coventry City	1-1	23,407	Whiteside
42	09/05/87	ASTON VILLA	3-1	35,179	Blackmore, Duxbury, Robson

Season: 1987/88

No	Date	Opponents	Score	Att	Scorers
1	15/08/87	Southampton	2-2	21,214	Whiteside 2
2	19/08/87	ARSENAL	0-0	42,890	
3	22/08/87	WATFORD	2-0	38,582	McGrath, McClair
4	29/08/87	Charlton Ath	3-1	14,046	McClair, Strachan, Whiteside
5	31/08/87	CHELSEA	3-1	46,478	McClair, Strachan, Whiteside
6	05/09/87	Coventry City	0-0	27,125	
7	12/09/87	NEWCASTLE UTD	2-2	45,137	Olsen, McClair
8	19/09/87	Everton	1-2	38,439	Whiteside
9	26/09/87	TOTTENHAM	1-0	47,601	McClair
10	03/10/87	Luton Town	1-1	9,137	McClair
11	10/10/87	Sheffield Wednesday	4-2	32,779	McClair 2, Robson, Blackmore
12	17/10/87	NORWICH CITY	2-1	39,345	Davenport, Robson
13	25/10/87	West Ham United	1-1	19,863	Gibson
14	31/10/87	NOTT'HAM FOREST	2-2	44,669	Robson, Whiteside
15	15/10/87	LIVERPOOL	1-1	47,106	Whiteside
16	21/10/87	Wimbledon	1-2	11,532	Blackmore
17	05/12/87	Queens Park Rgrs	2-0	20,632	Davenport, Robson
18	12/12/87	OXFORD UTD	3-1	34,709	Strachan 2, Olsen
19	19/12/87	Portsmouth	2-1	22,207	Robson, McClair
20	26/12/87	Newcastle United	0-1	26,461	
21	28/12/87	EVERTON	2-1	47,024	McClair 2
22	01/01/88	CHARLTON ATH	0-0	37,257	
23	02/01/88	Watford	1-0	18,038	McClair
24	16/01/88	SOUTHAMPTON	0-2	35,716	
25	24/01/88	Arsenal	2-1	29,392	Strachan, McClair
26	06/02/88	COVENTRY CITY	1-0	37,144	O'Brien
27	10/02/88	Derby County	2-1	20,016	Whitside, Strachan
28	13/02/88	Chelsea	2-1	25,014	Bruce, O'Brien
29	23/02/88	Tottenham Hotspurs	1-1	25,731	McClair
30	05/03/88	Norwich City	0-1	19,129	
31	12/03/88	SHEFFIELD W'DAY	4-1	33,318	McClair 2, Blackmore, Davenport
32	19/03/88	Nottingham Forest	0-0	27,598	
33	26/03/88	WEST HAM UTD	3-1	37,269	Strachan, Anderson, Robson
34	02/04/88	DERBY COUNTY	4-1	40,146	McClair 3, Gibson
35	04/04/88	Liverpool	3-3	43,497	Robson 2, Strachan
36	12/04/88	LUTON TN	3-0	28,830	McClair, Robson, Davenport
37	30/04/88	QUEENS PARK RGRS	2-1	35,733	Bruce, Parker
38	02/05/88	Oxford United	2-0	8,966	Anderson, Strachan
39	07/05/88	PORTSMOUTH	4-1	35,105	McClair 2, Davenport, Robson
40	09/05/88	WIMBLEDON	2-1	28,040	McClair 2

Season: 1988/89

No	Date	Opponents	Score	Att	Scorers
1	27/08/88	QUEENS PARK RGRS	0-0	46,377	
2	03/09/88	Liverpool	0-1	42,026	
3	10/09/88	MIDDLESBROUGH	1-0	40,422	Robson
4	17/09/88	Luton Town	2-0	11,010	Davenport, Robson
5	24/09/88	WEST HAM UTD	2-0	39,941	Davenport, Hughes
6	01/10/88	Tottenham Hotspurs	2-2	29,318	Hughes, McClair
7	22/10/88	Wimbledon	1-1	12,143	Hughes
8	26/10/88	NORWICH CITY	1-2	36,998	Hughes
9	30/10/88	Everton	1-1	27,005	Hughes
10	05/11/88	ASTON VILLA	1-1	44,804	Bruce
11	12/11/88	Derby County	2-2	24,080	Hughes, McClair
12	19/11/88	SOUTHAMPTON	2-2	37,277	Robson, Hughes
13	23/11/88	SHEFFIELD W'DAY	1-1	30,867	Hughes
14	27/11/88	Newcastle United	0-0	20,350	
15	03/12/88	CHARLTON ATH	3-0	31,113	Milne, McClair, Hughes
16	10/12/88	Coventry City	0-1	19,936	
17	17/12/88	Arsenal	1-2	37,422	Hughes
18	26/12/88	NOTT'HAM FOREST	2-0	39.582	Milne, Hughes
19	01/01/89	LIVERPOOL	3-1	44,745	McClair, Hughes, Beardsmore
20	02/01/89	Middlesbrough	0-1	24,411	
21	14/01/89	MILLWALL	3-0	40,931	Blackmore, Gill, Hughes
22	21/01/89	West Ham United	3-1	29,822	Strachan, Martin, McClair
23	05/02/89	TOTTENHAM	1-0	41,423	McClair
24	11/02/89	Sheffield Wednesday	2-0	34,820	McClair 2
25	25/02/89	Norwich City	1-2	23,155	McGrath
26	12/03/89	Aston Villa	0-0	28,332	
27	25/03/89	LUTON TN	2-0	36,335	Milne, Blackmore
28	27/03/89	Nottingham Forest	0-2	30,092	
29	02/04/89	ARSENAL	1-1	37,977	og
30	08/04/89	Millwall	0-0	17,523	
31	15/04/89	DERBY COUNTY	0-2	34,145	
32	22/04/89	Charlton Ath	0-1	12,055	
33	29/04/89	COVENTRY CITY	0-1	29,799	
34	02/05/89	WIMBLEDON	1-0	23,368	McClair
35	06/05/89	Southampton	1-2	17,021	Blackmore
36	08/05/89	Queens Park Rgrs	2-3	10,017	Bruce, Blackmore
37	10/05/89	EVERTON	1-2	26,722	Hughes
38	13/05/89	NEWACSTLE UTD	2-0	30,379	McClair, Robson

Season: 1989/90

No	Date	Opponents	Score	Att	Scorers
1	19/08/89	ARSENAL	4-1	47,245	Bruce, Hughes, Webb, McClair
2	22/08/89	Crystal Palace	1-1	22,423	Robson
3	26/08/89	Derby County	0-2	22,175	
4	30/08/89	NORWICH CITY	0-2	39,610	
5	09/09/89	Everton	2-3	37,916	McClair, Beardsmore
6	16/09/89	MILLWALL	5-1	42,746	Hughes 3, Robson, Sharpe
7	23/09/89	Manchester City	1-5	43,246	Hughes
8	14/10/89	SHEFFIELD W'DAY	0-0	41,492	
9	21/10/89	Coventry City	4-1	19,605	Hughes 2, Bruce, Phelan
10	28/10/89	SOUTHAMPTON	2-1	37,122	McClair 2
11	04/11/89	Charlton Ath	0-2	16,065	
12	12/11/89	NOTT'HAM FOREST	1-0	34,182	Pallister
13	18/11/89	Luton Town	3-1	11,141	Wallace, Blackmore, Hughes
14	25/11/89	CHELSEA	0-0	46,975	
15	03/12/89	Arsenal	0-1	34,484	
16	09/12/89	CRYSTAL PALACE	1-2	33,514	Beardsmore
17	16/12/89	TOTTENHAM	0-1	36,230	
18	23/12/89	Liverpool	0-0	37,426	
19	26/12/89	Aston Villa	0-3	41,247	
20	30/12/89	Wimbledon	2-2	9,622	Hughes, Robins
21	01/01/90	QUEENS PARK RGRS	0-0	34,824	
22	13/01/90	DERBY COUNTY	1-2	38,985	Pallister
23	21/01/90	Norwich City	0-2	17,370	
24	03/02/90	MANCHESTER CITY	1-1	40,274	Blackmore
25	10/02/90	Millwall	2-1	15,491	Wallace, Hughes]
26	24/02/90	Chelsea	0-1	29,979	
27	03/03/90	LUTON TN	4-1	35,327	McClair, Hughes, Wallace, Robins
28	14/03/90	EVERTON	0-0	37,398	
29	18/03/90	LIVERPOOL	1-2	46,629	og
30	21/03/90	Sheffield Wednesday	0-1	33,260	
31	24/03/90	Southampton	2-0	20,510	Gibson, Robson
32	31/03/90	COVENTRY CITY	3-0	39,172	Hughes 2, Robins
33	14/04/90	Queens Park Rgrs	2-1	18,997	Robins, Webb
34	17/04/90	ASTON VILLA	2-0	44,880	Robins 2
35	21/04/90	Tottenham Hotspurs	1-2	33,317	Bruce
36	30/04/90	WIMBLEDON	0-0	29,281	
37	02/05/90	Nottingham Forest	0-4	21,186	
38	05/05/90	CHARLTON ATH	1-0	35,389	Pallister

Season: 1990/91

No	Date	Opponents	Score	Att	Scorers
1	25/08/90	COVENTRY CITY	2-0	46,715	Bruce, Webb
2	28/08/90	Leeds United	0-0	29,172	
3	01/09/90	Sunderland	1-2	26,105	McClair
4	04/09/90	Luton Town	1-0	12,576	Robins
5	08/09/90	QUEENS PARK RGRS	3-1	43,427	McClair, Robins 2
6	16/09/90	Liverpool	0-4	35,726	
7	22/09/90	SOUTHAMPTON	3-2	41,228	McClair, Blackmore, Hughes
8	29/09/90	NOTT'HAM FOREST	0-1	46,766	
9	20/10/90	ARSENAL	0-1	47,232	
10	27/10/90	Manchester City	3-3	36,427	Hughes, McClair 2
11	03/11/90	CRYSTAL PALACE	2-0	45,724	Webb, Wallace
12	10/11/90	Derby County	0-0	21,115	
13	17/11/90	SHEFFIELD UTD	2-0	45,903	Bruce, Hughes
14	25/11/90	CHELSEA	2-3	37,836	Wallace, Hughes
15	01/12/90	Everton	1-0	32,400	Sharpe
16	08/12/90	LEEDS UTD	1-1	40,927	Webb
17	15/12/90	Coventry City	2-2	17,106	Hughes, Wallace
18	22/12/90	Wimbledon	3-1	9,744	Bruce 2(pens), Hughes
19	26/12/90	NORWICH CITY	3-0	39,801	Hughes, McClair 2
20	29/12/90	ASTON VILLA	1-1	47,485	Bruce (pen)
21	01/01/91	Tottenham Hotspurs	2-1	29,399	Bruce(pen), McClair
22	12/01/91	SUNDERLAND	3-0	45,934	Hughes 2, McClair
23	19/01/91	Queens Park Rgrs	1-1	18,544	Phelan
24	03/02/91	LIVERPOOL	1-1	43,690	Bruce(pen)
25	26/02/91	Sheffield United	1-2	27,570	Blackmore(pen)
26	02/03/91	EVERTON	0-2	45,656	
27	09/03/91	Chelsea	2-3	22,818	Hughes, McClair
28	13/03/91	Southampton	1-1	15,701	Ince
29	16/03/91	Nottingham Forest	1-1	23,859	Blackmore
30	23/03/91	LUTON TN	4-1	41,752	Bruce 2, Robins, McClair
31	30/03/91	Norwich City	3-0	18,282	Bruce 2(1 pen), Ince
32	02/04/91	WIMBLEDON	2-1	36,660	Bruce, McClair
33	06/04/91	Aston Villa	1-1	33,307	Sharpe
34	16/04/91	DERBY COUNTY	3-1	32,776	Blackmore, McClair, Robson
35	04/05/91	MANCHESTER CITY	1-0	45,286	Giggs
36	06/05/91	Arsenal	1-3	40,229	Bruce(pen)
37	11/05/91	Crystal Palace	0-3	25,301	
38	20/05/91	TOTTENHAM	1-1	46,791	Ince

Season: 1991/92

No	Date	Opponents	Score	Att	Scorers
1	17/08/91	NOTTS COUNTY	2-0	46,278	Hughes, Robson
2	21/08/91	Aston Villa	1-0	39,995	Bruce(pen)
3	24/08/91	Everton	0-0	36,085	
4	28/08/91	OLDHAM ATH	1-0	42,078	McClair
5	31/08/91	LEEDS UTD	1-1	43,778	Robson
6	03/09/91	Wimbledon	2-1	13,824	Blackmore, Pallister
7	07/09/91	NORWICH CITY	3-0	44,946	Irwin, McClair, Giggs
8	14/09/91	Southampton	1-0	19,264	Hughes
9	21/09/91	LUTON TN	5-0	46,491	McClair 2, Ince, Hughes, Bruce
10	28/09/91	Tottenham Hotspurs	2-1	35,087	Hughes, Robson
11	06/10/91	LIVERPOOL	0-0	44,997	
12	19/10/91	ARSENAL	1-1	46,594	Bruce
13	26/10/91	Sheffield Wednesday	2-3	38,260	McClair 2
14	02/11/91	SHEFFIELD UTD	2-0	42,942	og, Kanchelskis
15	16/11/91	Manchester City	0-0	38,180	
16	23/11/91	WEST HAM UTD	2-1	47,185	Giggs, Robson
17	30/11/91	Crystal Palace	3-1	29,017	Webb, McClair, Kanchelskis
18	07/12/91	COVENTRY CITY	4-0	42,549	Bruce, Webb, McClair, Hughes
19	15/12/91	Chelsea	3-1	23,120	Irwin, McClair, Bruce
20	26/12/91	Oldham Ath	6-3	18,947	Irwin 2, McClair 2, Kanchelskis, Giggs
21	29/12/91	Leeds United	1-1	32,638	Webb
22	01/01/92	QUEENS PARK RGRS	1-4	38,554	McClair
23	11/01/92	EVERTON	1-0	46,619	Kanchelskis
24	18/01/92	Notts County	1-1	21,055	Blackmore(pen)
25	22/01/92	ASTON VILLA	1-0	45,022	Hughes
26	01/02/92	Arsenal	1-1	41,703	McClair
27	08/02/92	SHEFFIELD W'DAY	1-1	47,074	McClair
28	22/02/92	CRYSTAL PALACE	2-0	46,347	Hughes 2
29	26/02/92	CHELSEA	1-1	44,872	Hughes
30	29/02/92	Coventry City	0-0	23,967	
31	14/03/92	Sheffield United	2-1	30,183	McClair, Blackmore
32	18/03/92	Nottingham Forest	0-1	28,062	
33	21/03/92	WIMBLEDON	0-0	45,428	
34	28/03/92	Queens Park Rgrs	0-0	22,603	
35	31/03/92	Norwich City	3-1	17,489	Ince 2, McClair
36	07/04/92	MANCHESTER CITY	1-1	46,781	Giggs
37	16/04/92	SOUTHAMPTON	1-0	43,972	Kanchelskis
38	18/04/92	Luton Town	1-1	13,410	Sharpe
39	20/04/92	NOT'HAM FOREST	1-2	47,576	McClair
40	22/04/92	West Ham United	0-1	24,197	
41	26/04/92	Liverpool	0-2	38,669	
42	02/05/92	TOTTENHAM	3-1	44,595	Hughes 2, McClair

FA Premier League

Season: 1992/93

No	Date	Opponents	Score	Att	Scorers
1	15/08/92	Sheffield United	1-2	28,070	Hughes
2	19/08/92	EVERTON	0-3	31,901	
3	22/08/92	IPSWICH TN	1-1	31,704	Irwin
4	24/08/92	Southampton	1-0	15,623	Dublin
5	29/08/92	Nottingham Forest	2-0	19,694	Hughes, Giggs
6	02/09/92	CRYSTAL PALACE	1-0	29,736	Hughes
7	06/09/92	LEEDS UTD	2-0	31,296	Kanchelskis, Bruce
8	12/09/92	Everton	2-0	30,002	McClair, Bruce (pen)
9	19/09/92	Tottenham Hotspurs	1-1	33,296	Giggs
10	26/09/92	QUEENS PARK RGRS	0-0	33,287	
11	03/10/92	Middlesbrough	1-1	24,172	Bruce (pen)
12	18/10/92	LIVERPOOL	2-2	33,243	Hughes 2
13	24/10/92	Blackburn Rovers	0-0	20,305	
14	31/10/92	WIMBLEDON	0-1	32,622	
15	07/11/92	Aston Villa	0-1	39,063	
16	21/11/92	OLDHAM ATH	3-0	33,497	McClair 2, Hughes
17	28/11/92	Arsenal	1-0	29,739	Hughes
18	06/12/92	MANCHESTER CITY	2-1	35,408	Ince, Hughes
19	12/12/92	NORWICH CITY	1-0	34,500	Hughes
20	19/12/92	Chelsea	1-1	34,464	Cantona
21	26/12/92	Sheffield Wednesday	3-3	37,708	McClair 2, Cantona
22	28/12/92	COVENTRY CITY	5-0	36,025	Giggs, Hughes, Cantona (pen), Sharpe, Irwin
23	09/01/93	TOTTENHAM	4-1	35,648	Cantona, Irwin, McClair, Parker
24	18/01/93	Queens Park Rgrs	3-1	21,117	Ince, Giggs, Kanchelskis
25	27/01/93	NOTT"HAM FOREST	2-0	36,085	Ince, Hughes
26	30/01/93	Ipswich Town	1-2	22,068	McClair
27	06/02/93	SHEFFIELD UTD	2-1	36,156	McClair, Cantona
28	08/02/93	Leeds United	0-0	34,166	
29	20/02/93	SOUTHAMPTON	2-1	36,257	Giggs 2
30	27/02/93	MIDDLESBOROUGH	3-0	36,251	Giggs, Irwin, Cantona
31	06/03/93	Liverpool	2-1	44,374	Hughes, McClair
32	09/03/93	Oldham Ath	0-1	17,106	
33	14/03/93	ASTON VILLA	1-1	36,163	Hughes
34	20/03/93	Manchester City	1-1	37,136	Cantona
35	24/03/93	ARSENAL	0-0	37,301	
36	05/04/93	Norwich City	3-1	20,582	Giggs, Kanchelskis, Cantona
37	10/04/93	SHEFFIELD W'DAY	2-1	40,102	Bruce 2
38	12/04/93	Coventry City	1-0	24,429	Irwin
39	17/04/93	CHELSEA	3-0	40,139	Hughes, Clarke (og), Cantona
40	21/04/93	Crystal Palace	2-0	30,115	Hughes, Ince

Season: 1993/94

No	Date	Opponents	Score	Att	Scorers
1	15/08/93	Norwich City	2-0	19,705	Giggs, Robson
2	18/08/93	SHEFFIELD UTD	3-0	41,949	Keane 2, Hughes
3	21/08/93	NEWCASTLE UTD	1-1	41,829	Giggs
4	23/08/93	Aston Villa	2-1	39,624	Sharpe 2
5	28/08/93	Southampton	3-1	16,189	Sharpe, Cantona, Irwin
6	01/09/93	WEST HAM UTD	3-0	44,613	Sharpe, Cantona (pen), Bruce
7	11/09/93	Chelsea	0-1	37,064	
8	19/09/93	ARSENAL	1-0	44,009	Cantona
9	25/09/93	SWINDON TN	4-2	44,583	Kanchelskis, Cantona, Hughes2
10	02/10/93	Sheffield Wednesday	3-2	34,548	Hughes 2, Giggs
11	16/10/93	TOTTENHAM	2-1	44,655	Keane, Sharpe
12	23/10/93	Everton	1-0	35,455	Sharpe
13	30/10/93	QUEENS PARK RGRS	2-1	44,663	Cantona, Hughes
14	07/11/93	Manchester City	3-2	35,155	Cantona 2, Keane
15	20/11/93	WIMBLEDON	3-1	44,748	Pallister, Hughes, Kanchelskis
16	24/11/93	IPSWICH TN	0-0	43,300	
17	27/11/93	Coventry City	1-0	17,009	Cantona
18	04/12/93	NORWICH CITY	2-2	44,694	Giggs, McClair
19	07/12/93	Sheffield United	3-0	26,744	Hughes, Sharpe, Cantona
20	11/12/93	Newcastle United	1-1	36,332	Ince
21	19/12/93	ASTON VILLA	3-1	44,499	Cantona 2, Ince
22	26/12/93	BLACKBURN RVRS	1-1	44,511	Ince
23	29/12/93	Oldham Ath	5-2	16,708	Kanchelskis, Cantona (pen), Bruce, Giggs
24	01/01/94	LEEDS UTD	0-0	44,724	
25	04/01/94	Liverpool	3-3	42,795	Bruce, Giggs, Irwin
26	15/01/94	Tottenham Hotspurs	1-0	31,343	Calderwood (og)
27	22/01/94	EVERTON	1-0	44,750	Giggs
28	05/02/94	Queens Park Rgrs	3-2	21,267	Kanchelskis, Cantona, Giggs
29	25/02/94	West Ham United	2-2	28,832	Hughes, Ince
30	05/03/94	CHELSEA	0-1	44,745	
31	16/03/94	SHEFFIELD W'DAY	5-0	43,669	Giggs, Hughes, Ince, Cantona 2
32	19/03/94	Swindon Town	2-2	18,102	Keane, Ince
33	22/03/94	Arsenal	2-2	36,203	Sharpe 2
34	30/03/94	LIVERPOOL	1-0	44,751	Ince
35	02/04/94	Blackburn Rovers	0-2	20,866	
36	04/04/94	OLDHAM ATH	3-2	44,686	Giggs, Dublin, Ince
37	16/04/94	Wimbledon	0-1	28,553	
38	23/04/94	MANCHESTER CITY	2-0	44,333	Cantona 2
39	27/04/94	Leeds United	2-0	41,127	Kanchelskis, Giggs
40	01/05/94	Ipswich Town	2-1	22,478	Cantona, Giggs
41	04/05/94	SOUTHAMPTON	2-0	44,705	Kanchelskis, Hughes
42	08/05/94	COVENTRY CITY	0-0	44,717	

Season: 1994/95

No	Date	Opponents	Score	Att	Scorers
1	20/08/94	QUEENS PARK RGRS	2-0	43,214	Hughes, McClair
2	22/08/94	Nottingham Forest	1-1	22,072	Kanchelskis
3	27/08/94	Tottenham Hotspurs	1-0	24,502	Bruce
4	31/08/94	WIMBLEDON	3-0	43,440	Cantona, McClair, Giggs
5	11/09/94	Leeds United	1-2	39,120	
6	17/09/94	LIVERPOOL	2-0	43,740	Kanchelskis, McClair
7	24/09/94	Ipswich Town	2-3	22,553	Cantona, Scholes
8	01/10/94	EVERTON	2-0	43,803	Kanchelskis, Sharpe
9	08/10/94	Sheffield Wednesday	0-1	32,616	
10	15/10/94	WEST HAM UTD	1-0	43,795	Cantona
11	23/10/94	Blackburn Rovers	4-2	30,260	Cantona (pen), Kanchelskis 2 Hughes
12	29/10/94	NEWCASTLE UTD	2-0	43,795	Pallister, Gillespie
13	06/11/94	Aston Villa	2-1	32,136	Ince, Kanchelskis
14	10/11/94	MANCHESTER CITY	5-0	43,738	Cantona, Kanchelskis 3, Hughes
15	19/11/94	CRYSTAL PALACE	3-0	43,788	Irwin, Cantona, Kanchelskis
16	26/11/94	Arsenal	0-0	38,301	
17	03/12/94	NORWICH CITY	1-0	43,789	Cantona
18	10/12/94	Queens Park Rgrs	3-2	18,948	Scholes 2, Keane
19	17/12/94	NOTT'HAM FOREST	1-2	43,744	Cantona
20	26/12/94	Chelsea	3-2	31,139	Hughes, Cantona (pen), McClair
21	28/12/94	LEICESTER CITY	1-1	43,789	Kanchelskis
22	31/12/94	Southampton	2-2	15,204	Butt, Pallister
23	03/01/95	COVENTRY CITY	2-0	43,120	Scholes, Cantona (pen)
24	15/01/95	Newcastle United	1-1	34,471	Hughes
25	22/01/95	BLACKBURN RVRS	1-0	43,742	Cantona
26	25/01/95	Crystal Palace	1-1	18,224	May
27	04/02/95	ASTON VILLA	1-0	43,795	Cole
28	11/02/95	Manchester City	3-0	26,368	Ince, Kanchelskis, Cole
29	22/02/95	Norwich City	2-0	21,824	Ince, Kanchelskis
30	25/02/95	Everton	0-1	40,011	
31	04/03/95	IPSWICH TN	9-0	43,804	Keane, Cole 5, Hughes 2, Ince
32	07/03/95	Wimbledon	1-0	18,224	Bruce
33	15/03/95	TOTTENHAM	0-0	43,802	
34	19/03/95	Liverpool	0-2	38,906	
35	22/03/95	ARSENAL	3-0	43,623	Hughes, Sharpe, Kanchelskis
36	02/04/95	LEEDS UTD	0-0	43,712	
37	15/04/95	Leicester City	4-0	21,281	Sharpe, Cole 2, Ince
38	17/04/95	CHELSEA	0-0	43,728	
39	01/05/95	Coventry City	3-2	21,858	Scholes, Cole 2
40	07/05/95	SHEFFIELD W'DAY	1-0	43,868	May
41	10/05/95	SOUTHAMPTON	2-1	43,479	Cole, Irwin (pen)
42	14/05/95	West Ham United	1-1	24,783	McClair

Season: 1995/96

No	Date	Opponents	Score	Att	Scorers
1	19/08/95	Aston Villa	1-3	34,655	Beckham
2	23/08/95	WEST HAM UTD	2-1	31,966	Scholes, Keane
3	26/08/95	WIMBLEDON	3-1	32,226	Keane 2, Cole
4	28/08/95	Blackburn Rovers	2-1	29,843	Sharpe, Beckham
5	9/09/95	Everton	3-2	39,496	Sharpe 2, Giggs
6	16/09/95	BOLTON WDRS	3-0	32,812	Scholes 2, Giggs
7	23/09/95	Sheffield Wednesday	0-0	34,101	
8	1/10/95	LIVERPOOL	2-2	34,934	Butt, Cantona
9	14/10/95	MANCHESTER CITY	1-0	35,707	Scholes
10	21/10/95	Chelsea	4-1	31,019	Scholes 2, Giggs, McClair
11	28/10/95	MIDDLESBROUGH	2-0	36,580	Pallister, Cole
12	4/11/95	Arsenal	0-1	38,317	
13	18/11/95	SOUTHAMPTON	4-1	39,301	Scholes, Cole, Giggs 2
14	22/11/95	Coventry City	4-0	23,400	Irwin, McClair 2, Beckham
15	27/11/95	Nottingham Forest	1-1	29,263	Cantona
16	2/12/95	CHELSEA	1-1	42,019	Beckham
17	9/12/95	SHEFFIELD W'DAY	2-2	41,849	Cantona,
18	17/12/95	Liverpool	0-2	40,549	Cantona 2
19	24/12/95	Leeds United	1-3	39,801	Cole
20	27/12/95	NEWCASTLE UTD	2-0	42,024	Cole, Keane
21	30/12/95	QUEENS PARK RGRS	2-1	41,890	Cole, Giggs
22	1/01/96	Tottenham Hotspur	1-4	32,852	Cole
23	13/01/96	ASTON VILLA	0-0	42,667	
24	22/01/96	West Ham United	1-0	24,197	Cantona
25	3/02/96	Wimbledon	4-2	25,380	Cole, Cantona 2, og
26	10/02/96	BLACKBURN RVRS	1-0	42,681	Sharpe
27	21/02/96	EVERTON	2-0	42,459	Keane, Giggs
28	25/02/96	Bolton Wanderers	6-0	21,381	Beckham, Bruce, Cole, Scholes 2, Butt
29	4/03/96	Newcastle United	1-0	36,584	Cantona
30	16/03/96	Queens Park Rgrs	1-1	18,817	Cantona
31	20/03/96	ARSENAL	1-0	50,028	Cantona
32	24/03/96	TOTTENHAM	1-0	50,157	Cantona
33	6/04/96	Manchester City	3-2	29,688	Cantona, Cole, Giggs
34	8/04/96	COVENTRY CITY	1-0	50,332	Cantona
35	13/04/96	Southampton	1-3	15,262	Giggs
36	17/04/96	LEEDS UTD	1-0	48,382	Keane
37	28/04/96	NOTT'HAM FOREST	5-0	53,926	Scholes, Beckham 2, Giggs, Cantona
38	5/05/96	Middlesbrough	3-0	29,921	May, Cole, Giggs

Miscellaneous

Managers

Ernest Mangnall (1903-1912)

Football League champions	1907/8, 1910/11
Division Two runners-up	1905/06
FA Cup winners	1909

John Robson (1914-1921)

The first person to assume the title of Manager – Mangnall's official title had been Secretary.

John Chapman (1921-1926)

| Division Two runners–up | 1924/25 |

Although full details were never made known, the FA suspended Chapman from football in 1926.

Clarence Hilditch (1926-1927)

The only player–manager in United's history.

Herbert Bamlett (1927-1931)

Made history by being the youngest man ever to referee an FA Cup Final – in 1914 aged 32. As a manager he guided United into their worst ever spell.

Walter Crickmer (1931-1932)

Another never to assume the title of manager although he was responsible for team selection. Crickmer was one of the victims of the Munich Air Crash.

Scott Duncan (1932-1937)

| Division Two champions | 1935/36 |

Walter Crickmer (1937-1945)

Sir Matt Busby (1945-1969)

Football League champions	1951/52, 1955/56, 1956/57, 1964/65, 1966/67
Division One runners–up	1946/47, 1947/48, 1948/49, 1950/51, 1958/59, 1963/64, 1967/68
FA Cup winners	1948, 1963
FA Cup runners–up	1957
European champions	1967/68

Jimmy Murphy (1958)

In the absence of Matt Busby, seriously injured in the Munich Air Crash, Jimmy Murphy took over for six months from February to August 1958. During that time he led the makeshift team to an FA Cup Final appearance.

| FA Cup runners–up | 1958 |

Wilf McGuinness (1969-70)

United's only attempt to promote from within. Two League Cup semi–finals and one FA Cup semi–final were not sufficient to keep him in the job.

Frank O'Farrell (1971-72)

At Christmas of his first season in charge, United were five points clear at the top of the league when there were only two points for a win but they slumped to finish eighth. He soon paid the penalty.

Tommy Docherty (1972-77)

Division Two champions	1974/75
FA Cup winners	1977
FA Cup runners–up	1976

Dave Sexton (1977-1981)

FA Cup runners–up	1979
First Division runners–up	1979/80

Tommy Docherty was the first manager to offer Dave Sexton a chance in management when he appointed Sexton as his coach at Stamford Bridge. Sexton was later to replace Docherty at both Chelsea and Manchester United.

Ron Atkinson (1981-1986)

FA Cup winners	1983, 1985
League Cup runners–up	1983

Looked likely to succeed in bringing the Holy Grail back to Old Trafford when his side began the 1985/86 campaign with ten straight league victories but it wasn't to be.

Alex Ferguson (1986-)

FA Premier League champions	1992/93, 1993/94, 1995/96
FA Premier League runners–up	1994/95
Division One runners–up	1987/88, 1991/92
FA Cup winners	1990, 1994, 1996
FA Cup finalists	1995
League Cup winners	1992
League Cup runners–up	1991, 1994
European Cup Winners' Cup winners	1991

The Manchester 'Derby'

The following is a complete history of the Manchester 'derby' matches since they began, along with United's scorers and the attendances.

League Games

No	Date	Venue	Score	Scorers	Att
1	03/11/1894	(a)	5-2	Smith 4, Clarkin	14,000
2	05/01/1895	(h)	4-1	Clarkin 2, Donaldson, Smith	12,000
3	05/10/1895	(h)	1-1	Clarkin	12,000
4	07/12/1895	(a)	1-2	Cassidy	18,000
5	03/10/1896	(a)	0-0		20,000
6	25/12/1896	(h)	2-1	Donaldson, Smith	18,000
7	16/10/1897	(h)	1-1	Gillespie	20,000
8	25/12/1897	(a)	1-0	Cassidy	16,000
9	10/09/1898	(h)	3-0	Cassidy, Boyd, Collinson	20,000
10	26/12/1898	(a)	0-4		25,000
11	25/12/1902	(h)	1-1	Pegg	40,000
12	10/04/1903	(a)	2-0	Peddie, Schofield	30,000
13	01/12/1906	(a)	0-3		40,000
14	06/04/1907	(h)	1-1	Roberts	40,000
15	21/12/1907	(h)	3-1	A.Turnbull, Wall	35,000
16	18/04/1908	(a)	0-0		40,000
17	19/09/1908	(a)	2-1	Halse, J.Turnbull	40,000
18	23/12/1908	(h)	3-1	Livingstone 2, Wall	40,000
19	17/09/1910	(h)	2-1	A.Turnbull, West	60,000
20	21/01/1911	(a)	1-1	A.Turnbull	40,000
21	02/09/1911	(a)	0-0		35,000
22	30/12/1911	(h)	0-0		50,000
23	07/09/1912	(h)	0-1		40,000
24	28/12/1912	(a)	2-0	West 2	38,000
25	06/12/1913	(a)	2-0	Anderson 2	40,000
26	11/04/1914	(h)	0-1		36,000
27	05/09/1914	(h)	0-0		20,000
28	02/01/1915	(a)	1-0	West	30,000
29	11/10/1919	(a)	3-3	Hodge, Hopkin, Spence	30,000
30	18/10/1919	(h)	1-0	Spence	40,000
31	20/11/1920	(h)	1-1	Miller	63,000
32	27/11/1920	(a)	0-3		35,000
33	22/10/1921	(a)	1-4	Spence	24,000
34	29/10/1921	(h)	3-1	Spence 3	56,000
35	12/09/1925	(h)	1-1	Rennox	62,994
36	23/01/1926	(h)	1-6	Rennox	48,657
37	01/09/1928	(a)	2-2	Johnston, Wilson	61,007

38	05/01/1929	(h)	1-2	Rawlings	42,555
39	05/10/1929	(h)	1-3	Thomas	57,201
40	08/02/1930	(a)	1-0	Reid	64,472
41	04/10/1930	(a)	1-4	Spence	41,757
42	07/02/1931	(h)	1-3	Spence	39,876
43	12/09/1936	(h)	3-2	Bamford, Bryant, Manley	68,796
44	09/01/1937	(a)	0-1		64,862
45	20/09/1947	(a)	0-0		1,364
46	07/04/1948	(h)	1-1	Rowley	71,690
47	11/09/1948	(a)	0-0		64,502
48	22/01/1949	(h)	0-0		66,485
49	03/09/1949	(h)	2-1	Pearson 2	47,760
50	31/12/1949	(a)	2-1	Delaney, Pearson	63,704
51	15/09/1951	(a)	2-1	Berry, McShane	52,571
52	19/01/1952	(h)	1-1	Carey	54,245
53	30/08/1952	(a)	1-2	Downie	56,140
54	03/01/1953	(h)	1-1	Pearson	47,883
55	05/09/1953	(a)	0-2		53,097
56	16/01/1954	(h)	1-1	Berry	46,379
57	25/09/1954	(a)	2-3	Blanchflower, Taylor	54,105
58	12/02/1955	(h)	0-5		47,914
59	03/09/1955	(a)	0-1		59,162
60	31/12/1956	(h)	2-1	Taylor, Viollet	60,956
61	22/09/1956	(h)	2-0	Whelan, Viollet	53,525
62	2/02/1957	(a)	4-2	Edwards, Viollet, Taylor, Whelan	63,872
63	31/08/1957	(h)	4-1	Edwards, Viollet, Taylor, Berry	63,347
64	28/12/1957	(a)	2-2	Charlton, Viollet	70,483
65	27/09/1958	(a)	1-1	Charlton	62,912
66	16/02/1959	(h)	4-1	Bradley 2, Goodwin, Scanlon	59,846
67	19/09/1959	(a)	0-3		58,300
68	06/02/1960	(h)	0-0		59,450
69	31/12/1960	(h)	5-1	Dawson 3, Charlton 2	61,213
70	04/03/1961	(a)	3-1	Dawson, Charlton, Pearson	50,479
71	23/09/1961	(h)	3-2	Stiles, Viollet, Ewing og	56,345
72	10/02/1962	(a)	2-0	Herd, Chisnall	49,959
73	15/09/1962	(h)	2-3	Law 2	49,193
74	15/05/1963	(a)	1-1	Quixall	52,424
75	17/09/1966	(h)	1-0	Law	62,085
76	21/02/1967	(a)	1-1	Foulkes	62,983
77	30/09/1967	(a)	2-1	Charlton	62,942
78	27/03/1968	(h)	1-3	Best	63,004
79	17/08/1968	(a)	0-0		63,052
80	08/03/1969	(h)	0-1		63,264

81	15/11/1969	(a)	0-4		63,013
82	28/03/1970	(h)	1-2	Kidd	59,777
83	12/12/1970	(h)	1-4	Kidd	52,636
84	05/05/1971	(a)	4-3	Best 2, Law, Charlton	43,626
85	06/11/1971	(a)	3-3	Gowling, Kidd, McIlroy	63,326
86	12/04/1972	(h)	1-3	Buchan	56,362
87	18/11/1972	(a)	0-3		52,050
88	21/04/1973	(h)	0-0		61,676
89	13/03/1974	(a)	0-0		51,331
90	27/04/1974	(a)	0-1		56,996
91	27/09/1975	(a)	2-2	Macari, McQueen	46,931
92	04/05/1976	(h)	2-0	Hill, McIlroy	59,517
93	25/09/1976	(a)	3-1	Coppell, Daly, McCreery	48,861
94	05/03/1977	(h)	3-1	Coppell, Hill, Pearson	58,595
95	10/09/1977	(a)	1-3	Nicholl	50,856
96	15/03/1978	(h)	2-2	Hill 2	58,398
97	30/09/1978	(h)	1-0	Jordan	55,301
98	10/02/1979	(a)	3-0	Coppell 2, Ritchie	46,151
99	10/11/1979	(a)	0-2		50,067
100	22/03/1980	(h)	1-0	Thomas	56,387
101	27/09/1980	(h)	2-2	Albiston, Coppell	55,918
102	21/02/1981	(a)	0-1		50,114
103	10/10/1981	(a)	0-0		52,037
104	27/02/1982	(h)	1-1	Moran	57,830
105	23/10/1982	(h)	2-2	Stapleton 2	57,334
106	05/03/1983	(h)	2-2	Stapleton 2	45,400
107	14/09/1985	(a)	3-0	Albiston, Duxbury, Robson	48,773
108	22/03/1986	(h)	2-2	C.Gibson, Strachan	51,274
109	26/10/1986	(a)	1-1	Stapleton	32,440
110	07/03/1987	(h)	2-0	Robson, Reid og	48,619
111	23/09/1989	(a)	1-5	Hughes	43,246
112	03/02/1990	(h)	1-1	Blackmore	40,274
113	27/10/1990	(a)	3-3	Hughes, McClair 2	36,427
114	04/05/1991	(h)	1-0	Giggs	45,286
115	16/11/1991	(a)	0-0		38,180
116	07/04/1992	(h)	1-1	Giggs	46,781
117	06/12/1992	(h)	2-1	Ince, Hughes	35,408
118	20/03/1993	(a)	1-1	Cantona	37,136
119	07/11/1993	(a)	3-2	Cantona 2, Keane	35,155
120	23/04/1994	(h)	2-0	Cantona 2	44,333
121	10/11/1994	(h)	5-0	Cantona, Kanchelskis 3, Hughes	43,738
122	11/02/1995	(a)	3-0	Ince, Kanchelskis, Cole	26,368
123	14/10/1995	(h)	1-0	Scholes	35,707
124	06/04/1996	(a)	3-2	Cantona (pen), Cole, Giggs	29,688

FA Cup

1	27/03/1926	(n)	0-3		46,450
2	29/01/1954	(a)	0-2		75,000
3	24/01/1970	(h)	3-0	Kidd 2, Morgan	63,417
4	10/01/1987	(h)	1-0	Whiteside	54,294
5	17/02/1996	(h)	2-1	Cantona (pen), Sharpe	42,692

League Cup

1	03/12/1969	(a)	1-2	Charlton	55,799
2	17/12/1969	(h)	2-2	Edwards, Law	63,418
3	09/10/1974	(h)	1-0	Daly	55,159
4	12/11/1975	(a)	0-4		50,182

FA Charity Shield

1	24/10/1956	(a)	1-0	Viollet	30,495

Post War Average Attendances

Season	Home	Away	Season	Home	Away
46/47	43,615	31,364	71/72	45,999	44,085
47/48	53,660	40,493	72/73	48,623	41,171
48/49	46,023	44,720	73/74	42,721	35,337
49/50	41,455	46,172	74/75	48,388	25,556
50/51	37,159	38,091	75/76	54,750	37,037
51/52	41,870	40,945	76/77	53,710	35,357
52/53	35,737	37,068	77/78	51,938	30,424
53/54	33,637	37,096	78/79	46,687	30,498
54/55	34,077	35,865	79/80	51,562	34,101
55/56	38,880	32,872	80/81	45,055	29,849
56/57	45,192	39,772	81/82	44,685	27,214
57/58	45,583	45,352	82/83	41,583	25,294
58/59	53,258	44,028	83/84	42,534	24,936
59/60	47,288	41,026	84/85	43,010	27,884
60/61	37,807	34,139	85/86	44,422	28,204
61/62	33,490	33,964	86/87	40,625	25,221
62/63	40,317	34,894	87/88	39,155	23,041
63/64	43,753	38,697	88/89	36,488	23,713
64/65	45,990	41,377	89/90	39,078	26,666
65/66	38,456	38,171	90/91	43,241	25,020
66/67	53,984	45,577	91/92	44,985	27,893
67/68	57,759	45,802	92/93	35,132	28,254
68/69	51,121	44,295	93/94	44,240	28,868
69/70	51,115	43,997	94/95	43,692	27,331
70/71	44,754	41,695	95/96	41,683	29,976

The First Great United Side

Manchester United were not always the force they are nowadays. Indeed, they were virtual also rans until Ernest Mangnall came to the club and produced the first truly great United side to put himself in the same category as Sir Matt Busby and Alex Ferguson. Mangnall joined United in 1903 and slowly built his team up until they captured the Championship in 1908, the FA Cup the following season and a second title in 1910-11.

The players who made up the FA Cup Final team were regarded as some of the finest in the country at the time but won surprisingly few international caps due to a reputation of taking on the establishment.

Harry MOGER was one of Mangnall's first signings when the Southampton goalkeeper was regarded as the finest outside of the Football League and quickly proved to be one of the best in it once he was given a chance at United in 1903. Well over six feet tall, Moger dominated the aerial battles and from the reports of the time brought confidence to his fellow defenders in much the same way that Schmeichel does today. Moger played 264 games for United and was a member of both Championship winning sides as well as keeping a clean sheet against Bristol City in the 1908 FA Cup Final. Despite his success with United, Moger surprisingly never won an international cap.

George STACEY was a full back who hailed from South Yorkshire where Rotherham, Barnsley and Sheffield had reputations of producing men of steel and coal. Stacey was no exception, nor should he have been for he had connections with all three having been born in Rotherham, joining Sheffield Wednesday as a junior and being signed by United from Barnsley. Mangnall paid £400 for Stacey's services mainly to provide cover on the run in to the club's first title. Stacey, however, quickly forced himself into the team and stayed there playing in the last thirteen games after making five other appearances earlier in the campaign. He could play on either flank and, like Moger, was in both Championship sides as well as the FA Cup Final team. Also like Moger he never won a cap although he did play in a trial. He was with United until the outbreak of World War One playing 267 games and scoring nine goals. After the War he returned to his old job as a coal miner.

Vince HAYES was the other full back in the FA Cup Final side but missed out on the two Championships. Hayes had two spells with United having been with the club in their days as Newton Heath. He was in and out of the team under Mangnall who eventually let him go to Brentford in 1905. After United won their first title, Mangnall re-signed Hayes and he became a regular in the line up the season the club won the FA Cup and the following season as well during which time he played for the Football League representative side. But he then found himself out of favour again and played just one game, a 2-1 defeat at Nottingham Forest, in United's second Championship year. After a combined total of 128 games and two goals, Hayes moved to Bradford Park Avenue where he ended his playing career in 1912.

351

After the First World War, Hayes returned to football for a brief spell as manager of Preston North End.

Dick DUCKWORTH was one of United's earliest 'greats', the engine room around whom Mangnall built his side. He was an integral part of the half back line of Duckworth, Roberts, and Bell that put fear into every other English club of the time. United were his one and only Football League club and he played over 250 games scoring eleven goals and was another who played in both Championship sides and the 1908 FA Cup Final. The local lad was amazingly yet another of the first great United team to fail to win international recognition although he did appear in a Commonwealth game against South Africa and also played for the Football League. When both Bell and Roberts left United in 1912/13, Duckworth announced his retirement but was persuaded to stay on for one more season before finishing for good. Charlie ROBERTS captained the side to their glories after Mangnall signed the Darlington born player from Grimsby Town for £400 in 1904. He was a central defender but scored 23 goals from 299 appearances through his ability to ghost into the opposition's penalty area. It wasn't, however, that ability that earned him his nickname of 'The ghost in boots' but his whiter than white complexion. He had immense stamina from working on trawlers in Grimsby but was also exceptionally fast, being timed at 11 seconds for the 100 yards when the World record was about 10 seconds. Roberts gained just three England caps mainly because he was one of the founders of the Players Union and an early Chairman of the organisation. Never afraid to speak his mind on behalf of the players, Roberts was not one of officialdom's favourite sons and his international career suffered accordingly. He left United for Oldham Athletic in 1913 and managed the 'Latics briefly after the First World War but soon quit as he said he couldn't bear to watch.

Alex BELL was born in South Africa of Scottish parents and was signed by Mangnall in 1903 for £700 from Scottish non-league side Ayr Parkhouse. This was a colossal sum in those days for a non-league player but the manager's judgement was rewarded with over 300 appearances in the ten years Bell served the club. The left hand side of the Duckworth, Roberts and Bell half back line, the Scot was generally considered the quiet man of the trio. Bell won one Scottish cap as well as his two Championship medals and Cup Final appearance before moving to Blackburn Rovers in 1913 for £1,000. After the First World War he became trainer at Coventry City and then Manchester City and he was still working with United's great rivals when he died at the early age of 51.

Billy MEREDITH was the first truly great winger in the British game with his international career spanning an astonishing 25 years whilst his overall career lasted almost thirty years! He won 48 Welsh caps when internationals were more or less limited to the three Home internationals a season and clocked up over 700 games in total including some 332 for United. Although he was a class finisher, Meredith scored only 35 goals for United but managed over 300 in his career including the goal that won Manchester City the FA Cup in 1904. When United signed Meredith, he was still serving a suspension along with several other Manchester City players incurred over an illegal payments inquiry conducted by the FA and it was seven months before he could make his debut.

Harold HALSE played his early football in the South with Barking, Clapton Orient and Southend United before Mangnall brought him North in 1908 to finish off his team building. He had time to play six games during the run- in to United's first Championship scoring four goals, including one on his debut in a 4-1 win over Sheffield Wednesday. The following season he played a big part in the only goal of the FA Cup Final as it was his shot which hit the bar and bounced down for Sandy Turnbull to give United the famous Trophy for the first time. Halse added a Championship medal in 1911 before moving on to Aston Villa and Chelsea where he won an FA Cup-winners medal with both! It was whilst with United that he won his only England cap against Austria in 1909 when he scored twice in an 8-1 victory.

Jimmy TURNBULL was yet another who learned his football trade down South and it was from Clapton Orient that Mangnall signed Turnbull in May 1907. He was to form a lethal partnership with Sandy Turnbull (no relation) and he scored 42 goals in only 76 games. In United's first Championship success he notched up only 10 goals to add to Sandy's 25 but five of them were points winners. In the following campaign, as United inexplicably faded to 13th in the League, Turnbull hit 17 goals in 22 outings but, crucially, it was his two goals in the quarter final of the FA Cup that gave United a 3-2 victory on the way to winning the trophy for the first time.

Sandy TURNBULL was another of the banned Manchester City players to sign for United as Mangnall sought to land the title and he was one of four City players to make their debut on 1st January 1907 once their bans were finished. Turnbull, playing alongside former City team-mates Billy Meredith, Jimmy Bannister and Herbert Burgess, scored the only goal of the game against Aston Villa. Sandy Turnbull's 25 goals the following campaign were to prove vital to the landing of United's first title and he was to go on to score exactly 100 goals in 272 appearances. He also scored the only goal of the 1909 FA Cup Final and had earlier in the competition scored a hat-trick against Blackburn Rovers. He won a second Championship medal in 1911 scoring 18 goals and continued playing for United until the First World War where he met his death in action on 3rd May 1917 in France.

George WALL hailed from the North East but it was from Barnsley that United signed him in 1906. He scored the only goal of the game on his debut against Clapton Orient and was to share in both Championship successes and the FA Cup Final victory. A free scoring left winger, Wall scored no fewer than 98 goals from just over 300 appearances, a fabulous strike rate for a winger which won him seven England caps. He continued playing for United right up to the outbreak of World War One but after hostilities ceased he signed for Oldham Athletic before moving to Hamilton Academicals. He had a brief stay at Rochdale before hanging up his boots with over 500 league games to his credit.

That, then, was the backbone of the first truly great United side.

Although now a household name in most countries of the world where football is played, Manchester United's beginnings were, extremely humble and on at least two occasions they were nearly forced out of business. The origins of the club can be traced back to 1878 and a railway carriage making department at the Newton Heath works of the Lancashire and Yorkshire Railway Company. Not surprisingly, the workmen who formed the first side called themselves Newton Heath Lancashire and Yorkshire Railway.

The first ground was by the side of a clay pit in North Road, Newton Heath but there was no running straight out on to the pitch in those days. The players changed in a pub called the Three Crowns about eight hundred yards up the road from the ground but, nevertheless, the side were easily the best railway side in the area at that time and other works teams failed to give the Newton Heath side a decent game on most occasions. Soon, Newton Heath were looking further afield for matches. By the time professionalism was legalised in 1885, Newton Heath were on the fringe of the better class of sides in the area such as Bootle and Bolton Wanderers. In order to progress, Newton Heath decided to begin recruiting professionals who could also be offered work in the carriage department to boost their soccer earnings. This double-barrelled bargaining point enabled Newton Heath to attract some quite decent players including several Welsh internationals.

Indeed, no fewer than five Newton Heath players appeared for Wales in an international against Scotland in 1888. No matter that the Welsh side were beaten 5-1 in that game, the fact was that Newton Heath were growing in stature. Jack and Roger Doughty had been recruited from the top Welsh side of the day, Druids, whilst Jack Powell, who signed in 1886, became captain. Many is the player these days who says he would *"walk to Old Trafford for the privilege of playing for United"*. In the late 1880's a Scot by the name of Patrick O'Donnell did just that (except of course it was then Newton Heath). The distance from Glasgow to Manchester, however, was the same those days as a century later and he was rewarded for his epic walk with a job at the railway as well as playing football.

It may seem nonsensical now but, on the first occasion United (Newton Heath) applied for membership of the Football League in 1891, they received just one vote. They therefore turned their attentions in the direction of the Football Alliance and were promptly accepted. They won their first game against Sunderland Albion 4-1 and beat Small Heath 9-1 in their first campaign but struggled away, winning just twice on their travels, a feat they were to repeat in their second season. The third term of Alliance soccer got under way with yet another away beating but this disguised the course of events that lay ahead. When a second application to join the Football League was made, they could hardly have fared worse than on the first occasion but they did with Newton Heath not receiving a single vote of support. After this set back and an opening day defeat at Burton, few could have forecast the success that was to arrive in the 1891/92 season. After the loss at Burton, Newton

Heath remained unbeaten in their next fifteen outings and lost only twice more all season to secure runners-up spot behind Notts Forest who drew a crowd of 16,000 to North Road on New Year's Day 1892. At the end of that season, the Football League decided to enlarge and the Football Alliance were virtually encompassed en bloc. Newton Heath and Forest, as the Alliance's top two teams, went straight into the First Division and, now in the big time, the LYR was dropped from the club's title and the first full time Secretary, A.H.Albut appointed.

Thus, United began their Football League life under the name Newton Heath with a 4-3 defeat at Blackburn Rovers and, a week later, First Division football came to Manchester for the first time when Burnley visited North Road and went home with a 1-1 draw under their belts. It took Newton Heath seven games to notch their first ever Football League victory but it was done in some style. Strangely, their first ever win, 10-1 against Wolves remains today, well over 3,600 games later, their record score in the Football League! The big victory, however, was just a flash in the pan and Newton Heath finished rock bottom to be saved from relegation only by a 'Test Match' defeat of Small Heath. Newton Heath were, however, out of their depth in the First Division and finished bottom yet again the following campaign. They were relegated after losing their 'Test Match' to a side that were going to become, a century later, one of United's chief protagonists, Liverpool.

By now, Newton Heath had moved to pastures new at Bank Street but crowds were disappointing and, starved of cash, Newton Heath remained by and large a struggling Second Division outfit. There were highlights, however, including what almost was a record Football League scoreline of 14-0 over Walsall. The Midlanders, though, were obviously gluttons for punishment as they put in a protest, which was upheld, and when the game was replayed, Newton Heath could only find the net nine times!

Although nowadays a fashionable shirt to wear, the green and gold halves were dropped and the team kitted out in white but the side still languished in the lower reaches. By the turn of the century, the club were in serious financial trouble but were saved in bizarre fashion by a Bazaar by a St Bernard dog. The Bazaar had been organised to raise much needed money for the club and the captain of the side, Harry Stafford, tied a collection box to the neck of his St Bernard and allowed it to roam freely about the hall. Unfortunately, or, as it turned out, very fortunately, the dog wandered off out of the building and was eventually found by a wealthy businessman, John Davies. He became the club's first saviour.

On hearing of Newton Heath's plight, Davies paid off the club's debts of £2,500 (an astronomical sum in those days) and put in a further £500 to get some new players. He immediately became Chairman, decreed a change of name to Manchester United and bought a new kit – the famous red and white!

The first game under the new name was at Gainsborough Trinity in September 1902 and ended in a 1-0 victory. The season was to see another, much more, significant development, however, with the appointment of James Mangall as Secretary. Although his official title was Secretary, Mangnall is accepted as the first manager of the club as he was responsible for team selection and policy. It is a sign of how significant this move was, that Mangnall ranks with Sir Matt Busby and, latterly, Alex Ferguson in the top three managers the club has ever had.

In modern day parlance, Mangnall quite simply *"turned the club round"*. After finishing fifth in the Second Division in his first season (Manchester City, unfortunately for United supporters, won it) a crowd of over 40,000 turned out for the opening game of the 1903/04 campaign. For the next two seasons United were to just miss out on promotion but in 1905/06, after twice finishing third, United returned to the top flight after an absence of twelve years. They were about to embark on their most successful era and one that would not be repeated until another forty years had elapsed.

The strength of the team lay in the midfield, or half back line as it was then known, with Duckworth, Bell and Roberts acknowledged as the finest to be seen in English football until the 1940s. Mangnall also recruited the unrelated Sandy and James Turnbull along with Harold Halse and the legendary Billy Meredith. Halse was to play in FA Cup Finals for three different clubs in a seven year period (United, Villa and Chelsea) and it was his goal that brought United an FA Cup Final appearance for the first time in 1909. Meredith and Sandy Turnbull were part of a deal that saw United sign five players from Manchester City in 1906 with suspensions still to be served until 1907 over an illegal payments row. It wasn't, therefore, until the start of the 1907/08 season that Mangnall could at last get the team he wanted out on to the field but when he did, it was to prove a resounding success.

They won 14 of their first 15 league games in 1907/08, the only set back being a 2-1 reverse at Middlesbrough in the third game of the campaign. In those 15 games, Sandy Turnbull found the net 19 times, Meredith 8 and Jack Turnbull scored six after missing the opening five matches through injury. United dominated the Championship, finishing nine points (when there were only two points awarded for a win) clear of second placed Aston Villa who themselves were only thirteen points off bottom spot! Given that domination, United surprisingly didn't figure at all in the following season's Championship but they did put their appaling FA Cup record behind them by lifting the famous trophy for the first time.

United had never been beyond the quarter-final stage, indeed they had only reached the last eight on three occasions, and they needed an inordinate slice of luck to get past that stage on their way to capturing the Cup. They were losing 1-0 at Burnley with only eighteen minutes play left when a blizzard put paid to the game. When the replay took place, United won 3-2 and were then fortunate to tackle in the semi-final the most successful FA Cup side of that era, Newcastle United, when the Geordies were reduced to ten men with Halse scoring the only goal. Halse also had a big role to play in the final, for it was his shot that hit the Bristol City crossbar before bouncing down for Sandy Turnbull to score the only goal.

Satisfied with the success that his money had brought, John Davies now put in a further £60,000, a colossal amount in that period, to build a new stadium that would match the brilliance of the team his money had enabled Mangnall to establish. United played their last game at Clayton, ending with a 5-0 victory against Spurs and in February 1910, Old Trafford was born. The last game at Clayton was witnessed by a crowd of only 7,000 but in true Old Trafford tradition the opening of the new stadium attracted 45,000!

The first game was a hard pill to swallow as arch enemies Liverpool spoiled the party with a 4-3 success after United had led 3-1. The first full campaign in the stadium, which matched the best anywhere in the country, saw the crowds flock to Old Trafford to watch United take their second Championship, but whereas their first title had been all over bar the shouting a long way from home, this one went right to the finishing line. Again, Villa were the nearest challengers and going into the penultimate game of the season United had a two point lead. They lost at Villa Park which put Villa level on 50 points and a game in hand, a game which they proceeded to draw. The final day saw United at home to Sunderland whilst Villa, with a superior goal average, played Liverpool who were languishing in the bottom half of the table and with nothing to play for. United had to win and Villa lose, or alternatively, United win by a large score whilst Villa drew. The public showed what they thought of United's chances when only 10,000 turned up but United did their bit by winning 5-1 and then, with communications not as good as they are today, it was a case of sit and wait. For once, probably to their eternal sorrow, Liverpool did United a favour by beating Villa 3-1 and the title came to Old Trafford. But two World Wars were to pass before Old Trafford saw success again.

Mangnall left in 1912 as he saw his great team beginning to age and United were not to appoint a successor until John Robson in December 1914. The First World War, however, then intervened but when the country opened for football again in 1919, Old Trafford was inundated with crowds and the record league gate, 70,504 was set in 1920 for the visit of Aston Villa who won 3-1. United, however, were only a shadow of their former selves and Robson resigned after two seasons of mid-table mediocrity. His replacement, John Chapman, would doubtless have settled for a mid-table position as his first season in charge saw United relegated to the Second Division!

The relegation brought one of football's most famous names of the time, Frank Barson, to Old Trafford in an effort to regain a place in the top flight and a change of colours to all white with a red 'V'. But success was not achieved overnight and United had to wait until 1925 before gaining promotion behind Leicester City setting, in the process, a defensive record of just 23 goals conceded, a total never beaten before or since in the Second Division. Once again, however, the issue was not settled until the very last game of the campaign with United needing a point from their game with Barnsley to secure promotion in front of Derby County. They got the necessary point in a goalless draw at Barnsley but, in the event, County failed to win so United would have gone up anyway.

Back in the First Division, United had a reasonable season finishing ninth but they also had some bitter disappointments. There was a 5-0 hiding at Huddersfield and an even bigger 7-0 trouncing (then a record, later equalled but never surpassed) at Blackburn. Manager Chapman was quickly dismissed when the FA suspended him over a charge of "improper conduct", the exact details of which were never made known but, perhaps, the biggest blow of all was the FA Cup semi-final defeat at Bramall Lane against Manchester City. Another little piece of Old Trafford history was made with the appointment of Clarrie Hilditch as player/manager to replace Chapman, the only occasion the club have ever had such a position. No sooner was 1926 out of the way than the death of John Davies, who had done so much to first of all save, then resurrect, United was announced. The appointment of Hilditch had never been intended as anything other than temporary and 1927 saw the appointment of Herbert Bartlett along with a return to the familiar red shirts.

All these changes put United firmly on a downward road and the club headed towards oblivion. After four terms of being bottom half material, United had probably their worst ever season, being relegated back to the Second Division with a paltry 22 points and also set a Football League record that still exists when they lost all their first twelve games of 1930/31 season. In consecutive home games against Huddersfield Town and Newcastle United, the Reds conceded thirteen goals whilst in an away game at Stamford Bridge immediately prior to those two home disasters, Chelsea had also breached the United defence, if one could call it that, six times. Later in the season, Huddersfield Town and Derby County were also to find the net six times against United who, altogether, conceded 115 goals. Bamlett resigned but with the poor form, allied to the recession, attendances plummetted and the club was again financially crippled. With no John Davies to turn to, United were now saved by another local businessman, James Gibson, whose son Alan is still a Vice-President of the club.

He cleared the more pressing debts, paid the outstanding wages, injected a reported £20,000 to buy players and hired a new manager, Scott Duncan at a salary rumoured to be almost £1,000 a year. Duncan quickly spent the £20,000 recruiting his players mainly from his homeland, Scotland. Despite the vast expenditure he incurred, Duncan's early stewardship was a disaster and in 1933/34 they reached an all time low when they were just one game away from relegation to the Third Division North. United travelled to play Millwall in their final match of the season knowing they had to win in order to avert relegation. Lincoln City were already down but the Reds were in 21st spot with 32 points. Immediately above United were Millwall with 33 points but their problem had been picking up points away from home. At the Den they had a good home record, better in fact than the Champions, Grimsby Town and, as United travelled to London, the unthinkable was very much on the cards. Despite, or because of, using no fewer than 38 players (no substitutes in those days) during the campaign United looked doomed. In the event, United surprised everybody, including most probably themselves, and won 2-0 with goals from Cape and Manley. The Reds had, in fact, gone five games unbeaten at the end of the campaign to save themselves.

Immediately after this escape, Duncan made probably his best buy, capturing George Mutch from Arbroath for £800. He was leading scorer in his first term and when, twelve months later, United won the Second Division title thanks to an unbeaten run of 19 games stretching from 4th January, when Bradford City beat them 1-0, until the end of the season, it was Mutch's 21 goals that led the way. Mutch went on to be transferred for £5,000 to Preston North End and is still shown on television scoring the only goal of the 1938 FA Cup Final from the penalty spot in the last minute. Duncan was rewarded with a new five year contract for gaining promotion but the directors should have waited – twelve months later the Reds were back in the Second Division! Almost as bad was the fact that Manchester City had won the First Division title! Duncan resigned and moved to Ipswich Town whom he immediately proceeded to take into the Football League.

As the saying goes, football is a funny old game. The following season United won promotion back to the First whilst, almost unbelievably, Manchester City created history by being the first, and to date, only Champions to be immediately relegated. The boot was very firmly on the other foot! But, once again, it was a nail-biting climax that went to the last day. Aston Villa were up as Champions and Sheffield United were second with 53 points having finished their programme. United and Coventry City were level in third place, two points behind Sheffield, with United's goal average just the better. A crowd of over 50,000 saw United clinch promotion with a 2-0 victory whilst Coventry finished fourth when they only drew their last fixture. In this new look United were several unknowns who were not to remain unknown after World War Two – the era of Johnny Carey, Stan Pearson and Jack Rowley was beginning to unfold.

By the end of the war, Matt Busby had been named as manager but United had no ground. Old Trafford, situated in the heart of Manchester's main industrial complex, Trafford Park, had been destroyed as the Germans targeted factories in the area for almost daily bombings. Whilst in the Army, Busby had been in charge of an army side in Italy and had been helped out by Jimmy Murphy. Busby immediately turned to his war-time colleague and invited him to become his assistant. The partnership was to take United to great heights.

United had arguably the best team in the land but couldn't prove it with a title as they finished runners-up four times in the first five post-war championships. They did, however, lift the FA Cup for the second time nearly forty years after their first success in 1909. The 1948 Wembley victory came without playing anybody outside of the top flight. The Third Round tie against Aston Villa was a classic as the home side went in front in under 20 seconds only for United to lead 5-1 at half-time. Anybody who thought the game was over had another think coming. The Reds scraped home 6-4 in one of the classic FA Cup confrontations of all time. By the time they reached the Twin Towers, the Reds had scored eighteen goals but so had their opponents, Blackpool. With just over twenty minutes left it looked like United were going to be bridesmaids as Blackpool led 2-1 but Rowley equalised and goals from Pearson and Anderson secured the coveted trophy.

The crowds were returning in dramatic fashion and United, with their ground rebuilt, left their temporary home at Maine Road to return to Old Trafford in the knowledge that they had repaid all debts. The way was clear for progress. Despite being invited to take over the Italian National side, Busby remained at Old Trafford and by 1952 had landed his first Championship. It then seemed as if United could follow City in to the record books by getting relegated immediately after winning the title when, at the end of October they were bottom – not that City fans were laughing – they were next to bottom! To halt the rot, Busby introduced many of his young reserve team, Whitefoot, Pegg, Edwards, Viollett, Foulkes, Jones and Blanchflower. In addition he bought Tommy Taylor from Barnsley for £29,999, the missing £1 being because Busby didn't want the youngster being burdened with the tag of becoming the first £30,000 player. Another youngster, Roger Byrne, who had played in the Championship side as a left winger was switched to left back on the retirement of Carey and was to become one of the most astute captains ever to lead United.

The youngsters learned their trade under Busby and Murphy for two years, finishing fourth and fifth, before becoming the most dominant team of their era. The 1955/56 title was a one horse race when they took the title by eleven points (in the days of two points for a win) from Blackpool. There was no nail biting finish this time with the Championship nicely wrapped up as early as 7th April when the Reds beat their nearest rivals 2-1 at Old Trafford in front of almost 63,000 adoring fans. Only winger Johnny Berry and Roger Byrne, still a youngster himself, remained from the team that won the title just four years earlier and the average age was an incredible 22. Just Berry and Taylor had cost sizeable fees with almost the entire squad having come through the Youth ranks. Indeed, it was not uncommon for crowds of over 25,000 to turn out to watch the Youth team as it won the FA Youth Cup in each of the first five occasions it was competed for. The aggregate scores of 9-3, 7-1 and 8-2 in three of the Finals demonstrated how outclassed the opposition were in this competition whilst it took great goalkeeping by an unknown youngster, Gordon Banks, to keep United down to four in the 1956 Final against Chesterfield. Indeed, although the 25,000 plus crowd at that Final didn't realise it at the time, they were watching two players who were to become household names throughout the world, let alone England, in Banks and Bobby Charlton.

United ignored an FA request not to enter the newly instituted European Cup (Chelsea had obliged the FA the previous season) and, without floodlights, they played their home games at Maine Road. Having won the First Leg against Belgian champions, Anderlecht, barely 40,000 turned up to see one of most polished performances given by any team in the world. Anderlecht were not a bad team but they had no answer to United on that evening as the Reds ran riot scoring ten which would have been significantly more had several players refused to score, preferring instead to try to give a goal to Pegg, who didn't get on the scoresheet despite setting up many chances for his colleagues. In the league, United took their unbeaten run of fourteen games at the end of the previous campaign to 26 before Everton surprisingly put five past the Reds at Old Trafford. The title was wrapped up by eight points and there were high hopes of a treble as United reached the FA Cup Final and the semi-finals of the European Cup thanks to a momentous night at Maine Road. United were trailing by two goals to Spanish champions, Atletico Bilbao, from the first leg but overcame the deficit in an electric atmosphere.

United were now to embark on nine months that was nothing but grief. A truly great Real Madrid side containing players such as Di Stefano, Gento, Santamaria and Kopa drew 2-2 in Old Trafford's first European competitive game to knock United out 5-3 on aggregate. In the FA Cup Final, United's hopes were dashed by what today would have been an automatic sending off but McParland, after breaking 'keeper Wood's jaw stayed on to score both Aston Villa's goals against stand in custodian, Jackie Blanchflower. United were left with just the Championship in a season which marked the two goal debut of Bobby Charlton against, strangely, Charlton Athletic, whom he scored a hat-trick against in the return fixture!

United didn't quite dominate the 1957/58 title race as they had in the previous two seasons but, after winning a classic 5-4 encounter at Arsenal on 1st February, after putting seven past Bolton Wanderers in the previous match, everything seemed on course for a third successive championship. The Reds left Arsenal in good spirits to travel to Red Star Belgrade confident of protecting a 2-1 First Leg lead to reach the semi-finals of the European Cup for a second successive time. The game finished 3-3 but, as the whole football world knows, tragedy was to wipe out most of the team at a stroke. Attempting to take off for a third time following a refuelling stop at Munich, an iced up wing caused the plane to veer off the runway and crash. Roger Byrne, Eddie Colman, Mark Jones, David Pegg, Billy Whelan, Tommy Taylor and a reserve player, Geoff Bent were amongst those killed instantly. Duncan Edwards, as one would expect from such a giant, fought for life against overwhelming odds for almost two weeks before losing the one sided battle. When he died in his 21st year, he already held 18 full caps, two championship medals and an FA Cup Final medal.

Miraculously, United beat AC Milan 2-1 in the first leg of the European Cup semi-final and reached the FA Cup Final, but won only one more league match (against Sunderland 2-1, away) as not surprisingly they fell down the table to finish ninth. As Matt Busby fought successfully for his life, Jimmy Murphy, who had not been on the ill fated trip due to his commitments with the Welsh national side, took charge and produced a team for the first match after Munich, a 5th Round FA Cup-tie against Sheffield Wednesday, containing only two players, Harry Gregg and Billy Foulkes, who had played in the previous round, three weeks earlier against Ipswich Town. Ian Greaves, Ronnie Cope, Mark 'Pancho" Pearson, Shay Brennan and Alex Dawson were boys who became men overnight. Two reserve players who had played in the first team previously, Colin Webster and Freddie Goodwin made up the side along with two signings, Ernie Taylor and Stan Crowther, who were given special dispensation by the FA to play as they had already appeared for Blackpool and Aston Villa in that season's competition. Carried along on a wave of emotion, the cobbled together side won 3-0 with two goals from Brennan and one from Dawson. The Sixth Round saw a Colin Webster goal dispose of West Bromwich Albion on another emotional night after a 2-2 draw at the Hawthorns in a match that saw the arrival back of Bobby Charlton – little could he have known then what responsibility he was going to have thrust on him over the next few years. Fulham (and a young Jimmy Hill) almost put United out in the semi-final but two Charlton goals saved the day and a Dawson treble in the Highbury replay did the rest. Incredibly, the ravaged United were in the FA Cup Final.

Unbelievably, United were to have their 'keeper injured for the second Final in succession when Lofthouse quite blatantly bundled both Gregg and the ball into the net for Bolton's second and decisive goal. Charlton had hit the post for United and had had another fine effort saved by England 'keeper Eddie Hopkinson but the Reds became the first side in the 20th century to lose two successive FA Cup Finals. Eleven days later, their European dreams also crashed when they lost 4-0 in Milan.

Amazingly, the following season United finished runners-up to Wolverhampton Wanderers as Denis Viollet broke the club scoring record for a campaign with 32 strikes. But the momentum began to wane and United had some average seasons finishing seventh twice and then 15th as well as being humiliated 7-2 at home in the FA Cup by Sheffield Wednesday. In 1963 it looked for much of the time as if they would be relegated but a draw in the third last game of the season at Maine Road virtually kept the Reds up and City down. The FA Cup, however, redeemed an otherwise forgettable year with United completely outclassing Leicester City who had finished fifteen places above them in the First Division. Goals from David Herd (two) and Denis Law brought the Cup back to Old Trafford.

Just as almost thirty years earlier when the near drop into the Third Division galvanised United, so did the threat of relegation in 1963. The following year saw the introduction of a youngster from Northern Ireland, George Best, who became an instant hit with the fans. United finished runners-up to Liverpool and reached the semi-final of the FA Cup only to be beaten by a Bobby Moore inspired West Ham on a quagmire at Hillsborough just days after finally overcoming Sunderland at the third attempt on another bog at Leeds Road, Huddersfield. But the biggest disappointment was reserved for the Cup-winners Cup where everyone went home after a 4-1 first-leg victory over Sporting Lisbon thinking all United had to do was to turn up in Portugal. Apparently, the players also thought along those lines for they crashed 5-0 in one of the biggest ever turn rounds in European history.

The crowds flocked back to Old Trafford as United boasted three of the world's best players, Law, Best and Charlton on display every Saturday afternoon. United won the 1964/65 title on goal difference from Leeds United although it wasn't quite as close as that as they already had the title sewn up when they lost their last game at Aston Villa. Leeds had the last laugh, however, when they beat United in the semi-final of the FA Cup after two games. United were also destined to lose in the semi-final of the Inter-Cities Fairs Cup over three matches to the Hungarian outfit, Ferencvaros.

United were now back on the big stage of the European Cup itself and the dream was shortly to become reality but not before more disappointment. Best became christened 'El Beatle' after demolishing Benfica 5-1 in the Stadium of Light. After such a performance United were considered very serious contenders for the European crown but the soldiers of Partisan Belgrade surprised everybody with a 2-0 home win that United could not overcome in the return. Busby presumably thought his dream had vanished for ever. But his side bounced back to grab the title once more in 1966/67 with a relentless run of twenty games unbeaten to the end of the season culminating in a 6-1 celebration at Upton Park. The boys were back!

The following season they lost their title of Champions but the fact that it was Manchester City who deprived them of top spot made it hurt just that little bit more. However, there was a glittering prize that was more than ample consolation.

Comparatively easy wins over Hibernians of Malta, Sarajevo, and Gornik saw United up against Real Madrid in the semi-final. A George Best goal gave United a slender advantage to take to the Bernabeau Stadium but surely it wasn't enough. And so it looked with a quarter of an hour left as United trailed 3-1 but then, as in all fairy stories, came the unlikeliest of heroes. Billy Foulkes had started down the European road in United's first ever tie in 1956. Twelve years later he was to inspire United from adversity to their golden goal. In a career spanning almost 700 games, Foulkes rarely ventured over the half way line and scored just nine goals in a 17 year career. Suddenly, he rose above the Madrid defence to head a Crerand free-kick on for Sadler to convert and, then, three minutes later appeared from nowhere to stab home the equaliser on the night and the winner on aggregate.

On a nostalgic night that nobody who was present will ever forget, United finally overcame Benfica 4-1 in extra time at Wembley. Even that game, however, could have gone the other way had Stepney not made a great save from Eusebio in normal time. Best was a wizard, Charlton scored a rare goal with his head, and Kidd celebrated his 19th birthday with a goal but the lad who played the game of his life that night was the one who was the target of the boo boys for much of the campaign, John Aston, whose pace tore the Portuguese side apart.

United were unable to retain their new title the following year when they lost 2-1 to AC Milan and Busby handed over the reins to Wilf McGuinness. It heralded an era of managerial change at Old Trafford and with McGuinness soon departed, Busby took over again temporarily before Frank O'Farrell experienced an even worse time than McGuinness. In 1972, with relegation once more a very real prospect, Tommy Docherty was brought in. He saved them from the immediate threat but couldn't keep them up the following season which had a sting in the tail, for it was former United hero Denis Law, now returned to Manchester City, who back heeled the goal at Old Trafford that confirmed the relegation. Law took no pleasure from the act and did not join in the City celebrations. The following day he announced his retirement – his last league goal had put United down. At least the Board kept faith with Docherty and he rewarded them with probably the best 'flair' team to play between Busby's 1967 championship side and Ferguson's 1992 Champions. Gordon Hill and Steve Coppell patrolled the wings and scored goals at the same time, Martin Buchan had developed into a fine defender as well as a fine leader and there were talents such as Macari and McIlroy. They were lucky with injuries and, by the end of the season, no fewer than ten players had played over 30 games. They won their first game at Orient and were never headed.

Back in the First Division, Docherty saw his young side more than hold their own and they also reached Wembley where they were hot favourites to dispose of Southampton, then a mid-table Division Two side. On the day, United never performed and a good strike by Bobby Stokes sealed victory for the 'Saints'. The following year they were back at the Twin Towers but very much in the role that Southampton had adopted twelve months previously. Liverpool had won the League and Wembley was merely a stopping off point on the way to a unique treble as they were also to take the European crown. Unfortunately for the Anfield club, nobody had given United a copy of the script and two goals in a five minute second half spell gave United a victory as unexpected as their defeat in the previous final. Two months after this success, Docherty was dismissed for undertaking a relationship with the wife of the United physio, Laurie Brown.

After flirting in more ways than one with the outgoing personality of Docherty, United turned back to the quiet and unassuming type in Dave Sexton even though their experience with O'Farrell should have been sufficient to let the Board know it was not what the fans wanted. Sexton, to an extent, was unlucky for he saw his team come second in one of the best modern FA Cup Finals. United fought back from 2-0 down to level against Arsenal in the last four minutes of the 1979 Wembley spectacular only to immediately concede a third goal themselves. The following campaign saw United level with Liverpool at the top of the First Division on the final Saturday of the season but Liverpool beat Villa whilst United lost at Elland Road. 1980/81 saw the end of Sexton's reign and he must look back and think it was a case of so near, yet so far. Sadly, for a man of immense integrity, he left with the millstone of his £1 million plus signing, striker Gary Birtles, around his neck – Birtles had failed to find the net in the 25 league games he played under Sexton.

United's hierarchy realised they had to give the fans someone with charisma and in those stakes they didn't come much bigger than Ron Atkinson. Where Sexton and O'Farrell had struggled in communication with the fans, Atkinson, like Docherty, loved the publicity and banter. He also had a flair for producing attractive sides and United looked good again. He took twelve months to settle in and then gave the Reds their first ever League Cup Final but it ended in defeat against Liverpool after extra-time. Just weeks later the Red hordes were back at Wembley for the FA Cup Final against Brighton. That, too, almost finished in disaster as Bailey made a great reflex save to deny Brighton the winner with virtually the last kick of the match. Brighton had had their opportunity and paid heavily in the replay, losing to a 4-0 scoreline that flattered them. In these games Alan Davies created what will surely be a record that stands for all time. He only played two FA Cup ties for United, both of which were FA Cup Finals! Two years later United made FA Cup history again when Kevin Moran became the first player to be sent off in a FA Cup Final as United beat Everton with a Norman Whiteside goal in extra-time.

The coveted title still eluded United but, in 1985, it looked to be on its way as United won their first ten matches. It all went sadly wrong, however, and a bad start to the next campaign left Atkinson to rue that two Cup wins in three seasons was no compensation for not winning the Championship. United appointed Alex Ferguson, destined to become the first man since Busby to land the title, but it took him six years to end the obsession. In November 1986, just weeks after Ferguson's arrival, United were in 21st position but had recovered to finish 11th by the end of the season. In 1987/88 they improved to finish second but near misses were no good to United followers and 1988/89 brought only disappointment. Indeed, many United fans were beginning to see Ferguson in the mould of Sexton and O'Farrell and there were distant rumblings. The league performance in 89/90 was tantamount to disillusionment for many Old Trafford faithful and the rumblings were getting very much closer to home and almost reached a crescendo when a United side that had cost Ferguson £11m were crushed like schoolboys 5-1 by Manchester City. Off the field, United were almost becoming a laughing stock with Robert Maxwell expressing interest in buying the club and then a ball juggling Michael Knighton appearing out of the blue in a bid to become Chairman. United finished 13th but Ferguson was probably saved by an incredible cup run. United were drawn away in every round, drew 3-3 with Oldham Athletic in the semi-final and, amazingly, drew by the same scoreline in the Final itself with Crystal Palace. In the replay, the only FA Cup goal ever scored by Lee Martin brought Ferguson his first trophy.

Having broken his duck at last, Ferguson collected prizes for fun. Although they slipped up badly against Sheffield Wednesday (and Ron Atkinson) in the Final of the Rumbelows' League Cup, United lifted their second European honour when they beat Barcelona 2-1 in Rotterdam in the Cup-Winners Cup. The next year it was the League Cup with Nottingham Forest the victims but the Reds let the league title slip away to Leeds. Still the ultimate prize eluded them but then in the late autumn of 1992 with his side again failing to set the world alight, Ferguson, quite out of character, took an immense gamble. He purchased from Leeds United the volatile Frenchman, Eric Cantona. Most pundits agreed that Ferguson had flipped his lid but, in fact, the last piece of the jigsaw had just been slotted into place. On a stage fit for world class acts, Cantona became one. The bald statistics show just what a bargain Ferguson landed for £1m. In the Frenchman's first fifty games, United lost just twice! The title was won at last, and by ten points, but it was never that easy. Indeed, at 4.45 on 10th April 1993, United appeared to have lost the lead to Aston Villa for they trailed Sheffield Wednesday by 1-0 at Old Trafford whilst title rivals Villa (and Ron Atkinson) were winning. In the next minute Villa dropped two valuable points and United gained three as Steve Bruce scored twice in time added on for injury to the referee! The five point turn around in that decisive moment proved vital and United went on to win their last seven games as Villa fell away. Strangely, just twenty four hours earlier, central defender Bruce had said on TV that it was about time he started scoring again following a run of over 30 games without finding the net! The Holy Grail came back to Old Trafford in a carnival atmosphere as United entertained Blackburn Rovers on 3rd May but nobody mentioned Harry Stafford and his dog!

The return of the Holy Grail, however, was only the prelude to the most successful season ever in the club's history. Never in with a realistic hope of European Cup success due to the 'foreign players' rule, it was still a major surprise to see the Reds go out to little known Turkish side Galatasary after holding a 3-1 lead at one stage in the first leg at Old Trafford. But this proved to be almost a blessing in disguise as the dismissal enabled United to concentrate their minds on the domestic scene. And how they concentrated! A massive lead by Christmas in the League gave the Old Trafford outfit the opportunity to pour everything into the two home Cup competitions. The Coca Cola League Cup that did not figure on their hit list whilst they were still in Europe now assumed more importance and progress was made in the FA Cup. The club were rocked in January by the death of Sir Matt Busby and it seemed with his passing that the team were blown off course. By the end of March, Hughes, Cantona (in successive games), Schmeichel, and Kanchelskis were all sent off, United's once substantial lead in the League was whittled away to nothing by Blackburn and former Red boss Ron Atkinson tactically outmanoeuvred United in the Coca Cola League Cup Final.

United's campaign seemed to be doomed to insignificant failure with just one minute of extra time in the FA Cup semi-final against Oldham Athletic left. The hoardes that United had taken to Wembley were silent, almost unbelieving, as they pondered how so much could have gone wrong so quickly. Then came the one moment in time that saved United's season as Mark Hughes volleyed a last gasp equaliser out of nothing. Had they lost that game, many fervently believe they would have ended up with nothing.

As it was, their season resumed what had been assumed for many months to be its destiny. Having stared the precipice in the face, the Reds somehow became revitalised, thrashing Oldham in the replay and gaining the League title as Blackburn faltered. A 4-0 victory over Chelsea in FA Cup Final was not as easy as the scoreline suggests but it was good enough to give Alex Ferguson the double, the first United team to accomplish the feat – and how near they had come to a treble after becoming the first club in English Football history to win the Championship and appear in both major domestic Cup Finals. A fitting memory to Sir Matt.

But after the high of 1993/94 United fell victim in 1994/95 to the Eric Cantona saga of Crystal Palace where the Frenchman attacked a so-called supporter and was banned for nine months. Despite this set-back the Reds only narrowly failed to repeat their double of the previous season, finishing runners-up in both League and FA Cup. Ferguson then rocked the football world by selling three of the integral parts of the team that had done so well for him and many people saw the departure of Mark Hughes, Paul Ince and Andrei Kanchelskis as the beginning of the end for the United boss. Their thoughts appeared to be well founded just 45 minutes into the campaign when United were three down at Villa Park but the roller coaster ride that is Manchester United was about to turn yet another upward curve. Despite that defeat, the youngsters brought in to replace the departed stars hung on in the title race until the return of Cantona from suspension in October and, after going twelve points adrift of Newcastle in January, a brilliant run of 19 victories and one draw in their last 21 games from the end of January saw United capture their second double in three years to become the first club ever to perform the feat.

1909	–	After winning the FA Cup, United are given the then huge sum of £60,000 to purchase a new site and build a modern (for the times) stadium.
19/02/1910	–	United leave their old ground in Clayton and play their first ever game at Old Trafford. The visitors are Liverpool and 45,000 fans turn up but go home disappointed as United lose 4-3 after twice leading by two goals.
29/04/1911	–	United beat Sunderland 5-1 on the final day of the season at Old Trafford to take the First Division title by one point. Two World Wars would be waged before it landed back at Old Trafford again.
1911	–	The new stadium is quickly rewarded as the Football Association choose it for the FA Cup replay between Bradford City and Newcastle United. The Yorkshire club win their one and only FA Cup, beating the Geordies 1-0.
1915	–	Old Trafford hosts the FA Cup Final to end a 19 year association with Crystal Palace as the venue. With war clouds over Europe, the Final became known as "The Khaki Final" as the terraces were packed with soldiers at home on leave for the weekend. Sheffield United beat Chelsea 3-0.
27/12/1920	–	The record attendance for a League game is set at 70,504 for the visit of Aston Villa who win 3-1.
1922	–	Old Trafford stages the FA Charity Shield match between Huddersfield Town and Liverpool which goes to the Yorkshire side 1-0.
17/04/1926	–	The last England v. Scotland full International to be played in England outside of Wembley Stadium takes place at Old Trafford. The Scots win with the only goal of the game from Jackson.
Sept 1930	–	United concede thirteen goals in successive home games four days apart when Huddersfield hit them for six and Newcastle United knock in seven. In the worst ever start by any Football League club, United's first point of the campaign does not come until November when Birmingham City are beaten 2-0 at Old Trafford after twelve straight defeats.
16/11/1938	–	The ground witnesses the fastest ever hat–trick in International football as Willie Hall (Spurs) nets a treble inside three and a half minutes against Ireland. He goes on to score five times in succession thus equalling the England record in a 7-0 rout.

25/03/1939	–	The ground's record attendance of 76,962 is set when Old Trafford stages the FA Cup semi–final between Portsmouth and Grimsby Town. The 'Mariners' lose their 'keeper very early in the match and Portsmouth take full advantage to win 5-0.
11/03/1941	–	The ground, situated on the perimeter of Manchester's vast Trafford Park industrial complex, is virtually demolished as Hitler's bombs target the area to halt engineering production for Britain's war effort.
8/01/1949	–	United play their first FA Cup tie at Old Trafford for ten years when they hammer Bournemouth 6-0. Their last tie at Old Trafford had been a Third Round replay on 11th January 1939 when West Bromwich Albion had beaten the Reds 5-1.
1951	–	The first foreign team to play United at Old Trafford are Red Star Belgrade in a fixture organised to celebrate the Festival of Britain. The match finishes 1-1 with Jack Rowley equalising from the penalty spot late in the game.
26/04/1952	–	United swamp Arsenal, the only team who can catch them, 6-1 in the final game of the season to capture the title for the first time since 1911. Rowley nets a hat–trick.
24/01/1955	–	The longest ever FA Cup tie is finally resolved at Old Trafford when Stoke City eventually beat Bury 3-2 after nine hours twenty–two minutes.
07/04/1956	–	United clinch their third ever First Division title by beating Blackpool 2-1 at Old Trafford in front of their biggest crowd of the season, 62,277.
30/04/1956	–	The programme for the First Leg of the FA Youth Cup Final at Old Trafford against Chesterfield contains the following pen picture of a Chesterfield youngster. *"Gordon Banks (Goalkeeper), a Sheffield boy in his second year at the club. Has played several games in the Reserves recently and acquitted himself well".*
6/10/1956	–	In a strange coincidence, Bobby Charlton makes his debut at Old Trafford against his namesake team, Charlton Athletic. He scores twice and in the return game hits a hat–trick!
20/10/1956	–	United lose 5-2 to Everton at Old Trafford where they had been unbeaten for eighteen months. The last team to beat them at home had also been Everton in March 1955.
25/03/1957	–	United play their first ever game at Old Trafford under floodlights but fail to celebrate as they go down 2-0 in a league match to Bolton Wanderers.

08/04/1957	–	United's Youth team lose 3-2 to Southampton at Old Trafford in the semi–final of the FA Youth Cup. It is their first ever defeat in the competition since it was formed in 1952 but they still go on to win it again as they had won the first leg at the Dell 5-1.
25/04/1957	–	Old Trafford stages its first ever European cup tie as Real Madrid provide stiff resistance in a 2-2 draw which sees them through to the Final having beaten United 3-1 in Spain. All United's previous home games in the European Cup had been played at Maine Road.
2/10/1957	–	Shamrock Rovers become United's first ever Old Trafford European victims when they are beaten 3-2 in the European Cup.
30/10/1957	–	Brian Clough becomes the second player to score five goals in a Representative game at Old Trafford when he goes 'nap' for an FA XI against the Army.
30/11/1957	–	Having never been beaten by a London club at Old Trafford since October 1938 when Charlton Athletic won 2-0, United finally lose 4-3 to Spurs. United then proceeded to lose their very next home game to another London outfit, Chelsea!
19/02/1958	–	United's first game after the Munich Air Crash takes place in an emotional atmosphere at Old Trafford. The FA Cup Fifth Round tie is won 3-0 with a make shift team of youngsters. Shay Brennan's opening goal was in fact United's first ever FA Cup goal against Wednesday as the Yorkshire side had been victorious in all the previous encounters by scores of 6-0, 1-0 and 2-0.
14/01/1961	–	United beat Spurs 2-0 at Old Trafford – the only occasion that the famous Tottenham 'double' side failed to score all season.
1961	–	Old Trafford stages the first ever League Cup semi–final replay when Aston Villa beat Burnley 2-1.
1966	–	Old Trafford is selected to host three of the Group games in the World Cup. Portugal, who England went on to defeat in the semi–final score their first ever goal in World Cup Finals stages when Augusto nets in a 3-1 win over Hungary at Old Trafford.
26/11/1966	–	David Herd scores one of the most unusual hat-tricks ever when Sunderland visit Old Trafford. Each of his three goals was put past a different 'keeper! He scored first of all against Jim Montgomery who was injured and then against his replacement, central defender Charlie Hurley. The Sunderland management then decided the team pattern was better served by Hurley reverting to his outfield position and he was replaced by John Parke against whom Herd completed his treble!

1967/68	–	United, with Best, Law and Charlton in the side set an average attendance record for the season at Old Trafford (and the Football League) of 57,758.
17/12/1969	–	Old Trafford sets a record attendance for the League Cup when United draw 2-2 with neighbours Manchester City in the second leg of a semi–final tie. A crowd of 63,418 see City reach the Final, having won the first leg 2-1.
1970	–	Old Trafford stages its third FA Cup Final when Leeds United and Chelsea replay there after a 2-2 draw at Wembley. The game finishes 2-1 to Chelsea after extra–time.
1972	–	Bobby Moore saves a penalty at Old Trafford in the League Cup 2nd Replay between West Ham United and Stoke City. He had to go in net when the 'Hammers' 'keeper Ferguson was taken off injured but although Moore saved the spot kick, Bernard followed up to convert. When Conroy scored the winner for Stoke, the tie had been under way for seven hours.
1977	–	Old Trafford sees League Cup history made when Aston Villa beat Everton in a League Cup Final 2nd Replay by 3-2. They become the first club to win the trophy three times.
1978	–	The League Cup Final is back again at Old Trafford with Nottingham Forest defeating Liverpool 1-0 via a hotly disputed John Robertson penalty.
22/03/1980	–	The 100th 'Derby' match with Manchester City takes place at Old Trafford. A Micky Thomas goal gives the Reds victory.
14/10/1980	–	Old Trafford hosts the England 'B' international with the United States. The home side win 1-0.
12/12/1984	–	Celtic are ordered to replay their European tie with Rapid Vienna at Old Trafford after crowd trouble on their own ground and are well beaten by the Austrians.
22/04/1989	–	The Women's FA Cup Final takes place at Old Trafford and is televised for the first time. Leasowe Pacific beat Fulham 3-2.
21/10/1989	–	Rugby League history is made at Old Trafford when Paul Newlove becomes the youngest Great Britain international at the age of 18 years and 72 days in the 24-16 reverse at the hands of New Zealand.

Awards

European Footballer of the Year

| 1964 | Denis Law | 1966 | Bobby Charlton | 1968 | George Best |

NB – The only other British club to have had a player voted European Footballer of the Year are Blackpool whose Stanley Matthews won the first award in 1956.

Footballer of the Year

| 1949 | Johnnie Carey | 1966 | Bobby Charlton | 1968 | George Best |
| 1996 | Eric Cantona | | | | |

PFA Player of the Year

| 1989 | Mark Hughes | 1991 | Mark Hughes | 1992 | Gary Pallister |
| 1994 | Eric Cantona | | | | |

NB – Mark Hughes is the only player to have won this award on more than one occasion.

PFA Young Player of the Year

| 1985 | Mark Hughes | 1991 | Lee Sharpe | 1992 | Ryan Giggs |
| 1993 | Ryan Giggs | | | | |

(NB – Ryan Giggs is the only player to have won this award in successive seasons. United are the only club to have had three successive winners)

PFA Merit Awards

| 1974 | Bobby Charlton | 1975 | Denis Law | 1980 | Sir Matt Busby |
| 1993 | 1968 Manchester United team | | | | |

Manager of the Year

| 1968 | Sir Matt Busby | 1993 | Alex Ferguson | 1994 | Alex Ferguson |
| 1996 | Alex Ferguson | | | | |

Barclay's Young Eagle of the Year

| 1992 | Ryan Giggs |

Squad Performances 1995-96

Reserves

Pontins League Division One

Date	Fixture	Score	Goalscorers
16/08/95	Bolton Wanderers (h)	1-0	Tomlinson
30/08/95	Notts County (h)	2-2	Giggs, McGibbon
02/09/95	Liverpool (a)	2-3	Giggs, Appleton
06/09/95	Blackburn Rovers (a)	1-1	Wallwork
27/09/95	Oldham Athletic (a)	2-0	Tomlinson, Casper
07/10/95	Leeds United (h)	2-0	Tomlinson, Cooke

(The attendance for this match was 21,502 due to Eric Cantona's appearance)

Date	Fixture	Score	Goalscorers
12/10/95	West Bromwich Albion (a)	4-2	Kirovski 3, Cooke
18/10/95	Birmingham City (a)	3-0	Tomlinson 2, Cooke
25/10/95	Nottingham Forest (a)	1-1	Cooke
01/11/95	Sheffield Wednesday (a)	3-5	Kirovski 2, Sharpe
15/11/95	Sheffield United (h)	6-0	McClair, Kirovski, Tomlinson, Appleton, Beckham, Blount og
20/11/95	Wolves (h)	2-0	Cooke, Sharpe
29/11/95	Tranmere Rovers (a)	3-1	Tomlinson, Cooke, Kirovski
06/12/95	Leeds United (a)	2-1	Tomlinson, McGibbon
14/12/95	Oldham Athletic (h)	2-2	Kirovski, Baker
20/12/95	Derby County (h)	3-1	Kirovski, Mustoe, Sutton og.
03/01/96	Newcastle United (a)	0-2	
09/01/96	Everton (a)	1-0	Casper
16/01/96	Liverpool (h)	2-1	Scholes, McGibbon
24/01/96	Bolton Wanderers (a)	2-0	Beckham, Scholes
31/01/96	Blackburn Rovers (h)	2-1	Kirovski, Thornley
15/02/96	Everton (h)	2-0	Kirovski, Thornley
26/02/96	Sheffield United (a)	3-0	Davies 2, G Neville
07/03/96	Sheffield Wednesday (h)	2-1	Clegg, Kirovski
19/03/96	Derby County (a)	1-2	Kirovski
28/03/96	Stoke City (a)	1-1	Cooke
04/04/96	Notts County (a)	1-0	Wood
10/04/96	West Bromwich Albion (h)	4-1	O'Kane, Scholes, Appleton, Kirovski
20/04/96	Notts Forest (h)	4-0	Kirovski 2, Cooke 2
22/04/96	Birmingham City (a)	0-1	
24/04/96	Newcastle United (h)	2-0	Kirovski, Baker
29/04/96	Stoke City (h)	1-0	Kirovski
01/05/96	Tranmere Rovers (h)	2-3	Kirovski 2
06/05/96	Wolves (a)	2-3	Kirovski, O'Kane

'A' Team

19/08/95	Morecambe Reserves (h)	8-0
26/08/95	Tranmere Rovers 'A' (h)	0-0
2/09/95	Blackburn Rovers 'A' (h)	2-2
9/09/95	Blackpool 'A' (a)	2-1
16/09/95	Wrexham 'A' (h)	3-2
7/10/95	Crewe Alexandra Res (h)	0-1
14/10/95	Tranmere Rovers 'A' (a)	2-0
21/10/95	Everton 'A' (h)	5-1
28/10/95	Stoke City 'A' (a)	0-2
11/11/95	Marine Res (a)	6-1
18/11/95	Manchester City 'A' (h)	0-0
24/11/95	Morecambe Reserves (a)	2-0
2/12/95	Wrexham 'A' (a)	2-0
16/12/95	Liverpool 'A' (h)	3-1
6/01/96	Preston North End 'A' (h)	5-0
13/01/96	Crewe Alexandra Res (a)	0-2
20/01/96	Blackburn Rovers 'A' (a)	5-0
3/02/96	Manchester City 'A' (a)	1-0
17/02/96	Oldham Athletic 'A' (h)	3-0
24/02/96	Marine Res (h)	3-1
2/03/96	Bury 'A' (h)	2-0
9/03/96	Burnley 'A' (a)	0-1
16/03/96	Preston North End 'A' (a)	2-1
23/03/96	Everton 'A' (a)	2-0
30/03/96	Burnley 'A' (h)	2-0
6/04/96	Stoke City 'A' (h)	1-3
13/04/96	Liverpool 'A' (a)	1-0
20/04/96	Oldham Athletic 'A' (a)	2-1
24/04/96	Bury 'A' (a)	6-1
27/04/96	Blackpool 'A' (h)	0-1

'B' Team

19/08/95	Preston North End 'B' (h)	2-2
21/08/95	Bolton Wanderers 'A'	5-2
26/08/95	Rochdale 'A' (h)	6-1
29/08/95	Blackburn Rovs 'B' (h)	1-1
2/09/95	Stockport County 'A'(a)	1-1
9/09/95	Everton 'B' (a)	2-3
16/09/95	Oldham Athletic 'B' (h)	2-0
23/09/95	Burnley 'B' (h)	5-1

7/10/95	Liverpool 'B' (h)	4-2
14/10/95	Blackburn Rovers 'B' (a)	1-3
21/10/95	Blackpool 'B' (h)	6-0
28/10/95	Wigan Athletic 'A' (a)	3-2
4/11/95	Bury 'B' (h)	5-0
11/11/95	Manchester City 'B' (a)	2-1
18/11/95	Crewe Alexandra 'A' (h)	2-2
25/11/95	Oldham Athletic 'B' (a)	2-0
2/12/95	Carlisle Utd 'A' (h)	0-0
9/12/95	Chester 'A' (a)	0-2
16/12/95	Tranmere Rovers 'B' (h)	5-0
6/01/96	Marine Youth (a)	4-0
13/01/96	Rochdale 'A' (a)	1-1
20/01/96	Wigan Athletic 'A' (h)	3-2
10/02/96	Manchester City 'B' (h)	1-0
17/02/96	Everton 'B' (h)	0-3
24/02/96	Liverpool 'B' (a)	1-3
2/03/96	Bury 'B' (a)	3-1
9/03/96	Carlisle United 'A' (a)	2-1
16/03/96	Tranmere Rovers 'B' (a)	1-0
23/03/96	Crewe Alexandra 'A' (a)	4-1
30/03/96	Burnley 'B' (a)	4-1
6/04/96	Chester 'A' (h)	2-1
13/04/96	Preston North End 'B' (a)	3-0
17/04/96	Stockport County 'A' (h)	2-0
20/04/96	Bolton Wanderers 'A' (h)	6-1
27/04/96	Marine Youth (h)	7-0
4/05/96	Blackpool 'B' (a)	6-1

Youth Team

FA Youth Cup

21/11/95	Rotherham United (h)	3-1	Wallwork, Brebner, Baker.
10/01/96	Sunderland (a)	4-1	Wilson, Brown, Baker (2 pens)
13/02/96	Norwich City (h)	1-0	Wilson
5/03/96	Liverpool (a)	2-3	Brebner, Twiss

Lancs FA Youth Cup

12/12/95	Oldham Athletic (a)	1-1	Wallwork
3/04/96	Oldham Athletic (h)	4-0	Mulryne, Macken, Wilson 2
22/04/96	Tranmere Rovers (a)	3-0	Mulryne, Macken, Wilson
30/04/96	Blackburn Rovers (h) (Final)	3-2	Ford, Macken, Brebner

4-Year Form & Match Guide

Here's your guide to the 1995-96 season. It includes details of previous Premiership encounters plus a few pointers as to what you can expect from the match. Dates are subject to change what with Cup matches, TV requirements and bad weather – so always double check along with kick-off times. Enjoy the games!

No	Date	Opponents	92/3	93/4	94/5	95/6
1	17/08/96	**WIMBLEDON (Away)**	2-1	0-1	1-0	4-2

United will be looking to improve on their very average away form when meeting Wimbledon whom they have beaten only five times in ten trips.

2	21/8/96	**EVERTON (Home)**		0-3	1-0	2-0	2-0

Everton were the first side to beat United at Old Trafford in the FAPL but haven't scored there in three attempts since.

3	24/8/96	**BLACKBURN ROVERS (Home)**	3-1	1-1	1-0	1-0

Blackburn have felt hard done by on their last three trips to Old Trafford and will be well wound up as they attempt to beat United for the first time at the ground in the FAPL. History is against them, however, with only eight wins in 35 visits.

4	4/9/96	**DERBY COUNTY (Home)**	–	–	–	–

A first trip to Old Trafford in the FAPL for Derby County where the Rams had only eight successes in 38 attempts in the Football League.

5	7/9/96	**LEEDS UNITED (Away)**	0-0	2-0	1-2	1-3

Just one win in four trips to Elland Road in the FAPL and the last two visits have seen poor performances from United. It could be another tricky encounter this time round.

6	14/9/96	**NOTTINGHAM FOREST (Home)**	2-0	–	1-2	5-0

Possibly United's best home performance of last season but Forest are usually made of sterner stuff and it will surely be much closer this time. Just nine wins in 46 visits for the Midlands oufit.

7	21/9/96	**ASTON VILLA (Away)**	0-1	2-1	2-1	1-3

United will be out to revenge the stuffing they got in last season's opening game but they don't have a good record at Villa Park in the league, having won only 16 times in 63 visits. By contrast they have never lost a semi-final at the ground.

8	28/9/96	**TOTTENHAM H (Home)**	4-1	2-1	0-0	1-0

Spurs have tightened up considerably in defence since Gerry Francis took over and the days of pulsating games between these two sides seem to be gone. This is the sixtieth Old Trafford league meeting between the clubs with the London side successful just ten times.

9   12/10/96   LIVERPOOL (Home)   2-2   1-0   2-0   2-2

Two wins and two draws at Old Trafford. Last season this game marked the return of Eric Cantona who fittingly scored the equalising goal.

10   19/10/96   NEWCASTLE UNITED (Away)   –   1-1   2-0   1-0

With Newcastle's fabulous home record in the FAPL it must really hurt them to know that United are the only team to win a league fixture at St James' Park in either of the past two seasons.

11   26/10/96   SOUTHAMPTON (Away)   1-0   3-1   2-2   1-3

Last season's fixture saw the demise of United's notorious grey kit when they switched shirts at the interval after going three down. Prior to that United had not lost at the Dell in their previous six visits and will be hoping for a return to that sort of form.

12   2/11/96   CHELSEA (Home)   3-0   0-1   0-0   1-1

Chelsea have a better record than anyone against United at Old Trafford where the Reds haven't beaten the Pensioners since 92/3. The Londoners also only lost 13 times in 50 Football League visits.

13   16/11/96   ARSENAL (Home)   0-0   1-0   3-0   1-0

The Reds have a good record at home to the Gunners who have yet to score a goal at Old Trafford in the FAPL. Arsenal have won only 12 of 77 league visits and haven't tasted success at Old Trafford in a league game since October 1990.

14   23/11/96   MIDDLESBROUGH (Away)   1-1   –   –   3-0

A happy first ever visit to the new Riverside Stadium last season for United as they clinched the title with a 3-0 victory. The Reds will be looking for a repeat win.

15   30/11/96   LEICESTER CITY (Home)   –   –   1-1   –

This will be Leicester's fiftieth visit to United in which time they have only won on five occasions. However, the draw they snatched in their only previous FAPL fixture at Old Trafford was to cost United the title. There won't be a slip up this time.

16   7/12/96   WEST HAM UNITED (Home)   –   3-0   1-0   2-1

A 100% home FAPL record against the Hammers should be maintained as the London outfit have not won even a point at the ground since August 1986.

17   14/12/96   SHEFF WEDNESDAY (Away)   3-3   3-2   0-1   0-0

Only one victory at Hillsborough for the Reds since the formation of the FAPL which is in keeping with their generally poor record at a ground where they have only won a dozen times in 52 league fixtures.

18   21/12/96   SUNDERLAND (Home)   –   –   –   –

A first FAPL visit to Old Trafford for Sunderland who almost undid United's double bid at the first hurdle in the FA Cup last season when only a late Eric Cantona goal earned the Reds a replay at Roker Park. Just eleven wins in 48 previous visits for Sunderland.

19 26/12/96 NOTTINGHAM FOREST (Away).

United are undefeated at the City Ground in the FAPL bu
their last two visits and overall don't have a great record with on
46 league trips. Expect another close encounter.

20 28/12/96 LEEDS UNITED (Home) 2-0 0-0 0-0 1-0

Leeds, under Howard Wilkinson, regularly come to Old Trafford merely to
defend in numbers. They have yet to score at Old Trafford in the FAPL but
even if that record is extended it doesn't mean the Reds will win. Could be
the bore of the season.

21 1/1/97 ASTON VILLA (Home) 1-1 3-1 1-0 0-0

Was always considered one of the best games of the season but under Brian
Little Villa have become very defensive away from home and this is likely to
be another dour battle as in 95/6. Villa still win at Old Trafford in the FAPL

22 11/1/97 TOTTENHAM H (Away) 1-1 1-0 1-0 1-4

United got a real New Year's Day drubbing last season and will be looking
for revenge. They could be successful as they had lost only once in their
previous eight visits to White Hart Lane prior to suffering their biggest defeat
in the FAPL.

23 18/1/97 COVENTRY CITY (Away) 1-0 1-0 3-2 4-0

United had a poor record at Highfield Road in the Football League with just
eight wins in 28 visits but that has all changed since the formation of the
FAPL with United holding a 100% record on their trips to Coventry.

24 1/2/97 SOUTHAMPTON (Home) 2-1 2-0 2-1 4-1

A 100% home record in the FAPL against the Saints should be maintained.
United in fact have not dropped a point to Southampton at home in the last
seven meetings.

25 15/2/97 MIDDLESBROUGH (Home) 3-0 – – 2-0

No goals for Middlesbrough in either of their two visits to Old Trafford on
FAPL business and only eight wins in 39 attempts on United territory. Not
likely to improve on that record.

26 22/2/97 CHELSEA (Away) 1-1 0-1 3-2 4-1

Stamford Bridge has proved to be a happy hunting ground over the years for
United. The Reds have lost only 15 times in 55 visits and enjoyed an
excellent victory there last season.

27 1/3/97 COVENTRY CITY (Home) 5-0 0-0 2-0 1-0

Like Arsenal, Coventry have yet to score at Old Trafford in the FAPL. Indeed
the Sky Blues have yet to beat United in the FAPL and that record is unlikely
to change this season.

28 4/3/97 ARSENAL (Away) 1-0 2-2 0-0 0-1

Always a dour game between these two sides at Highbury and that isn't likely
to change this season. The Gunners beat United in the FAPL in the
corresponding game last season for the first time.

handful of clubs to which United have conceded
their travels. Just a dozen wins in nearly fifty
Roker Park but the Reds should improve on that.

...F WEDNESDAY (Home)   2-1   5-0   1-0   2-2
their first Old Trafford FAPL point in last season's
fixture but have an abysmal record when visiting United on
...ss with just six wins in over fifty trips. Not likely to improve on

... ...3/97   EVERTON (Away)   2-0   1-0   0-1   3-2
Three wins from four visits to Goodison Park for United but Joe Royle has
stiffened up the home side since his arrival and if Andrei Kanchelskis repeats
his fine 95/96 form for the Merseyside club then the Reds could be in for a
tough game.

32   29/3/97   WIMBLEDON (Home)   0-1   3-1   3-0   3-1
After their shock humbling of United in 1992/93 the Dons have not caused
the Reds many problems at Old Trafford since and this encounter should
provide the Champions with three points.

33   5/4/97   DERBY COUNTY (Away)   –   –   ¬   –
The Baseball Ground has not been a favourite haunt of United over the years
with just nine league victories in 38 games during which the Reds conceded
84 goals. They failed to beat County on any of their last three trips in the
Football League and failed to score in the last two.

34   12/4/97   BLACKBURN ROVERS (Away)   0-0   0-2   4-2   2-1
The Reds have won on their last two trips to Ewood Park but it has been close
on both occasions. Expect another tight finish.

35   19/4/97   LIVERPOOL (Away)   2-1   3-3   0-2   2-0
Always one of United's toughest fixtures and Liverpool will be seeking
revenge for that FA Cup Final defeat in front of their own supporters.

36   23/4/97   NEWCASTLE UNITED (Home)   –   1-1   2-0   2-0
Newcastle still looking for their first win at Old Trafford since the formation
of the FAPL and their overall record when visiting United isn't good either
with only nine victories in almost sixty attempts.

37   3/5/96   LEICESTER CITY (Away)   –   4-0   –
United have a surprisingly poor record at Filbert Street with only 13
successes in 49 visits but it will be a major disappointment if the Reds fail to
take three points from this one.

38   11/5/97   WEST HAM UNITED (Away)   –   2-2   1-1   1-0
United look on Upton Park with mixed emotions for it was there, of course,
that they were pipped by Blackburn for the 94/5 title when the Hammers held
them to a draw whilst last season's 1-0 success set United off on a storming
run to the Championship. But that victory was only United's eighth in 43
league meetings at the ground.